Thomas Sternhold, John Hopkins

The Whole Book of Psalms

Collected Into English Metre

Thomas Sternhold, John Hopkins

The Whole Book of Psalms

Collected Into English Metre

ISBN/EAN: 9783744784955

Printed in Europe, USA, Canada, Australia, Japan

Cover: Foto ©Lupo / pixelio.de

More available books at **www.hansebooks.com**

THE WHOLE BOOK
OF
PSALMS,
Collected into
Englifh Metre,
BY
Thomas Sternhold, John Hopkins,
and Others.

Set forth and allowed to be Sung in all Churches, of all the People together, before and after Morning and Evening Prayer; and alfo before and after Sermon; and moreover in private Houfes, for their Godly Solace and Comfort: laying apart all ungodly Songs and Ballads, which tend only to the nourifhing of Vice, and corrupting of Youth.

If any be afflicted, let him pray; and if any be merry, let him fing Pfalms. James v. 13.
Let the Word of God dwell plenteoufly in you, in all Wifdom, teaching and exhorting one another in Pfalms, Hymns, and Spiritual Songs, finging unto the Lord with Grace in your Hearts. Coloff. iii. 16.

(By Permiffion of the Stationer's Company.)

BIRMINGHAM,
Printed by JOHN BASKERVILLE, 1762.
(Price One Shilling and Sixpence in Sheets.)

An Alphabetical TABLE, shewing how to find each PSALM by its Beginning.

A.	Psalm.	L.	Psalm.
ALL Laud and	30	Lord, in thy	6
All People	49	Lord, keep me,	16
Attend my People	78	Lord, be my Judge,	26
Among the Princes	82	Lord, plead my	35
All People that	100	Like as the Hart	42
B.		Let God arise, and	68
Be Light and	81	Lord, give thy	72
Blessed are they	119	Lord, bow thy Ear	86
Blessed art thou	128	Lord God of Health,	88
Behold and have	134	Lord, unto thee I	130
Blest be the Lord	144	Lord, save me from	140
D.		Lord, hear my	143
Do not, O God	83	**M.**	
E.		My Shepherd is	23
Except the Lord	127	My Heart doth	45
G.		My Soul to God shall	62
Give to the Lord	29	My Lord, my God,	71
Grudge not to	37	My Soul give Laud	103
Great is the Lord,	48	My Soul, praise the	104
God save me for	54	My Soul, praise thou	146
Give Praises unto	105	**N.**	
Give Thanks unto	107	Not unto, Lord,	115
Give Laud unto	148	Now Israel	124
H.		**O.**	
Help, Lord, for	12	O Lord, how are	3
How long wilt	13	O God that art	4
Have Mercy on me,	51	O Lord my God, I	7
Have Mercy on me,	56	O God our Lord,	8
Have Mercy on us,	67	O Lord, give Ear	17
How pleasant is thy	84	O God, my Strength	18
He that within the	91	O Lord, how joyful	21
Hear thou my Pray'r,	102	O God, my God,	22
I.		O Lord, I put my	31
Incline thine Ears,	5	Our Ears have	44
In God the Lord	11	O Lord, consider	51
In Trouble and	20	O God, give Ear,	55
I lift my Heart to	25	O Lord, thou didst	60
I will give Laud and	34	O God, my God,	63
I said, I will look	39	O Lord, unto my	64
I waited long and	40	O God, to me take	70
Judge and defend my	43	O God, the Gentiles	79
I with my Voice to	77	O Lord, thou dost	94
It is a Thing both	92	O come let us lift	95
In God the Lord	100	O sing ye now unto	98
I Mercy will and	101	O God, my Heart	108
In speechless Silence	109	O all ye Nations of	117
I love the Lord	116	O give ye Thanks	118
In Trouble and in	120	O Thou that in the	123
I lift my Eyes to	121	Oft they, now Israel	129
I did in Heart	122	O Lord, I am not	131

An Alphabetical TABLE, &c.

	Psalm.		Psalm.
O what a happy	133	To sing the Mercies	89
O praise the Lord,	135	Thou, Lord, hast	90
O laud the Lord	136	The Lord doth reign,	93
O Lord, thou hast	139	The Lord doth reign,	97
O Lord, upon thee	141	The Lord doth reign,	99
P.		The Lord did say	110
Put me not to	38	The Man is blest	112
Praise ye the	106	Those that do	125
Praise ye the Lord,	136	Thee will I praise	138
Praise ye the Lord,	147	Thee will I laud,	145
R.		**U.**	
Regard, O Lord,	61	Unto the Lord	142
Remember	132	**W.**	
S.		Why did the	2
Send Aid and save	59	With Heart	9
Save me, O God,	69	What is the Cause	10
Sing ye with Praise	96	Within thy	15
Such as in God the	125	Why dost thou	52
Sing ye unto the	149	Why art thou, Lord,	74
T.		With Heart I do	111
The Man is blest	1	When Israel by	114
There is no	14	When that the	126
The Heav'ns and	19	When as we did	137
The Lord is only	23	**Y.**	
The Earth is all the	24	Ye Righteous in	33
The Lord is both my	27	Ye People all,	47
Thou art, O Lord,	28	Ye Rulers that are	58
The Man is blest,	32	Ye Men on Earth,	66
The wicked by his	36	Ye Children which	113
The Man is blest that	41	Yield unto God,	150
The Lord is our	46		
The mighty God,	50	*These are after the Psalms.*	
The God of Gods,	50	Veni Creator.	
The foolish Man	53	The humble Suit of a Sinner.	
Take Pity for thy	57	The Song of Zacharias.	
Thy Praise alone, O	65	The Song of the blessed Virgin Mary.	
Truly the Lord is	73	The Lamentation of a Sinner,	
To thee, O God,	75	A Thanksgiving after the receiving of	
To all that now	76	The Creed.	
Thou Shepherd that	80	Preserve us Lord,	
Thou hast been	85	The Lord's Prayer.	
That City shall full	87	Gloria Patri.	

The

The PSALMS of DAVID, in Metre.

PSALM I.   T. S.

THE Man is bleſt that hath not lent   to wicked Men his Ear:
Nor led his Life as Sinners do,   nor ſat in Scorners Chair.
2 But in the Law of God the Lord   doth ſet his whole Delight:
And in the ſame doth exerciſe   himſelf both Day and Night.

3 He ſhall be like a Tree that is   planted the Rivers nigh:
Which in due Seaſon bringeth forth   its Fruit abundantly.
4 Whoſe Leaf ſhall never fade nor fall,   but flouriſhing ſhall ſtand:
Even ſo all Things ſhall proſper well   that this Man takes in Hand.

5 As for ungodly Men, with them   it ſhall be nothing ſo:
But as the Chaff which by the Wind   is driven to and fro.
6 Therefore the wicked Men ſhall not   in Judgment ſtand upright:
Nor in Aſſembly of the Juſt   ſhall Sinners come in Sight.

7 For why the Way of godly Men   unto the Lord is known:
Whereas the Way of wicked Men   ſhall quite be overthrown.

PSALM II.   T. S.

1 **W**HY did the Gentiles Tumults raiſe?   what Rage was in their Brain?
Why do the People ſtill contrive   a Thing that is but vain?
2 The Kings and Rulers of the Earth   conſpire, and are all bent
Againſt the Lord, and Chriſt his Son,   whom he among us ſent.

3 Shall we be bound to them? ſay they,   let all their Bonds be broke:
And of their Doctrine and their Law   let us reject the Yoke.
4 But he that in the Heav'n doth dwell,   their Doings will deride:
And make them all his Mocking-ſtocks,   throughout the World ſo wide.

5 For in his Wrath he ſhall reprove   their Pride and ſcornful Ways
And in his Fury trouble them,   and unto them ſhall ſay,
6 I have anointed him my King   upon my holy Hill:
I will therefore, Lord, preach thy Law   according to thy Will.

7 The Law whereof the Lord himſelf   hath thus ſaid unto me,
Thou art my only Son, this Day   have I begotten thee.
8 All People I will give to thee,   as Heirs at thy Requeſt:
The Ends and Coaſts of all the Earth   by thee ſhall be poſſeſt.

9 Thou ſhalt them bruiſe, even like to thoſe   that under Foot are trod:
And as a Potter's Veſſel break   them with an Iron Rod.
10 Now ye, O Kings and Rulers all,   be wiſe therefore, and learn'd:
By whom the Matters of the World   are judged and diſcern'd.

11 See that ye ſerve the Lord above,   in Trembling and in Fear:
See that with Rev'rence ye rejoice   when you to him draw near.
12 See that ye do embrace and kiſs   his Son without Delay:
Leſt in his Wrath ye ſuddenly   periſh from the right Way.

13 If once his Wrath (but little) ſhall   be kindled in his Breaſt:
Then only they that truſt in him,   ſhall happy be and bleſt.

PSALM III.   T. S.

1 **O** Lord, how are my Foes increas'd,   who vex me more and more!
They break my Heart when as they ſay   God can him not reſtore.

PSALM IV, V.

2 But thou, O Lord, art my Defence, when I am hard beftead:
My Worſhip and my Honour both, and thou hold'ſt up my Head.
3 Then with my Voice upon the Lord I did both call and cry;
And he out of his holy Hill did hear me ſpeedily.
4 I laid me down, and quietly I ſlept and roſe again:
For why? I know aſſuredly, the Lord did me ſuſtain.
5 If thouſands up againſt me riſe, I will not be afraid;
For thou art ſtill my Lord and God, my Saviour and my Aid.
6 Riſe up therefore, ſave me my God, to thee I make my Pray'r:
For thou haſt broke the Cheeks and Teeth of all that wicked are.

7 Salvation only doth belong to thee, O Lord, above:
Who on thy People doſt beſtow thy Bleſſing and thy Love.

PSALM IV. T. S.

1 O God that art my Righteouſneſs, Lord, hear me when I call:
Thou haſt ſet me at Liberty when I was bound in Thrall.
2 Have Mercy, Lord, therefore on me, and grant me my Requeſt:
For unto thee inceſſantly to cry I will not reſt.

3 O mortal Man, how long will ye my Glory thus deſpiſe?
Why wander ye in Vanity, and follow after Lies?
4 Know ye that good and godly Men the Lord doth take and chuſe:
And when to him I make Complaint, he doth me not refuſe.

5 Sin not, but ſtand in Awe therefore, examine well your Heart:
And in your Chamber quietly ſee ye yourſelves convert.
6 Offer to God the Sacrifice of Righteouſneſs and Praiſe:
And look that in the living Lord you put your Truſt always.

7 The greater Sort crave worldly Goods, and Riches do embrace:
But, Lord, grant us thy Countenance, thy Favour and thy Grace.
8 For thou thereby ſhalt make my Heart more joyful and more glad,
Than they that of their Corn and Wine full great Increaſe have had.

9 In Peace therefore lie down will I, taking my Reſt and Sleep:
For thou only doſt me, O Lord, preſerve and ſafely keep.

PSALM V. T. S.

1 INCLINE thine Ears, O Lord, and let my Words have free Acceſs
To thee, who art my God and King, from whom I ſeek Redreſs.
2 Hear me betime, Lord, tarry not, for I will have Reſpect,
My Supplication in the Morn to thee for to direct.

3 And I will patiently ſtill truſt in thee my God alone:
Thou art not pleas'd with Wickedneſs, and Ill with thee dwells none.
4 Such as the Fooliſh ſhall not ſtand in Sight of thee, O Lord:
Vain Workers of Iniquity thou haſt always abhorr'd.

5 The Lyars and baſe Flatterers ſhall be deſtroy'd by thee:
Blood-thirſty and deceitful Men likewiſe ſhall hated be.
6 Therefore will I come to thy Houſe, truſting upon thy Grace:
And rev'rently will worſhip thee towards thy holy Place.

7 Lord, lead me in thy Righteouſneſs, for to confound my Foes:
Alſo the Way that I ſhall walk, before my Face diſcloſe.
8 For in their Mouths there is no Truth, their inward Filth is great:
Their Throat an open Sepulchre, and Tongues full of Deceit.

9 Deſtroy

PSALM VI, VII.

Destroy their false Conspiracies, that they may come to nought:
Subvert them in their Heaps of Sin, who have Rebellion wrought.
But those that put their Trust in thee, let them be glad always:
And render Thanks for thy Defence. and give thy Name the Praise.

1 For thou with Favour wilt increase the Just and Righteous still:
And with thy Grace, as with a Shield, defend him from all Ill.

PSALM VI. T. S.

LORD, in my Wrath reprove me not, tho' I deserve thine Ire:
Nor yet correct me in thy Rage, O Lord, I thee desire.
For I am weak, therefore, O Lord, of Mercy me forbear:
And heal me, Lord, for why? thou know'st my Bones do quake for fear.

My Soul is troubled very sore, and vex'd exceedingly:
But, Lord, how long wilt thou delay to cure my Misery?
Lord, turn thee to thy wonted Grace, some Pity on me take:
O save me not for my Deserts, but for thy Mercies sake.

For why? no Man among the Dead remembreth thee at all:
O who shall worship thee, O Lord, that in the Pit do fall?
So grievous is my Plaint and Moan, that I grow wond'rous faint:
All the Night long I wash my Bed with Tears of my Complaint.

My Sight is dim, and waxeth old, with Anguish of my Heart:
For fear of them that be my Foes, and would my Soul subvert.
But now depart from me, all ye that work Iniquity:
Because the Lord hath heard the Voice of my Complaint and Cry.

He heard not only the Request and Pray'r of my sad Heart:
But it received at my Hands, and took it in good Part.
o And now my Foes that vexed me, the Lord will soon defame:
And suddenly confound them all, with great Rebuke and Shame.

PSALM VII. T. S.

O Lord my God, I put my Trust and Confidence in thee:
Save me from them that me pursue, and still deliver me.
Left like a Lion he me tear, and rend in Pieces small:
While there is none to succour me, and rid me out of Thrall.

O Lord my God, if I have done the Thing that is not right:
Or else if I be found in Fault, or guilty in thy Sight;
Or to my Friend rewarded ill, or left him in Distress:
Who me pursu'd most cruelly, and hated me causeless;

Then let my Foe pursue my Soul, let him my Life down thrust
Unto the Earth, and also lay my Honour in the Dust.
Stand up, O Lord, in Wrath, because my Foes do rage so fast:
Awake for me to the Judgment which thou commanded hast.

Then shall great Nations come to thee, and know thee by this Thing
If thou declare for Love of them, thyself as Lord and King.
And as thou art of all Men Judge, O Lord, now judge thou me
According to my Righteousness, and my Integrity.

PART II.

Lord, cease the Hate of wicked Men, and be the just Man's Guide:
By whom the Secrets of all Hearts are searched and descry'd.
o I take my Help to come of God in all my Pain and Smart:
Who doth preserve all those that be of pure and perfect Heart.

PSALM VIII, IX.

11 The juſt Man and the wicked both God judgeth by his Pow'r:
So that he feels his mighty Hand even ev'ry Day and Hour.
12 Except he change his Mind, I die, for even as he thinks fit
He whets his Sword, he bends his Bow, aiming where he may hit.
13 And doth prepare his mortal Darts, his Arrows keen and ſharp:
For them that do me perſecute, and do at Miſchief harp.
14 But lo, tho' he in Travail be of his Dev'liſh Forecaſt:
And of his Miſchief once conceiv'd, yet brings forth nought at laſt.
15 He digs a Ditch and makes it deep, in Hope to hurt his Brother:
But he ſhall fall into the Pit that he digg'd up for other.
16 Thus wrong returneth to the Hurt of him in whom it bred:
And all the Miſchief that he wrought, ſhall fall on his own Head.
17 I will give Thanks to God therefore, that judgeth righteouſly:
And with my Song will praiſe the Name of him that is moſt high.

PSALM VIII. T. S.

1 O God our Lord, how wonderful are thy Works ev'ry where!
Thy fame ſurmounts in Dignity the higheſt Heav'ns that are.
2 Even by the Mouth of ſuckling Babes thou wilt confound thy Foes:
For in thoſe Babes thy Might is ſeen, thy Graces they diſcloſe.
3 And when I ſee the Heav'ns above, the Works of thy own Hand:
The Sun, the Moon and all the Stars, in order as they ſtand;
4 Lord! what is Man, that thou of him tak'ſt ſuch abundant Care?
Or what the Son of Man, whom thou to viſit doſt not ſpare?
5 For thou haſt made him little leſs than Angels in Degree:
And thou haſt alſo crowned him with glorious Dignity.
6 Thou haſt preferr'd him to the Lord of all thy Works, and thou
Haſt in Subjection unto him put all Things here below.
7 As Sheep, and Neat, and all Beaſts elſe, that in the Fields do feed:
Fowls of the Air, Fiſh in the Sea, and all that therein breed.
8 O God our Lord, how excellent is thy moſt glorious Name
In all the Earth! Therefore we do praiſe and adore the ſame.

PSALM IX. T. S.

1 WITH Heart and Mouth to thee, O Lord, will I ſing Laud and Praiſe:
And ſpeak of all thy wond'rous Works, and them declare always.
2 I will be glad and much rejoice in thee, O God, moſt high:
And make my Songs extol thy Name above the ſtarry Sky.
3 Becauſe my Foes are driven back, and turned unto Flight:
They do fall down, and are deſtroy'd by thy great Pow'r and Might.
4 Thou haſt revenged all my Wrong, my Grief and all my Grudge:
Thou doſt with Juſtice hear my Cauſe, moſt like a righteous Judge.
5 Thou doſt rebuke the Heathen Folk, and Wicked ſo confound.
That afterward the Memory of them cannot be found.
6 Deſtructions to an End are come, and Cities overthrown:
With them likewiſe is periſhed their Fame and great Renown.
7 Know thou that he who is above, for evermore ſhall reign,
And in the Seat of Equity true Judgment will maintain.
8 With Juſtice he will keep and guide the World and ev'ry Wight:
And ſo will yield with Equity to every Man his Right.

PSALM X.

9 He is Protector of the Poor,
   He is in all Adverſity
10 And they that know thy holy Name,
   For thou forſakeſt not their Suit
what Time they be oppreſt:
their Refuge and their Reſt.
therefore ſhall truſt in thee:
in their Neceſſity.

PART II.

11 Sing Pſalms therefore unto the Lord,
   Among the People all declare
12 For he is mindful of the Blood
   Forgetting not the humble Man
who dwells on Sion Hill:
his noble Acts and Will.
of them that be oppreſt:
that ſeeks to him for Reſt.

13 Have Mercy, Lord, on me, becauſe
   Who from the Gates of Death are wont
14 In Sion that I may ſet forth
   And that in thy Salvation great,
my Foes do yet remain:
to raiſe me up again.
thy Praiſe with Heart and Voice
my Soul may ſtill rejoice.

15 The Heathen ſtick faſt in the Pit,
   And in the Net that they did hide,
16 By Judgments great the Lord is known,
   And faſt entangled in the Work
which they themſelves prepar'd:
their own Feet are enſnar'd.
whilſt wicked Men are caught,
which their own Hands have (wrought.

17 The wicked and deceitful Men
   And all the People of the World,
18 But ſure the Lord will not forget
   The patient People never look
go down to Hell below:
that God refuſe to know.
the poor Man's Grief and Pain s
for Help of him in vain.

19 O Lord, ariſe, leſt Men prevail
   And let the Heathen Folk receive
20 Lord, ſtrike ſuch Terror, Fear and Dread,
   They will be forced to confeſs
that be of worldly Might:
their Judgment in thy Sight:
into their Hearts, and then
themſelves to be but Men.

PSALM X. T. S.

1 **W**HAT is the Cauſe that thou, O Lord,
   Why hideſt thou thy Face in Time
2 The Poor do periſh by the Proud,
   Let them be taken in the Craft
ſo far off now doſt ſtand?
when Trouble is at Hand?
and wicked Mens Deſire:
which they themſelves conſpire.

3 For in the Luſt of his own Heart
   So doth the Wicked praiſe himſelf,
4 He is ſo proud, that Right and Wrong
   Nay, nay, there is no God, ſaith he,
th' Ungodly doth delight:
and doth the Lord deſpite.
he ſetteth all apart:
for thus he thinks in Heart.

5 Becauſe his Ways do proſper ſtill,
   And with a Blaſt do puff againſt
6 Tuſh, tuſh, ſaith he, I have no Dread,
   And why? for all Adverſity
he doth thy Laws neglect:
ſuch as would him correct.
leſt my Eſtate ſhould change:
to him is very ſtrange.

7 His Mouth is full of Curſedneſs,
   Under his Tongue there Nothing is
8 He lieth hid in Ways and Holes,
   Againſt the Poor that paſs by him
of Fraud, Deceit, and Guile:
but what is baſe and vile.
to ſlay the Innocent:
his cruel Eyes are bent.

9 And like a Lion privily
   That he may ſnare them in his Net,
10 With cunning Craft and Subtilty
   So are great Heaps of poor Men made
lies lurking in his Den:
and ſpoil poor harmleſs Men.
he croucheth down alway:
by his ſtrong Pow'r a Prey.

PART II.

11 Tuſh, God forgetteth this, ſaith he,
   His Countenance is caſt aſide,
therefore I may be bold:
he doth it not behold.

PSALM XI, XII.

12 Arise, O Lord our God, in whom the poor Man's Hope doth rest:
Lift up thy Hand, do not forget the Poor that be opprest.
13 Why should the proud and wicked Man blaspheme God's holy Name
Whilst in his Heart he crieth, Tush, God cares not for the same.
14 But thou seest all their Wickedness, and well dost understand,
That Friendless and poor Fatherless, are left into thy Hand.
15 Of wicked and malicious Men then break the Pow'r alway:
That they with their Iniquity may perish and decay.
16 The Lord shall reign for evermore as King and God alone:
And he will chase out of the Land the Heathen Folk each one.
17 Thou hearest, Lord, the Poor's Complaint, their Pray'r and their Request:
Their Hearts thou wilt confirm, until thine Ears to hear be prest.
18 To judge the Poor and Fatherless, and help them to their Right:
That they may be no more opprest by Men of worldly Might.

PSALM XI. T. S.

1 IN God the Lord I put my Trust, why say ye to my Soul,
Unto the Mountain swiftly fly, as doth the winged Fowl?
2 Behold, the Wicked bend their Bows, their Arrows they prepare
To shoot in secret at those who sincere and upright are.
3 Of worldly Hope all stays were shrunk, and clearly brought to nought
Alas, the just and upright Man, what Evil hath he wrought?
4 But he that in his Temple is, most holy and most high:
And in the highest Heav'ns doth sit in royal Majesty.
5 The poor and single Man's Estate considers in his Mind,
And searcheth out full narrowly the Manners of Mankind;
6 And with a chearful Countenance the righteous Man will use:
But in his Heart he doth abhor all such as Mischief muse.
7 And on the Sinners casteth Snares as thick as Hail or Rain:
Brimstone and Fire, and Whirlwinds great, appointed for their Pain.
8 Ye see then how a righteous God doth Righteousness embrace:
And unto just and upright Men shews forth his pleasant Face.

PSALM XII. T. S.

1 HELP, Lord, for good and godly Men do perish and decay:
And Faith and Truth from worldly Men is parted clean away.
2 Whoso doth with his Neighbour talk, 'tis all but Vanity:
For ev'ry Man bethinketh how to speak deceitfully.
3 But flatt'ring and deceitful Lips, and Tongues that be so stout
To speak proud Words, and make great Brags, the Lord soon cuts them out.
4 For they say still, We will prevail, our Lips shall us extol:
Our Tongues are ours, we ought to speak, what Lord shall us controul?
5 But for the great Complaint and Cry of those that are opprest,
I will arise now, saith the Lord, and them restore to Rest.
6 God's Word is like to Silver pure, that from the Dross is try'd,
Which hath not less than seven Times in the Fire been purify'd.
7 Now since thy Promise is to help, Lord, keep thy Promise then:
And save us now and evermore from this ill Kind of Men.
8 For now the wicked World is full of Mischiefs manifold:
Whilst Vanity with worldly Men so highly is extol'd.

PSALM

PSALM XIII, XIV, XV, XVI.

PSALM XIII. T. S.

1 HOW long wilt thou forget me, Lord? shall it for ever be?
How long doſt thou intend to hide thy Face away from me?
2 In Heart and Mind how long ſhall I with Care tormented be?
And how long ſhall my deadly Foe thus triumph over me?

3 Behold me now, O Lord my God, and hear me ſore oppreſt:
Lighten mine Eyes, leſt I do ſleep, as one by Death poſſeſt:
4 Leſt that my Enemy do ſay, behold, I do prevail:
Leſt they alſo that hate my Soul, rejoice to ſee me fail.

5 But from thy Mercy and Goodneſs my Hope ſhall not depart:
In thy Relief and ſaving Health right glad ſhall be my Heart.
6 I will give Thanks unto the Lord, and Praiſes to him ſing;
Becauſe he hath heard my Requeſt for ev'ry needful Thing.

PSALM XIV. T. S.

1 THERE is no God, do fooliſh Men affirm in their mad Mood:
Their Drifts are all corrupt and vain, not one of them doth good.
2 The Lord beheld from Heav'n moſt high, the whole Race of Mankind:
And ſaw not one that ſought indeed the living God to find.

3 They went all wide, and were corrupt, and truly there was none
That in the World did any good, no not ſo much as one.
4 Is all their Judgment ſo far loſt, that all work Miſchief ſtill?
Eating my People even as Bread, not one to ſeek God's Will.

5 When they thus rage, then ſuddenly great Fear on them ſhall fall:
For God doth love the righteous Man, and will preſerve them all.
6 Ye mock the doings of the Poor, to their Reproach and Shame:
Becauſe they put their truſt in God, and call upon his Name.

7 But who ſhall give the People Health? and when wilt thou fulfill
Thy Promiſe made to Iſrael, from out of Sion's Hill?
8 For when thou ſhalt reſtore again ſuch as were captive led,
Then Jacob ſhall therein rejoice, and Iſrael be glad.

PSALM XV. T. S

1 WITHIN thy Tabernacle Lord, who ſhall inhabit ſtill?
Or whom wilt thou receive to dwell in thy moſt holy Hill?
2 The Man whoſe Life is uncorrupt, whoſe Works are juſt and ſtraight:
Whoſe Heart doth think the very truth and Tongue ſpeaks no Deceit.

3 That to his Neighbour doth no Ill, in Body, Goods, or Name;
Nor willingly doth Slanders raiſe, which might impair the ſame.
4 That in his Heart regardeth not malicious wicked Men:
But thoſe that love and fear the Lord, he maketh much of them.

5 His Oath and all his Promiſes that keepeth faithfully,
Altho' he make his Cov'nant ſo, that he doth loſe thereby.
6 That putteth not to Uſury his Money and his Coin:
Nor for to hurt the Innocent doth bribe or elſe purloin.

7 Whoſo doth theſe Things faithfully, and turneth not therefrom,
Shall never periſh in this World, nor that which is to come.

PSALM XVI. T. S.

1 LORD, keep me, for I truſt in thee, and do confeſs indeed,
Thou art my God, and of my Goods thou haſt not any Need.

2 There-

PSALM XVII.

2 Therefore I give them to the Saints that in the World do dwell:
Namely, unto the faithful Flock in Virtue that excel.
3 Their Sorrows shall be multiply'd, who run so hastily,
To offer to the Idol-Gods, that are but vanity.
4 As for the bloody Sacrifice, and Off'rings of that sort,
I will not touch, neither thereof shall my Lips make Report.
5 For why? the Lord the Portion is of my Inheritance:
And he it is that doth preserve my Lot from all Mischance.
6 The Place wherein my Lot is fall'n, in Beauty doth excel:
My Heritage assign'd to me, doth please me wond'rous well.
7 I thank the Lord that caused me to understand the right:
For by his Means my secret Thoughts do teach me in the Night.
8 I set the Lord still in my Sight, and trust him over all:
For he doth stand on my Right-hand, therefore I shall not fall.
9 Wherefore my Heart and Tongue also rejoice exceedingly:
My Flesh likewise doith rest in hope to rise again, for why?
10 Thou wilt not leave my Soul in Hell, because thou lovest me:
Nor yet will give thy holy One Corruption for to see;
11 But wilt me shew the Way to Life, where there is Joy in Store:
And where at thy Right-hand there are Pleasures for evermore.

PSALM XVII. T. S.

1 O Lord, give ear to my just Cause, attend unto my Cry:
  And hear the Pray'r I offer up to thee unfeignedly.
2 And let the Judgment of my Cause proceed always from thee:
And let thine Eyes behold, and clear Truth and Simplicity.
3 Thou hast well try'd me in the Night, and yet could'st Nothing find,
That I have spoken with my Tongue that was not in my Mind,
4 As for the Works of wicked Men, and Paths perverse and ill,
For love of thy most holy Name, I have refrained still.
5 Then in thy Paths that be most pure guide me, Lord, and preserve:
That from the Way wherein I walk my Steps may never swerve.
6 For I do call to thee, O Lord, surely thou wilt me aid:
Then hear my Pray'r, and weigh right well the Words that I have said.
7 O thou the Saviour of all them that put their Trust in thee,
Declare thy Strength on them that spurn against thy Majesty.
8 O keep me as thou wouldest keep the Apple of thine Eye:
And under covert of thy Wings defend me secretly.

PART II.

9 From wicked Men that trouble me, and daily me annoy:
And from my Foes that go about my Soul for to destroy,
10 Who wallow in their worldly Wealth, and are so full and fat,
That in their Pride they do not spare to speak they care not what.
11 They lie in wait where I should pass, with Craft me to confound:
And musing Mischief in their Minds, to cast me to the Ground.
12 Much like a Lion greedily, that would his Prey embrace:
Or lurking like a Lion's Whelp, within some secret Place.
13 Up, Lord, in haste, prevent my Foe, and cast him at my Feet:
Save thou my Soul from the ill Man, and with thy Sword him smite.

14 Deliver

PSALM XVIII.

14 Deliver me, Lord, by thy Pow'r,   out of these Tyrants Hands,
Who now so long Time reigned have,   and kept us in their Bands.

15 I mean from worldly Men, who do   in worldly Goods abound:
That have no Hope or Joy but what   in this Life can be found,
16 Thou of thy Store their Bellies fill'st,   with Pleasure to their Mind:
Their Children have enough, and leave   the rest to theirs behind.

17 But as for me, I will behold   thy Face in Righteousness:
And shall be satisfy'd when I   awake with thy Likeness.

PSALM XVIII. T. S.

1 O God, my Strength and Fortitude,   of force I must love thee:
Thou art my Castle and Defence   in my Necessity.
2 My God, my Rock, in whom I trust,   the Worker of my Wealth:
My Refuge, Buckler, and my Shield,   the Horn of all my Health.

3 When I 'sing Laud unto the Lord,   most worthy to be serv'd,
Then from my Foes I am right sure,   that I shall be preserv'd.
4 The Pangs of Death did compass me;   and bound me ev'ry where:
The flowing Waves of Wickedness   did put me in great Fear.

5 The sly and subtle Snares of Hell   were round about me set:
And for my Life there was prepar'd   a deadly trapping Net.
6 I thus beset with Pain and Grief,   did pray to God for Grace:
And he forthwith heard my Complaint,   out of his holy Place.

7 Such is his Pow'r that in his Wrath   he made the Earth to quake,
Yea, the Foundation of the Mount   of Basan for to shake.
8 And from his Nostrils went a Smoke,   when kindled was his Ire:
And from his Mouth went burning Coals   of hot consuming Fire.

9 The Lord descended from above,   and bow'd the Heav'ns most high:
And underneath his Feet he cast   the Darkess of the Sky.
10 On Cherubs and on Cherubims   full royally he rode:
And on the Wings of all the Wind   came flying all abroad.

PART II.

11 And like a Den most dark he made   his hid and secret Place:
With Waters black, and airy Clouds,   encompassed he was.
12 At his bright Presence did thick Clouds   in Haste away retire:
And in the stead thereof did come   Hail-stones and Coals of Fire.

13 The fiery Darts and Thunder-bolts,   disperse them here and there:
And with his frequent Lightnings he   doth put them in great Fear.
14 When thou, O Lord, with great Rebuke   thy Anger dost declare,
The Springs and the Foundations of   the World discover'd are.

15 And from above the Lord sent down   to fetch me from below:
And pluck'd me out of Waters great,   that would me overflow.
16 And me deliver'd from my Foes   that sought me to enthral:
Yea, from such Foes as were too strong   for me to deal withal.

17 They did prevent me evermore   in Time of my great Grief:
But yet the Lord is my Defence,   my Succour and Relief.
18 He brought me forth in open Place,   that so I might be free:
And kept me safe, because he had   a Favour unto me.

19 According to my Innocence,   so did he me regard:
And to the Cleanness of my Hands   he gave me my Reward;

PSALM XVIII.

20 For that I walked in his Ways, and in his Paths have trod:
And not departed wickedly from him that is my God.

PART III.

21 'But evermore I have Respect to his Law and Decree:
His Statutes and Commandments I cast not away from me.
22 But pure, and clean, and uncorrupt, appear'd before his Face:
And did refrain from Wickedness and Sin in ev'ry Case.
23 The Lord therefore will me reward, as I have done aright:
And to the Cleanness of my Hands appearing in his Sight.
24 For, Lord, with him that holy is, wilt thou be holy too:
And with the good and virtuous Man, thou wilt uprightly do:
25 And for the loving and Elect thy Favour wilt reserve:
And thou wilt use the wicked Men as wicked Men deserve.
26 For thou dost save the simple Folk in Trouble when they lie;
And dost bring down the Countenance of them that look full high.
27 The Lord will light my Candle so, that it shall shine full bright:
The Lord my God will make also my Darkness to be Light.
28 For by thy Help an Host of Men discomfit, Lord, I shall:
By thee I scale and over-leap the Strength of any Wall.
29 Unspotted are the Ways of God, his Word is purely try'd:
He is a sure Defence to such as in his Faith abide.
30 For who is God, except the Lord? for other there is none:
Or else who is Omnipotent, saving our God alone?

PART IV.

31 The God that girdeth me with Strength, is he that I do mean:
That all the Ways wherein I walk, did evermore keep clean.
32 That made my Feet like to the Harts, in Swiftness of my Pace:
And for my Safety brought me forth into an open Place.
33 He did in Order put my Hands in Battle for to fight:
To break in sunder Bars of Brass, he gave my Arms the Might.
34 Thou teachest me thy saving Health; thy Right-hand is my Tow'r:
Thy Love and Gentleness also doth still increase my Pow'r.
35 And under me thou makest plain the Way where I should go:
So that my Feet shall never slip, nor wander to and fro.
36 And fiercely I pursue and take my Foes that me annoy'd:
And from the Field do not return till they be all destroy'd.
37 So I suppress and wound my Foes that they can rise no more:
For underneath my Feet they fall, I wound them all so sore.
38 For thou hast girded me with Strength unto the Battle, and
Thou wilt throw down my Enemies that do against me stand.
39 Lord thou hast giv'n me the Necks of all my Enemies:
That so I might destroy all those that up against me rise.
40 They call'd for Help but none gave ear, nor came to their Relief:
Yea, to the Lord they call'd for Aid, yet heard he not their Grief.

PART V.

41 And still like Dust before the Wind, I drive them under Feet:
And sweep them out like filthy Dirt that lieth in the Street.

PSALM XIX, XX.

42 Thou keep'st me from seditious Folk, that still in Strife are led:
And thou dost of the Heathen Folk appoint me to be Head.
43 A People strong, to me unknown, and yet they shall me serve:
And at the first obey my Word, whereas my own will swerve.
44 I shall be irksome to mine own, they will not see my Light
But wander wide out of the Way, and hide them out of Sight.
45 But blessed be the living Lord, most worthy of all Praise,
He is my Rock and saving Health, praised be he always.
46 For it is he that gave me Pow'r, revenged for to be:
And with his holy Word subdu'd the People unto me.
47 And from my Foe deliver'd me, and set me over those,
That cruel and ungodly were, and up against me rose.
48 And for this Cause, O Lord my God, to thee give thanks I shall:
And sing out Praises to thy Name among the Gentiles all.
49 Deliv'rance great thou giv'st the King, and dost reserve in Store,
Mercy for thine Anointed, and his Seed for evermore.

PSALM XIX. T. S.

1 THE Heav'ns and Firmament on high do wond'rously declare
God's Glory and Omnipotence, his Works and what they are.
2 The wond'rous Works of God appear by ev'ry Day's Success:
The Nights likewise, which their Race run, the self-same Thing express.
3 There is no Language, Tongue or Speech, where their Sound is not heard:
In all the Earth and Coasts thereof their Knowledge is conferr'd.
4 In them the Lord made for the Sun a Place of great Renown:
Who like a Bridegroom ready trimm'd, comes from his Chamber down.
5 And as a valiant Champion who would to Honour rise,
With Joy doth haste to take in Hand some noble Enterprise.
6 And all the Sky from End to End he compasseth about:
Nothing can hide it from his Heat, but he will find it out.
7 How perfect is the Law of God! his Covenant is sure:
Converting Souls, and making wise the Simple and Obscure.
8 The Lord's Commands are righteous, and rejoice the Heart; likewise
His Precepts are most pure, and do give Light unto the Eyes.
9 The Fear of God is excellent, and ever doth endure:
The Judgments of the Lord also most righteous are and pure.
10 And more to be desired are than much fine Gold alway:
The Honey and the Honey-comb are not so sweet as they.
11 By them thy Servant is forewarn'd to have God in regard:
And in performance of the same there shall be great Reward.
12 But, Lord, what earthly Man doth know the Errors of his Life?
Then cleanse me from my secret Sins, which are in me most rife.
13 And keep me, that presumptuous Sins prevail not over me:
And so shall I be innocent and great Offences flee.
14 Accept my Mouth and Heart also, my Words and Thoughts each one:
For my Redeemer and my Strength, O Lord thou art alone.

PSALM XX. T. S.

1 IN Trouble and Adversity the Lord God hear thee still:
The Majesty of Jacob's God defend thee from all Ill.

2 And

PSALM XXI, XXII.

2 And send thee from his holy Place　　　his Help at every Need:
And so in Sion 'stablish thee,　　　　　and make thee strong indeed.
3 Remembring well the Sacrifice　　　　that now to him is done:
And so receive most graciously　　　　thy Offerings each one:
4 According to thy Heart's Desire,　　　the Lord grant unto thee:
And all thy Counsel and thy Mind,　　 full well perform may he.
5 We will rejoice when thou us sav'st　and Banners shall display
Unto the Lord, who thy Requests　　　 fulfilled hath alway.
6 The Lord will his Anointed save,　　 I know well by his Grace:
And send him Help by his Right-hand　out of his holy Place.
7 In Chariots some put Confidence,　　 and some in Horses trust:
But we remember God our Lord,　　　　 who keepeth Promise just.
8 They all fall down, but we do rise　and stand up stedfastly:
O save and help us, Lord and King,　 when we to thee do cry.

PSALM XXI. T. S.

1 O Lord, how joyful is the King　　　in thy Strength and thy Pow'r
Exceedingly he doth rejoice　　　　　in thee his Saviour.
2 For thou hast given unto him　　　　his godly Heart's Desire:
To him thou Nothing hast deny'd　　　of that he did require.
3 Thou didst prevent him with thy Gifts　and Blessings manifold:
And thou hast set upon his Head　　　a Crown of perfect Gold.
4 And when he asked Life of thee,　　 therefore thou mad'st him sure:
To have long Life, yea, such a Life　as ever shall endure.
5 Great is his Glory by thy Help,　　 thy Benefit and Aid:
Great Worship and great Honour both　thou hast upon him laid.
6 Thou wilt give him Felicity　　　　　that never shall decay:
And with thy chearful Countenance　　will comfort him alway.
7 Because the King doth strongly trust　in God for to prevail:
Therefore his Goodness and his Grace　to save him will not fail.
8 Thy Enemies shall feel thy Force,　 and those that thee withstand:
Find out thy Foes, and let them feel　the Pow'r of thy Right-hand.
9 And like an Oven burn them, Lord,　in fiery Flame and Fume:
Thy Anger shall destroy them all,　　and Fire shall them consume.
10 And thou shalt root out of the Earth　their Fruit that should increase:
And from the Number of thy Folk,　　 their Seed shall end and cease.
11 For they much Mischief did contrive　against thy holy Name:
Yet did they fail, and had no Pow'r　for to perform the same.
12 But as a Mark thou shalt them set　in a most open Place:
And charge thy Bow-strings readily　 against their very Face.
13 Be thou exalted, Lord, in thy　　　 own Strength, which is our Tow'r:
So shall we sing right solemnly,　　 praising thy Might and Pow'r.

PSALM XXII. T. S.

1 O God, my God, wherefore dost thou　forsake me utterly?
And helpest not when I do make　　　 my great Complaint and Cry?
2 To thee, my God, even all Day long,　I do both cry and call:
I cease not all the Night, and yet　 thou hearest not at all.
3 But thou that in thy holy Place　　 for evermore dost dwell,
Thou art the Joy, the Comfort and　　Glory of Israel.

PSALM XXII.

4 And he in whom our Fathers old   had all their Hope and Stay,
Who when they put their Trust in thee,   deliver'dst them alway.
5 They were preserved ever when   they called on thy Name:
And for the Faith they had in thee,   they were not put to Shame.
6 But I am now become more like   a Worm than to a Man:
An Out-cast, whom the People scorn   with all the Spite they can.
7 All Men despise as they behold   me walking on the Way:
They grin, make Mouths, and nod their Heads,   and on this wise do say;
8 This Man did glory in the Lord,   his Favour and his Love:
Let him redeem and help him now,   his Pow'r if he will prove.
9 But from the Prison of the Womb   I was by thee releast:
Thou didst preserve me still in hope,   whilst I did suck the Breast.
10 I was committed from my Birth,   with thee to have Abode:
Since I came from my Mother's Womb,   thou hast been still my God.

PART II.

11 Then, Lord, depart not now from me   in this my present Grief,
Since I have none to be my Help,   my Succour and Relief.
12 For many Bulls do compass me   that be full strong of Head:
Yea, Bulls so fat, as tho' they had   in Basan Field been fed.
13 They gape upon me greedily,   as though they would me slay:
Much like a Lion roaring out,   and ramping for his Prey.
14 But I drop down like Water shed,   my Joints in sunder break:
My Heart doth in my Body melt   like Wax, I am so weak.
15 My Strength doth like a Potsherd dry,   my Tongue it cleaveth fast
Unto my Jaws, and I am brought   to Dust of Death at last.
16 For many Dogs do compass me,   in Council they do meet:
Conspiring still against my Life,   piercing my Hands and Feet.
17 I was tormented, so that I   might all my Bones have told:
Whilst they do look and stare at me,   when they do me behold.
18 My Garments they divided have   in Parts among them all:
And for my Coat they did cast Lots,   to whom it should befall.
19 Therefore, I pray thee, be not far   from me at my great Need:
But rather, since thou art my Strength,   to help me, Lord, make Speed.
20 And from the Sword save thou my Soul   by thy Might and thy Pow'r:
And ever keep my darling Dear   from Dogs that would devour.
21 And from the Lion's Mouth, that would   me all in sunder tear:
From midst the Horns of Unicorns,   O Lord, thou didst me hear.
22 Then shall I to my Brethren all   thy Majesty record:
And in thy Church shall praise the Name   of thee the living Lord.

PART III.

23 All ye that fear him, praise the Lord,   thou Jacob him adore:
And all ye Seed of Israel,   fear him for evermore,
24 For he despiseth not the Poor,   he hideth not away
His Countenance when they do call,   but hears them when they pray.
25 Among the Folk that fear the Lord,   I will therefore proclaim
Thy Praise, and keep my Promise made   for setting forth thy Name.
26 The Poor shall eat and be suffic'd,   such as their Minds do give
To seek the Lord, shall praise his Name,   their Hearts shall ever live.

27 The

PSALM XXIII, XXIV.

27 The Coasts of all the Earth shall praise
the Lord, and seek his Grace:
The Heathen Folk shall worship all
before his blessed Face.
28 The Kingdoms of the Heathen Folk,
the Lord shall have therefore:
And he shall be their Governor,
and King for evermore.

29 The rich Men of his goodly Gifts
shall taste and feed also:
And in his Presence worship him,
and bow their Knees full low.
30 And all that do go down to Dust,
of Life by him shall taste:
A Seed shall serve and worship him
till Time away shall waste.

31 They shall declare and plainly shew
his Truth and Righteousness,
Unto a People yet unborn,
who shall his Name confess.

PSALM XXIII. W. W.

1 THE Lord is only my Support,
and he that doth me feed:
How can I then lack any Thing
whereof I stand in Need?
2 In Pastures green he feedeth me,
where I do safely lie:
And after leads me to the Streams
which run most pleasantly.

3 And when I find myself near lost,
then doth he me Home take;
Conducting me in his right Paths,
ev'n for his own Name's sake.
4 And tho' I were ev'n at Death's Door,
yet would I fear no Ill:
For both thy Rod and Shepherd's Crook
afford me Comfort still.

5 Thou hast my Table richly spread
in Presence of my Foe:
Thou hast with Balm my Head refresh'd,
my Cup doth overflow.
6 And finally while Breath doth last,
thy Grace shall me defend:
And in the House of God will I
my Life for ever spend.

Another of the same by T. S.

1 MY Shepherd is the living Lord,
Nothing therefore I need:
In Pastures fair, near pleasant Streams, he setteth me to feed.
2 He shall convert and glad my Soul,
and bring my Mind in Frame:
To walk in Paths of Righteousness,
for his most holy Name.

3 Yea, tho' I walk in Vale of Death,
yet will I fear no Ill:
Thy Rod and Staff do comfort me,
and thou art with me still.
4 And in the Presence of my Foes
my Table thou shalt spread:
Thou wilt fill full my Cup, and thou
anointed hast my Head.

5 Thro' all my Life thy Favour is
so frankly shew'd to me,
That in thy House for evermore
my Dwelling-place shall be.

PSALM XXIV. J. H.

1 THE Earth is all the Lord's, with all
her Store and Furniture:
Yea, his is all the World, and all
that therein doth endure.
2 For he hath fastly founded it
above the Seas to stand:
And plac'd below the liquid Floods,
to flow beneath the Land.

3 Who is the Man, O Lord, that shall
ascend unto thy Hill?
Or pass into thy holy Place,
there to continue still?
4 Even he whose Hands and Heart are pure,
which Nothing doth defile:
His Soul not set on Vanity,
and hath not sworn to Guile.

5 Him that is such a one, the Lord
most highly will regard:
And from his God and Saviour shall
receive a just Reward.
6 This is the Generation of
them that do seek his Grace:
Ev'n them that with an upright Heart
O Jacob, seek thy Face.

7 Ye

PSALM XXV.

7 Ye Gates and everlasting Doors, lift up your Heads on high:
Then shall the King of glorious State come in triumphantly.
8 Who is the King of glorious State? the great and mighty Lord:
The mighty Lord in Battle strong, and Trial of the Sword.

9 Ye Gates and everlasting Doors, lift up your Heads on high:
Then shall the King of glorious State come in triumphantly.
10 Who is the King of glorious State? the Lord of Hosts it is:
The Kingdom and the Royalty of glorious State is his.

PSALM XXV. T. S.

1 I Lift my Heart to thee, my God and Guide most just:
Now suffer me to take no Shame, for in thee do I trust.
2 Let not my Foes rejoice, nor make a Scorn of me:
And let them not be overthrown that put their Trust in thee.

3 But Shame shall them befall who harm them wrongfully:
Therefore thy Paths and thy right Ways unto me, Lord, descry.
4 Direct me in thy Truth, and teach me, I thee pray:
Thou art my Saviour and my God, on thee I wait alway.

5 Thy Mercies manifold remember, Lord, I pray:
In Pity thou art plentiful, and so hast been alway,
6 Remember not the Faults and Frailty of my Youth:
Call not to Mind how ignorant I have been of thy Truth.

7 Nor after my Desires let me thy Mercy find:
But of thine own Benignity, Lord, have me in thy Mind.
8 His Mercy is full sweet his Truth a perfect Guide:
Therefore the Lord will Sinners teach, and such as go aside.

9 The Humble he will teach his Precepts to obey:
He will direct in all his Paths the lowly Man alway.
10 For all the Ways of God both Truth and Mercy are,
To them that do his Covenant and Statutes keep with Care.

PART II.

11 Now for thy holy Name, O Lord, I thee intreat,
To grant me Pardon for my Sin, for it is wond'rous great.
12 Whoso doth fear the Lord, by him he shall be kept,
To lead his Life in such a Way as he doth best accept.

13 His Soul shall evermore in Goodness dwell and stand:
His Seed and his Posterity inherit shall the Land.
14 All those that fear the Lord know his secret intent:
And unto them he doth declare his Will and Testament.

15 My Eyes and thankful Heart to him I will advance,
That pluckt my Feet out of the Snare of Sin and Ignorance.
16 With Mercy me behold, to thee I make my Moan:
For I am poor and desolate, and comfortless alone.

17 The Troubles of my Heart are multiply'd indeed:
Bring me out of this Misery, Necessity and Need.
18 Behold my Poverty, my Anguish and my Pain:
Remit my Sin and my Offence, and make me clean again.

19 O Lord, behold my Foes, how they do still increase:
Pursuing me with deadly Hate, that fain would live in Peace.

PSALM XXVI, XXVII.

20 Preserve and keep my Soul, and still deliver me:
And let me not be overthrown, because I trust in thee.
21 Let Truth and Uprightness for ever wait on me:
Because my Hope and Confidence hath always been in thee.
22 Deliver, Lord, thy Folk, and send them some Relief:
I mean thy Chosen Israel, from all their Pain and Grief.

PSALM XXVI. T. S.

1 LORD, be my Judge, and thou shalt see my Paths be right and plain:
I trust in God and hope that he with Strength will me sustain.
2 Prove me, my God, I thee desire, my Ways to search and try:
As Men do prove their Gold with Fire, my Heart and Reins espy.
3 Thy Loving-kindness in my Sight I do behold always:
I ever walked in thy Truth, and will do all my Days.
4 I do not love to haunt or use with Men whose Deeds are vain,
To come in House I do refuse with the deceitful Train.
5 I much abhor the wicked Sort, their Deeds I do despise:
I do not once to them resort that hurtful Things devise.
6 My Hands I wash, and do proceed in Works to walk upright:
Then to thy Altar I make Speed, to offer there in Sight.
7 That I may speak and preach the Praise that doth belong to thee:
And so declare how wond'rous Ways thou hast been good to me.
8 O God, thy House I love most dear, to me it doth excell:
My chief Delight is to be near the Place where thou dost dwell.
9 O shut not up my Soul with them in Sin that take their Fill:
Nor yet my Life among those Men that seek much Blood to spill.
10 For in their Hands much Mischief is, their Lives therewith abound:
And Nothing else in their Right-hand but Bribes is to be found.
11 But I resolve in Righteousness my Time and Days to spend,
Therefore that I may not transgress, let thy Grace me defend.
12 My Foot is staid for all Assays, it standeth well and right:
Wherefore to God will I give Praise in all the People's Sight.

PSALM XXVII. J. H.

1 THE Lord is both my Health and Light, shall Man make me dismay'd?
Since God doth give me Strength and Might, why should I be afraid?
2 While that my Foes, with all their Strength, began with me to brawl,
Thinking to eat me up, at length themselves be caught to fall.
3 Tho' they in Camp against me lie, my Heart is not afraid:
And if in Battle they will try, I trust in God for Aid.
4 One Thing of God I do require, that he will not deny:
For which I pray, and will desire till he to me apply.
5 That I within his holy Place my Life thro'out may dwell:
To see the Beauty of his Face, and view his Temple well.
6 In Time of Dread he shall me hide within his Place most pure:
And keep me secret by his Side, as on a Rock most sure.
7 At length I know the Lord's good Grace shall make me strong and stout,
My Foes to foil and clean deface, that compass me about.
8 Therefore within his House will I give Sacrifice of Praise:
With Psalms and Songs I will apply to laud the Lord always.

PART

PSALM XXVIII, XXIX.
PART. II.

9 Lord, hear the Voice of my Requeſt, for which to thee I cry:
Have Mercy, Lord, on me oppreſt, and help me ſpeedily.
10 My Heart confeſſeth unto thee, I ſue to thee for Grace:
Then ſeek my Face, ſaidſt thou to me, Lord, I will ſeek thy Face.

11 In Wrath turn not thy Face away, nor ſuffer me to ſlide:
My Help thou haſt been to this Day, be ſtill my God and Guide.
12 When both my Parents me forſake, and caſt me off at large:
Ev'n then the Lord himſelf doth take of me the Care and Charge.

13 Teach me, O Lord, the Way to thee, and lead me on forth right:
For fear of ſuch as watch for me, to trap me, if they might,
14 O leave me not unto the Will of them that be my Foes:
For they ſurmiſe againſt me ſtill falſe Witneſs to depoſe.

15 I utterly ſhould faint, but that this Hope ſupporteth me,
That in the Land wherein I live God's Goodneſs I ſhall ſee.
16 Truſt ſtill in God, whoſe Whole thou art, his Will abide thou muſt:
He will ſupport and eaſe thy Heart. if thou in him do truſt.

PSALM XXVIII. T. S.

1 THOU art, O Lord, my Strength and Stay, the Succour which I crave:
Neglect me not, left I be like them that are laid in Grave.
2 My Voice and Supplications hear when unto thee I cry:
When I lift up my Hands unto thy holy Ark moſt high.

3 Repute me not among thoſe Men in Sin that take their Fill:
That ſpeak right fair unto their Friends, but think in Heart full ill.
4 According to thoſe wicked Deeds which they did moſt regard,
And after their Inventions, Lord, let them receive Reward.

5 Becauſe they never mind the Works of God, he will therefore,
Inſtead of building of them up, deſtroy them evermore.
6 To render Thanks unto the Lord how great a Cauſe have I,
My Voice, my Pray'r and my Complaint, that heard ſo willingly.

7 He is my Shield and Fortitude, my Buckler in Diſtreſs:
My Heart rejoiceth greatly, and my Song ſhall him confeſs.
8 He is our Strength and our Defence, our Foes for to reſiſt:
The Health and the Salvation of his own Elect by Chriſt.

9 Thy People and thy Heritage, Lord, bleſs, guide and preſerve:
Increaſe them, Lord, and rule their Hearts, that they may never ſwerve.

PSALM XXIX. T. S.

1 GIVE to the Lord, ye Potentates, give ye with one Accord,
All Praiſe and Honour, Might & Strength, unto the living Lord.
2 Give Glory to his holy Name, and honour him alone:
Give Worſhip to his Majeſty within his holy Throne.

3 His Voice doth rule the Waters all, as he himſelf doth pleaſe:
He doth prepare the Thunder-claps, and governs all the Seas.
4 The Voice of God is of great Force, and wond'rous excellent:
It is moſt mighty in Effect, and moſt magnificent.

5 The Voice of God doth rend and break the Cedar-trees ſo long:
The Cedar-trees of Lebanon, which are both high and ſtrong.
6 And makes them leap like as a Calf, or as the Unicorn;
Not only Trees, but Mountains great, whereon the Trees are born.

PSALM XXX, XXXI.

7 His Voice divides the Flames of Fire, and shakes the Wilderness
   It makes the Desart quake for Fear, that Cades called is.
8 It makes the Hinds for Fear to calve, and Coverts plain appear:
   And in his Temple ev'ry Man speaks of his Glory there.
9 The Lord doth sit upon the Floods, their Fury to restrain:
   And he likewise as Lord and King, for evermore shall reign.
10 The Lord will give his People Strength, whereby they shall increase:
   And he will bless his chosen Flock. with everlasting Peace.

PSALM XXX. J. H.

1 ALL Laud and Praise with Heart and Voice, O Lord, I give to thee:
   Who didst not make my Foes rejoice, but hast exalted me.
2 O Lord my God to thee I cry'd in all my Pain and Grief;
   Thou gav'st an Ear, and didst provide to ease me with Relief.
3 Thou, Lord, hast brought my Soul from Hell, and thou the same didst save
   From them that in their Pit do dwell, and kept'st me from the Grave.
4 Sing Praise, ye Saints, that prove and see the Goodness of the Lord:
   In Honour of his Majesty rejoice with one Accord.
5 For why? his Anger but a Space doth last, ceasing again:
   But in his Favour and his Grace always doth Life remain.
6 Tho' Heaviness and Pangs full sore abide with us all Night,
   The Lord to Joy shall us restore before the Day be light.
7 When I enjoy'd the World at Will, thus would I boast and say,
   Tush, I am sure to feel no Ill, my Wealth shall not decay.
8 For thou, O Lord, of thy good Grace didst send me Strength and Aid:
   But when thou turn'dst away thy Face, my Mind was sore dismay'd.
9 Wherefore again then did I cry to thee, O Lord of Might:
   And my Complaints did multiply, praying both Day and Night.
10 What Gain is in my Blood, said I, if Death destroy my Days?
   Can Dust declare thy Majesty, or give thy Truth its Praise?
11 Wherefore, my God, some Pity take, O Lord, I thee desire:
   Do not, O Lord, my Soul forsake, of thee Help I require.
12 Then didst thou turn my Grief and Woe into a chearful Voice:
   My Sackcloth didst take off also, and mad'st me to rejoice.
13 Wherefore my Soul incessantly shall sing unto thy Praise:
   My Lord, my God, to thee will I give Laud and Thanks always.

PSALM XXXI. J. H.

1 O Lord, I put my Trust in thee, let Nothing work me Shame:
   As thou art just, deliver me, and set me free from Blame.
2 Hear me, O Lord, and that anon, to help me make good Speed:
   Be thou my Rock and House of Stone, my Fence in Time of Need.
3 For why? as Stones thy Strength is try'd, thou art my Fort and Tow'r:
   For thy Name's Sake be thou my Guide, and lead me in thy Pow'r.
4 Pluck thou my Feet out of the Snare which they for me have laid:
   Thou art my Strength, and all my Care is for thy mighty Aid.
5 Into thy Hands, Lord, I commit my Soul, which is thy Due:
   Because thou hast redeemed it, O Lord my God most true.
6 I hate such Folk as will not part from Things to be abhorr'd:
   When they on Trifles set their Heart, my Trust is in the Lord.

PSALM XXXII.

7 For I will in thy Mercy joy, I fee it doth excell:
Thou feeſt when ought would me annoy, and know'ſt my Soul full well.
8 Thou haſt not left me in their Hand that would me overcharge:
But thou haſt ſet me out of Band, to walk abroad at large.

PART II.

9 Great Grief, O Lord, doth me aſſail, ſome Pity on me take:
My Eyes wax dim, my Sight doth fail, my Heart with Fear doth ake.
10 My Life is worn with Grief and Pain, my Years in Woe are paſt:
My Strength is gone, and thro' Diſdain my Bone corrupt and waſte.
11 Among my Foes I am a Scorn, my Friends are all diſmay'd:
My Neighbours and my Kinſmen born, to ſee me are afraid.
12 As Men once dead are out of Mind, ſo am I now forgot:
As little Uſe of me they find, as of a broken Pot.
13 I heard the Brags of all the Rout, their Threats my Mind did fray:
How they conſpir'd and went about to take my Life away.
14 But, Lord, I truſt in thee for Aid, not to be overtrod:
For I confeſs, and ſtill have ſaid, thou art the Lord my God.
15 The Length of all my Life and Age, O Lord is in thy Hand:
Defend me from the Wrath and Rage of them that me withſtand.
16 To me thy Servant, Lord, expreſs and ſhew thy joyful Face:
And ſave me, Lord, for thy Goodneſs, thy Mercy and thy Grace.

PART III.

17 Lord, let me not be put to Shame, becauſe on thee I call:
But let the Wicked bear the Blame, and into the Grave fall.
18 O Lord, make dumb their Lips out-right, who given are to Lyes:
And cruelly with Pride and Spight againſt the Juſt deviſe.
19 How plentiful thy Mercies be laid up for thy Children,
That fear and put their Truſt in thee before the Sons of Men!
20 Thy Preſence ſhall them fence and guide from all proud Brags and Wrongs:
Within thy Place thou ſhalt them hide from all the Strife of Tongues.
21 Thanks to the Lord that hath declar'd on me his Grace ſo far,
Me to defend with Watch and Ward, as in a Town of War,
22 Thus did I ſay both Day and Night, when I was ſore oppreſt,
Lo, I am clean caſt out of Sight, yet heard'ſt thou my Requeſt.
23 Ye Saints, love ye the Lord alway, the Faithful he doth guide:
And to the Proud he doth repay according to their Pride.
24 Be of good Courage, all ye Juſt, on God your Strength depend:
For thoſe in him that put their Truſt, he ever will defend.

PSALM XXXII. T. S.

1 THE Man is bleſt whoſe Wickedneſs the Lord forgiven hath:
And he whoſe Sin is likewiſe hid, and cover'd from his Wrath.
2 And bleſt is he to whom the Lord imputeth not his Sin:
Who in his Heart hath hid no Guile, nor Fraud is found therein.
3 For whilſt that I kept cloſe my Sin in Silence and Conſtraint,
My Bones did wear and waſte away with daily Moan and Plaint.
4 Both Night and Day thy Hand on me ſo grievous was and ſmart,
My Moiſture like the Summer's Heat, to Dryneſs did convert.
5 I did therefore confeſs my Faults, and all my Sins reveal:
Then thou, O Lord, didſt me forgive, and all my Sins conceal.

PSALM XXXIII.

6 The humble Man shall pray therefore, and seek thee in due Time:
So that the Floods of Waters great shall have no Pow'r on him.
7 When Trouble and Adversity do compass me about,
Thou art my Refuge and my Joy, and thou dost rid me out.
8 Come hither and I will thee teach, how thou shalt walk aright;
I thee will guide, as I myself have learn'd by Proof and Sight.
9 Be not so rude and ignorant as is the Horse and Mule:
Whose Mouth without a Rein or Bit, from Harm thou canst not rule.
10 The wicked Man shall manifold Sorrows and Grief sustain:
But unto him that trusts in God, his Goodness shall remain.
11 Be merry therefore in the Lord, ye Just lift up your Voice:
And ye of pure and perfect Heart, with Chearfulness rejoice.

PSALM XXXIII. J. H.

1 YE Righteous in the Lord rejoice, it is a seemly Sight,
That upright Men with thankful Voice, shall praise the Lord of Might.
2 Praise ye the Lord with Harp, and sing to him with Psaltery:
With Ten-string'd founding Instruments praise ye the Lord most high.
3 Sing to the Lord a Song most new, with Courage give him Praise:
For why? his Word is ever true, his Works and all his Ways.
4 Both Judgment, Equity, and Right, he ever lov'd and will:
And with his Gifts he doth delight the Earth throughout to fill.
5 For by the Word of God alone the Heav'ns above were wrought:
Their Hosts and Powers ev'ry one, his Breath to pass hath brought.
6 The Waters great gather'd hath he on Heaps within the Shore:
And hid them in the Depth to be, as in a House of Store.
7 Let all the Earth then fear the Lord, and keep his righteous Law:
And all the World with one Accord dread him, and stand in Awe.
8 What he commanded, wrought it was at once with utmost Speed:
What he doth will, is brought to pass with full Effect indeed.
9 The Counsels of the Nations rude, the Lord doth bring to nought;
He doth defeat the Multitude of their Device and Thought.
10 But his Decrees continue still, they never slack nor swage:
The Motions of his Mind and Will take Place in ev'ry Age.

PART II.

11 Blessed are they to whom the Lord as God and Guide is known:
Whom he doth chuse of meer Accord, to take them as his own.
12 The Lord from Heav'n did cast his Sight on Men mortal by Birth:
Beholding from his Seat of Might the Dwellers on the Earth.
13 The Lord, I say, whose Hand hath wrought Man's Heart, and doth it frame;
'Tis he alone doth know the Thought and working of the same.
14 A King that trusteth in his Host, shall nought prevail at length:
The Man that of his Might doth boast, shall fail for all his Strength.
15 The Troops of Horsemen all shall fail, their sturdy Steeds shall swerve:
The Strength of Horse shall not prevail the Rider to preserve.
16 But lo, the Eyes of God attend and watch to aid the Just:
With such as fear him to offend and on his Goodness trust.
17 That he of Death and great Distress may set their Souls from Dread:
And if that Dearth their Land oppress, in Hunger them to feed.

18 Where

PSALM XXXIV.

18 Wherefore our Soul doth whole depend on God our Strength and Stay
    He is our Shield us to defend, and drive all Darts away.
19 Our joyful Souls always proclaim his Power and his Might:
    For why? in his most holy Name we hope and much delight.
20 Therefore let thy Goodness, O Lord, still present with us be,
    As we always with one Accord do only trust in thee.

PSALM XXXIV. T. S.

1 I Will give Laud and Honour both unto the Lord always:
    My Mouth also for evermore shall speak unto his Praise.
2 I do delight to laud the Lord in Soul, in Heart, in Voice:
    That humble Men may hear thereof, and heartily rejoice.
3 Therefore see that ye magnify with me the living Lord:
    Let us exalt his holy Name always with one accord.
4 For I my self besought the Lord, he answer'd me again:
    And me deliver'd speedily from all my Fear and Pain.
5 Whoso they be that him behold, shall see his Light most clear:
    Their Countenance shall not be dasht, they never need to fear.
6 The poor distressed Man for Help, unto the Lord doth call:
    Who doth him hear without Delay, and rid him out of Thrall.
7 The Angel of the Lord doth pitch his Tents in ev'ry Place:
    To save all such as do him fear, that Nothing them deface.
8 Taste and consider well therefore, that God is good and just:
    O happy Man that maketh him his only Stay and Trust.
9 O fear the Lord, all ye his Saints, who is a mighty King:
    For they that fear the living Lord, are sure to lack Nothing.
10 The Lions shall be hunger-bit, and pin'd with Famine much:
    But as for them that fear the Lord, no Lack shall be to such.

PART II.

11 Come near to me, my Children, and unto my Words give ear:
    I will you teach the perfect Way, how ye the Lord shall fear.
12 Who is the Man that would live long, and lead a happy Life?
    See thou refrain thy Tongue and Lips from all Deceit and Strife.
13 Turn back thy Face from doing Ill, and do the godly Deed:
    Enquire for Peace and Quietness, and follow it with Speed.
14 For why? the Eyes of God above unto the Just are bent:
    His Ears likewise to hear the Cry of the poor Innocent.
15 But he doth frown and bend his Brows upon the wicked Train:
    And cuts away the Memory that should of them remain.
16 But when the Just do call and cry, the Lord doth hear them so.
    That out of Pain and Misery forthwith he lets them go.
17 The Lord is ever nigh to them that broken-hearted are:
    And for the contrite Spirit he Salvation doth prepare.
18 Full many be the Miseries that righteous Men endure:
    But of Deliv'rance from them all the Lord doth them secure.
19 The Lord doth so preserve and keep their very Bones alway,
    That not so much as one of them doth perish or decay.
20 The Sin shall slay the wicked Man, which he himself hath wrought:
    And such as hate the righteous Man, shall soon be brought to nought.

PSALM XXXV.

21 But they that fear the living Lord, are ever safe and found.
And as for those that trust in him, Nothing shall them confound.

PSALM XXXV. J. H.

1 LORD, plead my Cause against my Foes, confound their Force and Might:
And take my Part against all those that seek with me to fight.
2 Lay hold upon the Spear and Shield, thyself in Armour dress:
Stand up with me to fight the Field, and help me from Distress.
3 Gird on thy Sword, and stop the Way, my Enemies withstand:
That thou unto my Soul may'st say, I am thy Help at Hand.
4 Confound them with Rebuke and Blame that seek my Soul to spill:
Let them turn back and flee with Shame, that think to work me ill.
5 Let them disperse and flee abroad, as Wind doth drive the Dust:
That so the Angel of our God, their Might away may thrust.
6 Let all their Ways be void of Light, and slipp'ry like to fall:
And send thy Angel with thy Might, to persecute them all.
7 For why? without my Fault have they in secret set their Gin:
And digg'd a Pit in my Path-way, to take my Soul therein.
8 When they think least, and have no Care, O Lord, destroy them all:
Let them be caught in their own Snare, and in their Mischief fall.
9 But let my Soul, my Heart, and Voice, in God have Joy and Wealth:
That in the Lord I may rejoice, and in his saving Health.
10 Then all my Bones shall speak and say, (my Parts shall all agree)
O thou great God of Heav'n and Earth, what Man is like to thee?

PART II.

11 Thou dost defend the Weak from them that are both stout and strong:
And rid the Poor from wicked Men, that spoil and do them Wrong.
12 My cruel Foes against me rise, to witness Things untrue:
And to accuse me they devise, of Things I never knew.
13 When I to them did shew good Will, they quit me with Disdain:
That they should pay my Good with Ill, my Soul doth sore complain.
14 When they were sick I mourn'd therefore, myself in Sackcloth clad:
With Fasting I was faint full sore, and prayed with Heart full sad.
15 As they had been my Brethren dear, I did myself behave:
As one that mourneth heavily about his Mother's Grave.
16 But they in my Adversity did gather in a Rout:
Yea, abject Slaves reproachfully at me did mock and flout.
17 The Belly-Gods and flatt'ring Train, that all good Things deride,
At me did grin with great Disdain, turning their Mouths aside.
18 Lord, when wilt thou for me appear? why dost thou stay and pause?
O rid my Soul, my darling Dear, out of these Lions claws.
19 And then will I give Thanks to thee before the Church always:
And where most of the People be, there will I shew thy Praise.
20 Let not my Foes prevail on me, which hate me for no Fault:
Neither let them wink with their Eyes, that causeless me assault.

PART III.

21 Of Peace no Word they think or say, their Talk is all untrue:
They still consult how to betray all those that Peace pursue.
22 With open Mouth they run at me, their Fury is like Fire:
Well, well, say they, our Eye doth see the Thing that we desire.

23 But,

PSALM XXXVI, XXXVII.

23 But, Lord, thou fee'ft what Ways they take, and what they do intend:
Be not far off, nor me forfake, but fpeedy Help me fend.
24 Awake, arife, and ftir abroad, defend me in my Right:
Revenge my Caufe, O Lord my God, and aid me with thy Might.
25 According to thy Righteoufnefs, O Lord God, fet me free:
And let them not their Pride exprefs, nor triumph over me.
26 Let not their Hearts rejoice, nor cry, ev'n fo we would it have:
Nor give them Caufe to fay on high, he's funk into the Grave.
27 Confound them all that do rejoice when they my Trouble fee:
Let them be cloathed with Rebuke, that boaft with Scorn at me.
28 But let them heartily rejoice who love my upright Way:
Let them all Times with Heart and Voice ftill praife the Lord and fay,
29 Great is the Lord, and doth excell, and he doth much delight
To fee his Servants profper well, it is his pleafant Sight.
30 Wherefore my Tongue I will apply thy Righteoufnefs to praife:
To thee the Lord my God will I give Laud and Thanks always.

PSALM XXXVI. J. H.

1 THE Wicked by his Works unjuft doth thus perfwade my Heart,
That in the Lord he hath no Truft, his Fear is fet apart.
2 Yet doth he joy in his Eftate to walk as he began,
So long till he deferve the Hate of God as well as Man.
3 His Words are wicked, vile, and nought, his Tongue no Truth can tell:
Yet at no Hand will he be taught, which Way he may do well.
4 When he fhould fleep, then doth he mufe his Mifchiefs to fulfil:
No wicked Way doth me refufe, nor any Thing that's ill.
5 But, Lord, thy Goodnefs doth afcend above the Heav'ns moft high:
So doth thy Truth itfelf extend unto the cloudy Sky.
6 Much more than Hills both high and fteep, thy Juftice is expreft:
Thy Judgments like to Seas moft deep, thou fav'ft both Man and Beaft.
7 Thy Mercy is above all Things, O God, it doth excell:
In Truft whereof, as in thy Wings, the Sons of Men that dwell.
8 Within thy Houfe they fhall be fed with Plenty at their Will:
Of all Delights they fhall be fped, and take thereof their Fill.
9 Becaufe the Well of Life moft pure doth ever flow from thee:
And in thy Light we are full fure eternal Light to fee.
10 From fuch as thee defire to know, let not thy Grace depart:
Thy Righteoufnefs declare and fhow to Men of upright Heart.
11 Let not the Proud on me prevail, O Lord of thy good Grace:
Nor let the Wicked me affail, to throw me out of Place.
12 But they in their Device fhall fall, that wicked Works maintain:
They fhall be certainly caft down, and never rife again.

PSALM XXXVII. W. W.

1 GRUDGE not to fee the wicked Men in Wealth to flourifh ftill:
Nor envy fuch as ill to do have bent and fet their Will.
2 For as the Grafs and the green Herb do wither and decay:
So fhall their great Profperity foon fade and pafs away.
3 Truft thou therefore in God alone, to do well give thy Mind:
So fhalt thou have the Land as thine, and there fure Food fhalt find.

PSALM XXXVII.

4 In God let all thy Heart's Delight,
  Or elſe canſt wiſh in all the World,
  and look what thou wouldſt have:
  thou need'ſt it not to crave.
5 Caſt both thyſelf and thy Affairs
  And then thou ſhalt with Patience ſee
  on God with perfect Truſt:
  th' Effect both ſure and juſt.
6 Thy perfect Life and godly Name
  So that the Sun, even at Noon-day,
  he will clear as the Light:
  ſhall not ſhine half ſo bright.
7 Be ſtill therefore and ſtedfaſtly
  Nor ſhrinking for the proſp'rous State
  on God ſee thou wait then:
  of lewd and wicked Men.
8 Shake off Deſpite, Envy and Hate,
  That thou mayſt not be drawn into
  let not thine Anger riſe:
  ſome ſinful Enterpriſe.
9 For ev'ry wicked Man will God
  But ſuch as truſt in him are ſure
  moſt certainly deſtroy:
  the Land for to enjoy.
10 Wait but a while, and thou ſhalt ſee
   No, not ſo much as Houſe or Place
   no more the wicked Train:
   where once he did remain.

PART II.

11 But merciful and humble Men
   In Reſt and Peace they ſhall rejoice,
   enjoy ſhall Sea and Land:
   for nought ſhall them withſtand.
12 The lewd Men and malicious do
   They gnaſh their Teeth at him, as Men
   againſt the Juſt conſpire:
   who do his Bane deſire.
13 But while ungodly Men thus think,
   For he doth ſee the Time approach,
   the Lord laughs them to ſcorn;
   when they ſhall ſigh and mourn.
14 The wicked have their Sword out drawn,
   To overthrow and kill the Poor,
   their Bow is alſo bent,
   whoſe Life is innocent.
15 But the ſame Sword ſhall pierce their Heart,
   So ſhall the Bow in Shivers break,
   which was to kill the Juſt:
   wherein they put their Truſt.
16 Doubtleſs the juſt Man's poor Eſtate
   Than all the lewd and wicked Man's
   is to be valu'd more,
   rich Pomp and heaped Store.
17 For tho' their Power be moſt ſtrong
   Where contrary he doth preſerve
   God will it overthrow:
   the humble Men and low.
18 He ſees by his great Providence
   And will give them Inheritance
   the Godly's upright Way:
   which never ſhall decay.
19 Diſcouraged they ſhall not be
   When others ſhall be hunger-bit,
   when ſome are hard beſtead:
   they ſhall be clad and fed.
20 For whoſoever wicked is,
   Shall like the Fat of Lambs conſume;
   and Enemy to God,
   or Smoke that flies abroad.

PART III.

21 Behold, the Wicked borrows much,
   Whereas the Juſt by lib'ral Gifts
   and payeth not again:
   the Needy doth ſuſtain.
22 For they whom God doth bleſs, ſhall have
   And they whom he doth curſe, likewiſe
   the Land for Heritage:
   ſhall periſh in his Rage.
23 The Lord the juſt Man's Steps doth guide,
   To ev'ry Thing he takes in Hand,
   and all his Ways doth bleſs:
   he giveth good Succeſs.
24 Tho' he do fail, yet he is ſure
   For God upholds him with his Hand,
   not utterly to ſink:
   and from him will not ſhrink.
25 I have been young, but now am old
   The juſt Man left, neither his Seed
   but never yet ſaw I
   reduc'd to Beggary.
26 He gives always moſt lib'rally,
   By which he doth from God ſecure.
   and lends where there is Need:
   a Bleſſing to his Seed.

27 Therefore

PSALM XXXVIII.

27 Therefore flee Vice and Wickedness
 So God shall grant thee long to have
28 For God so loveth Equity,
 That he preserveth them, but doth
29 Whereas the good and godly Men
 Having as Lords all Things therein,
30 The just Man's Mouth doth ever speak
 His Tongue doth talk of Judgment, and
31 For in his Heart the Law of God
 So that wherever he doth go,
32 The Wicked like a greedy Wolf,
 By all Means seeking him to kill,

and Virtue do embrace:
on Earth a dwelling Place.
and shews to his such Grace,
cut off the wicked Race.
inherit still the Land:
in their own Pow'r and Hand.
of Matters wise and high:
of Truth and Equity.
doth evermore abide:
his Foot shall never slide.
the just Man doth beset:
and take him in his Net.

PART IV.

33 But tho' he fall into his Hands,
 Tho' Men against him Sentence give,
34 Wait thou on God and keep his Way,
 The Earth to rule, and thou shalt see
35 The Wicked have I seen most strong,
 Spreading himself, and flourishing
36 But suddenly he past away,
 Then I him sought, but could not find
37 Mark and behold the upright Man,
 For the just Man shall have at length,
38 As for Transgressors, woe to them,
 God will cut off their budding Race,
39 But the Salvation of the Just
 Who in their Trouble sends them Aid
40 God evermore delivers them
 And still will save them, whilst that they

God will him Succour send:
yet God will him defend.
he shall preserve thee then:
destroy'd these wicked Men.
and plac'd in high Degree:
as doth the Lawrel-tree.
and lo he was quite gone:
the Place where dwelt such one.
how God doth him increase:
great Joy with Rest and Peace.
destroy'd they all shall be:
and rich Posterity.
doth come from God above,
of his meer Grace and Love.
form lewd Men and unjust:
in him do put their Trust.

PSALM XXXVIII. J. H.

1 PUT me not to Rebuke, O Lord,
 And in thy Wrath correct me not
2 Thy Arrows do stick fast in me,
 And in my Flesh no Health at all
3 And all this is by Reason of
 Nor any Rest is in my Bones,
4 For lo, my wicked Doings, Lord,
 A greater Load than I can bear,
5 My Wounds do stink and are corrupt,
 Which all thro' my own Foolishness
6 And I in careful wise am brought
 That I go wailing all the Day
7 My Loins are fill'd with sore Disease,
 I feeble am and broken sore,
8 Thou know'st, Lord, my Desire, my Groans
 My Heart doth pant, my Strength doth fail,
9 My Lovers and my wonted Friends
 My Kinsmen they do far away:

in thy provoked Ire:
I humbly thee desire.
thy Hand doth press me sore:
appeareth any more.
thy Wrath that I am in:
by Reason of my Sin.
above my Head are gone:
they lie me sore upon.
and loathsome are to see:
doth happen unto me.
into such great Distress,
in doleful Heaviness.
my Flesh hath no whole Part:
and roar for Grief of Heart.
are open in thy Sight:
my Eyes have lost their Light.
stand looking on my Woe:
from me depart also.

D
          10 They

PSALM XXXIX.

10 They that do seek my Life lay Snares, and they that go the Way
To do me Hurt, speak Lies, and think on Mischief all the Day.

PART II.

11 But as a deaf Man I became, that cannot hear at all:
And as one dumb, that opens not his Mouth to speak withal.
12 For all my Confidence, O Lord, I wholly place in thee:
Therefore, O Lord, who art my God, do thou give ear to me,
13 This do I crave that they my Foes triumph not over me:
For when my Foot doth slip, then they rejoice my Fall to see.
14 And I am ready for to halt, I cannot stand upright:
Also my grievous Heaviness is ever in my Sight.
15 For while that I my Wickedness in humble wise confess,
And while I for my sinful Deeds my Sorrows do express,
16 My Foes do still remain alive, and mighty are I know:
And they that hurt me wrongfully in Number largly grow.
17 They stand against me that my Good with Evil do repay:
Because that good and honest Things I do pursue alway.
18 Forsake me not, O Lord my God, be thou not far away:
Make Haste to help me, O my God, my Safety and my Stay.

PSALM XXXIX. J. H.

1 I Said, I will look to my Ways, for Fear I should go wrong:
I will take heed all Times that I offend not with my Tongue.
2 As with a Bit I will keep fast my Mouth with Force and Might:
Nor once to whisper all the While the Wicked are in Sight.
3 I held my Tongue and spake no Word, but kept me close and still:
Yea, from good Talk I did refrain, but sore against my Will.
4 My Heart grew hot within my Breast with Musing, Thought, and Doubt:
Which did increase and stir the Fire; at last these Words burst out:
5 Lord, number out my Life and Days, which yet I have not past:
So that I may be certify'd how long my Life shall last.
6 For thou hast pointed out my Life in Length much like a Span:
My Age is Nothing unto thee, so vain is ev'ry Man.
7 Man walketh like a Shade, and doth in vain himself annoy,
In getting Goods, and cannot tell who shall the same enjoy.
8 Therefore, O Lord, what wait I for, what Help do I desire?
Truly my Hope is even in thee, I Nothing else require.

PART II.

9 From all the Sins that I have done, Lord, quit me out of Hand,
And make me not a Scorn to Fools, that Nothing understand.
10 I was so dumb, that to complain no Trouble could me move:
Because I knew it was thy Work, my Patience for to prove.
11 Lord, take from me thy Scourge and Plague, I cannot them withstand:
I faint and pine away for fear of thy most heavy Hand.
12 When thou for Sin dost Man rebuke, he waxeth pale and wan,
As doth a Cloth that Moths have fret, so vain a Thing is Man.
13 Lord, hear my Suit, and give good Heed, regard my Tears that fall:
I sojourn like a Stranger here, as did my Fathers all.
14 O spare a little, give me Space my Strength for to restore,
Before I go away from hence, and shall be seen no more.

PSALM

PSALM XL.

PSALM XL. J. H.

1 I Waited long, and fought the Lord, and patiently did bear:
 At Length to me he did accord my Voice and Cry to hear.
2 He brought me from the dreadful Pit, out of the Mire and Clay:
 Upon a Rock he set my Feet, and he did guide my Way.
3 To me he taught a Pfalm of Praife, which I muft fhew abroad:
 And fing new Songs of Thanks always unto the Lord our God.
4 When all the Folk thefe Things fhall fee, as People much afraid:
 Then they unto the Lord will flee, and truft upon his Aid.
5 Bleffed is he whofe Hope and Heart doth in the Lord remain:
 That with the Proud doth take no Part, nor fuch as Lies maintain.
6 For, Lord my God, thy wond'rous Deeds in Greatnefs far do pafs:
 Thy Favour towards us exceeds all Things that ever was.
7 When I intend and do devife thy Works abroad to fhow,
 To fuch a Reck'ning they do rife, thereof no End I know.
8 Burnt-offerings thou delight'ft not in, I know thy whole Defire,
 With Sacrifice to purge his Sin, thou doft no Man require.
9 Meat-offering and Sacrifice thou would'ft not have at all:
 But thou, O Lord, haft open made my Ears to hear withal.
10 But then, faid I, Behold and look, I come with Heart moft free,
 For in the Volume of thy Book thus it is faid of me;
11 That I, O God, fhould do thy Mind, which Thing doth pleafe me well:
 For in my Heart thy Law I find, faft placed there to dwell.
12 Thy Righteoufnefs and Juftice I in great Affemblies tell:
 Behold, my Tongue no Time doth ceafe, O Lord, thou knoweft well.

PART II.

13 I have not hid within my Breaft thy Goodnefs as by Stealth:
 But I declare, and have expreft thy Truth and faving Health.
14 I kept not clofe thy loving Mind, that no Man fhould it know
 The Truft that in thy Truth I find, to all the Church I fhow.
15 Thy tender Mercy, Lord, from me withdraw thou not away:
 But let thy Love and Verity preferve me Night and Day.
16 For I with many Troubles am encompaffed about:
 My Sins fo greatly do increafe, I cannot fpy them out.
17 For why? in Number they exceed, the Hairs upon my Head:
 My Heart doth faint for very Fear, that I am almoft dead.
18 With Speed fend Help, and fet me free, O Lord, I thee require:
 Make Hafte with Aid to fuccour me, O Lord, at my Defire.
19 Confound them with Rebuke and Shame that feek my Soul to fpill:
 Drive back my Foes, and them defame that wifh me any Ill.
20 For their ill Feats do them defcry, that would deface my Name;
 Always at me they rail and cry, Fie on him, fie for Shame.
21 Let them in thee have Joy and Wealth, that feek to thee always:
 That thofe that love thy faving Health, may fay, To God be Praife.
22 But as for me, I am but poor, oppreft, and brought full low:
 Yet thou, O Lord, wilt me reftore to Health full well I know.
23 For why? thou art my Hope and Truft, my Refuge, Help and Stay:
 Wherefore, my God, as thou art juft, with me no Time delay.

PSALM XLI, XLII.

PSALM XLI. T. S.

1 THE Man is blest that doth provide for such as needy be:
   For in the Season perilous the Lord will set him free,
2 And he will keep him safe, and make him happy in the Land:
   And not deliver him into his Enemies strong Hand.
3 And from his Bed of languishing the Lord will him restore:
   For thou, O Lord, wilt turn to Health his Sickness and his Sore.
4 Then in my Sickness thus said I, Have Mercy, Lord, on me:
   And heal my Soul, which grieved is, that I offended thee.
5 My Foes did wish me ill in Heart, and thus of me did say,
   When shall he die, that so his Name may perish quite away?
6 And when they come to visit me, they ask if I do well:
   But in their Hearts they Mischief hatch and then abroad it tell.
7 All they that hate me do conspire against me craftily:
   And still devise how to procure my Hurt and Misery.
8 Some grievous Sin hath brought him to this Sickness, say they plain:
   He is so low, that without Doubt he cannot rise again.
9 The Man also that I did trust, with me did use Deceit:
   Who at my Table did eat Bread, the same for me laid Wait.
10 Have Mercy, Lord, on me therefore, and let me be preserv'd:
    That I may render unto them the Things they have deserv'd.
11 By this I know assuredly to be belov'd of thee,
    Because my Foes no Power have to triumph over me.
12 But in my Right thou hast me kept, and it maintained well:
    And in thy Presence Place assign'd where I shall ever dwell.
13 The Lord the God of Israel, be praised evermore:
    Ev'n so be it, Lord, will I say, praise ye the Lord therefore.

PSALM XLII. J. H.

1 LIKE as the Hart doth pant and bray the Well-springs to obtain:
   So doth my Soul desire alway, with thee, Lord, to remain.
2 My Soul doth thirst, and would draw near the living God of Might:
   Oh when shall I come and appear in Presence of his Sight?
3 The Tears all Times are my Repast which from my Eyes do slide:
   Whilst wicked Men cry out so fast, where now is God thy Guide?
4 Alas, what Grief is it to think the Freedom once I had:
   Therefore my Soul, as at Pit's Brink, most heavy is and sad.
5 For I did march in good Array, with joyful Company:
   Unto the Temple was our Way, to praise the Lord most high.
6 My Soul, why art thou sad always and frett'st thus in my Breast?
   Trust still in God, for him to praise I hold it ever best.
7 By him I Succour have at Need against all Pain and Grief:
   He is my God, who with all Speed doth haste to send Relief.
8 My Soul is vexed in me, and therefore, O Lord, I will
   Remember thee from Jordan's Land, and Hermon's little Hill.

PART II.

9 One Grief another in doth call, as Clouds burst out their Voice:
   The Floods of Evil that doth fall, run over me with Noise.

10 Yet

PSALM XLIII, XLIV.

10 Yet I by Day felt his Goodness,
    Likewise at Night I did not cease
11 I am perswaded thus to say
    O Lord thou art my Guide and Stay,
12 Why do I then in Pensiveness,
    While that my Enemies oppress
13 For why? they pierce my inward Parts
    When they cry out with stubborn Hearts,
14 So soon, my Soul, why dost thou faint,
    Why do sad Thoughts without Restraint,
15 Trust in the Lord thy God always,
    To give him Thanks with Laud and Praise,

and Help at all Assays:
the living God to praise.
to him with Reverence,
my Rock and sure Defence.
hanging the Head, thus walk,
and vex me with their Talk?
with Pains to be abhorr'd:
Where now is God thy Lord?
with Pain and Grief opprest?
thus rage within my Breast?
and thou the Time shalt see,
for Health restor'd to thee.

PSALM XLIII. T. S.

1 JUDGE and defend my Cause, O Lord,
    From wicked and deceitful Men,
2 For of my Strength thou art the God,
    Why walk I heavily, whilst that
3 O Lord, send out thy Light and Truth,
    Which may conduct me to thy Hill,
4 Then shall I to thine Altar go,
    And on my Harp give Thanks to thee,
5 Why art thou then so sad, my Soul,
    Still trust in God, for him to praise
6 By him I have Deliverance
    He is my God who doth always.

'gainst them that evil be:
O Lord, deliver me.
why am I put from thee?
my Foe oppresseth me?
and lead me with thy Grace,
and to thy Dwelling-place.
with Joy to worship there:
O God, my God most dear.
and frett'st thus in my Breast?
I hold it always best.
from all my Pain and Grief:
at Need send me Relief.

PSALM XLIV. T. S.

1 OUR Ears have heard our Fathers tell,
    The wond'rous Works that thou hast done
2 How thou didst drive the Heathen out
    Planting our Fathers in their Place,
3 They conquer'd not by their own Sword,
    But by thy Hand, thy Arm and Grace,
4 Thou art my King, O God, who sav'st
    Led with thy Pow'r, we threw down such
5 I trusted not in Bow nor Sword,
    Thou kept'st us from our Foes great Rage,
6 And still we boast of thee our God,
    Yet now thou go'st not with our Host,
7 Thou mad'st us flee before our Foes,
    They did us rob, and spoil our Goods,
8 Thou hast us given to our Foes,
    Amongst the Heathen ev'ry where
9 Thy People thou hast sold like Slaves,
    For Profit none thou hadst thereby,
10 And to our Neighbours thou hast made
    And those that round about us dwell,

and rev'rently record,
in ancient Time, O Lord.
with a most pow'rful Hand,
and gav'st to them their Land.
the Land wherein they dwell:
because thou lov'dst them well.
Jacob in sundry wise:
as did against us rise.
they could not save me found:
and didst them all confound.
and praise thy holy Name:
but leavest us to Shame.
so were we over-trod:
we were disperst abroad.
as Sheep for to be slain:
scatter'd we do remain.
and as a Thing of nought:
no Gain at all was sought.
of us a Laughing-stock:
at us do grin and mock.

PART II.

11 Thus we serve for no other Use,
    They mock, they scorn, and shake their Heads,

but for a common Talk:
where-ever they do walk.

PSALM XLV.

12 With Shame and great Confusion I afflicted am full sore:
Yea, so I blush that all my Face with Red is cover'd o'er.
13 For why? we hear such sland'rous Words, such false Reports and lies,
That Death it is to see their Wrongs, their Threat'nings and their Cries.
14 For all this we forget not thee, nor yet thy Cov'nant brake:
We turn'd not back our Hearts from thee, nor did thy Paths forsake.
15 Yet thou hast trod us down to Dust, where Dens of Dragons be:
And cover'd us with Shade of Death, and great Adversity.
16 If we God's Name forgotten have, and Help of Idols sought,
Shall he not search and find this out? for he doth know our Thought.
17 But 'tis for thy Name's Sake, O Lord, we always are slain thus:
As Sheep unto the Shambles sent, ev'n so they deal with us.
18 Up, Lord, why sleepest thou? awake, for ever leave us not:
Why hidest thou thy Countenance? our Thrall thou hast forgot.
19 Ev'n to the Dust our Soul is brought, our Troubles so increase:
Our Belly cleaveth to the Ground, our Grief no Time doth cease.
20 Rise up therefore for our Defence, and help us, Lord, at Need:
We thee beseech, for thy Goodness, to rescue us with Speed.

PSALM XLV. J. H.

1 MY Heart doth take in Hand, some godly Song to sing:
The Praise that I shall shew therein, pertaineth to the King.
2 My Tongue shall be as quick his Honour to indite,
As is the Pen of any Scribe that useth fast to write.
3 O fairest of all Men, thy Lips with Grace are pure:
For God hath blessed thee with Gifts, for ever to endure.
4 About thee gird thy Sword, O Prince of Might elect:
With Honour, Glory, and Renown, thou art most richly deckt.
5 Go forth with godly Speed, with Meekness, Truth, and Right:
And thy Right-hand shall thee instruct in Works of dreadful Might.
6 Thy Arrows sharp and keen, their Hearts so sore shall sting,
That they shall crouch and kneel to thee, yea, all thy Foes, O King.
7 Thy Royal Seat, O Lord, for ever shall remain:
Because the Sceptre of thy Realm doth Righteousness maintain.
8 Because thou lov'st the Right, and didst the Ill detest:
Therefore hath God anointed thee with Joy above the rest.
9 With Myrrh and Savours sweet thy Clothes are all bespread,
When thou dost from thy Palace pass, thereby to make thee glad.
10 Kings Daughters do attend in fine and rich Array:
At thy Right-hand the Queen doth stand in Gold and Garments gay.

PART II.

11 O Daughter, take good Heed, incline and give good Ear:
Thou must forget thy Kindred all, and Father's House most dear.
12 Then shall the King desire thy Beauty more and more:
He is the Lord thy God, whom thou must worship and adore.
13 The Daughters then of Tyre, with Gifts full rich to see,
And all the Wealthy of the Land shall make their Suit to thee.
14 The Daughter of the King is glorious to behold:
Within her Closet she doth sit all deckt in beaten Gold.

PSALM XLVI, XLVII.

15 In Robes with Needle wrought, / and every pleasant Thing:
With Virgins fair on her to wait, / she cometh to the King.
16 Thus are they brought with Joy / and Mirth on ev'ry Side,
Into the Palace of the King, / and there they do abide.

17 Instead of Fathers thou / shalt Children multiply:
Whom thou may'st Princes make to rule / all Lands successively.
18 Wherefore thy holy Name / all Ages shall record:
The People shall give Thanks to thee / for evermore, O Lord.

PSALM XLVI. J. H.

1 THE Lord is our Defence and Aid, / the Strength whereby we stand:
When we with Woe are much dismay'd, / he is our Help at Hand.
2 Tho' the Earth move, we will not fear, / tho' Mountains high and steep
Be thrust and hurled here and there. / within the Sea so deep.

3 No, tho' the Sea do rage so sore, / that all the Banks it spills:
And tho' it overflow the Shore, / and beat down mighty Hills.
4 For one fair Flood doth send abroad / his pleasant Streams apace:
To glad the City of our God, / and wash his holy Place.

5 In Midst of her the Lord doth dwell, / she never can decay:
All Things against her that rebel, / the Lord will surely slay.
6 The Heathen Folk and Kingdoms fear, / the People make a Noise:
The Earth doth melt and disappear. / when God puts forth his Voice.

7 The Lord of Hosts doth take our Part, / to us he hath an Eye:
Our Hope of Health, with all our Heart, / on Jacob's God doth lie.
8 Come here, and see with Mind and Thought / the working of our God:
What Wonders he himself hath wrought, / in all the World abroad.

9 By him all Wars are husht and gone, / tho' Countries did conspire:
Their Bows and Spears he brake each one, / their Chariots burnt with Fire.
10 Be still therefore, and know that I / am God, and therefore will
Among the Heathen People be / highly exalted still.

11 The Lord of Hosts doth us defend / he is our Strength and Tow'r;
On Jacob's God we do depend / and on his mighty Pow'r.

PSALM XLVII. J. H.

1 YE People all, with one Accord, / clap Hands, shout and rejoice:
Be glad and sing unto the Lord / with sweet and pleasant Voice.
2 For high the Lord and dreadful is, / his Wonders manifold:
A mighty King he is likewise, / in all the Earth extoll'd.

3 The People shall he make to be / unto our Bondage Thrall:
And underneath our Feet shall he / the Nations make to fall.
4 For us the Heritage he chose, / which we possess alone:
The Excellency of Jacob, / his well-beloved one.

5 Our God ascended up on high / with Joy and pleasant Noise:
The Lord goes up above the Sky / with Trumpets royal Voice.
6 Sing Praises to our God, sing Praise, / sing Praises to our King:
For God is King of all the Earth, / all skilful Praises sing.

7 God on the Heathen reigns, and sits / upon his holy Throne
The Princes of the People have / them joined every one.
8 To Abram's People: for our God, / who is exalted high,
As with a Buckler doth defend / the Earth continually.

PSALM

PSALM XLVIII, XLIX.

PSALM XLVIII. J. H.

1 GREAT is the Lord, and with great Praife, to be advanced ftill,
Within the City of our God, upon his holy Hill.
2 Mount Sion is a pleafant Place. it gladdeth all the Land:
The City of the mighty King on her North-fide doth ftand.

3 Within the Palaces thereof God is a Refuge known:
For lo! the Kings are gather'd, and together they are gone.
4 But when they did behold it fo, they wond'red, and they were
Aftonifh'd much, and fuddenly were driven back with Fear.

5 Great Terror there on them did fall; for Grief of Heart they cry:
As doth a Woman when fhe fhall go travail fpeedily.
6 As thou with Eaftern Winds the Ships upon the Seas doft break:
They were deftroy'd, and ev'n as we have heard our Fathers fpeak.

7 So in the City of the Lord we faw as it was told:
Yet in the City which our God for ever will uphold.
8 O Lord we wait and do depend on thy good Help and Grace:
For which we do all Times attend within thy holy Place.

9 O Lord, according to thy Name, for ever is thy Praife:
And thy Right-hand, O Lord, is full of Righteoufnefs always.
10 For thy Judgments let Sion mourn be filled full with Joys:
Alfo of Judah, grant, O Lord, the Daughters to rejoice.

11 Go walk about all Sion Hill, yea, round about her go:
And tell the Towers that thereon are builded on a Row.
12 And mark ye well her Bulwarks all, behold her Towers there:
That ye may tell thereof to them that after fhall be here.

13 For this moft mighty God, our God for evermore is he:
And unto Death we are refolv'd, our Guide he ftill fhall be.

PSALM XLIX. J. H.

1 ALL People hearken and give ear to that which I fhall tell:
Both High and Low, both Rich and Poor, that in the World do dwell.
2 For why? my Mouth fhall make Difcourfe of many Things moft wife:
In Underftanding fhall my Heart its Study exercife.

3 I will incline mine Ear to know the Parable fo dark;
And open all my doubtful Speech in Metre on my Harp.
4 Wherefore fhould I Affliction fear, or any careful Toil?
Or elfe my Foes, which at my Heels do prefs my Life to fpoil.

5 For as for fuch as Riches have, wherein their Truft is moft:
And they who of their Treafures great proudly do brag and boaft;
6 There is not one of them that can his Brother's Life redeem:
Or give a Ranfome unto God, fufficient in Efteem.

7 It is too great a Price to pay, none can thereto attain:
So that he might his Life prolong, or not in Grave remain.
8 They fee wife Men as well as Fools are fubject to Death's Bands:
And being dead, Strangers poffefs their Houfes, Goods, and Land,

9 Their Care is to build Houfes fair, and fo determine fure:
To make their Names upon the Earth for ever to endure.
10 Yet fhall no Man always enjoy high Honour, Wealth, and Reft:
But muft at length fubmit to Death, as well as the Brute Beaft.

PART

PSALM L.
PART II.

11 And tho' they find their foolish Thoughts
    Their Children yet approve their Talk,
12 As Sheep into the Fold are brought,
    Death shall them eat, and in that Day
    to be most lewd and vain,
    and in like Sin remain.
    they shall be laid in Grave:
    the Just shall Lordship have.

13 Their Beauty and their royal Port
    When from their House unto the Pit
14 But God will surely me preserve
    Because he will of his good Grace,
    shall fade and quite decay:
    with Woe they pass away.
    from Death and endless Pain.
    my Soul receive again.

15 If any Man grow wondrous rich,
    Altho, the Glory of his House
15 For when he dies, of all these Things
    His Glory will not follow him,
    be not afraid therefore,
    increaseth more and more.
    Nothing shall he receive.
    his Pomp will take its Leave.

17 Yet in this Life he counts himself
    And others likewise flatter him,
18 But yet if he should live as long
    Yet must he needs at length give Place,
    th' happiest under Sun:
    saying, All is well done.
    as did his Fathers old,
    and be brought to Death's Fold.

19 Man that in Honour lives, and doth
    Compar'd unto the very Beasts,
    not understand, may be
    that perish utterly.

PSALM L. W. W.

1 THE mighty God,
    And all the World
    Even from the East,
    Out of Sion,
    God will appear
    Our God will come
    th' Eternal hath thus spoke.
    he will call and provoke:
    and so forth to the West.
    which Place he liketh best.
    in Beauty most excellent,
    before long Time be spent.

2 Devouring Fire
    A great Tempest
    Then shall he call
    To judge his Folk
    Saying, Go to,
    My Pact they keep,
    shall go before his Face,
    shall round about him trace:
    the Earth and Heav'ns bright,
    with Equity and Right:
    and now my Saints assemble:
    their Gifts do not dissemble.

3 The Heav'ns they shall
    For God is Judge
    Hear, my People,
    Lift, Israel,
    Thy God, thy God
    For not giving
    declare his Righteousness:
    of all Things more or less,
    for I will now reveal ;
    I'll from thee nought conceal:
    am I, and will not blame thee
    all sorts of Off'rings to me.

4 I have no Need
    Goats of thy Fold,
    For all the Beasts
    On thousand Hills
    I know for mine
    All Beasts mine are
    to take of thee at all
    or Calves out of thy Stall:
    are mine within the Woods,
    Cattle are mine own Goods.
    all Birds that are on Mountains,
    which haunt the Fields & Fountains.

5 Were I hungry
    For all is mine
    Eat I the Flesh
    Or drink the Blood
    Offer to God
    And pay thy Vows
    I would not thee it tell :
    that in the World doth dwell.
    of great Bulls or Bullocks?
    of Goats or of the Flocks ?
    Praise and hearty Thanksgiving,
    unto God ever-living.

6 Call

PSALM L.

6 Call upon me
Then will I help,
To the Wicked
Why doſt thou preach
Seeing thou haſt
And hat'ſt to be
when troubled thou ſhalt be:
and thou ſhalt honour me.
thus ſaith th' eternal God,
my Words and Laws abroad:
them with thy Mouth abuſed,
by Diſcipline reduced?

7 My Words, I ſay,
If that thou ſee'ſt
Thou runn'ſt with him,
And are all one
Thou giv'ſt thyſelf
And how thy Tongue
thou doſt reject and hate.
a Thief, as with thy Mate,
and ſo your Prey ſeek out;
with the adult'rous Rout.
to back-bite and to ſlander:
deceiveth, is a Wonder.

8 Thou ſitt'ſt muſing
And how to put
Theſe Things thou didſt,
Thou didſt me judge,
Like to thyſelf:
Once ſhalt thou feel
thy Brother how to blame,
thy Mother's Son to ſhame,
and while I held my Tongue,
becauſe I ſtay'd ſo long,
yet tho' I keep long Silence,
of thy Wrongs juſt Recompence.

9 Conſider this,
And fear not when
Left without Help,
But he that Thanks
Saith the Lord God,
I will him teach
ye that forget the Lord,
he threatneth with his Word,
I ſpoil you as a Prey,
offers, praiſeth alway,
and he that walks this Trace,
God's ſaving Health t'embrace.

Another of the ſame, by J. H.

1 THE God of Gods, the Lord,
From whence the Sun doth riſe, unto
2 From Sion his fair Place,
The perfect Beauty of his Grace,
hath call'd the Earth by Name,
the ſetting of the ſame.
his Glory bright and clear:
from thence it doth appear.

3 Our God ſhall come in Haſte,
Before him ſhall the Fire waſte
4 The Heav'ns which are ſo high,
He will call forth, that he may try
to ſpeak aloud, no doubt:
and Tempeſt round about.
the Earth below likewiſe,
the People that are his.

5 Bring forth my Saints, ſaith he,
Who are in Band and League with me,
6 And when theſe Things are try'd,
That God is juſt, and all muſt bide
my faithful Flock moſt dear:
my Law to love and fear.
then ſhall the Heav'ns record,
the Judgment of the Lord.

7 My People, now give Heed,
I am thy God, thy Help at Need,
8 I do not ſay to thee,
Thou offer'ſt daily unto me
Iſr'el to thee I cry:
thou can'ſt not it deny.
thy Sacrifice is ſlack:
much more than I do lack.

9 Think'ſt thou that I do need
Or elſe ſo much deſire to feed?
10 Nay, all the Beaſts are mine
And thouſands more of Neat and Kine
thy Cattle young or old:
on Goats out of thy Fold?
in Woods that eat their fills:
that run wild on the Hills.

PART II.

11 The Birds that build on high,
And Beaſts that in the Fields do lie,
12 Then tho, I hungred ſore,
Since that the Earth with her great Store,
on Hills and out of Sight:
are ſubject to my Might.
what Need I ought of thine?
and all therein, is mine.

13 To

PSALM LI.

13 To Bulls Flesh have I Mind
   Or such a Sweetness do I find
14 Give to the Lord his Praise,
   And see thou pay thy Vows always
to eat it, dost thou think?
the Blood of Goats to drink?
with Thanks to him apply:
unto the God most high.

15 Then seek and call to me,
   And I will sure deliver thee,
16 But to the wicked Train,
   And yet their Works are foul and vain.
when ought would work thee Blame:
that thou may'st praise my Name.
who talk of God each Day:
to them the Lord will say;

17 With what Face darest thou
   Why doth thy Words my Law allow
18 Whereas for to amend
   My Word the which thou dost pretend,
my Word once speak or name?
thy Deeds deny the same?
thy Life thou art so slack:
is cast behind thy Back.

PART III.

19 When thou a Thief dost see
   With him thou runn'st, and dost agree
20 When thou dost them behold
   Thou lik'st it well, and waxest bold
by Theft to live in Wealth,
likewise to thrive by Stealth.
that Wives and Maids defile,
to use that Life most vile.

21 Thy Lips thou dost apply
   Thy Tongue doth teach to cheat and lie,
22 Thou studiest to revile
   With Slander basely dost defile
to slander and defame:
and still doth use the same.
thy Friends to thee most near:
thy Mother's Son most dear.

23 Hereat while I do wink,
   Thou go'st on still and so dost think
24 But sure I will not let
   Thy Faults in Order I will set,
as tho' I did not see,
that I am like to thee.
to strike when I begin:
and open all thy Sin.

25 Mark this I you require
   Lest when I plague you in mine Ire,
26 He that doth give to me
   Doth please me well, and he shall see
who have not God in Mind:
your Help be far to find.
the Sacrifice of Praise,
to walk in godly Ways.

PSALM LI. W. W.

1 O Lord, consider my Distress,
   My Sins forgive, my Faults redress,
2 Wash me, O Lord, and make me clean,
   And purify me once again
and now with Speed some Pity take:
good Lord, for thy great Mercies Sake.
from this unjust and sinful Act:
from this foul Crime and bloody Fact.

3 Remorse and Sorrow do constrain
   Because my Sin doth still remain
4 Against thee only have I sinn'd,
   And if I should no Mercy find,
me to acknowledge my Excess:
before my Face without Release.
and done this Evil in thy Sight:
yet were thy Judgments just and right.

5 It is too manifest, alas!
   Yea, of my Mother so born was,
6 Also behold, Lord, thou dost love
   Therefore thy Wisdom from above
that first I was conceiv'd in Sin:
and yet, vile Wretch, remain therein.
the inward Truth of a pure Heart:
thou hast reveal'd, me to convert.

7 If thou with Hyssop purge this Blot,
   And if thou wash away my Spot,
8 Therefore, O Lord, such Joy me send,
   And that my Strength may now amend,
I shall be cleaner than the Glass:
the Snow in Whiteness I shall pass.
that I may praise thee with my Voice:
and broken Bones also rejoice.

9 Turn back thy Face and frowning Ire,
   And purge my Sins, I thee desire,
10 Make new my Heart within my Breast,
   And let thy Spirit in me rest,
for I have felt enough thine Hand:
which do in Number pass the Sand.
and frame it to thy holy Will:
which may my Soul with Comfort fill.

PART

PSALM LI.

PART II.

11 Cast me not, Lord, out from thy Sight, but speedily my Torments end:
Take not from me thy holy Spirit, which may from Dangers me defend.
12 Restore me to those Joys again, which I was wont in thee to find:
Let me thy free Spirit retain, which unto thee may draw my Mind.
13 Thus when I shall thy Mercies know, I shall instruct others therein:
And Men that are likewise brought low, by my Example shall flee Sin.
14 O God, that of my Health art Lord, do thou forgive my bloody Vice:
My Heart and Tongue shall then accord to sing thy Mercy and Justice.
15 Touch thou my Lips, my Tongue unite, O Lord, I do thee humbly pray:
And then my Mouth shall testify thy Praise and wond'rous Works alway.
16 And as for outward Sacrifice, I would have offer'd many one:
But thou esteem'st them at no Price, and therein Pleasure takest none.
17 The heavy Heart, the Mind opprest, O Lord, thou never dost reject:
This Sacrifice indeed is best, and that thou chiefly dost expect.
18 Lord, unto Sion turn thy Face, pour out thy Mercies on thy Hill:
And on Jerusalem thy Grace, build up the Walls, and love it still.
19 Thou shalt accept then our Off'rings of Peace and Righteousness alway,
Yea, Calves and many other Things, upon thy Altar we will lay.

Another of the same, by J. H.

1 HAVE Mercy on me, Lord, after thy great abounding Grace:
After thy Mercies multitude, do thou my Sins deface.
2 Yea, wash me clean from my Offence, and my Iniquity:
For I do own my Faults, and still my Sin is in my Eye.
3 Against thee, thee alone I have offended in this Case:
And evil have I done before the Presence of thy Face.
4 That in the Things that thou hast done, upright thou may'st appear:
And when thou judgest, all may see, that thou art very clear.
5 In Wickedness I formed was, when I began to be:
My Mother at the very first in Sin conceived me.
6 But lo, Truth in the inward Parts is pleasant unto thee:
And Secrets of thy Wisdom thou revealed hast to me.
7 With Hyssop, Lord, besprinkle me, I shall be cleansed so:
Yea, wash thou me, and then I shall be whiter than the Snow.
8 Of Joy and Gladness make thou me to hear the pleasant Voice:
That so the Bones which thou, O Lord, hast broken, may rejoice.
9 From the beholding of my Sins, Lord, turn away thy Face:
And all my Deeds of Wickedness do utterly deface.
10 O God, create in me a Heart unspotted in thy Sight:
Within my Bowels, Lord, renew a firm and stable Spirit.
11 Cast me not from thy Sight, nor take thy Spirit quite away:
The Comfort of thy saving Health give me again, I pray.
12 With thy free Spirit me support, then shall Transgressors be,
By my Instruction and Advice, converted unto thee.

PART II.

13 O God, that art God of my Health, from Blood deliver me:
That Praises of thy Righteousness my Tongue may sing to thee.
14 My Lips that yet fast closed be, do thou, O Lord, unloose:
The Praises of thy Majesty my Mouth shall then disclose.

PSALM LII, LIII, LIV.

15 I would have offer'd Sacrifice, if that had pleased thee:
But pleased with Burnt-offerings I know thou wilt not be.
16 A Spirit griev'd is Sacrifice delightful in thine Eyes:
A broken and a contrite Heart, Lord, thou wilt not despise.
17 In thy good Will deal gently, Lord, with Sion, and withal
Grant that of thy Jerusalem uprear'd may be the Wall.
18 Burnt-offerings, Gifts, and Sacrifice of Justice in that Day,
Thou shalt accept, and Calves they shall upon thy Altar lay.

PSALM LII. J. H.

1 WHY dost thou, Tyrant, boast abroad thy wicked Works to praise?
Dost thou not know there is a God? whose Mercies last always?
2 Why doth thy Mind yet still devise such wicked Wiles to warp?
Thy Tongue untrue in forging Lies, is like a Razor sharp.
3 On Mischief why sett'st thou thy Mind and wilt not walk upright?
Thou lovest more false Tales to find, than bring the Truth to Light.
4 Thou dost delight in Fraud and Guile, in Mischief, Blood, and Wrong.
Thy Lips have learn'd the flatt'ring Style, O false deceitful Tongue.
5 Therefore the Lord shall thee confound, and pluck thee from thy Place:
Thy Seed root out from off the Ground, and utterly deface.
6 The Just when they behold thy Fall, with Fear will praise the Lord:
And in reproach of thee withal, cry out with one Accord.
7 Behold the Man that did refuse the Lord for his Defence:
But in his Riches great did place his Trust and Confidence.
8 But I as Olive fresh and green, shall spring and spread abroad
Because my Trust all Times hath been upon the living God.
9 For this therefore will I give Praise to thee with Heart and Voice:
I will advance thy Name always, wherein thy Saints rejoice.

PSALM LIII. T. S.

1 THE foolish Man within his Heart blasphemously hath said,
There is not any God at all: why should we be afraid?
2 They are corrupt, and they also a heinous Work have wrought:
Among them all there is not one of Good that worketh ought.
3 The Lord look'd down from Heav'n upon the Sons of Men below,
To see if any were that sought the living God to know.
4 Out of the Way they all are gone. they all corrupted are:
There is not any that doth good, not one for God doth care.
5 Do not all wicked Workers know, that they do feed upon,
My People as they feed on Bread? the Lord they call not on.
6 Even there they were afraid, and stood with Trembling all dismay'd,
When as there was no Cause at all why they should be afraid.
7 For God his Bones that thee besieg'd, hath scatter'd all abroad:
He hath confounded them, for they rejected are of God.
8 O Lord, give to thy People Health, and thou, O Lord, fulfil
Thy Promise made to Israel, from out of Sion Hill.
9 When God his People shall restore, that once were captive led:
Then Jacob shall rejoice therein, and Israel be glad.

PSALM LIV. J. H.

1 GOD, save me for thy holy Name, and for thy Goodness sake:
Unto the Strength, Lord, of the same, I do my Cause betake.

2 Regard,

PSALM LV.

2 Regard, O Lord, and give an ear
to me when I do pray:
Bow down thyself to me, and hear
the Words that I do say.
3 For Strangers up against me rise,
and Tyrants vex me still:
Who have not God before their Eyes,
they seek my Soul to spill.
4 But lo, my God doth give me Aid,
the Lord is nigh at Hand:
With them by whom my Soul is staid,
the Lord doth ever stand.
5 With Plagues again repay all those
for me that lie in Wait:
And in thy Truth destroy my Foes
with their own Snare and Bait.
6 An Off'ring of free Heart and Will
then I to thee shall make:
And praise thy Name, for therein still
great Comfort I do take.
7 Thou, Lord, at length hast set me free
from them that Craft conspire:
And now my Eye with Joy doth see
on them my Heart's Desire.

PSALM LV. J. H.

1 O God, give ear, and speedily
hear me when I do pray:
And when to thee I call and cry,
hide not thyself away.
2 Take heed to me, grant my Request,
and answer me again:
With Grief I pray full sore opprest,
Sorrow doth me constrain.
3 Because my Foes with Threats and Cries
oppress me thro' Despite:
And so the wicked Sort likewise,
to vex me take Delight.
4 For they in Council do conspire
to charge me with some Ill:
And in their hasty Wrath and Ire
they do pursue me still.
5 My Heart doth faint for want of Breath,
it panteth in my Breast:
With Terror and the Dread of Death
my Soul is much opprest.
6 Such dreadful Fear on me doth fall,
that I therewith do quake:
Such Horror overwhelmeth me.
that I no Shift can make.
7 Oh that I had Wings like a Dove,
then would I swiftly flee
Away from hence unto a Place
where I at Rest should be.
8 Lo, then I would go far away,
to fly I would not cease:
And I would hide myself, and stay
in some great Wilderness.
9 I would be gone with Speed and Haste,
and not abide behind,
Till I had safely overpast
these Blasts of boistrous Wind.
10 Divide them, Lord, and from them pull
their false and double Tongues
For I have spy'd their City full
of Rapine, Strife and Wrong.
11 Both Day and Night they go about
within the City Wall:
In midst of her is Mischief wrought,
and Sorrow great withal.
12 Her inward Parts are wicked plain,
her Deeds they are most vile:
And in her Streets there doth remain
Nothing but Fraud and Guile.

PART II.

13 If that my Foes did seek my Shame,
I might it well abide:
Because from all their Check and Blame
somewhere I could me hide.
14 But thou it was my Fellow dear,
who Friendship didst pretend:
And didst my secret Counsel hear,
as a familiar Friend.
15 With whom I had Delight to talk
in Secret and Abroad:
And we together oft did walk
unto the House of God.
16 Let Death in Haste upon them fall,
and send them quick to Hell:
For Mischief doth abide in all
the Places where they dwell.
17 But I unto my God do cry,
to him for Aid I flee:
The Lord will help me speedily,
and he will succour me.

PSALM LVI, LVII.

18 At Morning, Noon, and Evening-tide,
 When I so constantly have cry'd,
 unto the Lord I pray:
 he did not say me nay.

19 To Peace he shall restore me yet,
 Altho' the Number be full great
 tho' War be now at Hand:
 that do against me stand.

20 The Lord that first and last doth reign,
 Will hear when I to him complain,
 both now and evermore,
 and punish them full sore.

21 For sure there is no Hope that they
 For why? they will not God obey,
 to turn will once accord:
 nor fear the living Lord.

22 Upon their Friends they laid their Hands,
 Of Friendship to neglect the Bands
 who were in Cov'nant knit:
 they do not care one Whit.

23 While they have War within their Hearts,
 And tho' they were as soft as Oyl,
 as Butter are their Words:
 they cut as sharp as Swords.

24 Cast thou thy Care upon the Lord,
 For in no wise will he accord
 and he shall nourish thee:
 the Just in Thrall to see.

25 But God shall cast them deep in Pit,
 He will no guileful Man permit
 who thirst for Blood always:
 to live out half his Days.

26 Tho' such be quite destroy'd and gone,
 I will depend his Grace upon,
 on him is all my Stay:
 with all my Heart alway.

PSALM LVI. J. H.

1 HAVE Mercy, Lord, on me, I pray,
 He fighteth with me Day by Day,
 for Man would me devour:
 and troubleth me each Hour.

2 My Foes do daily enterprise
 To fight against me many rise,
 to swallow me out-right:
 O thou Most High of Might.

3 When they would make me sore afraid,
 I trust in thee alone for Aid,
 with Boasts and Brags of Pride:
 by thee I will abide.

4 God's Promise I do mind and praise,
 I do not care at all Assays
 O Lord, I stick to thee:
 what Flesh can do to me.

5 What Things I either did or spake,
 And all the Counsel that they take,
 they wrest them at their Will:
 is how to work me Ill.

6 They all consent themselves to hide,
 They spy my Paths, and Snares have try'd
 close Watch for me to lay:
 to take my Life away.

7 Shall they escape on Mischief set?
 For in thy Wrath thou dost not let
 thou, God, on them wilt frown:
 to throw whole Kingdoms down.

8 Thou seest how oft they made me flee,
 Reserve them in a Glass by thee,
 and on my Tears dost look:
 and write them in thy Book.

9 When I do call upon thy Name,
 I well perceive it by the same,
 my Foes away do start.
 that God doth take my Part.

10 I glory in the Word of God,
 With Joy I will declare abroad
 to praise it I accord:
 the Promise of the Lord.

11 I trust in God the Lord, and say,
 The Lord he is my Help and Stay,
 as I before began,
 I do not care for Man.

12 I will perform my Heart most free
 And I, O Lord, all Times to thee
 my Vows to God always:
 will offer Thanks and Praise.

13 My Soul from Death thou dost defend,
 That I before thee may ascend
 and keep'st my Feet upright:
 with such as live in Light.

PSALM LVII. J. H.

1 TAKE Pity for thy Promise Sake,
 Because my Soul doth her betake
 have Mercy, Lord, on me:
 unto the Help of thee.

PSALM LVIII.

2 Within the Shadow of thy Wings: I set myself full fast:
Till Mischief, Malice, and like Things, be gone and over-past.
3 I call unto the God most high, to whom I stick and stand:
I mean the God that will stand by the Cause I have in Hand.
4 For he from Heav'n hath sent his Aid to save me from their Spite:
That to devour me have assay'd, ev'n Mercy, Truth, and Might.
5 I lead my Life with Lions fell, all set on Wrath and Ire:
And with such wicked Men I dwell, who fret like Flames of Fire.
6 Their Teeth are Spears and Arrows long, as sharp as I have seen:
They wound and cut with their quick Tongue, like Swords and Weapons keen.
7 Set up and shew thyself, O God, above the Heav'ns most bright:
Exalt thy Praise on Earth abroad, thy Majesty and Might.
8 They laid their Net, and did prepare a privy Cave and Pit:
Wherein they thought my Soul to snare, but are fall'n into it.
9 My Heart is set to laud the Lord, in him to joy always:
My Heart doth ever well accord to sing his Laud and Praise.
10 Awake my Joy, awake, I say, my Lute, my Harp, and String:
And I myself before the Day will rise, rejoice, and sing.
11 Among the People I will tell the Goodness of my God:
And shew his Praise, that doth excel in Heathen Lands abroad.
12 His Mercy doth extend as far as the Heav'ns all are high:
His Truth as high as any Star that shineth in the Sky.
13 Set forth and shew thyself, O God, above the Heav'ns most bright:
Exalt thyself on Earth abroad thy Majesty and Might.

PSALM LVIII. J. H.

1 YE Rulers that are put in Trust to judge of Wrong and Right,
Be all your Judgments true and just, regarding no Man's Might?
2 Nay, in your Hearts ye daily muse in Mischief to consent:
And where ye should true Justice use, your Hands to Bribes are bent.
3 The wicked Sort from their Birth-day have erred on this wise:
And from their Mothers Womb alway have used Craft and Lyes.
4 In them the Poison and the Breath of Serpents doth appear:
Yea, like the Adder that is deaf, and fast doth stop her Ear;
5 Because she will not hear the Voice of one that charmeth well:
No, tho' he were the chief of Choice, and therein did excel.
6 The Teeth, O Lord, which fast are set in their Mouth round about:
The Lion's Teeth that are so great, do thou, O Lord, break out.
7 Let them consume away and waste, as Water runs forth-right:
The Shafts that they do shoot in Haste, let them be broke in Flight.
8 As Snails do waste within the Shell, and unto Slime do run:
As one before his Time that fell, and never saw the Sun.
9 Before the Thorns that now are young as Bushes big shall grow,
Thy Storms of Anger waxing strong shall take them ere they know.
10 The Just shall joy, it doth them Good, that God doth Vengeance take:
And they shall wash their Feet in Blood of them that him forsake.
11 Then shall the World shew forth and tell, that good Men have Reward:
And that a God on Earth doth dwell, that Justice doth regard.

PSALM LIX, LX.

PSALM LIX. J. H.

1 SEND Aid, and save me from my Foes, O Lord, I pray to thee:
　Defend and keep me from all those that rise and strive with me.
2 O Lord, preserve me from those Men whose Doings are not good:
　And set me sure and safe from them that thirst still after Blood.

3 For lo, they wait my Soul to take they rage against me still:
　Yea, for no Fault that I did make, I never did them Ill.
4 They run and do themselves prepare when I no Whit offend:
　Arise, and save me from their Snare, and see what they intend.

5 Arise, O God of Israel, smite every Heathen Land:
　And pity none that do rebel, and in their Mischief stand.
6 At Night they run and seek about, like Dogs they howl also:
　And all the City quite thro'out, from Place to Place they go.

7 They speak of me with Mouth alway, but in their Lips are Swords:
　They have contriv'd my Death, and say, There's none doth hear our Words.
8 But, Lord, thou hast their Ways espy'd, and thou shalt them disgrace:
　The Heathen Folk thou dost deride, and mock them to their Face.

9 The Strength that does our Foes withstand, O Lord, doth come from thee:
　Thou art, O God, my Help at Hand, a Fort and Fence to me.
10 The Lord to me doth shew his Grace in great Abundance still:
　That I may see my Foes in Case such as my Heart doth will.

PART II.

11 Destroy them not at once, O Lord, lest it from Mind do fall:
　But with thy Strength drive them abroad, and so consume them all.
12 For their ill Words, and lying Tongue, confound them in their Pride:
　Their wicked Oaths, with Lyes and Wrong, let all the World deride.

13 Consume them in thy Wrath, O Lord, that nought of them remain:
　That Men may know thro'out the World, that Jacob's God doth reign.
14 At Ev'ning they return apace, as Dogs they grin and cry:
　Thro'out the Streets, in ev'ry Place, they run about and spy.

15 They seek about for Meat alway, but let them not be fed:
　Nor find a House wherein they may be bold to put their Head.
16 But I will shew thy Strength abroad, thy Goodness I will praise:
　For thou art my Defence and God in Time of Need always.

17 Thou art my Strength, thou hast me stay'd, O Lord, I sing to thee:
　Thou art my Fort, my Fence and Aid, a loving God to me.

PSALM LX. J. H.

1 O Lord, thou didst us clean forsake, and scatter all abroad:
　Such great Displeasure thou didst take: return to us, O God,
2 Thy Might did move the Land so sore, that it in sunder brake:
　The Health thereof, O Lord, restore, for it doth bow and quake.

3 With heavy Things thou plaguest thus the People that are thine:
　And thou hast given unto us a Drink of deadly Wine.
4 But yet to such as fear thy Name, a Banner thou dost shew:
　That they may triumph in the same, because thy Word is true.

5 So that thy Might may keep and save the Folk that serveth thee:
　That they thy Help at Hand may have, O Lord, grant this to me.
6 The Lord did speak from his own Place, this was his joyful Sound:
　I will divide Sichem by Pace, and mete out Succoth's Ground.

PSALM LXI, LXII.

7 Gilead is given to my Hand, Manaſſah mine beſide:
Ephraim the Strength of all my Land, my Law doth Judah guide.
8 In Moab I will waſh my Feet, o'er Edom caſt thy Shoe:
And thou, Philiſtia, ought'ſt to ſeek to me for Favour too.
9 But who will bring me at this Tide unto the City ſtrong?
Or who to Edom will me guide, ſo that I go not Wrong?
10 Lord, wilt not thou, who didſt forſake thy Folk, their Land and Coaſts?
Our Wars in Hand thou wouldſt not take, nor go forth with our Hoſts.
11 Give Aid, O Lord, and us relieve from them that us diſdain;
The Help that Hoſts of Men can give, is all but weak and vain.
12 But thro' our God we ſhall have Might to take great Things in Hand:
He will tread down and put to Flight all thoſe that us withſtand.

PSALM LXI. J. H.

1 REGARD, O Lord, for I complain, and make my Suit to thee:
Let not my Words return in vain, but give an Ear to me.
2 From out the Coaſts and utmoſt Parts of all the Earth I cry,
In Grief and Anguiſh of my Heart, to thee, O God, moſt high.

3 Upon the Rock of thy great Pow'r my woful Mind repoſe:
Thou art my Hope, my Fort and Tow'r, my Fence againſt my Foes.
4 Within thy Tent I long to dwell, there ever to abide:
Under thy Wings, I know right well, I ſhall me ſafely hide.

5 The Lord doth my Deſire regard, and doth fulfil the ſame:
With Riches great will he reward all thoſe that fear his Name:
6 The King ſhall he in Health maintain, and ſo prolong his Days,
That he from Age to Age may reign, with Honour great always.

7 That he may have a Dwelling-place before the Lord alway:
O let thy Mercy, Truth and Grace, defend him from Decay.
8 And then, O Lord, I ever will ſing Praiſe unto thy Name:
That all my Vows I may fulfil, and daily pay the ſame.

PSALM LXII. J. H.

1 MY Soul to God ſhall give good Heed, and him alone attend:
Becauſe my Health and Hope to ſpeed, doth whole on him depend.
2 For he alone is my Defence, my Rock, my Health and Aid:
He is my Stay, and no Pretence ſhall make me much diſmay'd.

3 O wicked Folk, how long will ye uſe Craft? ſure ye muſt fall:
For as a rotten Hedge ye be, and like a tott'ring Wall.
4 Whom God doth love, ye ſeek always to put him to the Worſe:
Ye love to lye, with Mouth ye praiſe, and yet your Heart doth curſe.

5 Yet ſtill my Soul doth whole depend on God my chief Deſire:
From all ill Fates me to defend, none but him I require.
6 He is my Rock, my Fort and Tow'r, my Health is of his Grace:
He doth ſupport me, that no Pow'r can move me out of Place.

7 My Glory and Salvation doth on him alone depend:
He is my Strength, my Stay, my Wealth, and ſtill doth me defend.
8 O put your Truſt in him alway, ye Folk with one Accord:
Pour out your Hearts to him, and ſay, Our Truſt is in the Lord.

9 The Sons of Men deceitful are, on Balance but a Sleight:
With Things moſt vain do them compare, for they can hold no Weight.
10 Truſt not in Wrong and Robbery, let vain Delights be gone:
Tho' Riches flow in ſuddenly, ſet not your Hearts thereon.

11 The

PSALM LXIII, LXIV, LXV.

11 The Lord long since one Thing did tell,
    He spake it oft, I heard it well,
12 And that thou, Lord, art good and kind
    So that all Sorts with thee shall find
which here to Mind I call:
that he alone doth all,
thy Mercy doth exceed:
according to their Deed.

PSALM LXIII. T. S.

1 O God, my God, I early seek
    For why? my Soul and Body both
2 And in this barren Wilderness,
    My Flesh is parcht for Thought of thee,
to come to thee in Haste:
do thirst of thee to taste.
where Waters there are none,
for thee I with alone.

3 That I might see yet once again
    As I was wont it to behold
4 For why? thy Mercies far surmount
    My Lips therefore shall give to thee,
thy Glory, Strength, and Might,
within thy Temple bright.
this Life and wretched Days:
due Honour, Laud, and Praise.

5 And whilst I live, I will not fail
    And in thy Name I will lift up
6 My Soul is as with Marrow fill'd,
    My Mouth therefore shall sing such Songs
to worship thee alway:
my Hands when I do pray.
which is both fat and sweet:
as are for thee most meet.

7 When in my Bed I think on thee,
    I under Covert of thy Wings
8 My Soul doth closely stick to thee,
    And those that seek my Soul to slay,
and in the wakeful Night:
rejoice with great Delight.
thy Right-hand is my Pow'r:
Death shall them soon devour.

9 The Sword shall them devour each one,
    The hungry Foxes, which do run
10 The King and all Men shall rejoice,
    For Lyars Mouths shall then be stopt,
their Carcases shall feed
their Prey to seek at Need.
that do profess God's Word:
and all their Ways abhorr'd.

PSALM LXIV. J. H.

1 O Lord, unto my Voice give Ear,
    And rid my Life and Soul from Fear
2 Defend me from that Sort of Men
    And from the frowning Face of them
when I complain and pray:
of Foes that threat to slay,
who in Deceit do lurk:
who all in Feats do work.

3 Who whet their Tongues as we have seen
    And shoot abroad their Arrows keen,
4 They privily do shoot their Shaft,
    The Innocent do strike by Craft,
Men whet and sharp their Swords:
I mean most bitter Words,
the upright Man to hit:
they care or fear no Whit.

5 A wicked Work they have decreed,
    To use Deceit let us not dread:
6 Which Way to hurt they talk and muse
    They all consult what Feats to use,
in Council thus they cry,
for none can it espy.
all Times within their Heart:
each doth invent his Part.

7 But yet all this shall not prevail:
    God with his Dart shall sure assail,
8 Their Crafts and their ill Tongues withal,
    That they who then behold their Fall,
when they think least thereon,
and wound them ev'ry one.
shall work themselves such Blame:
shall wonder at the same.

9 And all that see shall know right well,
    And praise his wond'rous Works, and tell
10 Yet shall the Just in God rejoice,
    So shall they joy with Mind and Voice,
that God the Thing hath wrought:
what he to pass hath brought.
still trusting in his Might:
whose Hearts are pure and right.

PSALM LXV. T. S.

1 THY Praise alone, O Lord, doth reign
    Their Vows to thee they do maintain,
in Sion shine own Hill:
and Promises fulfil.

PSALM LXVI.

2 For that thou doſt their Pray'rs ſtill hear, and doſt thereto agree:
The People all both far and near, with Truſt ſhall come to thee.
3 Our wicked Life ſo far exceeds, that we ſhall fall therein,
But, Lord, forgive our great Miſdeeds, and purge us from our Sin.
4 The Man is bleſt whom thou doſt chuſe within thy Courts to dwell:
Thy Houſe and Temple he ſhall uſe with Pleaſures that excel.
5 Of thy great Juſtice hear, O God, our Health of thee doth riſe:
The Hope of all the Earth abroad, and the Sea-coaſts likewiſe.
6 With Strength thou art beſet about, and compaſs'd with thy Pow'r:
Thou mak'ſt the Mountains ſtrong and ſtout, to ſtand in ev'ry Show'r.
7 The ſwelling Seas thou doſt aſſwage, making them very ſtill:
Thou doſt reſtrain the People's Rage, and rule them at thy Will.
8 The Folk that dwell thro'out the Earth, ſhall dread thy Signs to ſee:
Morning and Ev'ning, with great Mirth, ſend Praiſes up to thee.
9 When that the Earth is chapt and dry, and thirſteth more and more,
Then with thy Drops thou doſt ſupply, and much increaſe her Store.
10 The Flood of God doth overflow, and ſo doth cauſe to ſpring
The Seed and Corn which Men do ſow, for he doth guide the Thing.
11 With Rain thou doſt her Furrows fill, whereby her Clods do fall:
Thy Drops on her thou doſt diſtil, and bleſs her Fruit withal.
12 Thou deck'ſt the Earth of thy good Grace, with fair and pleaſant Crop:
The Clouds diſtil their Dew apace, great Plenty they do drop.
13 Whereby the Deſart ſhall begin full great Increaſe to bring:
The little Hills ſhall joy therein, much Fruit in them ſhall ſpring.
14 In Places plain the Flocks ſhall feed, and cover all the Earth:
The Vales with Corn ſhall ſo exceed, that they ſhall ſing with Mirth.

PSALM LXVI. T. S.

1 YE Men on Earth, in God rejoice, with Praiſe ſet forth his Name,
Extol his Might with Heart and Voice, give Glory to the ſame.
2 How wonderful, O Lord, ſay ye, in all thy Works thou art!
Thy Foes for fear ſhall ſeek to thee full ſore againſt their Heart.
3 All Men that dwell the Earth thro'out, ſhall praiſe the Name of God:
The Laud whereof the World about is ſhew'd and ſet abroad,
4 All Folk come forth, behold, and ſee what Things the Lord hath wrought:
Mark well the wond'rous Works that he for Man to paſs hath brought.
5 He laid the Sea like Heaps on high, therein a Way they had
On Foot to paſs, both fair and dry, whereof their Hearts were glad.
6 His Might doth rule the World alway, his Eyes all Things behold:
All ſuch as will him diſobey, by him ſhall be controll'd.
7 Ye People, give unto our God due Laud and Thanks always:
With joyful Voice declare abroad, and ſing unto his Praiſe.
8 Who doth endue our Souls with Life, and it preſerve withal;
He ſtays our Feet, ſo that no Strife can make us ſlip or fall.
9 The Lord doth prove our Deeds with Fire, whether they will abide:
As Workmen do, when they deſire to have their Metals try'd.
10 Altho' thou doſt us ſuffer long in Priſon to be caſt:
And there with Chains and Fetters ſtrong to lie in Bondage faſt.

PART II.

11 Altho', I ſay, thou ſuffer Men on us to ride and reign:
Tho' we thro' Fire and Water run with very Grief and Pain.

12 Yet

PSALM LXVII, LXVIII.

12 Yet sure thou dost, of thy good Grace, dispose it to the best :
  Bringing us out into a Place, to live in Wealth and Rest.
13 Unto thy House resort will I, to offer and to pray :
  And there I will myself apply my Vows to thee to pay.
14 The Vows, that with my Mouth I spake, in all my Grief and Smart :
  The Vows, I say, which I did make in Anguish of my Heart.
15 Burnt-offerings I will give to thee, of Oxen fat, and Rams :
  Yea, this my Sacrifice shall be of Bullocks, Goats and Lambs.
16 Come forth, and hearken here full soon, all ye that fear the Lord :
  What he for my poor Soul hath done, to you I will record.
17 Full oft I call to Mind his Grace, this Mouth to him doth cry :
  And thou, my Tongue, make speedy Pace to praise him joyfully.
18 But if I feel my Heart within in wicked Works rejoice :
  Or if I have Delight in Sin, God will not hear my Voice.
19 But surely God my Voice hath heard, and what I do require :
  My Pray'r also he doth regard, and granteth my Desire.
20 All Praise to him that hath not put, nor cast me out of Mind :
  Nor yet his Mercy from me shut, which I do ever find.

PSALM LXVII. J. H.

1 HAVE Mercy on us, Lord, and grant to us thy Grace :
  To shew to us do thou accord the Brightness of thy Face.
2 That all the Earth may know the Way to godly Wealth ;
  And all the Nations here below may see thy saving Health.
3 Let all the World, O God, give Praise unto thy Name :
  And let the People all abroad extol and laud the same.
4 Thro'out the World so wide, let all rejoice with Mirth :
  For thou with Truth and Right dost guide the Nations of the Earth.
5 Let all the World, O God, give Praise unto thy Name :
  And let the People all abroad extol and laud the same.
6 Then shall the Earth increase, great Store of Fruit shall fall :
  And then our God, the God of Peace, shall ever bless us all.
7 God shall us greatly bless, and then both far and near,
  The Folk which all the Earth possess, of him shall stand in fear.

PSALM LXVIII. T. S.

1 LET God arise, and then his Foes will turn themselves to flight :
  His Enemies for fear shall run, and scatter out of Sight.
2 And as Wax melts before the Fire, and Wind blows Smoke away :
  So in the Presence of the Lord the Wicked shall decay.
3 But righteous Men before the Lord, shall heartily rejoice :
  They shall be glad and merry all, and chearful in their Voice.
4 Sing Praise, sing Praise unto the Lord, who rideth on the Sky :
  Extol the great Jehovah's Name, and him still magnify.
5 The same is he that is above within his holy Place :
  That Father is of Fatherless, and Judge of Widow's Case.
6 Houses and Issue both he gives unto the Comfortless :
  He bringeth Bondmen out of Thrall, and Rebels to Distress.
7 When thou didst march before thy Folk th' Egyptians from among,
  And brought'st them thro' the Wilderness, which was both wide and long.

PSALM LXVIII.

8 The Earth did shake, the Heav'ns did drop, great Thunder-claps were heard:
Mount Sinai also moved was when Isr'el's God appear'd.
9 Thy Heritage with Drops of Rain abundantly was wash'd:
And if so be it barren was, by thee it was refresh'd.
10 Thy chosen Flock doth there remain, thou hast prepar'd that Place:
And for the Poor thou dost provide, of thy especial Grace.

PART II.

11 God will give Women Causes just to magnify his Name:
When as his People Triumphs make, and purchase mighty Fame.
12 Puissant Kings for all their Pow'r, shall flee and take the Foil:
And Women which remain at Home, shall help to part the Spoil.
13 And tho' ye were as black as Pots, your Hue shall pass the Dove:
Whose Wings and Feathers seem to have Silver and Gold above.
14 When in this Land God shall triumph o'er Kings both high and low:
Then shall it be like Salmon Hill, as white as is the Snow.
15 Tho' Basan be a fruitful Hill, and in height others pass:
Yet Sion, God's most holy Hill, doth far excel in Grace.
16 Why leap ye thus, ye Hills most high, and thus in Pride do swell?
The Hill of Sion God doth love and there will ever dwell.
17 God's Army twenty thousand is of Angels great and strong:
The Lord also in Sinai is present them among.
18 Thou didst, O Lord, ascend on high, and captive ledst them all:
Who in Times past thy chosen Flock in Bondage did inthrall.
19 Thou hast received Gifts for Men, ev'n for thine Enemies:
Unto the End that God the Lord might dwell with them likewise.
20 Now praised be the Lord, for that he pours on us such Grace:
From Day to Day he is the God both of our Health and Peace.

PART III.

21 He is the God from whom alone Salvation we obtain:
He is the God, by whom we 'scape all Dangers, Death and Pain.
22 And he shall wound the Head of all his Enemies; also
The hairy Scalp of such as on in Wickedness still go.
23 From Basan will I bring, said he, my People and my Sheep:
And all my own, as I have done, from Dangers of the Deep.
24 And make them dip their Feet in Blood of those that hate my Name:
The Tongues of Dogs they shall be red with licking of the same.
25 Thy Goings they have seen, O God, unto their own Disgrace:
How thou my God and King dost go within thy holy Place.
26 The Singers go before with Joy, the Minstrels make no Stay:
And in the midst the Damsels do with Timbrels sweetly play.
27 Now in the Congregations thou, O Isr'el, praise the Lord:
And Jacob's whole Posterity, give Thanks with one Accord.
28 Their chief was little Benjamin, but Judah made their Host:
With Zebulun and Naphthalim, who dwelt about their Coast.
29 Thy God hath sent forth Strength for thee, O God make firm and sure,
The Thing that thou has wrought in us, for ever to endure.
30 Then in thy Temple Gifts will we offer to thee, O Lord:
And in thy own Jerusalem praise thee with one accord.

PART

PSALM LXIX.
PART IV.

1 Yea, and strange Kings by us subdu'd, shall do like in those Days:
For unto thee they shall present their Gifts of Laud and Praise.
2 He shall destroy the Spearmen's Ranks, the Calves and Bulls of Might:
And make them Tribute pay, and daunt all such as love to fight.
3 Then shall the Lords of Egypt come, and Presents with them bring:
The Moors also stretch out their Hands to God their Lord and King.
4 Therefore, ye Kingdoms of the Earth, give Praise unto the Lord:
Sing Psalms to God with one Consent, thereto let all accord.
5 For he doth ride, and ever did, above the Heav'ns most bright:
And by his fearful Thunder-claps Men may well know his Might.
6 Therefore the Strength of Israel ascribe to God on high;
Whose Might and Pow'r doth far extend above the cloudy Sky.
7 O God, thy Holiness and Pow'r is dread for evermore:
The God of Isra'l gives us Strength, therefore his Name adore.

PSALM LXIX. J. H.

1 SAVE me, O God, and that with Speed, because the Waters do
So very nigh my Soul proceed, and enter thereinto.
2 I sink full deep in Mire and Clay, where I can feel no Ground:
And in deep Waters, where I may most suddenly be drown'd.
3 With crying I am weary, lo, my Throat is hoarse and dry:
My Sight doth fail, looking also for Help to God on high.
4 My Foes that guiltless do oppress my Soul, with hate are led:
In Number sure they are no less than Hairs upon my Head.
5 Tho' for no Cause they vex me sore they prosper and are glad:
They do compel me to restore the Things I never had.
6 What I thro' my Simplicity have done, Lord, thou canst tell:
And all my Faults in Privacy, to thee are known full well.
7 O God of Hosts, defend and stay all those that trust in thee:
Let no Man doubt or shrink away, for ought that chanceth me.
8 It is for thee, and for thy Sake, that I do bear this Blame:
In Spite to thee they would me make to hide my Face for Shame.
9 My Mother's Sons, my Brethren all, reject me with Disgrace:
And as a Stranger they me call, they will not know my Face.
10 Unto thy House such Zeal I bear, that it doth vex me much:
Their Cheeks and Taunts at thee to hear, my very Heart doth touch.

PART II.

11 Tho' I do fast my Flesh to tame, yea, if I weep and moan:
I am reproached for the same by Scorners ev'ry one.
12 If I for Grief and Pain of Heart in Sackcloth use to walk:
Reproachfully they it pervert, thereof they jest and talk.
13 Both High and Low, and all the throng that sit within the Gate:
They have me ever in their Tongue, of me they talk and prate.
14 They that sit in the Gate with spite against me all decree:
The Drunkards that in Wine delight, do make their Songs of me.
15 But unto thee, O Lord, I pray, that when it pleaseth thee:
For thy great Truth thou wilt alway send down thy Aid to me.
16 Pluck thou my Feet out of the Mire, from drowning do me keep:
From such as owe me Wrath and Ire, and from the Waters deep.

PSALM LXX.

17 Left with the Waves I should be drown'd, and Depth my Soul devour.
And left the Pit should me confound, and shut me in her Pow'r.
18 O Lord of Hosts, to me give ear, as thou art good and kind:
And as thy Mercy is most dear, Lord, have me in thy Mind

19 And do not from thy Servant hide, nor turn thy Face away:
I am opprest on ev'ry Side, in Haste give ear, I pray.
20 O Lord, unto my Soul draw nigh, the same with Aid repose:
Because of their great Tyranny, acquit me from my Foes.

PART III.

21 That I abide Rebuke and Shame, thou know'st, and thou canst tell:
For those that seek and work the same, thou see'st them all full well.
22 When with Reproach they break my Heart, some Help I fain would see:
But find no Friends to ease my Smart, not one to comfort me.

23 But in my Meat they gave me Gall, too cruel for to think:
And gave me in my Thirst withal, strong Vinegar to drink.
24 Lord, turn their Table to a Snare to take themselves therein:
And when they think full well to fare, then trap them in their Gin.

25 And let their Eyes be dark and blind, that they may Nothing see:
Bow down their Backs, and let them find themselves in Thrall to be.
26 Pour out thy Wrath as hot as Fire, that it on them may fall:
Let thy Displeasure in thine Ire take hold upon them all.

27 As Deserts dry their House disgrace. their Seed do thou expel:
That none thereof possess their Place, nor in their Tents once dwell.
28 If thou dost strike the Man to tame, on him they lay full sore:
And if that thou do wound the same. they seek to hurt him more.

29 Then let them heap up Mischief still, since they are all pervert:
That of thy Favour and Good-will they never have a Part.
30 And raze them clean out of thy Book of Life, of Hope, and Trust:
That for their Names they never look in Number of the Just.

PART IV.

31 Tho' I, O Lord, with Pain and Grief have been full sore opprest:
Thy Help shall give me such Relief that all shall be redrest.
32 That I might give thy Name the Praise that doth to thee belong:
I will extol the same always with a Thanksgiving Song.

33 Which is more pleasant unto thee, such Mind thy Grace hath born:
Than either Ox or Calf can be, that hath both Hoof and Horn.
34 When simple Folk do this behold, it shall rejoice them sure:
All ye that seek the Lord, your Life for ever shall endure.

35 For why? the Lord of Hosts doth hear the Poor when they complain:
His Prisoners are to him full dear, he doth them not disdain.
36 Wherefore the Sky and Earth below, the Sea, with Flood and Stream:
His Praise they shall declare and show, with all that live in them.

37 For sure our God will Sion save, and Judah's Cities build:
Much Folk Possession there shall have, her Streets shall all be fill'd.
38 His Servants Seed shall keep the same all Ages out of Mind:
And there all they that love his Name, a Dwelling-place shall find.

PSALM LXX. J. H.

1 O God to me take Heed, of Help I thee require:
O Lord of Hosts, with Haste and Speed help me I thee desire.

PSALM LXXI.

With Shame confound them all,
Let them be turned back and fall,
that seek my Soul to spill:
that think and wish me Ill.

Let them rewarded be
Who when Harm happens unto me,
But let them joyful be
Who only trust and seek to thee,
with Infamy and Shame,
do triumph at the same.
in thee with Joy and Wealth,
and to thy saving Health.

That they may say always,
All Glory, Honour, Laud and Praise,
But I am weak and poor,
Thou art my Stay and Help, therefore
in Mirth and one Accord:
be given to the Lord.
come, Lord, thy Aid I lack:
make Speed, and be not slack.

PSALM LXXI. J. II.

MY Lord my God, in all Distress
Then let no Shame my Soul oppress,
As thou art just, defend me, Lord,
Give ear, and to my Suit accord,
my Hope is whole in thee:
nor once take Hold on me.
and rid me out of Dread:
and send me Help at Need.

Be thou my Rock, to whom I may
Thy Promise is to help alway,
Save me, my God, from wicked Men,
From Folk unjust, and also them
for Aid all Times resort:
thou art my Fence and Fort.
and from their Strength & Pow'r:
that cruelly devour.

Thou art my Stay whereon I rest,
Ev'n from my Youth I thought it best
Thou hast me kept ev'n from my Birth,
Wherefore I will thee praise with Mirth
thou, Lord of Hosts, art he:
still to depend on thee.
and I thro' thee was born:
both Ev'ning and at Morn.

As to a Monster seldom seen,
But then art now, and still hast been
5 Wherefore my Mouth for ever shall
Also my Tongue shall never fail
much Folk about me throng:
my Fence and Aid most strong.
be filled with thy Praise:
to honour thee always.

9 Refuse me not, O Lord, I pray,
And when my Strength doth waste away,
10 Among themselves my Foes enquire
And they against me do conspire,
when Age my Limbs doth take:
do not my Soul forsake.
to take me thro' Deceit,
that for my Soul lay wait.

PART II.

11 Lay Hands upon him now, they said
Dispatch him quite, for to his Aid
12 Do not withdraw thyself away,
But that in Time of Grief I may
for God from him is gone:
most sure there cometh none.
O Lord, when Need shall be:
have speedy Help from thee.

13 With Shame confound and overthrow
Suppress them with Rebuke also,
14 But I will patiently abide
Still more and more, each Time and Tide,
all those that seek my Life:
that fain would work me Strife:
thy Help at all assays:
I will set forth thy Praise.

15 My Mouth thy Justice shall accord,
For thy great Benefits, O Lord,
16 Yet will I go and seek for one,
The saving Health of thee alone
that daily Help doth send:
no Numbers have nor End.
with thy good Help, O God,
to shew and set abroad.

17 For of my Youth thou took'st the Care,
Therefore thy Wonders do declare
18 And as in Youth from wanton Rage
Forsake me not in my old Age,
and dost instruct me still:
I have great Mind and Will.
thou didst me keep and stay:
and when my Head is gray.

F

PSALM LXXII.

PART III.

19 That I thy Strength and Might may fhow to them that now be here:
And that our Seed thy Pow'r may know hereafter many Year.
20 O Lord, thy Juftice doth exceed, thy Doings all may fee:
Thy Works are wonderful indeed, oh, who is like to thee!
21 Thou mad'ft me feel Affliction fore, and yet thou didft me fave:
Yea, thou didft help and me reftore, and took'ft me from the Grave.
22 And thou my Honour doft increafe, my Dignity maintain:
Yea, thou doft make all Grief to ceafe, and comfort'ft me again.

23 Therefore thy Faithfulnefs to praife I will with Viol fing:
My Harp fhall found thy Laud always, O Ifr'el's holy King.
24 My Mouth will joy with pleafant Voice, when I fhall fing to thee;
Alfo my Soul fhall much rejoice, for thou haft fet me free.

25 My Tongue thy Righteoufnefs fhall found, I daily fpeak it will:
For Grief and Shame doth them confound, that feek to work me Ill.

PSALM LXXII. J. H.

1 LORD, give thy Judgments to the King, therein inftruct him well:
And with his Son in ev'ry Thing, Lord, let thy Juftice dwell.
2 That he may govern uprightly, and rule thy Folk with Right:
And fo defend with Equity, the Poor that have no Might.

3 And let the Mountains that are high, unto thy Folk give Peace:
Let little Hills alfo apply, in Juftice to increafe.
4 That he may help the Weak and Poor with Aid, and make them ftrong:
And fo deftroy for evermore all thofe that do them Wrong.

5 And then from Age to Age fhall they regard and fear thy Might:
So long as Sun doth fhine by Day, or elfe the Moon by Night.
6 Lord, make the King unto the juft like Rain to Fields new mown:
And like to Drops that lay the Duft, refrefhing Land new fown.

7 The Juft fhall flourifh in his Days, and all fhall be at Peace:
Until the Moon fhall ceafe always to change, wafte, or increafe.
8 He fhall be Lord, and have Command from Shore to Shore thro'out:
And from the Floods within the Land, thro' all the Earth about.

9 The People that in Defarts dwell, fhall kneel to him full thick:
And all his Foes that do rebel, the Earth and Duft to lick.
10 The Lords of all the Ifles alfo great Gifts to him fhall bring:
Arabia and Saba's Kings give many coftly Thing.

PART II.

11 All Kings fhall feek with one Accord in his good Grace to ftand:
And all the People of the World obey at his Command.
12 For he the needy Sort doth fave, that unto him do call:
Alfo the fimple Folk that have no Help of Man at all.

13 He taketh Pity on the Poor that are with Need oppreft:
He doth preferve them evermore, and bring their Souls to Reft.
14 He fhall redeem their Lives from Dread, fromFraud,fromWrong, & Might.
Alfo their Blood that fhall be fhed is precious in his Sight.

15 But he fhall live, and they fhall bring to him of Saba's Gold:
He fhall be honour'd as a King, and daily be extoll'd.
16 The mighty Mountains of his Land, of Corn fhall bear fuch Throng:
That it like Cedar-Trees fhall ftand in Libanus full long.

PSALM LXXIII.

17 Their Cities alfo well fhall fpeed the Fruits thereof furpafs:
    In Plenty it fhall fo exceed, and fpring as green as Grafs.
18 For ever they fhall praife his Name, while that the Sun is light:
    And think them happy thro' the fame, all Folk fhall blefs his Might.

19 Praife ye the Lord of Hofts, and fing to Ifr'el's God each one:
    For he doth ev'ry wond'rous Thing, yea, he himfelf alone.
20 And bleffed be his holy Name, all Times eternally:
    Let all the Earth ftill praife the fame, Amen, Amen, fay I.

PSALM LXXIII. T. S.

1 TRULY the Lord is very good and kind to Ifrael:
    And to all fuch as fafely keep their Confcience pure and well.
2 But as for me I almoft flipt, my Feet began to' flide:
    Before that I was well aware my Steps did turn afide.

3 For when I faw fuch foolifh Men, I grudg'd with great Difdain:
    That wicked Men all Things fhould have without Turmoil and Pain.
4 They never fuffer Pains nor Grief, as if Death fhould them fmite:
    Their Bodies are full ftout and ftrong, and ever in good Plight.

5 Always free from Adverfity, and ev'ry fad Event:
    With other Men they take no Part of Plague or Punifhment.
6 Therefore Prefumption doth embrace their Necks as doth a Chain:
    They are ev'n wrapt as in a Robe, with Rapine and Difdain.

7. They are fo fed, that ev'n with Fat their Eyes oft-times out-ftart:
    And as for worldly Goods, they have more than can wifh their Heart.
8 Their Life is moft licentious, and they boaft much with their Tongue:
    How they the Poor and Simple have oppreffed with great Wrong.

9 They fet their Mouth againft the Heav'ns, and do the Lord blafpheme:
    They proudly boaft of worldly Things, no one they do efteem.
10 God's People often do turn back to fee their profp'rous State:
    And almoft drink the felf-fame Cup, and talk at the fame Rate.

PART II.

11 How can it be that God, fay they, fhould know or underftand
    Thefe worldly Things, fince wicked Men be Lords of Sea and Land?
12 For we may fee how wicked Men in Riches ftill increafe:
    Rewarded well with worldly Goods, and live in Reft and Peace.

13 Then why do I fo carefully from Wickednefs refrain?
    And wafh my Hands in Innocence, and cleanfe my Heart in vain?
14 And fuffer Scourges ev'ry Day, as fubject to all Blame?
    And ev'ry Morning from my Youth fuftain Rebuke and Shame?

15 Now I had almoft faid as they, mifliking my Eftate:
    But then I fhould thy Children judge as moft unfortunate.
16 Then I bethought me how I might this Matter underftand:
    But yet the Labour was too great for me to take in Hand;

17 Until the Time I went into thy holy Place, and then
    I underftood right perfectly the End of all thefe Men.
18 Namely, how that thou fetteft them upon a flipp'ry Place:
    And at thy Pleafure and thy Will thou doft them foon deface.

19 Then all Men mufe at that ftrange Sight, to fee how fuddenly
    They do confume, perifh, and come to endlefs Mifery.

PSALM LXXIV.

20 Much like a Dream when one awakes, so shall their Wealth decay:
Their famous Names in all Men's Sight, shall fail and pass away.

PART III.

21 Yet thus my Heart was grieved then, my Mind was much opprest:
So simple and so ignorant, ev'n as it were a Beast.
22 Nevertheless by my Right-hand thou hold'st me always fast:
And with thy Counsel shalt me guide to glory at the last.
23 What Thing is there that I can wish but thee in Heav'n above?
And in the Earth there Nothing is like thee that I can love.
24 My Flesh and Spirit both do fail, but God will me restore:
For of my Heart he is the Strength and Portion evermore.
25 But lo, all such as thee forsake, thou shalt destroy each one:
And those that trust in any Thing, saving in thee alone.
26 Therefore will I draw near to God, and ever with him dwell:
In God alone I put my Trust, his Wonders I will tell.

PSALM LXXIV. J. H.

1 **W**HY art thou, Lord, so long from us in all this Danger deep?
Why doth thy Anger kindle thus at thy own Pasture Sheep?
2 Lord, call the People to thy Thought which have been thine so long:
The which thou hast redeem'd, and brought from Bondage sore and strong.
3 Have Mind therefore, and think upon, remember it full well:
Thy pleasant Place, thy Mount Sion, where thou wast wont to dwell.
4 Lift up thy Feet and come in Haste, and all thy Foes deface:
Who now at Pleasure rob and waste within thy holy Place.
5 Amidst thy Congregations all, thy Foes do roar, O God:
They set as Signs on every Wall, Banners displ'ay'd abroad.
6 As Men with Axes hew down Trees that on the Hills do grow:
So thine the Bills and Swords of these within thy Temple now.
7 The Cieling fine, and carved Boards, with all the goodly Stones:
With Axes, Hammers, Bills and Swords, they beat them down at once.
8 Thy Places they consume with Flame, their Rage doth so abound:
The House appointed to thy Name, they raze ev'n to the Ground.
9 And thus they say within their Heart, Dispatch them out of Hand:
Then burn they up in ev'ry Part God's Houses thro' the Land.
10 Yet thou no Sign of Help dost send, our Prophets all are gone:
To tell when this our Plague shall end, among us there is none.
11 How long, Lord, shall thy Enemies thus boldly thee defame:
Shall they for evermore blaspheme thy great and holy Name?
12 Why dost thou thy Right-hand withdraw from us so long away?
Out of thy Bosom pluck it forth, with Speed thy Foes to slay.

PART II.

13 O God, thou art our King and Lord, and evermore hast been:
Yea, thy good Grace thro'out the World, for our great Help is seen.
14 The Seas that are so deep and dead, thy Might did make them dry:
And thou didst break the Serpent's Head, that he therein did die.
15 Yea, thou didst break the Heads so great, of Whales that are most fell:
And gav'st them to the Folk to eat that in the Desarts dwell.
16 Thou mad'st a Spring with Streams to rise from Rocks both hard and high:
Thy mighty Hand hath made likewise deep Rivers to be dry.

17 Both

PSALM LXXV, LXXVI.

7 Both Day and Night alfo are thine,
And thou likewife prepared haft
8 Thou didft appoint the Ends and Coafts
Both Summer Heats, and Winter Frofts,
by thee they were begun:
the Light of Moon and Sun.
of all the Earth about:
thy Hand hath found them out.

9 Think on, O Lord, no Time forget
And how the foolifh Folk are fet
10 Deliver not the Soul, O Lord,
Into their Hands, but Help afford
thy Foes that thee defame:
to rail upon thy Name.
of thy own Turtle Dove,
the Poor, whom thou doft love.

11 Regard, O Lord, thy Covenant,
All the dark Places of the Earth
12 Let not the fimple Man therefore,
But let the Needy evermore
behold our Mifery:
are full of Cruelty.
be turned back with Shame:
give Praife unto thy Name.

13 Arife, O Lord, and plead thy Caufe
Who daily do reject thy Laws,
14 The Voice forget not of thy Foes,
Is more and more increas'd of thofe
againft thy Enemies:
and them with Scorn defpife.
for the Prefumption high,
that hate thee fpitefully.

PSALM LXXV. J. H.

1 TO thee, O God, will we give Thanks,
Since thy Name is fo near, declare
2 I will uprightly judge, when get
The Earth is weak, and all therein,
we will give Thanks to thee:
thy wond'rous Works will we.
convenient Time I may:
but I her Pillars ftay.

3 I did to the mad People fay,
And unto the ungodly Ones,
4 I faid unto them, Set not up
And fee that with ftiff Neck you do
Deal not fo furioufly:
Lift not your Horns on high.
your raifed Horns on high:
not fpeak prefumptuoufly.

5 For neither from the Eaftern Parts,
Nor from forfaken Wildernefs,
6 But God, who rules both Heav'n and Earth,
It's he that puts down one, and fets
nor from the Weft likewife:
Promotion doth arife.
the righteous Judge alone:
another in the Throne.

7 For why? a Cup of mighty Wine
And all the Mixture of the fame,
8 As for the Lees and filthy Dregs
The Wicked of the Earth fhall drink
is in the Hand of God:
himfelf will pour abroad.
that do remain of it,
and fuck them ev'ry Whit.

9 But I will talk of God alway,
And will not ceafe to celebrate
10 In funder break the Horns of all
But then the Horns of righteous Men
and his great Name adore,
his Praife for evermore.
ungodly Men will I:
fhall be exalted high.

PSALM LXXVI. J. H.

1 TO all that now in Judah dwell,
His Name is great in Ifrael,
2 At Salem he hath pitch'd his Tent,
In Sion alfo he is bent
the Lord is clearly known:
a People of his own.
to tarry there a Space:
to fix his Dwelling place.

3 And there he brake both Shaft and Bow,
His Enemies did overthrow
4 Thou art moft worthy Honour, Lord,
Than in the ftrongeft of the World,
the Sword, the Spear, and Shield:
in Battle in the Field.
more Might in thee doth lie:
that rob on Mountains high.

5 But now the Proud are fpoil'd thro' thee,
Tho' Men of War no Help can be,
and they are fall'n afleep:
themfelves they could not keep.

PSALM LXXVII.

6 At thy Rebuke, O Jacob's God, when thou didst them reprove,
As half asleep their Chariots stood, no Horseman once did move.
7 For thou art dreadful, Lord, indeed, what Man the Courage hath
To bide thy Sight, and doth not dread when thou art in thy Wrath?
8 When thou dost make thy Judgments heard from Heav'n unto the Ground:
Then all the Earth, full sore afraid, in Silence shall be found.
9 And that when thou, O God, dost stand in Judgment for to speak,
To save th' Afflicted of the Land that feeble are and weak.
10 The Fury that in Man doth reign shall turn unto thy Praise:
Hereafter, Lord, do thou restrain their Wrath and Threats always.
11 Make Vows and pay them to our God, ye Folk that nigh him be;
Bring Gifts, all ye that dwell abroad, for dreadful sure is he.
12 For he doth take both Life and Might from Princes great of Birth:
And full of Terror is his Sight to all the Kings on Earth.

PSALM LXXVII.   J. H.

1 With my Voice to God did cry, who lent a gracious Ear:
My Voice I lifted up on high, and he my Suit did hear.
2 In Time of Grief I sought to God, by Night no Rest I took:
But stretcht my Hand to him abroad, my Soul Comfort forsook.
3 When I to think on God intend, my Trouble then is more:
I spake, but could not make an End, my Breath was stopt so sore.
4 Thou dost my Eyes so hold from Rest, that I always awake:
With Fear I am so sore opprest, my Sleep doth me forsake.
5 The Days of old in Mind I cast, and oft do think upon:
The Times and Ages that are past full many Years agone.
6 By Night my Songs I call to Mind, once made thy Praise to show
And with my Heart much Talk I find, my Spirits search to know.
7 Will God, said I, at once for all cast off his People thus,
So that henceforth no Time he shall be friendly unto us?
8 What, is his Goodness quite decay'd, and passed clean away?
Or is his Promise now delay'd? and doth his Truth decay?
9 And will the Lord our God forget his Mercies manifold?
Or shall his Wrath increase so hot, his Mercies to with hold?
10 At last I said, This surely is mine own Infirmity:
But his Right hand can help all this, and change it speedily.

PART II.

11 I will regard and think upon the Working of the Lord:
And all his Wonders past and gone, I gladly will record.
12 Yea, all his Works I will declare, and what he did devise:
To tell his Facts I will not spare, and all his Counsel wise.
13 Thy Works, O Lord, are all upright, and holy all abroad:
What one hath Strength to match the Might of thee the Lord our God?
14 Thou art a God that dost forth show thy Wonders ev'ry Hour.
And so didst make the People know thy Virtue and thy Pow'r.
15 And thy own Folk thou dost defend with an out-stretched Arm:
Those that from Jacob did descend, and Joseph's Seed, from Harm.
16 The Waters, Lord, perceived thee, the Waters saw thee well:
And they for Fear away did flee, the Depths on Trembling fell.

17 Th

PSALM LXXVIII.

17 The Clouds that were both thick and black   did rain full plenteously,
   The Thunder in the Air did crack,   thy Shafts abroad did fly.
18 Thy Thunder in the Air was heard,   thy Lightnings from above,
   With Flashes great, made Men afraid,   the Earth did quake and move.
19 Thy Ways within the Sea do lie,   thy Paths in Waters deep:
   Yet none can there thy Steps espy,   nor know thy Paths to keep.
20 Thou ledst thy Folk upon the Land   as Sheep on ev'ry Side:
   By Moses and by Aaron's Hand   thou didst them safely guide.

PSALM LXXVIII. J. H.

1 ATTEND, my People, to my Law,   and to my Words incline:
   My Mouth shall speak strange Parables,   and Sentences divine.
2 Which we ourselves have heard and learn'd,   ev'n of our Fathers old:
   And which for our Instruction   our Fathers have us told.

3 Because we should not keep it close   from them that after came:
   Who should God's mighty Pow'r declare,   and wond'rous Works proclaim.
4 To Jacob he Commandment gave   how Israel should live:
   Willing our Fathers should the same   unto their Children give.

5 That they and their Posterity   that were not sprung up then,
   Should have the Knowledge of the Law,   and teach it their Children.
6 That they might have the better Hope   in God that is above:
   And not forget to keep his Laws,   and his Commands in Love.

7 Not being as their Fathers, who   rebelled in God's Sight:
   And would not frame their wicked Hearts   to know their God aright.
8 How went the Sons of Ephraim   their Neighbours for to spoil:
   Shooting their Darts in Day of War,   and yet receiv'd the Foil?

9 For why? they did not keep with God,   the Cov'nant that was made:
   Nor yet would walk or lead their Lives   according as he said.
10 But put into Oblivion   his Counsel and his Will:
   And all his Works magnificent,   which he declared still.

PART II.

11 What Wonders to our Fore-fathers   did he himself disclose:
   In Egypt Land, within the Field   that call'd is Thaneos!
12 He did divide and part the Sea,   thro' which he made a Way:
   For them to pass, and on a Heap   the Water made to stay.

13 He led them secret in a Cloud   by Day when it was bright:
   And in the Night when it was dark,   with Fire he gave them Light.
14 He clave the Rocks in Wilderness,   and gave the People Drink:
   As plentiful as when the Deeps   do flow up to the Brink.

15 He drew forth Rivers out of Rocks   that were both dry and hard:
   In such abundance, that no Floods   to them might be compar'd.
16 Yet for all this against the Lord   their Sin they did increase:
   And did provoke the most Highest   to Wrath in Wilderness.

17 And in their Hearts they tempted God,   like People of Mistrust:
   Requiring such a Kind of Meat   as served to their Lust.
18 Yea, they against him spake, and thus   their Boldness did express:
   Can God prepare a Table in   this barren Wilderness?

19 Behold, he smote the stony Rock,   and Floods forthwith did flow:
   But can he now give to his Folk   both Bread and Flesh also?
                                                20 When

PSALM LXXVIII.

20 When God heard this, he waxeth Wrath with Jacob and his Seed:
His Indignation alfo did 'gainſt Iſrael proceed.

PART III.

21 Becauſe they did not faithfully believe, and hope that he
Could always help and ſuccour them in their Neceſſity.
22 Wherefore he did command the Clouds, forthwith they brake in ſunder:
And rain'd down Manna for to eat, a Food of mighty Wonder.

23 When earthly Men with Angels Food did plentifully feaſt:
He made the Eaſt-Wind blow away, and brought in the South-Weſt.
24 He rain'd down Fleſh as thick as Duſt, and Fowls as thick as Sand:
Which he did caſt amidſt the Place where all their Tents did ſtand.

25 Then did they eat exceedingly, and all Men had their Fills:
Yet more and more they did deſire to ſerve their Luſts and Wills.
26 But as the Meat was in their Mouths, his Wrath upon them fell:
And ſlew the Strength of all their Youth, and Choice of Iſrael.

27 Yet fell they to their wonted Sin, and ſtill they did him grieve:
For all the Wonders that he wrought, they would not him believe.
28 Their Days therefore he ſhortned, and did make their Honour vain:
Their Years did waſte and paſs away with Terror and with Pain.

29 But ever when he plagued them, they ſought him ſpeedily:
Remembring that he was their Strength, their Help and God moſt high.
30 Tho' with their Mouths they Nothing did but flatter with the Lord:
And with their Tongues, and in their Hearts, diſſembled ev'ry Word.

PART IV.

31 For why their Hearts were Nothing bent to him, nor what he ſaid:
Nor yet to keep or to perform the Covenant he made.
32 Yet was he ſtill ſo merciful when they deſerv'd to die,
That he forgave them, and would not them utterly deſtroy.

33 Yea, many Times he ſtav'd his Wrath, and did not them ſurpriſe:
And would not ſuffer that his whole Diſpleaſure ſhould ariſe.
34 Conſidering they were but Fleſh, or like to Wind and Rain,
Paſſing away, and never doth return and come again.

35 How often in the Wildernefs did they the Lord provoke?
How did they move and ſtir him up to plague them with his Stroke!
36 Yet did they turn again to Sin, and tempt him very ſoon:
Preſcribing to the mighty God whatThings theywould havedone.

37 Not thinking of his mighty Hand, nor of the Day when he
Deliver'd them out of the Hand of the fierce Enemy.
38 Nor how he wrought his Miracles (as they themſelves beheld)
In Egypt, and the Wonders that he did in Zoan Field.

39 Nor how he turned by his Pow'r their Waters into Blood,
That no Man might receive his Drink at River or at Flood.
40 Nor how he ſent them Swarms of Flies, which did them ſore annoy:
And fill'd their Country full of Frogs, which did their Land deſtroy.

PART V.

41 Nor how he did their Fruits unto the Caterpiller give:
And of the Labour of their Hands Locuſts did them deprive.
42 With Hail he did rove'd their Vines, ſo that they all were loſt:
And likewiſe their canes he did conſume with Froſt.

43 With

PSALM LXXVIII.

43 With Hail-ſtones alſo once again the Lord their Cattle ſmote:
 And all their Flocks and Herds likewiſe with Thunder-bolts full hot.
44 He caſt upon them his fierce Wrath, and Indignation ſore:
 Amongſt them evil Angels ſent, which troubled them yet more.
45 Then to his Wrath he made a Way, and ſpared not the leaſt:
 But gave unto the Peſtilence the Man as well as Beaſt.
46 He ſmote alſo all the Firſt-born that up in Egypt came:
 And all the Chief of Men and Beaſts within the Tents of Ham.
47 But as for his own People, he did them preſerve and keep,
 And carry'd them thro' Wilderneſs, even like a Flock of Sheep.
48 Without all Fear, both ſafe and ſound, he brought them out of Thrall:
 Whereas their Foes with Rage of Seas were overwhelmed all.
49 And brought them out into the Coaſts of his own holy Land:
 Ev'n to the Mount which he had got by his ſtrong Arm and Hand.
50 And there caſt out the Heathen Folk, and did the Land divide:
 And in their Tents he ſet the Tribes of Iſr'el to abide.
51 Yet for all this, the God moſt high they mov'd and tempted ſtill:
 And would not keep his Teſtament, nor yet obey his Will.
52 But as their Fathers turned back, ev'n ſo they went aſtray:
 Much like a Bow that will not bend, but ſlip and ſtart away.

PART VI.

53 And griev'd him with their Hill-altars, with Offerings and Fire:
 And with their Idols grievouſly provoked him to Ire.
54 For which his Wrath began again to kindle in his Breaſt:
 The Wickedneſs of Iſrael he did ſo much deteſt.
55 The Tabernacle he forſook of Silo, where he was
 Right converſant with earthly Men, ev'n as his Dwelling-place.
56 Then ſuffer'd he his Might and Pow'r in Bondage for to be,
 And gave the Honour of his Ark unto the Enemy.
57 And did commit them to the Sword, wroth with his Heritage:
 Their young Men were conſum'd with Fire, Maid· had no Marriage.
58 And with the Sword the Prieſts alſo did periſh ev'ry one:
 And not a Widow left alive, their Death for to bemoan.
59 Then did the Lord awake, as one whom Sleep could not confine:
 And like a mighty Giant, that refreſhed is with Wine.
60 With Em'rods in the hinder Parts his Enemies he ſmote:
 And put them unto ſuch a Shame, as ſhould not be forgot.
61 The Tent and Tabernacle he of Joſeph did refuſe:
 Alſo the Tribe of Ephraim he would in no wiſe chuſe.
62 But he the Tribe of Judah choſe, that he therein might dwell:
 Ev'n the moſt noble Mount Sion, which he did love ſo well.
63 And there he did his Temple build both ſumptuouſly and ſure:
 Like as the Earth, which he hath made for ever to endure.
64 Then choſe he David him to ſerve, his People for to keep:
 Whom he took up and brought away, ev'n from the Folds of Sheep.
65 From following the Ewes with Young the Lord did him advance:
 To feed his People Iſrael, and his Inheritance.
66 Thus David with a faithful Heart his Flock and Charge did feed:
 And prudently with all his Pow'r did govern them indeed.

PSALM

PSALM LXXIX, LXXX.
PSALM LXXIX. J. H.

1 O God, the Gentiles do invade   thy Heritage to fpoil :
    Jerufalem a Heap is made,   thy Temple they defile.
2 The Bodies of thy Saints moft dear,   abroad to Birds they caft :
    The Flefh of them that do thee fear,   the Beafts devour and wafte.
3 Their Blood thro'out Jerufalem   as Water fpilt they have :
    So that there is not one of them   to lay their dead in Grave.
4 Thus are we made a laughing-ftock   almoft the World thro'out :
    The Enemies at us do mock   who dwell our Coafts about.
5 How long, O Lord, wilt thou retain   thy Anger and thy Rage ?
    And fhall thy Wrath and Jealoufy   not any more affwage ?
6 Upon thofe People pour the fame   who did thee never know :
    The Realms which call not on thy Name,   confume and overthrow.
7 For they have got the Upper-hand,   and Jacob's Seed deftroy'd :
    His Habitation and his Land   they have laid wafte and void.
8 Bear not in Mind our former Faults,   with Speed fome Pity fhow :
    And aid us, Lord, in our Affaults,   for we are weak and low.

PART II.

9 O God, that giv'ft all Health and Grace,   on us declare the fame :
    Weigh not our Works, our Sins deface,   for Honour of thy Name.
10 Why fhould the Wicked thus alway,   to us as People dumb,
    In thy Reproach rejoice, and fay,   Where is their God become ?
11 Require, O Lord, as thou feeft good,   before our Eyes in Sight,
    Of all thefe Folk thy Servant's Blood   which they fpilt in Defpite.
12 Receive into thy Sight in Hafte,   the Clamours, Grief, and Wrong,
    Of fuch as are in Prifon caft,   and bound in Irons ftrong.
13 Thy Force and Strength to celebrate,   Lord, fet them out of Band :
    Who unto Death are deftinate,   and in their Foes ftrong Hand.
14 The Nations which have been fo bold   as to blafpheme thy Name,
    Into their Laps do thou fev'n-fold   repay again the fame.
15 So we thy Flock and Pafture Sheep   will praife thee evermore :
    And teach all Ages how to keep   for thee like Praife in Store.

PSALM LXXX. J. H.

1 THOU Shepherd that doft Ifr'el keep   give ear and take good Heed :
    Who leadeft Jofeph like a Sheep,   and doft him watch and feed.
2 And thou, O Lord, whofe Seat is fet   on Cherubims moft bright,
    Shew forth thyfelf, and do not let,   fend down thy Beams of Light.
3 Before Ephr'im and Benjamin,   Manaffes in likewife :
    To fhew thy Pow'r do thou begin,   come help us, Lord, arife.
4 Direct our Hearts by thy good Grace,   convert us unto thee :
    Shew us the Brightnefs of thy Face,   and then full fafe are we.
5 Lord God of Hofts of Ifrael,   how long wilt thou delay ?
    Againft thy Folk in Anger fwell,   and wilt not hear them pray ?
6 Thou doft them feed with Sorrows deep,   their Bread with Grief they eat :
    And drink the Tears that they do weep,   in Meafure full and great.
7 Thou haft us made a very Strife   to thofe that dwell about :
    Which much doth pleafe our Enemies,   they laugh and jeft it out.
8 O take us, Lord, unto thy Grace,   convert our Hearts to thee :
    Shew forth to us thy joyful Face,   and we full fafe fhall be.

PSALM LXXXI.

9 From Egypt, where it grew not well
   The Heathen Folk thou didst expel,
10 Thou didst prepare for it a Place,
   That it did grow and spring apace,

thou brought'st a Vine full dear:
and thou didst plant it there.
and set its Root so fast:
and fill'd the Land at last.

PART II.

11 The Hills were cover'd round about
   Also the Cedars strong and stout,
12 Why then didst thou her Walls destroy?
   That all the Folk that pass thereby,
13 The Boar out of the Wood so wild,
   The furious Beasts out of the Field
14 O Lord of Hosts, return again,
   Behold, and with thy Help sustain
15 Thy pleasant Vine, thy Israel,
   The same which thou didst love so well,
16 They lop and cut it off apace,
   And thro' the frowning of thy Face
17 Let thy Right-Hand be with him now,
   And with the Son of Man, whom thou
18 And so when thou hast set us free,
   Then will we never fall from thee,
19 O Lord of Hosts, thro' thy good Grace,
   Behold us with a pleasant Face,

with Shade that from it came:
with Branches of the same.
her Hedge pluck'd up thou hast:
the same do spoil and waste.
doth dig and root it out:
devour it all about.
from Heav'n do thou look down:
thy Vineyard overthrown.
which thy Right-hand hath set:
O Lord, do not forget.
they burn it down with Fire:
we perish in thine Ire.
whom thou hast kept so long:
to thee hast made so strong.
and saved us from Shame:
but call upon thy Name.
convert us unto thee:
and then full safe are we.

PSALM LXXXI. J. H.

1 BE light and glad, in God rejoice,
   Be joyful and lift up your Voice
2 Prepare your Instruments most meet,
   Strike up with Harp and Lute so sweet,
3 Blow as it were in the New-moon,
   As it is used to be done,
4 For this is unto Israel
   By Jacob's God, and must full well
5 This Clause with Joseph was decreed
   That as a Witness all his Seed
6 When God himself had so prepar'd
   Whereas the Speech which he had heard
7 I from his Shoulder took, saith he,
   And from the Furnace set him free,
8 When thou in Grief didst cry and call
   And I did answer thee withal
9 Yea, at the Waters of Discord
   Where thou the Anger of the Lord
10 Hear, O my People Israel,
   Regard and mark my Words full well,

who is our Strength and Stay:
to Jacob's God alway.
some joyful Psalm to sing:
on ev'ry pleasant String.
with Trumpets of the best:
at any solemn Feast.
a Statute which was made
be evermore obey'd.
when he from Egypt came:
should still observe the same.
to bring him from that Land:
he did not understand.
the Burden clean away:
from burning Brick of Clay.
I help'd thee speedily:
in Thunder from on high.
I did thee tempt and prove:
with Murmuring didst move.
what I do promise thee:
if thou wilt cleave to me.

PART II.

11 Thou shalt no God in thee reserve,
   And in no wise bow to or serve
12 I am the Lord thy God, and I
   Then ask of me abundantly,

of any Land abroad:
a strange and foreign God.
from Egypt set thee free:
and I will give it thee.

13 But

PSALM LXXXII, LXXXIII.

13 But yet my People would not hear my Voice when that I spake:
And Ifrael would not obey, but did me quite forfake.
14 Then did I leave them to their Will in Hardnefs of their Heart:
To walk in their own Counfels ftill, themfelves they did pervert.
15 O that my People would have heard the Word that I did fay:
And Ifrael with due Regard had walked in my Way!
16 I fhould have foon deftroy'd their Foes, and brought them down full low:
And turn'd my Hand againft all thofe that fought their Overthrow.
17 And they that at the Lord did rage as Liars fhould be found:
But for his Folk their Time and Age fhould with great Joys be crown'd.
18 I would have fed them with the Crop and fineft of the Wheat:
And made the Rock with Honey drop, that they their Fills might eat.

PSALM LXXXII. J. H.

1 AMONG the Princes, Men of Might, the Lord himfelf doth ftand:
To plead the Caufe of Truth & Right, with Judges of the Land.
2 How long, faith he, will you proceed falfe Judgment to award?
Why have you partially agreed the Wicked to regard?
3 Whereas of Right you fhould defend the Fatherlefs and Weak:
And when the poor Man doth contend, in Judgment juftly fpeak.
4 If ye be wife defend the Caufe of poor Men in their Right:
And rid the Needy from the Claws of Tyrants Force and Might.
5 They will not learn nor underftand, but ftill in Darknefs go:
All the Foundations of the Land are out of Courfe alfo.
6 I had decreed affuredly, as God's to take you all:
Children alfo of the moft High, for Love I did you call.
7 But notwithftanding ye fhall die as Men, and fo decay:
O Tyrants, you deftroy will I, and pluck you quite away.
8 Up, Lord, and let thy Strength be known, and judge the World with Might:
For why, all Nations are thy own, to take them as thy Right.

PSALM LXXXIII. J. H.

1 DO not, O God, refrain thy Tongue, in Silence do not ftay:
Withhold not, Lord, thyfelf fo long, and make no more Delay.
2 For why? behold thy Foes, and fee how they do rage and cry:
And thofe that bear a Hate to thee, hold up their Heads on high.
3 Againft thy Folk they ufe Deceit, and craftily require:
For thine Elect to lie in Wait, in Council they confpire.
4 Come on, fay they, let us expel and pluck this Folk away:
So that the Name of Ifrael may utterly decay.
5 They all confpire within their Hearts how they may thee withftand:
Againft the Lord to take a Part they are in League and Band.
6 The Tents of all the Edomites, the Ifm'elites likewife:
The Hagarenes and Moabites, their Plots do ftill devife.
7 Gebal and Ammon do likewife with Amaleck confpire:
The Philiftines againft thee rife, with them that dwell at Tyre.
8 Affur is alfo join'd to them in their Confpiracy:
And is become a Fence and Aid to Lot's Pofterity.
9 As thou didft to the Midianites, to ferve them, Lord, each one:
To Jabin and to Sifera, befide the Brook Kifon.

10 Whom

PSALM LXXXIV.

1 Whom thou in Endor didſt deſtroy,
That they like Dung on Earth did lie,
and waſte them thro' thy Might:
and that in open Sight.

PART II.

1 Make them now and their Lords appear
As Zeba and Zalmunna were,
2 Who ſaid, let us thro'out the Land,
Poſſeſs and take into our Hand,
like Zeb and Oreb then:
the Kings of Midian.
in all the Coaſts abroad:
the fair Houſes of God.

3 Turn them, O God, with Storms ſo faſt
Or like the Chaff which Men do caſt
4 Like as the Fire with Rage and Fume
And as the Flame doth quite conſume
as Wheels that have no Stay:
with Wind do fly away.
the mighty Foreſt ſpills:
the Mountains and the Hills;

5 So let the Tempeſt of thy Wrath
And of thy Wind and ſtormy Breath,
6 Lord, bring them all, I thee deſire,
That it may cauſe them to enquire,
upon their Necks be laid:
Lord, make them all afraid.
to ſuch Rebuke and Shame,
and learn to ſeek thy Name.

7 And let them daily more and more
And in Rebuke and Obloquy
8 That they may know and underſtand
And that thou doſt with mighty Hand
to Shame and Slander fall:
confound and ſeek them all.
thou art the God moſt high:
the World rule conſtantly.

PSALM LXXXIV. J. H.

HOW pleaſant is thy dwelling Place
The Tabernacles of thy Grace;
My Soul doth long full ſore to go
My Heart and Fleſh cry out alſo
O Lord of Hoſts, to me!
how pleaſant, Lord, they be!
into thy Courts abroad:
for thee the living God.

The Sparrows find a Room to reſt,
The Swallow alſo hath a Neſt
Theſe Birds full nigh thy Altar may
O Lord of Hoſts, thou art alway
and ſave themſelves from Wrong:
wherein to keep her Young,
have Place to fit and ſing:
my only God and King.

O they be bleſſed that may dwell
For they all Times thy Facts do tell,
Yea, happy ſure likewiſe are they,
Who to thy Houſe do mind the Way,
within thy Houſe always:
and ever give thee Praiſe.
whoſe Stay and Strength thou art:
and ſeek it in their Heart.

As they go thro' the Vale of Tears,
That as a Spring it all appears,
From Strength to Strength they go full faſt,
And ſo the God of Gods at laſt
they dig up Fountains ſtill:
and thou their Pits doſt fill.
no Faintneſs there ſhall be:
in Sion they do ſee.

O Lord of Hoſts, to me give Heed,
And let it thro' thine Ears proceed,
9 O God our Shield of thy good Grace,
Regard, O Lord, behold the Face
and hearken to my Cry:
O Jacob's God moſt high.
regard and ſo draw near:
of thy Anointed Dear.

1 For why? within thy Courts one Day
Than other where to keep or ſtay
2 Much rather had I keep a Door
Than in the Tents of Wickedneſs
is better to abide,
a thouſand Days beſide.
within the Houſe of God,
to ſettle my Abode.

3 For God the Lord, Light and Defence,
And no good Thing will he withhold
4 O Lord of Hoſts, that Man is bleſt,
That is perſwaded in his Breaſt
will Grace and Worſhip give:
from them that purely live.
and happy ſure is he,
to truſt all Times in thee.

PSALM LXXXV, LXXXVI.

PSALM LXXXV. J. H.

1 THOU haſt been merciful indeed,   O Lord, unto thy Land:
    For thou reſtoredſt Jacob's Seed   from Thraldom by ſtrong Hand.
2 The wicked Ways that they were in,   thou didſt them clean remit:
    And thou didſt hide thy People's Sin,   full cloſe thou cover'dſt it.

3 And thou thy Anger didſt aſſwage,   that all thy Wrath was gone:
    And ſo didſt turn thee from thy Rage   with them to be at one.
4 O God, our Help, do thou convert   thy People unto thee:
    Put all thy Wrath from us apart,   and angry ceaſe to be.

5 Shall thy fierce Anger never end,   but ſtill be pour'd on us?
    And ſhall thy Wrath itſelf extend   unto all Ages thus?
6 Wilt thou not rather turn again,   and quicken us, that we
    And all thy Folk that yet remain,   may glad and joyful be?

7 O Lord, on us do thou declare   thy Goodneſs to our Wealth:
    Shew forth to us and do not ſpare,   thy Aid and ſaving Health:
8 I'll hear what God the Lord doth ſay,   to his he ſpeaketh Peace:
    And to his Saints, that never they   return to Fooliſhneſs.

9 For why? his Help is ſtill at Hand   to ſuch as do him fear:
    Whereby great Glory in our Land   ſhall dwell and flouriſh there,
10 For Truth and Mercy there ſhall meet   in one to take their Place:
    And Peace ſhall Juſtice with Kiſs greet,   and there they ſhall embrace.

11 Truth from the Earth ſhall ſpring apace,   and flouriſh pleaſantly:
    So Righteouſneſs ſhall ſhew her Face,   and look from Heaven moſt high,
12 Yea, God himſelf doth take in Hand   to give us each good Thing:
    And thro' the Coaſts of all the Land   the Earth her Fruit ſhall bring.

13 Before his Face ſhall Juſtice go,   much like a Guide or Stay:
    He ſhall direct his Steps alſo,   and keep them in the Way.

PSALM LXXXVI. J. H.

1 LORD, bow thine Ear to my Requeſt,   and hear me ſpeedily:
    For with great Pain and Grief oppreſt,   full poor and weak am I.
2 Preſerve my Soul, becauſe my Ways   and Doings holy be:
    And ſave thy Servant, O my God,   that puts his Truſt in thee.

3 Thy Mercy upon me expreſs,   and me defend alway:
    For thro' the Day I do not ceaſe   to thee, O Lord, to pray.
4 Comfort thy Servant's Soul, I pray,   that now with Pain is pin'd.
    For unto thee I do alway   lift up my Soul and Mind.

5 For thou art good and bountiful,   thy Gifts of Grace are free:
    Alſo thy Mercy plentiful   to all that call on thee.
6 O Lord, likewiſe, when I do pray,   regard and give an Ear:
    Mark well the Words that I do ſay,   and my Petitions hear.

7 In Time when Trouble doth me move   to thee I do complain:
    For why? I know, and well do prove   thou anſwer'ſt me again.
8 Among the Gods, O Lord, is none,   with thee to be compar'd:
    And none can do as thou haſt done,   the like has not been heard.

PART II.

9 The Gentiles and the People all,   whom thou didſt make and frame
    Before thy Face on Knees ſhall fall,   and glorify thy Name.

PSALM LXXXVII, LXXXVIII

10 For why? thou art so much of Might,   all Power is thy own:
   Thou workest Wonders still in Sight,   for thou art God alone.
11 O teach me, Lord, thy Way, and I   shall in thy Truth proceed:
   O join my Heart to thee so nigh,   that I thy Name may dread.
12 To thee will I give Thanks and Praise,   O Lord, with all my Heart:
   And glorify thy Name always,   because my God thou art.
13 For why? thy Mercy shew'd to me   is great, and doth excel:
   Thou sett'st my Soul at Liberty   out from the lowest Hell.
14 O Lord, the Proud against me rise,   and Heaps of Men of Might:
   They seek my Soul, and in no wise   will have thee in their Sight.
15 Thou, Lord, art merciful and kind,   but very slow to Wrath:
   Thy Goodness is full great, I find   thy Truth no measure hath.
16 O turn to me, and Mercy show,   thy Strength to me apply:
   O help and save thy Servant now,   thy Hand-maid's Son am I.
17 On me some Sign of Favour show,   that all my Foes may see
   And be asham'd, because that thou   dost help and comfort me.

PSALM LXXXVII. J. H.

1 THAT City shall full well endure   her Ground-work still doth stay
   Upon the holy Hills full sure,   it can no Time decay.
2 God loves the Gates of Sion best,   his Grace doth there abide:
   He loves them more than all the rest   of Jacob's Tents beside.
3 Full glorious Things reported be   in Sion, and abroad:
   Great Things, I say, are said of thee,   thou City of our God.
4 On Rahab I will cast an Eye,   and bear in Mind the same:
   To Babylon also apply,   and them that know thy Name.
5 Lo, Palestine, and Tyre also,   with Ethiope likewise:
   A People old full long ago,   were born and there did rise.
6 Of Sion they shall say abroad,   that diverse Men of Fame
   Have there sprung up, and the high God   hath founded fast the same.
7 In their Records to them it shall   by him be made appear,
   Of Sion, that the chief of all   had his beginning there.
8 The Trumpeters with such as sing,   there in great Plenty be:
   My Fountains and my pleasant Springs   are all contain'd in thee.

PSALM LXXXVIII. J. H.

1 LORD God of Health, the Hope and Stay   thou art alone to me:
   I call and cry thro'out the Day,   and all the Night to thee.
2 O let my Pray'r with Speed ascend   unto thy Sight on high:
   Incline thine Ear, O Lord, attend   and hearken to my Cry.
3 For why? with Woe my Heart is fill'd,   and doth in Trouble dwell:
   My Life and Breath doth almost yield,   and draweth nigh to Hell.
4 I am esteem'd as one of them   that in the Pit do fall:
   And made as one among those Men   that have no Strength at all.
5 As one among the Dead, and free   from Things that here remain:
   It were more Ease for me to be   with them the which are slain.
6 As those that lie in Grave, I say,   whom thou hast clean forgot:
   The which thy Hand hath cut away,   and thou regard'st them not.
7 Yea, like to one shut up full sure   within the lowest Pit:
   In darksome Place, and all obscure,   and in the Depth of it.

PSALM LXXXIX.

8 Thy Anger and thy Wrath likewife
    full fore on me do lie:
  And all thy Storms againft me rife,
    my Soul to vex and try.
9 Thou putt'ft my Friends far off from me,
    and mad'ft them hate me fore:
  I am fhut up in Prifon faft,
    and can come forth no more.
10 My Sight doth fail thro' Grief and Woe,
    I call to thee, O God:
  Thro'out the Day my Hands alfo
    to thee I ftretch abroad.

PART II.

11 Doft thou unto the Dead daclare
    thy wond'rous Works of Fame?
  Shall Dead to Life again repair,
    and praife thee for the fame?
12 Or fhall thy loving Kindnefs, Lord,
    be fhewed in the Grave?
  Or fhall with them that are deftroy'd,
    thy Truth her Honour have?
13 Shall they that lie in Dark full low,
    fee all thy Wonders great?
  Or there fhall they thy Juftice know
    where Men all Things forget?
14 But I, O Lord, to thee alway
    do cry and call apace:
  My Pray'r alfo, ere it be Day,
    fhall come before thy Face.
15 Why doft thou, Lord, abhor my Soul,
    in Grief that feeketh thee:
  And now, O Lord, why doft thou hide
    thy Face away from me?
16 I am afflicted, dying ftill
    from Youth many a Year:
  Thy Terrors which do work me Ill,
    with troubled Mind I bear.
17 The Furies of thy wrathful Rage
    full fore upon me lie:
  Thy Terrors they do not affwage,
    but prefs me heavily.
18 All Day they compafs me about,
    as Water at the Tide:
  And all at once with Streams full great,
    befet me on each Side.
19 Thou fetteft far from me my Friends,
    and Lovers ev'ry one:
  Yea, and my old Acquaintance all
    out of my Sight are gone.

PSALM LXXXIX. J. H.

1 TO fing the Mercies of the Lord
    my Tongue fhall never fpare:
  My Mouth from Age to Age accord
    thy Truth for to declare.
2 For I have faid that Mercy fhall
    for evermore endure:
  Thy Faithfulnefs in the Heav'ns all
    is ftablifh'd firm and fure.
3 With mine Elect, faith God, have I
    a faithful Cov'nant made:
  And fworn to David folemnly,
    having to him thus faid:
4 Thy Seed for ever I will ftay,
    and ftablifh it full faft:
  And ftill uphold thy Throne alway,
    from Age to Age to laft.
5 The Heav'ns do fhew with Joy and Mirth
    thy wond'rous Works, O Lord,
  Thy Saints within the Church on Earth
    thy Faith and Truth record.
6 Who with the Lord is equal then
    in all the Clouds abroad?
  Among the Sons of Gods or Men,
    what one is like our God?
7 God in Affembly of the Saints
    is greatly to be dread:
  And over all that dwell about
    in Rev'rence to be had.
8 Lord God of Hofts, in all the World
    what one is like to thee?
  On ev'ry Side, moft mighty Lord,
    thy Truth is feen to be.
9 The Rage and Fury of the Sea
    thou ruleft at thy Will:
  And when the Waves thereof arife,
    thou mak'ft them calm and ftill.
10 And Egypt, Lord, thou haft fubdu'd,
    thou haft deftroy'd it quite:
  Thy Foes thou clofely haft purfu'd,
    and fcatter'd thro' thy Might.

PART II.

11 The Heav'ns are thine, and ftill have been,
    likewife the Earth and Land:
  The World, and all that is therein,
    thou foundedft with thy Hand.

12 But

PSALM LXXXIX.

12 Both North and South, with East and West, thyself didst make and frame:
Both Tabor Mount, and Hermon Hill, rejoice and praise thy Name.
13 Thy Arm is strong and full of Pow'r, all Might therein doth lie:
The Strength of thy Right-hand each Hour thou liftest up on high.
14 In Righteousness and Equity thou hast thy Seat and Place:
Mercy and Truth are still with thee, and go before thy Face.

15 That Folk is blest that knoweth right the joyful Sound, O God:
For in the Favour of thy Sight they walk full safe abroad.
16 And in thy Name thro'out the Day they greatly do rejoice:
And thro' thy Righteousness have they a pleasant Fame and Noise.

17 For why? their Glory, Strength, and Aid, in thee only doth lie:
And thy Goodness, which hath us staid, shall lift our Horn on high.
18 Our Strength that doth defend us well, the Lord to us doth bring:
The holy One of Israel, he is our Guide and King.

19 Sometimes thy will to holy Men in Visions thou didst show:
And thus didst say unto them then, thy Mind to make them know.
20 A Man of Might I have erect, your King and Guide to be:
And set him up whom I elect among the Folk to me.

PART III.

21 My Servant David I appoint to rule my People well:
And with my holy Oil anoint him King of Israel.
22 For why? my Hand is ready still with him for to remain:
And with my Arm also I will him strengthen and sustain.

23 The Enemies shall not oppress, they shall not him devour:
Nor shall the Sons of Wickedness on him have any Pow'r.
24 His Foes likewise I will destroy before his Face in Sight:
Those that him hate I will annoy, and strike them with my Might.

25 My Truth and Mercy shall likewise upon him ever lie:
And in my Name his Horn shall rise. and be exalted high.
26 His Kingdom I will set to be upon the Sea and Land:
Also the running Floods shall he embrace with his Right-hand.

27 He shall depend with all his Heart on me, and thus shall say,
My Father and my God thou art, my Rock, my Health and Stay.
28 As my First-born I will him take of all on Earth that springs:
His Might and Honour shall surmount above all earthly Kings.

29 My Mercy shall be with him still, as I myself have told:
My faithful Cov'nant to fulfill, my Promise I will hold.
30 Also his Seed I will sustain for ever strong and sure:
So that his Seat shall still remain while Heav'n and Earth endure.

PART IV.

1 If that his Sons forsake my Law, and so begin to swerve:
And of my Judgments have no Awe, and will not them observe;
2 Or if they do not use aright my Laws for them prepar'd,
But set all my Commandments light, and will not them regard:

3 Then with the Rod will I begin their Doings to amend:
And so will scourge them from their Sin whenever they offend.
4 But yet my Mercy and Goodness I will not take away
From him, nor let my Faithfulness in any wise decay.

PSALM XC.

35 But sure my Cov'nant I will hold, with all that I have spoke:
No Word the which my Lips have told shall alter or be broke.
36 Once sware I by my Holiness, and that perform will I:
With David I shall keep Promise, to him I will not lye.

37 His Seed for evermore shall reign, also his Throne of Might:
As doth the Sun, it shall remain for ever in my Sight.
38 And as the Moon within the Sky for ever standeth fast,
A faithful Witness from on high, so shall his Kingdom last.

39 But, Lord, thou dost him now reject, and put him in great Fear:
Yea, thou art wroth with thine Elect, thy own anointed Dear.
40 Thy Cov'nant with thy Servant made, thou hast quite overthrown:
And down upon the Ground hast laid, and cast his Royal Crown.

PART V.

41 His Hedges thou hast overthrown, his Walls destroy'd quite round:
All his strong Holds hast beaten down, and levell'd with the Ground.
42 That he is fore destroy'd and torn of Comers-by thro'out:
And so is made a Mock and Scorn to all that dwell about.

43 Thou their Right-hand hast arm'd with Pow'r, that him so sore annoy:
And all his Foes that him devour, lo, thou hast made to joy.
44 His Sword's Edge thou dost take away that should his Foes withstand:
To him in War no Victory thou giv'st, nor Upper-hand.

45 His Glory thou dost also waste, his Throne, his Joy, his Mirth,
By thee is overthrown, and cast full low upon the Earth.
46 Thou hast cut off, and made full short his Youth and joyful Days:
And rais'd of him an ill Report, to his Shame and Dispraise.

47 How long away from me therefore, for ever wilt thou turn?
And shall thy Anger evermore like Fire consume and burn?
48 O call to Mind, remember then, my Time consumeth fast:
Why hast thou made the Sons of Men as Things in vain to waste?

49 What Man is he that liveth, and Death never thinks to see?
Or from the Grave's devouring Hand shall he his Soul set free?
50 Where is, O Lord, thy great Goodness, so oft declar'd before:
Which by thy Truth and Uprightness to David thou hast swore?

51 The great Rebukes to Mind I call that on thy Servants lie:
The Railings of the People all, born in my Breast have I.
52 Wherewith, O Lord, thy Enemies blasphemed have thy Name:
The Steps of thy anointed One they cease not to defame.

53 All Praise be given unto thee, O God the Lord most high:
From this Time forth for evermore, Amen, Amen, say I.

PSALM XC. J. H.

1 THOU, Lord, hast been our sure Defence, our Place of Ease and Rest:
In all Times past, yea, so long since, as cannot be exprest.
2 Before was made Mountain or Hill, the Earth and World abroad:
From Age to Age, and always still, for ever thou art God.

3 Thou grindest Man thro' Grief and Pain, to Dust or Clay, and then
Thou unto them dost say again, Return ye Sons of Men.
4 The lasting of a thousand Years, what is it in thy Sight?
As Yesterday it doth appear, or as a Watch by Night.

5 So soon as thou dost scatter them, then is their Life and Trade
Even as a sleep, or like the Grass, whose Beauty soon doth fade.

PSALM XCI.

6 Which in the Morning shines full bright, but fadeth suddenly:
  And is cut down before the Night, all wither'd, dead, and dry.
7 For thro' thy Anger we consume, our Might is much decay'd:
  And of thy fervent Wrath, O Lord, we are full sore afraid.
8 The wicked Works that we have wrought, thou satt'st before thine Eye:
  Our privy Faults, yea, all our Thoughts, thy Countenance doth spy.
9 For thro' thy Wrath our Days do waste, thereof doth nought remain:
  Our Years consume as doth a Blast, and are not call'd again.
10 The Time of our Abode on Earth is threescore Years and ten:
   But if we come to fourscore Years, our Life is grievous then.

PART II.

11 For of this Time the Strength and Chief we dote so much upon:
   Is Nothing else but Pain and Grief, and we as Blasts are gone.
12 What Man doth know what Power, and what Might thy Anger hath?
   Or in his Heart who doth thee fear according to thy Wrath?
13 Instruct us, Lord, to know and try how long our Days remain:
   That so we may our Hearts apply true Wisdom to attain.
14 Return, O Lord, how long wilt thou in thy great Wrath proceed?
   Shew Favour to thy Servants now, and help them at their Need.
15 Refresh us with thy Mercy soon, then shall we joyful be:
   All Times so long as Life doth last, in Heart rejoice will we.
16 As thou hast plagued us before, now also make us glad:
   And for the Years wherein full sore Affliction we have had.
17 O let thy Work and Pow'r appear, and on thy Servants light:
   And shew unto thy Children dear, thy Glory and thy Might.
18 Lord, let thy Grace and Glory stand on us thy Servants thus:
   Confirm the Works we take in Hand, and prosper them to us.

PSALM XCI. J. H.

1 HE that within the secret Place of God most High doth dwell.
  Under the Shadow of his Grace he shall be safe and well.
2 Thou art my Hope and my strong Hold, I to the Lord will say:
  My God he is, in him will I my whole Affiance stay.

3 He shall defend thee from the Snare the which the Hunter laid,
  And from the deadly Plague and Care, whereof thou art afraid.
4 And with his Wings shall cover thee, and keep thee safely there:
  His Faith and Truth thy Fence shall be, as sure as Shield and Spear.

5 So that thou never shalt have Cause to fear or be affright:
  For all the Shafts that fly by Day, or Terrors of the Night.
6 Nor of the Plague that privily doth walk in Darkness fast,
  Nor yet of that which doth destroy, and at Noon-day doth waste.

7 Yea, at thy Side as thou dost stand, a Thousand dead shall be:
  Ten thousand more at thy Right-hand, and yet shalt thou be free.
8 But thou shalt see it for thy Part, thy Eyes shall well regard:
  According unto their Desert, the Wicked have Reward.

9 For why? O Lord, I only rest, and fix my Hopes on thee:
  In the most High I put my Trust, my sure Defence is he.
10 No Evil shalt thou need to fear, with thee it shall go well:
   No Plague shall ever once come near the House where thou dost dwell.

PSALM XCII, XCIII.

11 For why? unto his Angels all
That still in all thy Ways they shall
12 And in their Hands shall bear thee up,
Lest that thy Foot should happen for

with Charge commanded he,
preserve and prosper thee.
still waiting thee upon :
to dash against a Stone.

13 Upon the Lion thou shalt go,
On the young Lions tread also,
14 Because he sets his Love on me,
And him advance, because that he

the Adder fell and long :
with Dragons stout and strong.
I'll save him by my Might :
doth know my Name aright.

15 When he for Help to me doth cry,
And from his Grief take him will I,
16 With Length of Days and Years I will
And also my Salvation still

an Answer I will give :
in Glory for to live.
him fully satisfy :
shew him assuredly :

PSALM XCII. J. H.

1 IT is a Thing both good and meet,
And to thy Name, O thou most High,
2 To shew the Kindness of the Lord
And to declare his Truth abroad

to praise the highest Lord :
to sing with one Accord.
before the Day be light :
when it doth draw to Night.

3 Upon ten-stringed Instrument,
With all the Mirth you can invent,
4 For thou hast made me to rejoice
That I have Joy in Heart and Voice

on Lute and Harp so sweet :
of Instruments most meet.
in Things so wrought by thee :
thy handy Works to see.

5 O Lord, how glorious and how great
So deeply are thy Counsels set,
6 The Man unwise cannot tell how
And Fools also are most unfit

are thy Works round about :
that none can find them out.
this Work to pass to bring :
to understand this Thing.

7 When as the Wicked at their Will
And when they flourish in their Ill,
8 But thou art mighty, Lord most High,
In Glory and great Majesty,

like Grass do spring full fast,
they suddenly shall waste.
and thou dost reign therefore
both now and evermore.

9 Behold, O Lord, thy Enemies
And all that work Iniquity
10 But thou, like as an Unicorn,
With fresh and new prepared Oil

shall be destroy'd alway :
shall perish and decay.
shalt lift my Horn on high :
anointed King am I.

11 And of my Foes before my Eyes
Of all that do against me rise,
12 The Righteous flourish shall on high,
And as the Cedars multiply

shall see the Fall and Shame :
my Ears shall hear the same.
as Palm-trees bud and blow :
in Libanus that grow.

13 For they are planted in the Place,
Within his Courts they spring apace,
14 And in their Age much Fruit shall bring
And also shall both bud and spring

and Dwelling of our God :
and flourish all abroad.
most pleasant to be seen :
with Boughs and Branches green.

15 To shew that God is good and just,
He is my Rock, my Hope, and Trust,

and upright in his Will :
in him there is no Ill.

PSALM XCIII. J. H.

1 THE Lord doth reign and clothed is
And to declare his Strength likewise,
2 The Lord also the Earth hath made
No Might could make it move or fade,

with Majesty most bright :
hath girt himself with Might.
and shaped it most sure :
at Stay it doth endure.

PSALM XCIV.

3 Before the World was made or wrought,
   Beyond all Time that can be thought,
4 The Floods, O Lord, the Floods do rise,
   The Floods, I say, did enterprise,

5 Yea, tho' the Storms arise in Sight,
   The Lord is strong and more of Might,
6 O Lord, thy Testimonies great
   Doth Holiness become thy Seat

thy Seat was set before:
thou hast been evermore.
they roar and make a Noise:
and lifted up their Voice.

tho' Seas do rage and swell:
for he on high doth dwell.
are very sure, therefore
and House for evermore.

PSALM XCIV. J. H.

1 O Lord, thou dost revenge all Wrong,
   Since then it doth to thee belong,
2 Set forth thyself, for thou of Right
   Reward the Proud and Men of Might

3 How long shall wicked Men bear Sway,
   Shall proud and wicked Men alway
4 How long shall they with Brags burst out,
   Shall they rejoice that be so stout,

5 Thy Flock, O Lord, thy Heritage,
   Against thy People they do rage
6 The Widows which are comfortless
   They slay the Children fatherless,

7 And when they take these Things in Hand,
   Can Jacob's God thus understand?
8 O Folk unwise, and People rude,
   Ye Fools among the Multitude,

9 The Lord who made the Ear of Man,
   He made the Eye, all Things must then
10 The Lord doth all the World correct,
   Shall he not then your Deeds detect?

Vengeance belongs to thee:
declare that all may see.
the Earth doth judge and guide:
according to their Pride.

with lifting up their Voice?
thus triumph and rejoice?
and proudly talk their Fill?
whose Works are ever ill?

they spoil and vex full sore:
still daily more and more.
and Strangers they destroy:
and none doth put them by.

this Talk they have of thee:
tush, no, he cannot see.
some Knowledge now discern:
at length begin to learn.

he Needs of Right must hear:
before his Sight appear.
and make them understand:
how can ye scape his Hand?

PART II.

11 The Lord doth know the Heart of Man,
   And he his very Thoughts doth scan,
12 But, Lord, that Man is happy sure,
   And thro' Correction dost procure

13 Whereby he shall in quiet rest,
   When wicked Men shall be supprest,
14 For sure the Lord will not refuse
   His Heritage whom he did chuse,

15 Until that Judgment be decreed
   That all may follow her with Speed
16 But who upon my Part will stand
   Or who shall rid me from their Hand,

17 Except the Lord had been my Aid,
   My Soul and Life had now been laid
18 When I did say, My Foot doth slide,
   Thy Mercy, Lord, most ready was

19 When with myself I mused much,
   Then Lord, thy Goodness did me touch,

and sees the same full plain:
and findeth them but vain.
whom thou dost keep in Awe:
to teach him in thy Law.

in Time of Trouble fit
and fall into the Pit.
his People for to take:
he will no Time forsake;

to Justice to convert:
that are of upright Heart.
against the cursed Train?
that wicked Works maintain?

my Enemies to quell,
almost as low as Hell.
before that I could call,
to save me from the Fall.

and could not Comfort find:
and that did ease my Mind.

20 Wilt

20 Wilt thou accuſtom, Lord, thyſelf with wicked Men to ſit,
Who with Pretence inſtead of Law, much Miſchief do commit?
21 For they conſult againſt the Life of righteous Men and good:
And in their Counſels they are rife to ſhed the guiltleſs Blood.
22 But yet the Lord is unto me a ſure and ſtrong Defence:
To him I flee, becauſe he is my Strength and Confidence.
23 And he ſhall cauſe their Miſchiefs all themſelves for to annoy:
And in their Malice they ſhall fall, our God ſhall them deſtroy.

PSALM XCV. J. H.

1 O Come, let us lift up our Voice, and ſing unto the Lord:
In him our Rock of Health rejoice let us with one Accord.
2 Yea, let us come before his Face to give him Thanks and Praiſe:
In ſinging Pſalms unto his Grace let us be glad always.

3 For why? the Lord he is no Doubt, a great and mighty God:
A King above all Gods thro'out, in all the World abroad.
4 The Secrets of the Earth ſo deep and Corners of the Land:
The Tops of Hills that are moſt ſteep, he hath them in his Hand.

5 The Sea and Waters all are his, for he the ſame hath wrought:
The Earth, and all that therein is, his Hand hath made of nought.
6 Come let us bow and praiſe the Lord, before him let us fall:
And kneel to him with one Accord, the which hath made us all.

7 For why? he is the Lord our God, for us he doth provide:
We are his flock, he doth us feed, his Sheep, and he our Guide.
8 To-Day if ye his Voice will hear, then harden not your Heart:
As ye with grudging many a Year provok'd him in Deſart.

9 Whereas your Fathers tempted me, my Power for to prove:
My wond'rous Works when they did ſee, yet ſtill they would me move.
10 Twice twenty Years they did me grieve, which cauſed me to ſay:
They, err in Heart, and not believe, they have not known my Way.

11 Wherefore I ſware, when that my Wrath was kindled in my Breaſt:
That they ſhould never tread the Path, to enter in my Reſt.

PSALM XCVI. J. H.

1 SING ye with praiſe unto the Lord, new Songs with Joy and Mirth;
Sing unto him with one Accord, all People on the Earth.
2 Yea, ſing unto the Lord alway praiſe ye his holy Name:
Declare and ſhew from Day to Day, Salvation by the ſame.

3 Among the Heathen all declare his Honour round about:
To ſhew his Wonders do not ſpare in all the World thro'out.
4 For why? the Lord is much of might, and worthy of all Praiſe:
And he is to be dread of Right, above all Gods always.

5 For all the Gods of Heathen Folk are Idols that will fade:
Whereas our God, he is the Lord that Heav'n & Earth hath made.
6 All Praiſe and Honour alſo dwell ever before his Face:
Both Pow'r and Might likewiſe excel within his holy Place.

7 Aſcribe unto the Lord therefore, all Men with one Accord:
All Might and Worſhip evermore aſcribe unto the Lord.
8 Aſcribe unto the Lord alſo the Glory of his Name:
Into his Courts with Preſents go, and offer there the ſame.

PSALM XCVII, XCVIII.

PART II.

9 Fall down and worship ye the Lord
   Let all the People of the World
10 Tell all the World, be not afraid,
   Yea, he the Earth so fast hath stay'd,
       within his Temple bright:
       be fearful at his Sight.
       the Lord doth reign above:
       that it can never move.

11 And that it is the Lord alone
   To judge the Nations ev'ry one
12 The Heav'ns shall joyfully begin,
   The Sea with all that is therein,
       who rules with princely Might:
       with Equity and Right.
       the Earth likewise rejoice:
       shall shout and make a Noise.

13 The Fields shall joy and ev'ry Thing
   The Wood and ev'ry Tree shall sing
14 Before the Presence of the Lord,
   When he shall justly judge the World,
       that springeth on the Earth:
       with Gladness and with Mirth.
       and coming of his Might:
       and rule his Folk with Right.

PSALM XCVII. J. H.

1 THE Lord doth reign, for which the Earth may sing with pleasant Voice:
   Also the Isles with joyful Mirth   may triumph and rejoice.
2 Both Clouds and Darkness likewise swell, and round about him beat:
   Yea, Right and Justice ever dwell,   and bide about his Seat.

3 Yea, Fire and Heat at once do run,
   Which all his Enemies shall burn
4 His Lightnings great full bright did blaze,
   Whereat the Earth did look and gaze
       and go before his Face:
       abroad in ev'ry Place.
       and to the World appear:
       with Dread and deadly Fear.

5 The Hills like Wax did melt in Sight
   They fled before that Ruler's Might
6 The Heav'ns likewise declare and show
   That all the World may see and know
       and Presence of the Lord:
       who guideth all the World.
       his Justice forth abroad:
       the Glory of our God.

7 Confusion sure shall come to such
   Also to those that glory much
8 For all the Idols of the World,
   Shall feel the Power of the Lord,
       as worship Idols vain:
       dumb Pictures to maintain.
       which they their Gods do call,
       and down to him shall fall.

9 With Joy shall Sion hear this Thing,
   For at thy Judgments they shall sing
10 For thou, O Lord, art set on high
   And art exalted wond'rously
       and Judah shall rejoice:
       with a most chearful Voice.
       in all the Earth abroad:
       above each other God.

11 All ye that love the Lord, do this,
   For he doth keep the Souls of his
12 And Light doth spring up to the Just
   Gladness and Joy likewise to them
       hate all Things that are ill:
       from such as would them spill.
       with Pleasure for his Part:
       that are of upright Heart.

13 Ye Righteous in the Lord rejoice,
   And thankfully with Heart and Voice,
       his Holiness proclaim:
       be mindful of the same.

PSALM XCVIII. J. H.

1 O Sing ye now unto the Lord   a new and pleasant Song:
   For he hath wrought thro'out the World his Wonders great and strong.
2 With his Right-hand full worthily   he doth his Foes devour:
   And gets himself the Victory   with his own Arm and Pow'r.

3 The Lord doth make the People know
   And also doth his Justice show
4 His Grace and Truth to Israel
   And all the Earth hath seen right well
       his saving Health and Might:
       in all the Heathens Sight.
       in Mind he doth record:
       the Goodness of the Lord.

5 Be

PSALM XCIX, C.

5 Be glad in him with joyful Voice,
 Give Thanks to God, sing and rejoice
6 Upon the Harp unto him sing,
 Rejoice before the Lord our King,

all People on the Earth:
to him with Joy and Mirth.
give Thanks to him always:
with Trumpets sound his Praise.

7 Yea, let the Sea with all therein
 The Earth likewise let it begin,
8 And let the Floods rejoice their Fills,
 Yea, let the Mountains and the Hills

for Joy both roar and swell:
with all that therein dwell.
and clap their Hands apace:
triumph before his Face.

9 For he shall come to judge and try
 And rule the People mightily,

the World and ev'ry Wight:
with Justice and with Right.

PSALM XCIX. J. H.

1 THE Lord doth reign, altho' at it
  Yea, on the Cherubims doth sit,
2 The Lord that doth in Sion dwell,
 Above all Folk he doth excel,

the People rage full sore:
tho' all the World do roar.
is high and wond'rous great:
and he aloft is set.

3 Let all Men praise thy mighty Name,
 And let them magnify the same,
4 The Princely Power of our King
 Thou rightly rulest ev'ry Thing

for it is fearful sure:
that holy is and pure.
doth love Judgment and Right,
in Jacob thro' thy Might.

5 To praise the Lord our God devise,
 And at his Foot-stool worship him
6 Moses, Aaron, and Samuel,
 When they did pray, he heard them well,

and Honour to him shew:
that holy is and true.
as Priests on him did call:
and gave them Answer all.

7 Within the Cloud to them he spake,
 To keep such Laws as he did make,
8 O Lord our God thou didst them hear,
 But their Inventions punished,

then did they labour still:
according to his Will.
and answer them again:
which foolish were and vain.

9 O praise our God and Lord therefore
 For why? our God whom we adore,

upon his holy Hill:
is the most holy still.

PSALM C. J. H.

1 ALL People that on Earth do dwell,
  Him serve with Fear, his Praise forth tell
2 The Lord ye know is God indeed,
 We are his Flock, he doth us feed,

sing to the Lord with chearful Voice,
come ye before him and rejoice.
without our Aid he did us make:
and for his Sheep he doth us take.

3 O enter then his Gates with Praise,
 Praise, laud, and bless his Name always,
4 For why? the Lord our God is good,
 His Truth at all Times firmly stood,

approach with Joy his Courts unto:
for it is seemly so to do.
his Mercy is for ever sure:
and shall from Age to Age endure.

Another of the same, by J. H.

1 IN God the Lord be glad and light,
  Serve him, and come before his Sight
2 Know that the Lord our God he is,
 Not we ourselves, for we are his

praise him thro'out the Earth:
with Singing and with Mirth.
he did us make and keep:
own Flock and Pasture Sheep.

3 O go into his Gates always,
 Within his Courts set forth his Praise,
4 For why? the Goodness of the Lord
 From Age to Age thro'out the World

give Thanks within the same:
and laud his holy Name.
for evermore doth reign:
his Truth doth still remain.

PSALM CI, CII.

PSALM CI. N.

Mercy will and Judgment sing, O Lord God, unto thee:
O let me understand the Ways that good and holy be.
Within my House I daily will walk with an Heart upright:
And I no Kind of wicked Thing will set before my Sight.

I hate their Works that fall away, they shall not cleave to me:
From me shall go the froward Heart, no Evil will I see.
Him I'll destroy that slandereth his Neighbour privily:
The lofty Heart I cannot bear, nor him that looketh high.

My Eyes shall be on them within the Land that faithful be:
In perfect Way who walketh, shall be Servant unto me.
I will no guileful Person have within my House to dwell:
And in my Presence he shall not remain that Lies doth tell.

Betimes I will destroy ev'n all the Wicked of the Land:
That I may from God's City cut the wicked Worker's Hand.

PSALM CII. N.

HEAR thou my Pray'r, O Lord, and let my Cry come unto thee:
In Time of Trouble do not hide thy Face away from me.
Incline thine Ear to me, make haste to hear me when I call:
For as the Smoke doth fade, so do my Days consume and fall.

And as an Hearth my Bones are burnt, my Heart is smitten dead:
And withers like the Grass, that I forget to eat my Bread.
By Reason of my groaning Voice, my Bones cleave to my Skin:
As Pelican in Wilderness, such Case now am I in.

And as an Owl in Desart is, lo, I am such an one
I watch, and as a Sparrow on the House-top am alone.
5 For daily in reproachful wise my Foes they do me scorn:
And them that mad upon me are, against me they have sworn.

7 Surely with Ashes, as with Bread, my Hunger I have fill'd:
And mingled have my Drink with Tears that from my Eyes distill'd.
8 Because of thy Displeasure, Lord, thy Wrath and great Disdain:
For thou hast set me up on high, and cast me down again.

9 The Days wherein I pass my Life, are like the fleeting Shade:
And I am wither'd like the Grass that soon away doth fade.
10 But thou, O Lord, for ever dost remain in steady Place:
And thy Remembrance ever doth abide from Race to Race.

PART II.

11 Thou wilt arise, and Mercy thou to Sion wilt extend:
The Time of Mercy, now the Time foreset is come to End.
12 For in the very Stones thereof thy Servants do delight:
And on the Dust thereof they have Compassion in their Sight.

13 Then shall the Heathen People fear the Lord's most holy Name:
And all the Kings on Earth shall dread his Glory and his Fame.
14 Then when the Lord, the mighty God, again shall Sion rear:
And then when he most nobly in his Glory shall appear.

15 To Pray'r of the Poor destitute when he himself shall bend:
When he shall not disdain unto their Suits for to attend.

PSALM CIII.

16 This shall be written for the Age
 The People that are yet unborn,
17 From his high Sanctuary he
 And out of Heav'n most high he hath
18 That of the mourning Captive he
 And that he might deliver those

 that after shall succeed:
 the Lord's Renown shall spread.
 hath looked down below:
 beheld the Earth also.
 might hear the woful Cry:
 that were condemn'd to die.

19 That they in Sion may declare
 And in Jerusalem set forth
20 Then when the People of the Land,
 Shall be assembled to perform

 the Lord's most holy Name:
 the Praises of the same.
 and Kingdoms with Accord,
 their Service to the Lord.

PART III.

21 My former Force of Strength he hath
 And shorter he did cut my Days,
22 My God, in midst of all my Days,
 Thy Years endure eternally,

 abated in the Way:
 thus I therefore did say;
 now take me not away:
 and never do decay.

23 Thou the Foundations of the Earth
 The Heav'ns also they are the Work
24 They all shall perish and decay,
 And they shall all in Time wax old,

 before all Time hast laid:
 which thy own Hands have made.
 but thou remainest still:
 ev'n as a Garment will.

25 Thou as a Garment shalt them change
 But thou dost still abide the same,
26 The Children of thy Servants shall
 And in thy Sight their happy Seed

 and changed shall they be:
 thy Years do never flee.
 continue and endure:
 for ever shall stand sure,

PSALM CIII. T. S.

1 MY Soul, give Laud unto the Lord
 And all the Secrets of my Heart,
2 Praise thou the Lord, my Soul, who hath
 And suffer not his Benefits

 my Spirit do the same:
 praise ye his holy Name.
 to thee been very kind:
 to slip out of thy Mind.

3 That gave thee Pardon for thy Faults
 From all thy weak and frail Disease,
4 That did redeem thy Life from Death
 His Mercy and Compassion both

 and thee restor'd again:
 and heal'd thee of thy Pain.
 from which thou couldst not flee:
 he did extend to thee.

5 That fill'd with Goodness thy Desire,
 Like as the Eagle casts her Bill,
6 The Lord with Justice doth repay
 So that their Sufferings and Wrongs

 and did thy Youth prolong:
 again becoming young.
 all such as are opprest,
 are turned to the best.

7 His Ways and his Commandments all
 His Counsels and his valiant Acts
8 The Lord is kind and merciful
 The slowest to conceive a Wrath,

 to Moses he did show:
 the Isr'elites did know.
 when Sinners do him grieve:
 and readiest to forgive.

9 He will not always chiding be,
 Nor keeps our Faults in Memory,
10 According to our Sins also
 And after our Iniquities

 tho' we be full of Strife:
 for all our sinful Life.
 he doth us not regard:
 he doth us not reward.

11 But as the Space is wond'rous great
 So is his Goodness much more large
12 He doth remove our Sins from us,
 As far as the Sun-rising is

 'twixt Earth and Heav'n above,
 to them that do him love.
 and our Offences all,
 full distant from his Fall.

PART

PSALM CIV.

PART II.

13 And look what Pity Parents do
　Like Pity beareth God to such
　　　　unto their Children bear:
　　　　as worship him in Fear.
14 The Lord that made us knows our Shape,
　How weak and frail our Nature is,
　　　　our Mold and Fashion just;
　　　　and that we are but Dust.
15 And how the Time of mortal Men
　Or like the Flow'r right fair in Field,
　　　　is like the with'ring Hay:
　　　　that fades full soon away.
16 Whose Glofs and Beauty stormy Winds
　And make that after their Assaults
　　　　do utterly disgrace:
　　　　such Bloffoms have no Place.
17 But yet the Goodness of the Lord
　Their Children's Children do receive
　　　　with his shall ever stand:
　　　　his Righteousness at Hand.
18 I mean, who keep his Covenant
　And not forget to do the Thing
　　　　with all their whole Defire:
　　　　that he doth them require.
19 The Heav'ns most high are made the Seat
　And by his Pow'r Imperial
　　　　and Foot-stool of the Lord:
　　　　he governs all the World.
20 Ye Angels that are great in Pow'r,
　Who to obey and do his Will
　　　　praise ye and bless the Lord:
　　　　immediately accord.
21 Ye noble Hosts and Ministers,
　Who ready are to execute
　　　　cease not to laud him still:
　　　　his Pleasure and his Will.
22 Yea, all his Works in ev'ry Place,
　My thankful Heart my Mind and Soul,
　　　　praise ye his holy Name:
　　　　praise ye also the same.

PSALM CIV. W. K.

1 MY Soul praise the Lord,
　　O Lord our great God,
　So palling in Glory,
　Honour and Majesty
　　　　speak good of his Name:
　　　　how dost thou appear!
　　　　that great is thy Fame,
　　　　in thee shine most clear.

2 With Light as a Robe
　Whereby all the Earth
　The Heav'ns in such sort
　That they to a Curtain
　　　　thou hast thyself clad,
　　　　thy Greatness may see:
　　　　thou also hast spread,
　　　　compared may be.

3 His Chamber-beams lie
　Which as his Chariots
　And there with much Swiftnefs
　Upon the Wings riding
　　　　in the Clouds full sure,
　　　　are made him to bear:
　　　　his Course doth endure,
　　　　of Winds in the Air.

4 He maketh his Spirits
　And Lightnings to serve
　His Will to accomplish
　To save and consume Things,
　　　　as Heralds to go,
　　　　we see also prest:
　　　　they run to and fro,
　　　　as seemeth him best.

5 He groundeth the Earth
　That it once to move
　The Deep a fair Cov'ring
　Which by its own Nature
　　　　so firmly and fast,
　　　　none shall have such Pow'r:
　　　　for it made thou hast,
　　　　the Hills would devour.

6 But at thy Rebuke
　And so give due Place
　At thy Voice of Thunder
　That in their great raging
　　　　the Waters do flee,
　　　　thy Word to obey:
　　　　so faithful they be
　　　　they haste soon away.

7 The Mountains full high
　If they do but speak,
　　　　they then up ascend,
　　　　thy Word they fulfil:

PSALM CIV.

So likewise the Vallies
Where thou them appointest
8 Their Bounds thou hast set,
So that in their Rage
For God hath appointed
The Earth to destroy more,

most quickly descend,
remain they do still.
how far they shall run,
not that pass they can:
they shall not return
which made was for Man.

PART II.

9 He sendeth the Springs
Which run do full swift
Where both the wild Asses
And Beasts of the Mountains

to strong Streams or Lakes,
among the huge Hills:
their Thirst often slakes,
thereof drink their Fills.

10 By these pleasant Springs
The Fowls of the Air
Who moved by Nature
Among the green Branches

and Rivers most clear,
abide shall and dwell:
to hop here and there,
their Songs shall excel.

11 The Mountains to Moist
The Earth with his Works
So as the brute Cattle
But Grass doth provide them,

the Clouds he doth use,
is wholly replete:
he doth not refuse,
and Herb for Man's Meat.

12 Yea, Bread, Wine and Oil
His Face to refresh,
The Cedars of Liban
Which Trees he doth nourish

he made for Man's sake:
and Heart to make strong:
the great Lord did make,
that grow up so long.

13 In these may Birds build,
In Fir-trees the Storks
The high Hills are Succours
Also the Rock stony

and all make their Nests:
remain and abide.
for wild Goats to rest:
for Conies to hide.

14 The Moon then is set
The Days from the Night,
And by the descending
The Cold from Heat alway

her Seasons to run,
thereby to discern:
also of the Sun,
thereby we do learn.

15 When Darkness doth come
Then creep forth do all
The Lions range roaring
But yet, 'tis the Lord,

by God's Will and Pow'r,
the Beasts of the Wood
their Prey to devour,
who giveth them Food.

16 As soon as the Sun
To couch in their Dens
That Man to his Work may,
Till Night come and call him

is up, they retire,
then are they full fain:
as Right doth require,
to take Rest again.

PART III.

17 How sundry, O Lord,
With Wisdom full great
So that the whole World
And as for thy Riches

are all thy Works found,
they are indeed wrought:
of thy Praise doth sound,
they pass all Mens Thought.

18 So is the great Sea,
Where creeping Things swarm,
There mighty Ships sail,
The Whale huge and monstrous

which is large and broad,
and Beasts of each sort:
and some lie at Road,
there also doth sport.

PSALM CV.

9 All Things on thee wait, thou doſt them relieve,
And thou in due Time full well doſt them feed:
Now when it doth pleaſe thee the ſame for to give,
They gather full gladly thoſe Things which they need.

o Thou open'ſt thy Hand, and they find ſuch Grace,
That they with good Things are filled we ſee:
But ſore they are troubled if thou hide thy Face,
For if thou their Breath take, vile Duſt then they be.

1 Again, when thy Spirit from thee doth proceed,
All Things to appoint, and what ſhall enſue
Then are they created as thou haſt decreed,
And doſt by thy Goodneſs the dry Earth renew.

2 The praiſe of the Lord for ever ſhall laſt,
Who may in his Works by Right well rejoice:
His Look can the Earth make to tremble full faſt,
And likewiſe the Mountains to ſmoke at his Voice.

3 To this Lord and God will I ſing always,
So long as I live, my God praiſe will I:
Then am I moſt certain my Words ſhall him pleaſe,
I will rejoice in him, to him will I cry.

4 The Sinners, O Lord, conſume in thine Ire,
Alſo the Perverſe, them root out with Shame:
But as for my Soul now, let it ſtill deſire,
And ſay with the Faithful, praiſe ye the Lord's Name.

PSALM CV. N.

GIVE Praiſes unto God the Lord, and call upon his Name:
Among the People all declare his Works to ſpread his Fame,
Sing joyfully unto the Lord, yea, ſing unto him Praiſe:
And talk of all his wond'rous Works. that he hath wrought always.

In honour of his holy Name rejoice with one Accord:
And let the Heart alſo be glad of them that ſeek the Lord.
Seek ye the Lord, and ſeek the Strength of his eternal Might:
Yea, ſeek his Face inceſſantly, and Preſence of his Sight.

The wond'rous Works which he hath done, keep ſtill in mindful Heart:
Let not the Judgments of his Mouth out of your Mind depart.
Ye that of faithful Abraham his Servants are the Seed:
Ye his Elect, the Children that of Jacob do proceed.

For why? 'tis he alone that is the mighty Lord our God:
And his moſt righteous Judgments are in all the Earth abroad.
His Promiſe and his Covenant which he hath made to his,
He hath rememb'red evermore to thouſands of Degrees.

PART II.

The Covenant which he hath made with Abram long ago:
And faithful Oath which he hath ſworn to Iſaac alſo.
9 And did appoint it for a Law that Jacob ſhould obey:
And for eternal Covenant to Iſrael alway.

1 When thus he ſaid, Lo, I to you all Canaan Land will give:
The Lot of your Inheritance, wherein your Seed ſhall live.

PSALM CV.

12 Altho' their Number at that Time
Yea, very small, and in the Land
did very small appear:
they then but Strangers were.

13 While yet they went from Land to Land,
And while from sundry Kingdoms they
without a sure Abode:
did wander all abroad.

14 Yet wrong at no Oppressor's Hand
But ev'n the great and mighty Kings
he suffer'd them to take:
reproved for their Sake.

15 And thus he said, Touch ye not those
Nor do the Prophets any Harm
that my Anointed be:
that do pertain to me.

16 He call'd a Dearth upon the Land,
But yet against the Time of Need
of Bread destroy the Store:
did send a Man before.

PART III.

17 Ev'n Joseph, who had once been sold
Whose Feet they hurt in Stocks, whose Soul
to live a Slave in Woe:
the Iron pierc'd into.

18 Until the Time came when his Cause
The mighty Word of God the Lord
was known apparently:
his Innocence did try.

19 The King sent and deliver'd him
The Ruler of the People then
from Prison where he was:
did freely let him pass.

20 And over all his House he made
And of his Substance made him have
him Lord, to bear the Sway:
the Rule and all the Stay.

21 That he might to his Will instruct
And Wisdom teach his Senators
the Princes of the Land:
rightly to understand.

22 Then into the Egyptian Land
And Jacob in the Land of Ham
came Israel also:
did sojourn to and fro.

23 His People he exceedingly
And stronger than their Enemies,
in Numbers made to grow:
who sought their Overthrow.

24 Whose Heart he turned, that with Hate
And did his Servants wrongfully
they did his People treat:
abuse with base Deceit.

PART IV.

25 His faithful Servant Moses then,
He did command to go to them
and Aaron whom he chose,
his Message to disclose.

26 His wonderful and mighty Signs
And Wonders in the Land of Ham
among them he did show:
then did they work also.

27 Darkness he sent, and made it dark,
And his Commission and his Word
instead of brighter Day:
they did not disobey.

28 He turn'd their Waters into Blood,
Their Land brought Frogs ev'n in the Place
their Fish also did slay:
where their King Phar'oh lay.

29 He spake, and at his Voice there came
And all the Quarters of their Land
great Swarms of noisome Flies:
were fill'd with crawling Lice.

30 He gave them Cold and stony Hail,
And fiery Flames within their Land
instead of milder Rain:
he sent unto their Pain.

31 He smote their Vines, and all the Trees
And all the Trees within their Coasts
whereon the Figs did grow:
also did overthrow.

32 He spake, then Caterpillars did,
Eating the Grass in all their Land,
and Grashoppers abound:
and Fruit of all their Ground.

PART V.

33 The first-begotten in their Land
Yea, the beginning and First-fruit
with Death did likewise smite:
of all their Strength and Might.

34 With Gold and Silver caused his
And in the Number of their Tribes
from Egypt Land to pass:
no feeble One there was.

35 Egy

PSALM CVI.

35 Egypt was glad and joyful then, when they did thence depart:
For Terror and the Fear of them was fall'n upon their Heart.
36 To shroud them from the parching Heat, a Cloud he did display:
And Fire he sent to give them Light, when Night had hid the Day.
37 They asked, and he caused Quails to rain at their Request:
And fully with the Bread of Heav'n their Hunger he represt.
38 He opened the stony Rock, and Waters gushed out:
Also the dry and parched Ground like Rivers ran about.
39 For of his holy Cov'nant he was mindful evermore:
Which to his Servant Abraham he plighted long before.
40 He brought his People forth with Mirth, and his Elect with Joy:
Out of the cruel Land where they had liv'd in great annoy.
41 And of the Heathen Men he gave to them the fruitful Lands:
The Labours of the People did they take into their Hands.
42 That they his holy Statutes might observe for evermore:
And faithfully obey his Laws, praise ye the Lord therefore.

PSALM CVI. N.

1 PRAISE ye the Lord, for he is good, his Mercy lasts alway:
Who can express his noble Acts, or all his Praise display?
2 They blessed are that Judgment keep, and justly do alway:
With Favour of thy People, Lord, remember me, I pray.
3 And with thy saving Health, O Lord, vouchsafe to visit me:
That I the great Felicity of thine Elect may see.
4 And with thy People joy I may, a joyful Mind possess:
And may with thy Inheritance a chearful Heart express.
5 Both we and our Forefathers all, have sinned ev'ry one:
We have committed Wickedness, and very lewdly done.
6 The Wonders great which thou, O Lord, hast done in Egypt Land,
Our Fathers, tho' they saw them all, yet did not understand.
7 Nor yet thy Mercies Multitude did keep in Memory:
But at the Sea, yea, the Red-sea, rebell'd ungratefully.
8 Nevertheless he saved them for Honour of his Name:
That he might make his Power known, and spread abroad his Fame.
9 The Red-sea he did then rebuke, and forthwith it was dry'd:
As in the Wilderness, so thro' the Deep he did them guide.
10 He sav'd them from the cruel Hand of their most spiteful Foe:
And from their Enemies he did deliver them also.

PART II.

11 The Waters did them overthrow, not one was left alive:
Then they believ'd his Word, and Praise in Song they did him give.
12 But very soon ungratefully his Works they quite forgot:
And for his Counsel and his Will they did neglect to wait.
13 But sinned in the Wilderness with fond and greedy Lust:
And in the Desart tempted God, their only Stay and Trust.
14 Who when their wanton Minds Desire, did suffer them to have:
But wasting Leanness therewithal, into their Souls he gave.
15 Then when they lodged in their Tents, at Moses they did grutch:
Aaron the holy of the Lord, they also envy'd much.

16 Therefore

PSALM CVI.

16 Therefore the Earth did open wide, and Dathan did devour:
And all Abiram's Company did cover in that Hour.
17 In their Assembly kindled was a hot confuming Fire:
And wasting Flame did then burn up the Wicked in his Ire.
18 Upon the Hill of Horeb they an Idol-calf did frame:
And there the molten Image they did worship of the same.
19 Thus to the Likeness of a Calf which feedeth on the Grass,
They turned all their Glory, and their Honour did deface.
20 And God their only Saviour they unthankfully forgot,
Who many great and mighty Things in Egypt Land had wrought.

PART III.

21 And in the Land of Ham for them most wond'rous Works had done
And by the Red-sea dreadful Things performed long agone.
22 Therefore becaufe they shew'd themselves forgetful and unkind,
To bring Destruction on them all he purpos'd in his Mind.
23 Had not his chosen Moses stood before him in the Way,
To turn away his Wrath, lest he should them destroy and flay.
24 They did despife the pleasant Land that he to them did give:
Yea, and the Words that he had spoke, they did no Whit believe
25 But in their Tents with grudging Heart, they wickedly repin'd:
Nor to the Voice of God the Lord did give a heark'ning Mind.
26 Therefore against them lifted he his strong revenging Hand,
Them to destroy in Wilderness, before they saw the Land.
27 And to destroy their Seed among the Nations with his Rod:
And thro' the Kingdoms of the World to scatter them abroad.
28 To Baal-peor they did join themselves most wickedly:
The Sacrifices of the Dead eating most greedily.
29 Thus they with their Inventions did his Anger much provoke:
And in his sore enkindled Wrath the Plague upon them broke.
30 But Phinehas stood up with Zeal the Sinners vile to slay:
And Judgment he did execute, and then the Plague did stay.

PART IV.

31 It was imputed unto him for Righteousness that Day:
And from henceforth so counted is from Race to Race alway.
32 At Waters called Meribah they did him angry make:
Yea, so far forth, that Moses then was punish'd for their Sake.
33 Because they vex'd his Spirit so, that in impatient Heat
His Lips spake unadvifedly, his Fervor was so great.
34 Nor, as the Lord commanded them, did they the People slay:
But were among the Heathen mixt, and learn'd their wicked Way.
35 They did their Idols serve, which was their Ruin and Decay:
To Devils Sons, and Daughters did they offer up and slay.
36 Yea, with unkind and murd'ring Knife the guiltless Blood they spilt:
Yea, their own Sons and Daughters Blood, without all Cause of Guilt.
37 Whom they to Canaan Idols then offer'd with wicked Hand:
And so with Blood of Innocents defiled was the Land.
38 Thus were they stained with the Works of their own filthy Way:
And with their own Inventions did a whoring go astray.

33 Therefore

PSALM CVII.

39 Therefore against his People was his Anger kindled sore:
and ev'n his own Inheritance he did abhor therefore.
40 Into the Hands of Heathen Men he gave them for a Prey,
And made their Foes their Lord, whom they were forced to obey.

PART V.

41 Yea, and their hateful Enemies opprest them in their Land:
And they were humbly made to stoop as Subjects to their Hand.
42 Full oftentimes from Thrall had he deliver'd them before:
But they rebell'd against him, and provok'd him evermore.
43 Therefore they by their Wickedness were brought full low to lie:
Yet when he saw them in Distress, he heark'ned to their Cry.
44 He call'd to Mind his Covenant, which he to them had swore:
And by his Mercies Multitude repented him therefore.
45 And Favour he them made to find before the Sight of those,
That led them captive from their Land, tho' they had been their Foes.
46 Save us, O Lord, that art our God, we do thee humbly pray:
And from among the Heathen Folk, Lord, gather us away.
47 That we may triumph and rejoice in thy most holy Name:
That we may glory in thy Praise, and sounding of thy Fame.
48 The Lord the God of Israel be blessed evermore:
Let all the People say, Amen, praise ye the Lord therefore.

PSALM CVII. W. K.

1 GIVE Thanks unto the Lord our God, for very kind is he:
And that his Mercy hath no End, all mortal Men may see.
2 Such as the Lord redeemeth hath, with Thanks shall praise his Name:
And shew how they from Foes were freed, and how he wrought the same.
3 He gather'd them forth of the Lands that lay so far about:
From East to West, from North to South, his Hand did find them out.
4 They wand'red in the Wilderness, and strayed from the Way:
Finding no City where to dwell, that serve might for their Stay.
5 Whose Thirst and Hunger was so great within those Deserts void,
That Faintness them assaulted, and their Souls greatly annoy'd.
6 Then did they cry in their Distress unto the Lord for Aid:
Who did remove their troublous State according as they pray'd.
7 And by the Way which was most right he led them like a Guide:
That they might to their City go, and safely there abide.
8 Let them therefore before the Lord confess his Goodness then:
And shew the Wonders that he doth before the Sons of Men.
9 For he their empty Souls sustain'd, whom Thirst had made to faint:
Their hungry Souls with Goodness fed, and heard their sad Complaint.
10 Such as do dwell in Darkness deep, where they on Death do wait:
Fast bound to bear such grievous Pains as Iron Chains do threat.

PART II.

11 Because against the Words of God, they proudly did rebel:
Esteeming light his Counsel high, which doth so far excel.
12 But when he humbled them full low, they then fell down with Grief:
And none was found that could them help, or give them some Relief.
13 Then did they cry in their Distress unto the Lord for Aid:
Who did remove their troublous State according as they pray'd.

14 For

PSALM CVII.

14 For he from Darkness brought them out, and from Death's dreadful Shade:
Bursting with Force the Iron Bands which them before did lade.
15 Let Men therefore before the Lord confess his Goodness then;
And shew the Wonders that he doth before the Sons of Men.
16 For he threw down the Gates of Brass with strong and mighty Hand:
The Iron Bars in sunder brake, Nothing could him withstand.
17 The foolish Folks great Plague do feel, by Reason of their Sin:
And for the great Transgression which they still continue in.
18 Their Soul abhorr'd all Sorts of Meat, no Relish they could have:
By which Means they were almost brought unto the very Grave.
19 Then did they cry in their Distress unto the Lord for Aid:
Who did remove their troublous State according as they pray'd.
20 For then he sent to them his Word, which Health did soon restore:
And brought them from those Dangers deep wherein they were before.

PART III.

21 Let Men therefore before the Lord confess his Goodness then:
And shew the Wonders that he doth before the Sons of Men.
22 And let them offer Sacrifice to him most thankfully:
And speak of all his wond'rous Works with Gladness and with Joy.
23 Such as in Ships and brittle Barks into the Seas descend,
Their Merchandize thro' fearful Floods to compass and to end:
24 These Men are forced to behold the Lord's Works what they be;
And in the dreadful Deep the same most marvellous they see.
25 For at his Word the stormy Wind ariseth in a Rage,
And stirreth up the Surges so, that nought can them asswage.
26 Then are they lifted up so high, the Clouds they seem to gain:
And plunging down the Depth until their Souls confume with Pain;
27 And like a Drunkard to and fro, now here and there they reel:
As Men that had their Reason lost, and had no Sense to feel.
28 Then did they cry in their Distress unto the Lord for Aid:
Who did remove their troublous State according as they pray'd.
29 For with his Word the Lord doth make the sturdy Storms to cease:
So that the Waves from their great Rage are brought to Rest and Peace.
30 Then are they glad when Rest is come, which they so much did crave:
And to the Haven by him are brought, which they so fain would have.

PART IV.

31 Let Men therefore before the Lord confess his Goodness then:
And shew the Wonders that he doth before the Sons of Men.
32 Let them in Presence of the Folk with Praise extol his Name:
And where the Elders use to sit, there let them do the same.
33 The Wilderness he often makes with Water to abound:
And Water-springs he often turns to dry and parched Ground.
34 A fruitful Land with Pleasures deckt full barren doth he make:
When on their Sins that dwell therein he doth just Vengeance take.
35 Again, the Wilderness full rude he maketh Fruit to bear:
With clear and pleasant Water-springs, tho' none before were there.
36 Wherein such hungry Souls are set as he hath freely chose:
That they a City might them build to dwell in safe from Foes.
37 That they may sow their pleasant Land, and Vineyards also plant:
To yield them Fruits of such Increase, that they may have no Want.

38 The

PSALM CVIII, CIX.

38 They multiply exceedingly, the Lord doth bless them so
Who also maketh the brute Beasts in Numbers great to grow.
39 But when the Faithful are brought low by the Oppressors stout,
Diminishing thro' many Plagues that compass them about:
40 Then doth the Princes bring to Shame, which did them sore oppress
And likewise caused them to err, when in the Wilderness.
41 But yet the Poor he raised up out of his Troubles deep.
And often doth his Train augment much like a Flock of Sheep.
42 The Righteous shall behold this Sight, and also much rejoice:
Whereas the Wicked and Perverse with Grief shall stop their Voice.
43 But who is wise, that now full well he may these Things record:
For certainly such shall perceive the Kindness of the Lord.

PSALM CVIII. J. H.

1 O God, my Heart prepared is, my Tongue is likewise so:
I will advance my Voice in Song, that I thy Praise may show.
2 Awake my Viol and my Harp, sweet Melody to make:
And in the Morning I myself right early will awake.

3 By me among the People, Lord, still praised shalt thou be:
And I among the Heathen Folk will Praises sing to thee.
4 Because thy Mercy doth ascend above the Heav'ns most high:
Also thy Truth doth reach the Clouds within the lofty Sky.

5 Above the high and starry Heav'ns exalt thyself, O God:
Display likewise upon the Earth thy Glory all abroad.
6 That thy Beloved also may be set at Liberty,
Help, O my God, with thy Right-hand, and hear me speedily.

7 God in his Holiness hath spoke, wherefore my Joys abound:
Sichem I will divide and mete the Vale of Succoth's Ground.
8 And Gilead shall be my own, Manasses mine shall be:
My Head-strength Ephraim, and Law shall Judah give to me.

9 Moab my Wash-pot is, my Shoe o'er Edom I will throw:
Upon the Land of Palestine in triumph will I go.
10 Who to the City strong shall be Leader and Guide to me:
Also by whom to Edom's Land conveyed shall I be?

11 Is it not thou, O Lord, who late had'st us forsaken quite?
And wilt not thou, Lord, also go forthwith our Hosts to fight?
12 Give us, O Lord, thy saving Aid when Troubles do assail:
For all the Help of Man is vain, and can no Whit avail.

13 Thro' God we shall do valiant Acts, and worthy of Renown:
He shall subdue our Enemies, yea, he shall tread them down.

• PSALM CIX. N.

1 IN speechless Silence do not hold, O God, thy Tongue always:
Ev'n thou, O Lord, because thou art the God of all my Praise.
2 The wicked and the guileful Mouths on me disclosed be:
And they with false and lying Tongues have spoken unto me.

3 They did beset me round about with Words of hateful Spite:
Without all Cause of my Desert against me they did fight.
4 For my Good-will they were my Foes, then I began to pray:
My Good with Ill, my Friendliness with Hate they did repay.

5 Set

PSALM CIX.

5 Set thou the Wicked over him, to have the upper Hand:
At his Right-hand, Lord, suffer thou his hateful Foe to stand.
6 When he is judged, let him then condemned be therein:
And let the Pray'r that he doth make be turned into Sin.

7 Few be his Days, his Charge also let thou another take:
His Children let be Fatherless, his Wife a Widow make.
8 His Offspring let be Vagabonds, and ever beg their Bread:
In Places desolate and waste let them seek to be fed.

9 Let covetous Extortioners get all his Goods in Store:
And let the Stranger spoil the Fruit of all his Toil before.
10 Let there be none to pity him, let there be none at all,
That on his Children Fatherless will let their Mercy fall.

PART II.

11 Let his Posterity be quite destroy'd, and never breed:
Their Name cut-blotted in the Age that after shall succeed.
12 Let not his Father's Wickedness from God's Remembrance fall,
And never let his Mother's Sin be done away at all.

13 But in the Presence of the Lord let them for ever stay:
That from the Earth their Memory he may cut clean away.
14 Since Mercy he forgot to shew but did pursue with Spight
The troubled Man, and sought to slay the woful hearted Wight.

15 As he did Cursing love, it shall happen unto him so:
And as he did not Blessing love, far from him it shall go.
16 As he with Cursing clad himself, so it like Water shall
Enter his Bowels, and like Oil into his Bones shall fall.

17 As Garment let it be to him, to cover him withal:
And as a Girdle wherewith he always be girded shall.
18 Let this be the Reward from God, of him that is my Foe:
Yea, and of those that Evil speak against my Soul also.

19 But thou, O Lord, that art my God, deal graciously with me:
Deliver me for thy Name's-sake, for great thy Mercies be.
20 Because in Depth of great Distress I needy am and poor:
Also within my painted Breast my Heart is wounded sore.

PART III.

21 Even so do I depart away, as doth declining Shade:
And as the Grashopper, so I am shaken off, and fade.
22 With fasting long from needful Food, my Knees enfeebled are:
And all the Fatness of my Flesh is gone with Grief and Care.

23 And I also a vile Reproach to them am made to be:
And they that did upon me look, did shake their Heads at me.
24 Help me therefore, O God, I pray, my Aid and Succour be:
According to thy Mercies great, save and deliver me.

25 And they shall know thereby that this is thy most mighty Hand:
And that 'tis thou that hast it done, they well shall understand.
26 Altho' they curse with Spite, yet thou shalt bless with loving Voice
When they rise up and come to Shame, thy Servant shall rejoice.

27 Let them with Shame be clothed all, that are my Enemies:
And with Confusion as a Cloak be covered likewise.
28 But greatly I will with my Mouth give Thanks unto the Lord:
And I among the Multitude his Praises will record.

29 For

PSALM CX, CXI.

For he with Help at his Right-hand,
To fave him from the Man that would
will ftand the poor Man by,
condemn his Soul to die.

PSALM CX. N.

THE Lord did fay unto my Lord,
    Till I have made thy Foes a Stool
The Lord fhall out of Sion fend
Amidft thy mortal Foes be thou
fit thou on my Right-hand,
whereon thy Feet fhall ftand.
the Scepter of thy Might:
the Ruler in their Sight.

And in the Day on which thy Reign
Then Free-will-offerings fhall all
Yea, with an holy Worfhipping,
Thy Birth-dew is the Dew that doth
and Power they fhall fee,
the People give to thee.
then fhall they offer all:
from Womb of Morning fall.

The Lord hath fworn, and never will
By th' Order of Melchifedeck
The Lord thy God, on thy Right-hand,
Shall wound for thee the ftately Kings
repent what he doth fay,
thou art a Prieft alway.
that ftandeth for thy Stay,
in that his wrathful Day.

The Heathen he fhall judge, and fill
And over divers Countries fhall
And he fhall drink out of the Brook
Wherefore he fhall lift up on high
the Place with Bodies dead
in funder fmite the Head.
that runneth in the Way:
his Royal Head that Day.

PSALM CXI. N.

1 WITH Heart I do accord,
    In Prefence of the Juft:
For great his Works are found,
As do him love and truft.
To praife and laud the Lord,

To fearch them fuch are bound

2 His Works are glorious,
It ever doth endure:
His wond'rous Works he would
His Mercy is full fure,
And Righteoufnefs to us,

We ftill remember fhould,

3 Such as to him bear Love,
He hath up for them laid:
For this they fhall well find,
And keep them as he faid.
A Portion fair above

He will have them in Mind,

4 For he did not difdain,
By Lightnings and by Thunders:
When he the Heathens Land
Where they beheld his Wonders.
His Works to fhew them plain,

Did give into their Hand,

5 Of all his Works enfu'th
Whereto his Statutes tend:
They are decreed fure,
On which we may depend.
Both Judgment, Right and Truth,

For ever to endure,

6 Redemption great he gave
It alfo hath appear'd:
His Promife doth not fail,
His holy Name be fear'd.
His People for to fave,

But evermore prevail,

Whofo with Heart full fain
The Lord fear and obey:
Such as his Laws do keep,
His Praife fhall laft alway.
True Wifdom would attain,

Shall Knowledge have full deep,

PSALM CXII, CXIII, CXIV.

PSALM CXII. W. K.

1 THE Man is bleſt that God doth fear, And that his Law doth love indeed:
His Seed on Earth God will up rear, And bleſs ſuch as from him proceed;
His Houſe with Riches he will fill, His Righteouſneſs endure ſhall ſtill.

2 Unto the Righteous doth ariſe In Trouble Joy, in Darkneſs Light:
Compaſſion great is in his Eyes, And Mercy always in his Sight;
Yea, Pity moveth him to lend, He doth with Judgment Things expend.

3 And ſurely he ſhall never fail, For in Remembrance had is he:
Nor Tidings ill his Mind aſſail, Who in the Lord ſure Hope doth ſee;
His Heart is firm, his Fear is paſt, For he ſhall ſee his Foes down caſt.

4 He did well for the Poor provide, His Righteouſneſs doth ſtill remain:
And his Eſtate with Praiſe abide, Which wicked Men behold with Pain;
Yea, gnaſh their Teeth thereat ſhall they And ſo conſume and melt away.

PSALM CXIII. W. K.

1 YE Children which do ſerve the Lord, Praiſe ye his Name with one Accord:
Yea, bleſſed be always his Name;
Who from the Riſing of the Sun, Till it return where it begun,
Is to be praiſed with great Fame.

The Lord all People doth ſurmount, As for his Glory we may count
Above the higheſt Heav'ns to be.
With God the Lord who can compare, Whoſe Dwellings in the Heavens are?
Of ſuch great Pow'r and Force is he.

2 He doth abaſe himſelf we know, Things to behold on Earth below,
And alſo in the Heav'n above:
The Needy out of Duſt to draw, Alſo the Poor who Help none ſaw,
His Mercy only did him move.

And ſo did ſet him up on high, With Princes of great Dignity,
That rule his People with great Fame:
The Barren he doth make to bear, And with great Joy her Fruit to rear.
Therefore praiſe ye his holy Name.

PSALM CXIV. W. W.

1 WHEN Iſrael by God's Command, from Pharaoh's Land was bent:
And Jacob's Houſe the Strangers left, and in the ſame Train went;
2 In Judah God his Glory ſhew'd, his Holineſs moſt bright:
So did the Iſr'elites declare his Kingdom, Pow'r, and Might.

3 The Sea ſaw it, and ſuddenly, as all amaz'd, did fly:
The roaring Streams of Jordan's Flood, gave back immediately.
4 As Rams afraid, the Mountains ſkipt, their Birthright did them forſake:
And as the ſilly trembling Lambs, their Tops did beat and ſhake.

5 What aileth thee, O Sea, that thou ſo ſuddenly didſt fly?
Ye rolling Waves of Jordan's Flood why turn'd ye ſo ſwiftly?
6 Ye Mountains, ev'n as Rams afraid, why did your Strength ſo ſhake?
Why did your Tops, as trembling Lambs quiver with Fear and quake?

7 O Earth, confeſs thy Sov'reign Lord, and dread his mighty Hand:
Before the Face of Jacob's God, fear ye both Sea and Land.
8 I mean the God, who from hard Rocks cauſeth Floods to appear:
And from the ſtony Flint doth ſend Fountains of Water clear.

PSALM CXV, CXVI.

PSALM CXV. N.

1 NOT unto us, Lord, not to us,
  Both for thy Mercy and thy Truth,
  but to thy Name give Praise:
  that are in thee always.
2 Why shall the Heathen Scorners say,
  Our God he is in Heav'n, and what
  where is their God become?
  he will'd, that he hath done.

3 Their Idols Silver are and Gold,
  They have a Mouth, but do not speak,
  Work of Men's Hands they be:
  and Eyes, but do not see.
4 And they have Ears join'd to their Heads,
  Noses also they formed have,
  but do not hear at all:
  but not to smell withal.

5 And Hands they have, but handle not,
  A Throat they have, yet thro' the same
  and Feet, but cannot walk:
  they do not speak or talk.
6 They and their Makers are alike,
  O Israel, trust in the Lord,
  and those whose Trust they be:
  thy Help and Shield is he.

7 O Aaron's House, trust in the Lord,
  Ye that do fear him, trust in him,
  that still defendeth thee:
  your sure Defence is he.
8 The Lord of us hath mindful been,
  On Israel and Aaron's House
  and will us bless also:
  his Blessing he'll bestow.

9 Them that be Fearers of the Lord,
  Yea, he will bless them ev'ry one,
  he sure will bless them all:
  ev'n both the Great and Small.
10 To you alway the living Lord
  And also to the Children that
  will multiply his Grace:
  shall follow of your Race.

11 Ye are the Blessed of the Lord,
  Who both the Heav'n and Earth did make,
  ev'n of the Lord most high:
  and fix immoveably.
12 The Heav'ns above, the highest Heav'ns,
  The Earth unto the Sons of Men
  belong unto the Lord:
  he gave of free Accord.

13 They that be dead do not with Praise
  Nor any that into the Place
  set forth the Lord's Renown:
  of Silence do go down.
14 But we will praise the Lord our God
  He only worthy is of Praise,
  henceforth for evermore:
  praise ye the Lord therefore.

PSALM CXVI. N.

1 I Love the Lord, because the Voice
  I'll ever call on him, because
  of my Pray'r heard hath he:
  he bow'd his Ear to me.
2 Even when the Snares of cruel Death
  When Pains of Hell me caught, and when
  about beset me round:
  I Woe and Sorrow found.

3 Upon the Name of God the Lord,
  Deliver thou my Soul, O Lord,
  then did I call and say,
  I do thee humbly pray.
4 The Lord is very merciful,
  And in our God Compassion doth
  and just he is also:
  most plentifully flow.

5 The Lord in Safety doth preserve
  I was in woful Misery,
  all those that simple be:
  and he deliver'd me.
6 And now, my Soul, since thou art safe,
  For largely unto thee the Lord
  return unto thy Rest:
  his Bounty hath exprest.

7 Because thou hast delivered
  My moist'ned Eyes from mournful Tears,
  my Soul from deadly Thrall:
  my sliding Feet from Fall;
8 Before the Lord I in the Land
  I did believe, therefore I spake,
  of Life will walk therefore:
  but I was troubled sore.

PART II.

9 I said in my Distress and Fear,
  What shall I pay the Lord for all
  that all Men Liars be:
  his Benefits to me?

PSALM CXVII, CXVIII.

10 The wholsome Cup of saving Health
 And on the Name of God will call
11 I to the Lord will pay my Vows
 Now at this very present Time,
12 Right dear and precious in his Sight
 The Death of all his holy Ones,
13 Thy Servant, Lord, thy Servant, lo,
 Son of thy Handmaid, thou hast broke
14 Therefore I'll offer up to thee
 And I will call upon the Name
15 I to the Lord will pay my Vows
 Now at this very present Time,
16 Yea, in the Courts of God's own House,
 O thou Jerusalem: Therefore

I thankfully will take:
when I my Pray'rs do make.
with Joy and great Delight:
in all his Peoples Sight.
he always doth esteem
whatever Men do deem.
I do myself confess:
the Bonds of my Distress.
a Sacrifice of Praise:
of God the Lord always.
with Joy and great Delight,
in all his Peoples Sight;
and in the Midst of thee,
the Lord our God praise ye.

PSALM CXVII. N.

1 O All ye Nations of the World,
 And all ye People ev'ry where
2 For great his Kindness is to us,
 Wherefore praise ye the Lord our God,

praise ye the Lord always:
set forth his noble Praise.
his Truth doth not decay:
praise ye the Lord alway.

PSALM CXVIII. N.

1 O Give ye Thanks to God the Lord,
 Because his Mercy doth endure
2 Let Israel confess that his
 Let Aaron's House likewise confess
3 Let all that fear the Lord our God,
 The Mercy of the Lord our God
4 In Trouble and in Heaviness
 Who lovingly heard me at large,
5 The Lord himself is on my Side,
 Nor fear what Man can do to me,
6 The Lord doth take my Part with them
 Therefore I shall see my Desire
7 Better it is to trust in God,
 Or to put Confidence in Kings,
8 All Nations have enclosed me,
 But in the Name of God shall I
9 They kept me in on ev'ry Side,
 But in the Lord's most mighty Name
10 They came about me all like Bees,
 I quencht their Thorns that were on fire,

for ever kind is he:
unto Eternity.
Mercy doth ever dure:
his Mercy is most sure.
ev'n now confess and say
endureth still alway.
unto the Lord I cry'd:
my Suit was not deny'd.
I will not stand in Doubt:
when God stands me about.
that help to succour me:
upon my Enemy.
than in Man's mortal Seed:
or Princes in our Need.
and compassed me round:
my Enemies confound.
and did me quite surround:
I cast them to the Ground.
but in the Lord's great Name
and did destroy the same.

PART II.

11 They did with Force thrust sore at me,
 But thro' the Lord I found such Help,
12 The Lord is my Defence and Strength,
 And is become for me indeed
13 The Right-hand of the Lord our God
 He causeth Voice of Joy and Health
14 The Right-hand of the Lord doth bring
 His Hand hath the Preeminence,

that I indeed might fall:
as did them vanquish all.
my Joy, my Mirth, my Song:
a Saviour great and strong.
doth bring to pass great Things:
in righteous Men's Dwellings.
most mighty Things to pass:
his Force is as it was.

PSALM CXIX.

15 I shall not die, but ever live / to utter and declare
    The mighty Power of the Lord, / his Works, and what they are.
16 The Lord himself hath chastened, / and hath corrected me:
    But not me given over yet / to Death, as you may see.

17 Set open unto me the Gates / of Truth and Righteousness:
    That I may enter into them, / his Praise for to express.
18 This is the Gate of God the Lord, / which open shall be set:
    That good and righteous Men always / may enter into it.

PART III.

19 I will give Thanks to thee, O Lord, / and ever will praise thee,
    Who hast me heard, and art become / a Saviour unto me.
20 The Stone which formerly among / the Builders was refus'd,
    Is now become the Corner-stone, / and chiefly to be us'd.

21 This was the mighty Work of God, / it was the Lord's own Fact:
    And it is wond'rous to behold / that great and noble Act.
22 This is the joyful Day indeed, / which God himself hath wrought:
    Let us be glad and joy therein, / in Heart, in Mind, and Thought.

23 Now help us, Lord, and prosper us, / we wish with one Accord:
    Blessed is he that comes to us / in the Name of the Lord.
24 God is the Lord that shews us Light, / bind ye therefore with Cord
    Your Sacrifice to the Altar, / and give Thanks to the Lord.

25 Thou art my God, I will confess, / and render Thanks to thee:
    Thou art my God, and I will praise / thy Mercy towards me.
26 O give ye Thanks to God the Lord, / for very kind is he:
    Because his Mercy doth endure / unto Eternity.

ALEPH.   PSALM CXIX.   W. W.

1 **B**LESSED are they that perfect are, / and pure in Mind and Heart:
    Whose Lives and Conversations do / from God's Laws never start.
2 Blessed are they that give themselves / his Statutes to observe:
    Seeking the Lord with all their Heart, / and never from him swerve.

3 Doubtless such Men go not astray, / nor do a wicked Thing;
    But stedfastly walk in his Way, / without any wand'ring.
4 'Tis thy Commandment and thy Will, / that with attentive Heed,
    Thy Precepts, which are most divine, / we learn and keep indeed.

5 O would to God it might thee please / my Ways so to direct:
    That I might always keep thy Laws, / and never them reject.
6 So shall I not ashamed be, / whilst I thus set my Eyes:
    And bend my Mind always to muse / on thy Decrees most wise.

7 Then will I praise with upright Heart, / and magnify thy Name:
    When I shall learn thy Judgments just, / and also prove the same.
8 And wholly will I give myself / to keep thy Laws most right:
    Forsake me not for ever, Lord, / but shew thy Grace and Might.

BETH.   PART II.

9 By what Means may a young Man best / his Life learn to amend?
    If that he mark and keep thy Word, / and therein his Time spend.
10 Unfeignedly I have thee sought, / and thus seeking abide:
    Then never suffer me, O Lord, / from thy Commands to slide.

11 Within my Heart and secret Thoughts / thy Words I have hid still
    That I might not at any Time / offend thy holy Will.

PSALM CXIX.

12 We magnify thy Name, O Lord, and praise thee evermore:
Thy Statutes of most worthy Fame, O Lord, teach me therefore.
13 My Lips have never ceas'd to preach, and publish Day and Night:
The Judgments all which did proceed from thy Mouth full of Might.
14 Thy Testimonies and thy Ways much more my Heart rejoice,
Than all the Treasures of the Earth, which worldlings make their choice
15 Upon thy Precepts I will muse, and thereto frame my Talk:
As at a Mark so will I aim, how I thy Ways may walk.
16 My only Joy shall be so fixt, and on thy Laws so set:
That Nothing shall me so far blind, that I thy Words forget.

GIMEL. PART III.

17 Grant to thy Servant now such Grace, as may my Life prolong:
Thy holy Word then will I keep, both in my Heart and Tongue.
18 My Eyes, which are dim and shut up, so open and make bright:
That of thy Law and wond'rous Works I may have the clear Sight.
19 I am a Stranger on the Earth, wand'ring now here now there:
Thy Word therefore to me disclose, my Footsteps for to clear.
20 My Soul is ravisht with Desire, and never is at Rest:
But seeks to know thy Judgments high, and what may please thee best.
21 The proud and the malicious Men thou dost destroy each one:
And cursed are such as do not thy Laws attend upon.
22 Lord, turn from me Rebuke and Shame, which wicked Men conspire:
For I have kept thy Covenants with Zeal as hot as Fire.
23 The Princes great in Council sat, and did against me speak:
But then thy Servant thought how he thy Statutes might not break.
24 For why? thy Cov'nants are the Joy and Solace of my Heart:
They are my faithful Counsellors, from them I'll not depart.

DALETH. PART IV.

25 Alas, I am as brought to Grave, and almost turn'd to Dust:
Therefore restore my Life again, as thy Promise is just.
26 My Ways when I acknowledged, with Mercy thou didst hear:
Hear now also, and me instruct thy Laws to love and fear.
27 Make me, O Lord, to understand thy Precepts evermore:
Then on thy Works I'll meditate, and lay them up in Store.
28 My Soul I feel so sore opprest, that it doth melt for Grief:
According to thy Word therefore haste, Lord, to send Relief.
29 From lying and deceitful Lips let thy Grace me defend:
And that I may learn thee to love, thy holy Law me send.
30 The Way of Truth both straight and sure, I chosen have and found:
Before me I thy Judgments set, which keep me safe and found.
31 Since then, O Lord, I readily thy Covenants embrace:
Let me therefore have no Rebuke, nor Check in any Case.
32 Then will I run most joyfully where thy Word doth me call:
When thou enlarged hast my Heart, and rid me out of Thrall.

HE. PART V.

33 Instruct me, Lord, in the right Way of thy Statutes divine:
And them to keep unto the End my Heart I will incline.
34 Grant me the Knowledge of thy Law, and I shall it obey:
With Heart and Mind, and all my Might I will it keep alway.

PSALM CXIX.

35 In the right Paths of thy Commands, guide me, Lord, I require:
    No other Pleasure do I wish, nor greater Thing desire.
36 Incline my Heart thy Laws to keep, and Cov'nants to embrace:
    And from all filthy Avarice, Lord, shield me with thy Grace.
37 From vain Desires and worldly Lusts turn back my Eyes and Sight:
    And with thy Spirit strengthen me, to walk thy Ways aright.
38 Confirm thy gracious Promise, Lord, which thou hast made to me,
    Who am thy Servant, and do love and Nothing fear but thee.
39 Reproach and Shame, which I so fear, from me, O Lord, expel:
    For thou dost judge with Equity, and therein dost excel.
40 Behold my Heart's Desire is bent thy Laws to keep alway:
    O strengthen me so with thy Grace, that it perform I may.

VAU. PART VI.

41 Thy Mercies great and manifold, let me obtain, O Lord:
    Thy saving Health let me enjoy, according to thy Word.
42 So shall I stop the sland'rous Mouths of leud Men and unjust:
    For in thy faithful Word is all my Confidence and Trust.
43 The Word of Truth within my Mouth let evermore be prest:
    For in thy Judgments wonderful my Hope doth always rest.
44 And whilst that Breath within me doth this mortal Life preserve:
    Yea, till this World shall be dissolv'd, thy Law will I observe.
45 So walk will I as set at large, from Dread and Danger free:
    Because I study how to keep thy Precepts faithfully.
46 Thy noble Acts I will describe, as Things of most great Fame:
    Ev'n before Kings I will them blaze, and shrink no Whit for Shame.
47 I will rejoice then to obey thy just Commands and Will:
    Which evermore I have lov'd best, and so will love them still.
48 My Hands I will lift to thy Laws, which I have dearly sought:
    And practice thy Commandments all, in Word, in Deed, and Thought.

ZAIN. PART VII.

49 Thy Promise which thou mad'st to me, remember, Lord, I pray:
    For therein have I put my Trust and Confidence alway.
50 It is my Comfort and my Joy, when Troubles me assail:
    For were my Life not by thy Word, it suddenly would fail.
51 The Proud, and such as God contemn, still maketh me a Scorn:
    Yet will I not thy Law forsake, as if I were forlorn.
52 But call to Mind, Lord, thy great Work, shew'd to our Fathers old:
    Whereby I feel my Joys surmount my Grief a Hundred-fold.
53 Horror hath taken Hold on me, because the Wicked do
    Forsake thy righteous Law, and Will have no Regard thereto.
54 But as for me, I fram'd my Songs thy Statutes to exalt,
    When I among the Strangers dwelt, and Grief did me assault.
55 I thought upon thy Name, O Lord, by Night when others sleep:
    Thy Law also I kept always, and ever will it keep.
56 This Grace I did obtain, because thy Covenants most dear
    I did embrace, and also keep with Reverence and Fear.

CHETH. PART VIII.

57 O God, who art my Part and Lot, my Comfort and my Stay:
    I have decreed and promised thy Laws to keep alway.

58 With

PSALM CXIX.

58 With my whole Heart I humbly fu'd in Presence of thy Face:
   As thou therefore hast promised,   Lord, grant to me thy Grace.
59 My Life I have examined,   and try'd my secret Heart:
   Which to thy Statutes caused me   my Feet straight to convert.
60 I did not stay nor linger long,   as they that slothful are:
   But hastily thy Laws to keep   I did myself prepare.
61 The cruel Bands of wicked Men   have made me of their Prey:
   Yet would I not thy Law forget,   nor from thee go astray.
62 Thy righteous Laws and Judgments are so very great and high:
   That ev'n at Midnight I will rise   thy Name to magnify.
63 I am Companion of all them   who fear thee in their Heart:
   O therefore grant I never may   from thy Commandments start.
64 Thy Mercies, Lord, most plenteously the Earth throughout do fill:
   O teach me how I may obey   thy Statutes and thy Will.

TETH.   PART IX.

65 According to thy Promise, Lord,   so hast thou with me dealt:
   For of thy Grace in sundry Sorts, have I thy Servant felt.
66 Teach me to judge always aright,   and give me Knowledge sure:
   For stedfastly I do believe   thy Precepts are most pure.
67 Before that I afflicted was,   I err'd and went astray:
   But now I keep thy holy Word,   and make it all my Stay.
68 Thou art both good and gracious, Lord, and in thy Gifts most free:
   Thy Ordinances how to keep   therefore, O Lord, teach me.
69 The Proud and the Ungodly have   against me forg'd a Lie:
   Yet thy Commandments still observe with all my Heart will I.
70 Their Hearts are even like to Brawn, which is exceeding fat:
   But in thy Law do I delight,   and Nothing seek but that.
71 O happy Time, may I well say,   when thou didst me correct:
   That I thereby might learn thy Laws, and never them reject.
72 So that thy Word and Law to me   is dearer manifold,
   Than Gold and Silver in great Sums, or Ought that can be told.

JOD.   PART X.

73 Thy Hands have made and fashion'd me, thy Creature, Lord, am I:
   Make me to understand thy Law   and keep it faithfully.
74 So they that fear thee shall rejoice whenever they me see:
   Because I have learn'd by thy Word to put my Trust in thee.
75 I know, O Lord, thy Judgments all, most just and righteous be:
   And that in very Faithfulness,   thou hast afflicted me.
76 Now of thy Goodness, I thee pray, some Comfort to me send:
   And as thou hast me hitherto,   O Lord, still me defend.
77 Thy tender Mercies pour on me,   then shall I surely live:
   For Joy and Consolation both   thy Law to me doth give.
78 Confound the Proud, who do me seek, perversly to destroy:
   But as for me thy Laws to know   I will myself employ.
79 Whoso with Rev'rence do thee fear, to me let them retire:
   And such as know thy Covenants,   and them alone desire.
80 My Heart without all wavering,   let on thy Laws be bent:
   That no confusion come to me,   nor any Discontent.

CAPH.

PSALM CXIX.

CAPH.   PART XI.

81 My Soul doth faint, and ceaseth not   thy saving Health to crave:
     And for thy Word's Sake still I trust,   my Heart's Desire to have.
82 My Eyes do fail with looking for   thy Word, and thus I say,
     Oh when wilt thou me comfort, Lord?   why dost thou thus delay?
83 Like as a Bottle in the Smoke,   so am I parch'd and dry'd:
     Yet will I not out of my Heart   let thy Commandments slide.
84 How long, O Lord, shall I yet live,   before I see the Hour,
     That on my Foes who me torment,   thy Vengeance thou wilt pour?
85 Presumptuous Men have digged Pits,   thinking to make me sure:
     Thus quite contrary to thy Law,   my Hurt they do procure.
86 But thy Commandments are all true,   and causeless they me grieve:
     To thee therefore I do complain,   that thou may'st me relieve.
87 Almost they had me quite destroy'd,   and brought me to the Ground:
     Yet by thy Statutes I abode,   and therein Succour found.
88 Restore me, Lord, again to Life,   thy Mercies do excel:
     And so shall I thy Statutes keep,   till Death my Life expel.

LAMED.   PART XII.

89 In Heav'n, O Lord, where thou dost dwell,   thy Word is stablish'd sure:
     And shall to all Eternity   fast settled there endure.
90 From Age to Age thy Truth abides,   as doth the Earth witness:
     Whose Ground-work thou hast laid so sure,   as no Tongue can express.
91 Ev'n to this Day we may well see   how thou dost them preserve:
     According to thy Ordinance,   for all Things do thee serve.
92 Had it not been that in thy Law,   my Soul had Comfort sought:
     Long Time ere now, in my Distress,   I had been brought to Nought.
93 Therefore will I thy Precepts keep,   in Memory full fast:
     Because that thou by them, O Lord,   my Life restored hast.
94 No Man to me can Title make,   for I am only thine:
     Save me therefore, for to thy Laws,   my Ears and Heart incline.
95 The wicked Men that seek my Bane,   for me do lie in Wait:
     But I will meditate upon   thy Testimonies great.
96 For Nothing in this World I see,   which hath at length no End:
     But thy Commandments and thy Word   beyond all Time extend.

MEM.   PART XIII.

97 What great Desire and fervent Love   unto thy Law I bear:
     On it my daily Study is,   that so I may thee fear.
98 Thy Word hath taught me to exceed   in Wisdom all my Foes:
     For they are ever with me, and   do give me sweet Repose.
99 My Teachers who did me instruct,   in Knowledge I excel:
     Because I do thy Statutes keep,   and them to others tell.
100 In Wisdom I do far surpass   the ancient Men also:
     And that because I keep thy Laws,   and so resolve to do.
101 My Feet I have refrain'd likewise,   from ev'ry evil Way:
     That so I might thy Word observe   and keep without Delay.
102 I have not from thy Judgments swerv'd,   nor shrunk, as thou canst tell:
     Because thou hast me taught thereby   to live godly and well,
103 O Lord, how sweet unto my Taste   I find thy Words alway!
     Doubtless no Honey in my Mouth   doth taste so sweet as they.

PSALM CXIX.

104 Thy Laws have me such Wisdom learn'd, that I do hate therefore:
All wicked and ungodly Ways, and will do evermore.

NUN. PART XIV.

105 Ev'n as a Lantern to my Feet, so doth thy Word shine bright
And to my Paths where I do go, it is a flaming Light.
106 I have both sworn, and will perform in Truth and Faithfulness:
That I will keep thy Judgments just, and them in Life express.
107 Affliction hath me sore oppress'd, and brought me to Death's Do
O Lord, as thou hast promised, so me to Life restore.
108 The Free-will-offerings of my Mouth which I to thee do give:
Accept, and teach me how I may after thy Judgments live.
109 My Soul is ever in my Hand, great Dangers me assail:
Yet do I not thy Law forget, nor it to keep will fail.
110 Altho' the Wicked laid their Nets to make of me a Prey:
Yet from thy Precepts did I not once swerve or go astray.
111 Thy Law, O Lord, I taken have my Heritage to be:
Because such great Delight and Joy, it doth afford to me.
112 For evermore I have been bent thy Statutes to fulfil:
Ev'n so likewise unto the End I will continue still.

SAMECH. PART XV.

113 All Thoughts that vain and wicked are I do always detest:
But for thy Precepts and thy Laws, I ever love them best.
114 Thou art my hid and secret Place, my Shield and strong Defence
Therefore have I thy Promises look'd for with Confidence.
115 Therefore ye Evil doers all, away from me be gone:
For the Commandments will I keep of God my Lord alone.
116 As thou hast promis'd, so perform, that I may live and be
Never ashamed of the Hope which thou hast given me.
117 Uphold me, and I shall be safe, for ought they do or say:
And in thy Statutes Pleasure take, I will both Night and Day.
118 Under thy Feet thou hast trod such as do thy Statutes break:
For Nought avails their Subtlety, their Counsel is too weak.
119 Like Dross thou casts the Wicked out wherever they do dwell:
Therefore can I as thy Commands, love Nothing half so well.
120 My Flesh doth quake for fear of thee, my Soul is much dismay'd:
By Reason of thy Judgments great my Heart is sore afraid.

AIN. PART XVI.

121 I do the Thing that lawful is, and give to all Men Right:
Resign me not to them that would oppress me with their Might.
122 But for thy Servant Surety be in that Thing which is right:
And never let the Proud oppress me with their Rage and Spite.
123 My Eyes do fail with waiting for thy Health which I do crave,
And for thy righteous Promise, Lord, whereby thou wilt me save.
124 Entreat thy Servant lovingly, and Favour to him show:
And thy Commands most excellent teach me also to know.
125 Thy humble Servant, Lord, I am, grant me to understand,
How by thy Statutes I may know best what to take in Hand.
126 It is now Time, Lord, to begin, for Truth doth quite decay:
Thy Law likewise they have made void, and none doth it obey.

PSALM CXIX.

7 This is the Cause wherefore I love thy Laws much more than Gold,
Or Jewels fine, which are esteem'd most costly to be sold.
8 I thought thy Precepts all most just, and so them kept in Store:
All crafty and malicious Ways I greatly do abhor.

P E.   PART XVII.

9 Thy Covenants are wonderful, and full of Things profound:
My Soul therefore doth keep them sure, when they are try'd and found:
10 The Entrance of thy Word doth give to Men a Light most clear:
The Simple likewise understand, when they it read or hear.

1 My Mouth I open'd, and did pant, because my Soul did long
For thy Commandments, which always do guide my Heart and Tongue:
2 With Mercy and Compassion look upon me from above:
As thou art wont such to behold as thy Name fear and love.

3 Direct my Foot-steps by thy Word, that I thy Will may know:
And never let Iniquity thy Servant overthrow.
4 From sland'rous Tongue, and deadly Harms, preserve and keep me sure:
Thy Precepts then will I observe with Heart upright and pure.

5 Thy Countenance, which doth surpass the Sun in its bright Hue,
Let shine on me, and by thy Law teach me what to eschew.
6 Rivers of Waters from my Eyes incessantly do fall:
Because I see how wicked Men thy Laws keep not at all.

Z A D E.   PART XVIII.

7 In ev'ry Thing, Lord, thou art just, altho' the Wicked grudge:
And when thou dost Sentence pronounce, thou are a righteous Judge.
8 To render right and free from Guile are two chief Points most high:
And such as thou hast in thy Law commanded us strictly.

9 My Zeal hath ev'n consumed me, and I am pin'd away:
Because my Foes thy Word forget, and will it not obey.
10 Thy Word is very pure, and doth greatly my Heart rejoice:
Therefore thy Servant Nothing more can love, or make my Choice:

11 And tho' I be Nothing set by, as one of base Degree:
Yet I do not thy Laws forget, nor shrink away from thee.
12 Thy Truth and Righteousness, O Lord, for ever shall endure:
Also thy Law is Truth itself, most constant and most pure.

13 Anguish and Grief hath seiz'd on me, and brought me wond'rous low:
Yet of thy Precepts do I still delight to hear and know,
14 The Righteousness of thy Commands doth last for evermore:
Then teach them me, because in them my Life lies up in Store.

C O P H.   PART XIX.

15 With fervent Heart I call'd and cry'd, now answer me, O Lord:
That thy Commandments to observe I fully may accord.
16 To thee, my God, I make my Suit, save me, I humbly pray:
Thy Testimonies then will I always keep and obey.

17 To thee do I cry in the Morn, before the Day appear:
For in thy Word I put my Trust, and thee alone do fear.
18 My Eyes prevent the Night-watches, before they call I wake:
That meditating on thy Word, I might some Comfort take.

19 Incline thy Ears to hear my Voice, and Pity on me take:
As thou wast wont, so quicken me, lest Life should me forsake:

PSALM CXIX.

150 My Foes draw near, and greedily do after Mischief run :
Far from thy Law they are gone back, and wickedly it shun.
151 Therefore, O Lord, approach thou near, since Need doth so require
For all thy Precepts are most true, then help I thee desire.
152 Concerning thy Commandments I have learned long ago :
That they remain for evermore, thou hast them grounded so.

RESH. PART XX.

153 My Trouble and Affliction, Lord, consider and behold :
Deliver me, for of thy Law I ever take fast Hold.
154 Defend my good and righteous Cause, with Speed some Succour send :
From Death, as thou hast promised, Lord, ever me defend.
155 As for the Wicked, they are far from saving Health and Grace,
Because the Way thy Laws to know they enter not the Trace.
156 Great are thy Mercies, Lord, I grant, what Tongue can them explain ?
According to thy Judgments good, let me my Life obtain.
157 Tho' many Men did trouble me, and persecute me sore :
Yet from thy Laws I never shrunk, nor went aside therefore.
158 The great Transgressors I behold, which is a Grief to me :
Because they do not keep thy Word, nor ever seek to thee.
159 Behold, how I do love thy Laws, with a most upright Heart :
Then quicken me, O Lord, for thou most good and gracious art.
160 Thy Word from the Beginning hath been ever true and just :
Thy righteous Judgments ev'ry one always continue must.

SCHIN. PART XXI.

161 Princes have persecuted me without a Cause, but saw
It was in vain, for of thy Word my Heart did stand in Awe.
162 And surely of thy Word I was more joyful and more glad
Than he that of rich Spoils and Prey great Store and Plenty had.
163 But as for Lies and Fallities, them I hate and detest :
Because thy holy Law I do above all Things love best.
164 Sev'n Times a Day I praise thee, Lord, singing with Heart and Voice :
Because thy righteous Judgments do greatly my Heart rejoice.
165 Great Peace and Rest shall all such have, who do thy Statutes love :
No Danger shall their quiet State impair or once remove.
166 My only Health and Comfort, Lord, I look for at thy Hand :
And therefore have I done those Things which thou didst me command.
167 Thy Laws have been my Exercise, which my Soul most desir'd :
So much to them my Love was bent, that nought else I requir'd.
168 Thy Statutes and Commandments I have kept with Heart upright :
For all my Doings and my Ways are present in thy Sight.

TAU. PART XXII.

169 O Lord, let my Complaint and Cry, before thy Face appear :
And as thou hast me Promise made, so teach me thee to fear.
170 O let my Supplication, Lord, have free Access to thee :
And let me be delivered, as thou hast promis'd me.
171 Then shall my Lips thy Praises speak after most ample Sort :
When thou thy Statutes hast me taught, wherein stands my Comfort.
172 My Tongue shall freely preach thy Word, and evermore confess :
Thy famous Acts and noble Laws are Truth and Righteousness.

PSALM CXX, CXXI, CXXII.

3 Stretch out thy Hand, I thee befeech,
For thy Commandments to obferve
4 Of thee alone, Lord, I crave Health,
And in thy Law to meditate

and fpeedily me fave:
chofen, O Lord, I have.
for other I know none;
I do delight alone.

5 Grant me therefore long Days to live,
And of thy Judgments wonderful,
6 For I was loft and went aftray,
O feek me, for I have not fail'd

thy Name to magnify:
let me the Favour try.
much like a wand'ring Sheep:
thy Statutes for to keep.

PSALM CXX. T. S.

IN Trouble and in Thrall
And he doth me comfort:
Deliver me, I pray,
And Tongues of falfe Report.

Unto the Lord I call,

From lying Lips alway,

What 'Vantage, or what Thing
Thou falfe and flatt'ring Liar?
Thy Tongue doth hurt, 'tis feen,
Or hot confuming Fire.

Gett'ft thou thus for to fting,

No lefs than Arrows keen.

Alas! that I am fain
Which Kedar are by Name:
By whom the Flock Eleft
Are put to open Shame.

In thofe Tents to remain,

And all of Ifaac's Sect.

With them that Peace do hate,
And fet a quiet Life:
But when my Mind was told,
By them that loved Strife.

I came to meditate,

Caufelefs I was controll'd.

PSALM CXXI. W. W.

I Lift my Eyes to Sion Hill,
From whence I do attend,
The mighty God me fuccour will,
Who Heav'n and Earth did frame,

Till God me Succour fend:

And all Things therein name.

Thy Foot from Slip he will preferve,
And will thee fafely keep,
Lo, he that Ifr'el doth conferve,
Sleep never can furprize,

For he doth never fleep.

Nor flumber clofe his Eyes.

The Lord thy Keeper is alway,
On thy Right-hand is he,
The Sun fhall not thee parch by Day
Nor Moon, fcarce half fo bright,

A Shade to cover thee.

With Cold thee hurt by Night.

The Lord will keep thee from Diftrefs,
And will thy Life fure fave:
In all thy Bufinefs good Succefs;
When thou go'ft in or out,

Yea, thou fhalt alfo have

He'll compafs thee about.

PSALM CXXII. W. K.

I Did in Heart rejoice,
In Offering fo willingly:
For 'et us up, fay they,
Thus fpake the Folk with Amity.

To hear the People's Voice,

And in the Lord's Houfe pray:

Our Feet that wand'red wide,
O thou Jerufalem full fair:

Shall in thy Gates abide,

K

Which

PSALM CXXIII, CXXIV.

Which are so seemly set, Much like a City neat,
Whither the People do repair.

3 The Tribes with one Accord, To give Thanks to the Lord,
Are thither bent their Way to take;
So God before did tell, That there his Israel
Their Pray'rs they should together make.

4 For there are Thrones erect, And that for this Respect,
To set forth Justice orderly:
Which Thrones right to maintain, To David's House remain,
His Folk to judge with Equity.

5 To pray let us not cease, For Jerusalem's Peace,
Thy Friends God keep in Amity:
Peace be thy Walls about, And prosper thee thro'out
Thy Palaces continually.

6 For my Friends Sake will I Wish that Prosperity
May evermore abide in thee:
God's House doth me allure, Thy Wealth for to procure,
So much as lies in me.

PSALM CXXIII. T. S.

1 O Thou that in the Heav'ns dost dwell, I lift my Eyes to thee:
   Ev'n as a Servant lifteth his, his Master's Hand to see.
2 As Handmaids watch their Mistress Hand, some Grace for to atchieve:
   So we behold the Lord our God, till he do us forgive.
3 O grant to us Compassion, Lord, and Mercy in thy Sight:
   For we are fill'd and overcome with Hatred and Despite.
4 Our Minds are fill'd with great Rebuke, the rich and worldly wise
   Do make of us their Mocking-flocks, the Proud do us despise.

PSALM CXXIV. W. W.

1 NOW Israel may say, and that truly,
   If that the Lord had not our Cause maintain'd;
   If that the Lord had not our Right sustain'd,
   When all the World against us furiously
   Made their Uproars, and said we should all die.

2 Then long ago they had devour'd us all,
   And swallow'd quick, for all that we could deem;
   Such was their Rage, as we might well esteem,
   And as the Floods with mighty Force do fall,
   So had they now our Lives ev'n brought to Thrall.

3 The raging Streams, most proud in roaring Noise,
   Had long ago o'erwhelm'd us in the Deep;
   Praised be God, who doth us safely keep
   From bloody Teeth, and their most cruel Voice,
   Who as a Prey, to eat us would rejoice.

4 Ev'n as a Bird from Fowlers Gin or Pen,
   Escapes away, right so it fares with us:
   Broke are the Nets, and we escaped thus.
   God who made Heav'n and Earth is our Help then,
   His Name hath sav'd us from these wicked Men.

PSALM CXXV, CXXVI.

PSALM CXXV. W. K.

SUCH as in God the Lord do trust,
As Sion Mount shall firmly stand,
The Lord will count them right and just,
So that they shall be sure
And be removed at no Hand:
For ever to endure.

As many Mountains sure and great,
Jerusalem about do close,
Who on his godly Will do wait:
Such are to him so dear,
So will the Lord do unto those
They never need to fear.

For tho' the Righteous try doth he,
By making wicked Men his Rod,
It shall not always their Lot be.
Give, Lord, to us thy Light,
Lest they thro' Grief forsake their God,
Whose Hearts are true and right.

But as for such as turn aside
By crooked Ways which they out-sought,
With Workers vile they shall abide:
But Peace with Israel.
The Lord will surely bring to nought,
For evermore shall dwell.

Another of the same, by W. W.

THOSE that do place their Confidence
And flee to him for their Defence
Their Faith is sure still to endure,
Mov'd with no ill, but standeth sure,
Upon the Lord our God only,
In all their Need and Misery:
Grounded on Christ the Corner-stone,
stedfast like to the Mount Sion.

And as about Jerusalem
So that no Foes can come to them
So God indeed in ev'ry Need
Standing them by assuredly,
The mighty Hills do it compass,
To hurt that Town in any Case:
His faithful People doth defend,
From this Time forth World without End.

Right wise and good is our Lord God,
The Sinners and Ungodly's Rod
Lest they also from God should stray,
O Lord, defend both Night and Day
And will not suffer certainly,
To rest upon his Family:
Falling to Sin and Wickedness:
Thy little Flock, and them still bless.

O Lord, do Good to Christians all,
But such as from the Lord do fall,
Them will the Lord scatter abroad,
God will them send Pains without End,
That stedfast in thy Words abide:
And to false Doctrine daily slide,
With Hypocrites thrown down to Hell:
But, Lord, grant Peace to Israel.

PSALM CXXVI. W. W.

WHEN that the Lord
From Bondage great,
His Work was such
So that we were;
Our Mouths were all
Also our Tongues
again his Sion had forth brought
and also Servitude extreme.
as did surmount Man's Heart and Thought,
much like to them that use to dream.
with Laughter filled then,
did shew us joyful Men.

The Heathen Folk
How that the Lord
But much more we,
Wherefore to joy
O Lord, go forth,
Who to Deserts
were forced then for to confess
for them also great Things had done.
and therefore can confess no less:
we have good Cause, as we begun.
thou canst our Bondage end,
doft flowing Rivers send.

PSALM CXXVII, CXXVIII, CXXIX.

5 Full true it is,
A Time will come
They went and wept,
For that their Foes,
But their Return
Their Sheaves bring home,

that they which sow in Tears indeed,
when they shall reap in Mirth and Joy.
in bearing of their precious Seed,
full oftentimes did them annoy:
they joyfully shall see,
and not impaired be.

PSALM CXXVII. W. W.

1 EXCEPT the Lord the House doth make,
And thereunto doth set his Hand;
Likewise in vain Men undertake,
Cities and Holds to watch and ward,

What Men do build it cannot sta
Except the Lord be their Safeguar

2 Tho' in the Morn ye rise early,
And so at Night go late to Bed,
Your Labour is but Vanity:
But they whom God doth love and keep,

Eating with Carefulness your Bre
Enjoy all Things with quiet Slee

3 Therefore mark well when you do see
That Men have Heirs t' enjoy their Land,
For God doth multiply to these,
Of his great Liberality,

It is the Gift of God's own Hand
The Blessing of Posterity.

4 And when the Children come to Age,
They grow in Strength and Activeness,
So that a Shaft shot with Courage
Of one that hath a most strong Arm,

In Person and in Comeliness:
Flies not so swift, nor doth like Ha

5 O well is he that hath his Quiver
Furnish'd with such Artillery:
Such one shall never quake or shiver,
When he doth plead before the Judge,

For when in Peril he shall be
Against his Foes that bear him Grud

PSALM CXXVIII. T. S.

1 BLESSED art thou that fearest God,
For of thy Labour thou shalt eat,
2 Like fruitful Vines on thy House-side,
Thy Children stand like Olive-plants

and walkest in his Ways:
happy shall be thy Days.
so doth thy Wife spring out:
thy Table round about.

3 Thus art thou blest that fearest God,
The promised Jerusalem,
4 Thou shalt thy Children's Children see,
And likewise Grace on Israel,

and he shall let thee see
and her Felicity.
to thy great Joys increase:
Prosperity and Peace.

PSALM CXXIX. N.

1 OFT they, now Israel may say,
Oft they assail'd me from my Youth,
2 Upon my Back the Plowers plow'd,
The righteous Lord hath cut the Cords

me from my Youth assail'd
yet never have prevail'd.
and Furrows long did cast:
of wicked Men at last.

3 They that hate me shall be asham'd,
And made as Grass upon the House,
4 Whereof the Mower cannot find
Nor can he fill his Lap that goes

and turned back also:
which withers ere it grow;
enough to fill his Hand:
to glean upon the Land;

5 Nor Passers-by pray God on them
Nor say, we bless you in his Name

to let his Blessing fall:
that Lord is over all.

PSALM CXXX, CXXXI, CXXXII.
PSALM CXXX. W. W.

1 LORD, unto thee I make my Moan
   I call, I sigh, complain and groan,
   when Dangers me oppress:
   trusting to find Release.
2 Hearken, O Lord, to my Request,
   And let thine Ears, O Lord, be prest
   unto my Suit incline:
   to hear this Pray'r of mine.
3 O Lord our God, if thou survey
   Who shall escape? or who dare say,
   our Sins, and them peruse,
   I can myself excuse?
4 But thou art merciful and free,
   That we may always careful be
   and boundless in thy Grace:
   to fear before thy Face.
5 In God the Lord I put my Trust,
   His Promise is for ever just,
   my Soul waits on his Will:
   and I hope therein still.
6 My Soul to God hath great Regard,
   Much more than they that watch and ward
   wishing for him alway:
   to see the dawning Day.
7 O Israel trust in the Lord,
   And he doth plentiously afford
   with him their Mercy is:
   Redemption unto his
8 Ev'n he it is that Isr'el shall,
   Redeem from his Offences all,
   thro' his abundant Grace,
   and wholly them deface.

PSALM CXXXI. N.

1 O Lord, I am not puft in Mind,
   I do not exercise myself
   I have no scornful Eye:
   in Things that be too high.
2 But as a Child that weaned is,
   So have I, Lord, behav'd myself
   ev'n from his Mother's Breast:
   in Silence and in Rest.
3 O Israel, trust in the Lord,
   From this Time forth for evermore,
   let him be all his Stay:
   from Age to Age alway.

PSALM CXXXII. N.

1 REMEMBER David's Troubles Lord,
   And vow'd a Vow to Jacob's God,
   how unto thee he swore,
   to keep for evermore.
2 I will not come within my House,
   Nor let my Temples take their Rest,
   nor climb up to my Bed:
   nor Eyes within my Head:
3 Till I have found out for the Lord
   A House for Jacob's God to be
   a Place to fit thereon:
   an Habitation.
4 We heard of it at Ephrata,
   And in the Fields and Forests there
   there did we hear this Sound:
   these Voices first were found.
5 We will assay and go into
   Before his Footstool to fall down,
   his Tabernacle there:
   and worship him in Fear.
6 Arise, O Lord, arise, I pray,
   Thou and the Ark of thy great Strength,
   into thy Resting-place:
   the Presence of thy Grace.
7 Let all thy Priests be clothed, Lord,
   Let all thy Saints with Songs of Praise,
   with Truth and Righteousness:
   their Joyfulness express.
8 And for thy Servant David's Sake,
   The Face of thy Anointed, and
   refuse not, Lord, I pray,
   turn not from him away.

PART II.

9 The Lord to David swore in Truth,
   The Fruit that from thy Loins proceed,
   and will not shrink from it:
   upon thy Seat shall sit.
10 And if thy Sons my Laws will keep,
   Then shall their Sons for ever sit
   that I shall learn each one:
   upon thy princely Throne.
11 The Lord himself hath Sion chose,
   Saying, This is my Resting-place,
   and loves therein to dwell:
   I love and like it well.

PSALM CXXXVII.

2 The Lord of Lords praife ye, Whofe Mercies ever dure:
Great Wonders only he, Doth by his Power fure: For, &c.
3 Which God omnipotent By his great Wifdom he,
The Heav'n and Firmament Did frame, as we may fee: For, &c.

4 Yea, he the heavy Charge Of all the Earth did lay
Upon the Waters large, Remaining to this Day; For, &c.
5 Great Lights he made, for why His Mercy lafts alway:
The Sun moft glorioufly To rule the lightfome Day; For, &c.

6 Alfo the Moon fo clear, Which fhineth in our Sight:
And Stars that do appear, To guard the darkfome Night; For, &c.
7 With grievous Plagues & Sores, All Egypt fmote he then:
The Firft-born, lefs and more, He flew of Beafts and Men; For, &c.

8 And from amidft their Land His Ifrael forth brought:
Which he with mighty Hand, And out-ftretch'd Arm hath wrought; For, &c.
9 The Sea he cut in two, Which flood up like a Wall:
And made thro' it to go His chofen Children all; For, &c.

10 But overwhelm'd there then, The haughty King Phar'oh,
With his huge Hoft of Men, And Chariots alfo; For, &c.
11 Who led thro' Wildernefs His People fafe and found:
And for his Love endlefs Great Kings he brought to Ground: For, &c.

12 And with puiffant Hand Slew Kings of mighty Fame:
As of the Am'rites Land Sehon the King by Name; For, &c.
13 And Og the Giant large, Of Bafan King alfo:
Whofe Land of Heritage He gave his People to; For, &c.

14 Ev'n unto Ifrael His Servant dear, I fay:
That he therein might dwell, And there abide alway: For, &c.
15 Who us remembred when In our moft low Degree:
And from Oppreffors then In Safety us fet free; For, &c.

16 Who doth all Flefh with Food Abundantly fupply:
Wherefore let God moft good Be prais'd inceffantly;
For certainly His Mercies dure
Both firm and fure Eternally.

PSALM CXXXVII. W. W.

1 WHEN we did in Babylon, the Rivers round about:
Then in Remembrance of Sion, the Tears for Grief burft out.
2 We hang'd our Harps and Inftruments the Willow-Trees upon;
For in that Place Men for their Ufe had planted many one.

3 Then they to whom we Pris'ners were, faid to us tauntingly:
Now let us hear your Hebrew Songs, and pleafant Melody.
4 Alas! faid we, who can once frame his heavy Heart to fing
The Praifes of our loving God, thus under a ftrange King?

5 But yet if I Jerufalem out of my Heart let flide;
Then let my Fingers quite forget the warbling Harp to guide.
6 And let my Tongue within my Mouth be ty'd for ever faft,
If I rejoice before I fee thy full Deliv'rance paft.

7 Therefore, O Lord, remember now the curfed Noife and Cry,
That Edom's Sons againft us made, when they rais'd our City.
8 Remember, Lord, their cruel Words, when with a mighty Sound
They cried, Down, yea, down with it unto the very Ground.

9 Ev'n

PSALM CXXXVIII, CXXXIX.

9 Ev'n so shalt thou, O Babylon,   at length to Dust be brought:
And happy shall that Man be call'd,   that our Revenge hath wrought:
10 Yea, blessed shall that Man be call'd,   that takes thy little Ones,
And dasheth them in Pieces small   against the very Stones.

PSALM CXXXVIII. N.

1 THEE will I praise with my whole Heart, my Lord my God always:
Ev'n in the Presence of the Gods   I will advance thy Praise.
2 Towards thy holy Temple I   will look and worship thee:
And praised in my thankful Mouth   thy holy Name shall be.

3 Ev'n for thy Loving-kindness sake,   and for thy Truth withal:
For thou thy Name hast by thy Word   advanced over all.
4 When I did call, thou heardest me,   and thou hast made also:
The Power of increased Strength,   within my Soul to grow.

5 Yea, all the Kings on Earth shall give   Praise unto thee, O Lord:
For they of thy most holy Mouth   have heard the mighty Word.
6 They of the Ways of God the Lord   in Singing shall repeat:
Because the Glory of the Lord   is so exceeding great.

7 The Lord is high, but yet he doth   the lowly Man respect:
The Proud he knows far off, and them   with Scorn he doth reject.
8 Altho' in Midst of Trouble I   do walk, yet shall I stand:
Reviv'd by thee, for thou, O Lord,   wilt stretch out thy Right-hand:

9 Upon the Wrath of all my Foes,   and saved shall I be
By thy Right-hand. The Lord God will   perform his Work to me.
10 Thy Mercies last for evermore,   Lord, do me not forsake:
Forsake me not, who am the Work   which thy own Hand did make.

PSALM CXXXIX. N.

1 O Lord thou hast me try'd and known,   my sitting down dost know:
My rising up, and Thoughts far off,   thou understand'st also.
2 My Path, yea, and my Bed likewise,   thou art about always:
And by familiar Custom art   acquainted with my Ways.

3 No Word is in my Tongue, O Lord,   that is not known to thee:
Thou hast beset me round about,   and laid thy Hand on me.
4 Such Knowledge is too wonderful,   and past my Skill to gain:
It is so high, that I unto   the same cannot attain.

5 From thy all-seeing Spirit then,   Lord, whither shall I go:
Or whither shall I fly away   from thy Presence also?
6 For if to Heav'n I do climb up,   lo, thou art present there,
In Hell if I lie down below,   ev'n there thou dost appear.

7 Yea, let me take the Morning Wings,   and let me go and dwell
Ev'n in the very utmost Parts   where flowing Sea doth swell.
8 Yea certainly there also shall   thy Hand me lead and guide:
And thy Right-Hand shall hold me fast,   and make me to abide.

9 Or if I say, The Darkness shall   shroud me quite from thy Sight,
Ev'n then the Night that is most dark,   about me shall be Light.
10 The Darkness hideth not from thee,   but Night doth shine as Day:
To thee the Darkness and the Light   are both alike alway.

PART II.

11 For thou possessed hast my Reins,   and thou didst cover me
Within my Mother's Womb, when I   was there enclos'd by thee.

PSALM CXL, CXLI.

12 Thee will I praife; made fearfully and wond'roufly I am:
Thy Works are marvellous, right well my Soul doth know the fame,
13 My Bones they are not hid from thee altho' in fecret Place,
I have been made, and in the Earth beneath I fhaped was.
14 When I was formlefs, then thy Eye faw me; for in thy Book
Were all my Members written, and Nought after Fafhion took.
15 The Thoughts therefore of thee, O God, how dear are they to me!
And of them all, how very great the endlefs Number be!
16 If I fhould count them, lo, their Sum more than the Sand would be:
And whenfoever I awake, I prefent am with thee.
17 The Wicked and Ungodly thou moft certainly wilt flay:
Therefore now, all ye bloody Men, depart from me away.
18 Thefe are the Men, O Lord, who fpeak moft wickedly of thee:
And take thy Name in vain, becaufe thy Enemies they be.
19 Hate I not them that hate thee, Lord, and that in Earneft wife?
Am not I grieved with all thofe that up againft thee rife?
20 I hate them with a perfect Hate, ev'n as my utter Foes:
Try me, O God, and know my Heart, my Thoughts prove and difclofe.
21 Confider, Lord, if Wickednefs in me there any be:
And in thy Way, O God, my Guide, for ever lead thou me.

PSALM CXL. N.

1 LORD, fave me from the evil Man, and from his Pride and Spight:
And from all thofe alfo who do in Violence delight.
2 Who evermore on me make War, their Tongues, lo, they have whet
Like Serpents; underneath their Lips is Adders Poifon fet.
3 Keep me, O Lord, from wicked Hands, preferve me to abide
Free from the cruel Man, who means to caufe my Steps to flide.
4 The Proud have laid a Snare for me, and they have fpread a Net
With Cords in my Path-way, and Gins for me alfo have fet.
5 Therefore I faid unto the Lord, Thou art my God alone:
Hear me therefore, O hear the Voice wherewith I pray and moan.
6 O Lord my God, thou only art the Strength that faveth me:
My Head in Day of Battle hath been cover'd ftill by thee.
7 Let not, O Lord, the Wicked have the End of his Defire:
Perform not his ill Thought, left he with Pride be fet on Fire.
8 Of them that compafs me about, the chiefeft of them all:
Lord, let the Mifchief of their Lips upon their own Heads fall.
9 Let Coals fall on them, let them be caft in confuming Flame:
And in deep Pit, that never they may rife out of the fame.
10 For no Backbiters fhall on Earth be fet in ftable Plight:
And Evil to Deftruction ftill fhall haunt the cruel Wight.
11 I know the Lord th' Afflicted will revenge, and judge the Poor:
The Juft fhall praife thy Name, and fhall dwell with thee evermore.

PSALM CXLI. N.

1 O Lord, upon thee do I call, then hafte thee unto me:
And hearken thou unto my Voice when I do cry to thee.
2 As Incenfe let my Pray'rs ftill be directed in thy Eyes:
And the up-lifting of my Hands, as Even-facrifice.

3 For

PSALM CXLII, CXLIII.

3 For guiding of my Mouth, O Lord,
   And alfo of my moving Lips,
4 That I fhould wicked Works commit,
   With ill Men of their Delicates,

5 But let the Righteous fmite me, Lord,
   Let him reprove me, and the fame
6 Such Smiting fhall not break my Head,
   When I fhall in their Mifery,

7 And when in ftony Places down
   Then fhall they hear my Words, becaufe
8 Our Bones about the Pit's Mouth are
   As when one breaketh, and doth hew

9 But, O my Lord and God, my Eyes
   In thee is all my Truft, let not
10 Keep and preferve me from the Snare
   And from the Gins of wicked Men,

11 The Wicked into their own Nets
   While I do by thy Help efcape

   fet thou a Watch before:
   O Lord, keep thou the Door.
   incline thou not my Heart:
   Lord, let me eat no Part.

   for that is good for me:
   a precious Oil fhall be.
   the Time fhall fhortly fall,
   fend Pray'rs up for them all.

   their Judges fhall be caft,
   they have a pleafant Tafte.
   all fcattered and found,
   the Wood upon the Ground.

   do look up unto thee:
   my Soul forfaken be.
   which they for me have laid:
   whereof I am afraid.

   together let them fall:
   the Danger of them all.

PSALM CXLII. N.

1 UNTO the Lord God with my Voice
   And with my ftrained Voice unto
2 My Meditation in his Sight
   And in the Prefence of the Lord

3 Altho' perplexed was my Soul,
   In Way where I did walk, a Snare
4 I look'd and view'd on my Right-hand,
   All Refuge failed me, and for

5 Then cried I to thee, and faid,
   And in the Land of the Living,
6 Hear now my Cry, for I am brought
   From them that do me perfecute,

7 That I may praife thy Name, my Soul
   When thou art good to me, the juft

   I did fend out my Cry,
   the Lord God prayed I.
   to pour I did not fpare:
   my Trouble did declare.

   my Path was known to thee:
   they flily laid for me.
   but none there would me know:
   my Soul none Care did fhow.

   O Lord, my Hope thou art:
   my Portion and my Part.
   full low, deliver me
   for me too ftrong they be.

   from Prifon, Lord, bring out:
   fhall compafs me about.

PSALM CXLIII. N.

1 LORD hear my Pray'r and my Complaint which I do make to thee
   And in thy naked Truth, and in
2 In Judgment with thy Servant, Lord,
   For juftify'd be in thy Sight

3 The Enemy purfu'd my Soul,
   And laid me in the Dark, like them
4 Therefore my Spirit in me is
   My Heart within me is alfo

5 Yet I record Time paft, and on
   Yea, I do mufe upon the Works
6 To thee, O Lord my God, do I
   My Soul defireth after thee,

7 Hear me with Speed, my Spirit fails,
   Be like to them that in the Pit

   thy Juftice anfwer me.
   O enter not at all:
   not one that liveth fhall.

   my Life to Ground hath thrown:
   that are to Grave gone down.
   in great Perplexity:
   afflicted grievoufly.

   thy Works I meditate:
   that thy Hands have create.
   ftretch forth my craving Hands:
   as do the thirfty Lands.

   hide not thy Face, left I
   fink down, and there do lie.

PSALM CXLIV, CXLV.

8 Let me thy loving Kindnefs in the Morning hear and know:
For in thee is my Truft, fhew me the Way that I fhould go.
9 For unto thee I lift my Soul, O Lord, deliver me;
From all my Enemies, for I have hid myfelf with thee.
10 Teach me to do thy Will, for thou, thou art my God alway:
Let thy good Spirit to the Land of Mercy me convey.
11 For thy Name Sake with quick'ning Grace, alive do thou me make:
And out of Trouble bring my Soul, ev'n for thy Juftice Sake.
12 And of thy Mercy flay my Foes, let them deftroyed be
That do opprefs my Soul, for I a Servant am to thee.

PSALM CXLIV. N.

1 BLEST be the Lord my Strength, that doth inftruct my Hands to fight:
The Lord that doth my Fingers frame to Battle by his Might.
2 He is my Hope, my Fort and Tow'r, Deliverer and Shield:
In him I truft, my People he fubdues to me to yield.

3 O Lord, what Thing is Man, that him thou doft fo highly prize?
Or Son of Man, that upon him thou thinkeft on fuch wife?
4 Man is but like to Vanity, fo pafs his Days to end
As fleeting Shade. Bow down, O Lord, the Heav'ns, and thence defcend.

5 The Mountains touch, and they fhall fmoke, caft forth thy Lightning Flame.
And fcatter them; thy Arrows fhoot, confume them with the fame.
6 Send down thy Hand from Heav'n above, O Lord, deliver me:
Take me from Waters great, from Hand of Strangers fet me free.

7 Whofe fubtle Mouth of Vanity, with flatt'ring Words doth treat,
And their Right-hand is a Right-hand of Falfhood and Deceit.
8 A new Song will I fing to thee, O God the Lord moft high
And on a ten-ftring'd Lute alfo, praife thee moft joyfully.

9 Ev'n he it is that only gives Deliverance to Kings:
Unto his Servant David Help from hurtful Sword he brings.
10 From Stranger's Hand me fave and fhield, whofe Mouth talks Vanity:
And their Right-hand is a Right-hand of Guile and Subtlety.

11 That fo our Sons may be as Plants, which growing Youth doth rear;
Our Daughters as carv'd Corner-ftones, like to a Palace fair.
12 Our Garners full, and Plenty may of fundry Sorts be found:
Our Sheep bring thoufands, in our Streets ten Thoufands may abound.

13 Our Oxen be to labour ftrong, that none may us invade:
No Goings-out there be, nor Cries within our Streets be made.
14 The People happy are that with fuch Bleffings great are ftor'd:
Yea, bleffed all the People are, whofe God is God the Lord.

PSALM CXLV. N.

1 THEE will I laud, my God and King, and blefs thy Name alway:
For ever will I praife the fame, and blefs thee Day by Day.
2 Great is the Lord, moft worthy Praife, his Greatnefs none can reach:
From Race to Race they fhall thy Works Praife, and thy Power preach.

3 I of thy glorious Majefty thy Beauty will record:
And meditate upon thy Works, moft wonderful, O Lord.
4 And they fhall of thy Pow'r, and of thy fearful Acts declare:
And I to publifh all abroad thy Greatnefs will not fpare.

5 And they into the Mention fhall break of thy Goodnefs great:
And I aloud thy Righteoufnefs in finging will repeat.

6 The

PSALM CXLVI, CXLVII.

6 The Lord our God moſt gracious is, and merciful alſo:
Of great abounding Mercy, and to Anger he is ſlow.
7 Yea, good to all, and all his Works his Mercy doth exceed:
Lo, all thy Works do praiſe thee, Lord, and honour thee indeed.
8 Thy Saints do bleſs thee, and they do thy Kingdoms Glory ſhow:
And blaze thy Pow'r, to cauſe the Sons of Men the ſame to know.

PART II.

9 And of thy Kingdoms Majeſty do ſpread thy glorious Praiſe:
Thy Kingdom, Lord, a Kingdom is that doth endure always.
10 And thy Dominion thro' each Age endures without Decay:
The Lord upholdeth them that fall, their Sliding he doth ſtay.
11 The Eyes of all do wait on thee, thou doſt them all relieve:
And thou to each ſufficing Food, in Seaſon due doſt give.
12 Thou openeſt thy plenteous Hand, and bounteouſly doſt fill
All Things whatever that do live, with Gifts of thy Good-will.
13 The Lord is juſt in all his Ways, his Works are holy all:
And he is near all thoſe that do in Truth upon him call.
14 He the Deſires which they require that fear him will fulfil:
And he will hear them when they cry, and ſave them all he will.
15 The Lord preſerves all thoſe to him that bear a loving Heart:
But he all them that wicked are will utterly ſubvert.
16 My thankful Mouth ſhall gladly ſpeak the Praiſes of the Lord:
All Fleſh to praiſe his holy Name for ever ſhall accord.

PSALM CXLVI. J. H.

1 MY Soul, praiſe thou the Lord always, my God I will confeſs:
While Breath and Life prolong my Days, my Tongue no Time ſhall ceaſe.
2 Truſt not in worldly Princes then, tho' they abound in Wealth:
Nor in the Sons of mortal Men. in whom there is no Health.
3 For why? their Breath doth ſoon depart, to Earth anon they fall:
And then the Counſels of their Heart decay and periſh all.
4 Bleſſed and happy are all they, whom Jacob's God doth aid:
And he whoſe Hope doth not decay, but on the Lord is ſtaid.
5 Who made the Earth and Waters deep, the Heav'ns moſt high withal:
Who doth his Word and Promiſe keep in Truth, and ever ſhall.
6 With Right always doth he proceed for ſuch as ſuffer Wrong:
The Poor and Hungry he doth feed, and looſe the Fetters ſtrong.
7 The Lord doth ſend the Blind their Sight, the Lame to Limbs reſtore:
He loveth all that are upright, and juſt Men evermore.
8 He doth defend the Fatherleſs, and Stranger ſad in Heart:
He frees the Widow from Diſtreſs, and ill Men's Ways ſubvert.
9 The Lord thy God eternally, O Sion, ſtill ſhall reign
In Time of all Poſterity, for ever to remain.

PSALM CXLVII. N.

1 PRAISE ye the Lord, for it is good unto our God to ſing:
For it is pleaſant, and to praiſe it is a comely Thing.
2 The Lord his own Jeruſalem he buildeth up alone:
And the Diſpers'd of Iſrael doth gather into one.
3 He heals the Broken in their Heart, their Sores up doth he bind:
He counts the Number of the Stars. and names them in their Kind.

PSALM CXLVIII.

4 Great is the Lord, great is his Pow'r, his Wisdom infinite:
   The Lord relieves the Meek, and throws to Ground the wicked Wight.
5 Sing unto God the Lord with Praise, unto the Lord rejoice:
   And to our God upon the Harp advance your singing Voice.
6 He covers Heav'n with Clouds, and for the Earth prepareth Rain:
   And on the Mountains he doth make the Grass to grow again.
7 He gives to Beasts their Food, and to young Ravens when they cry:
   His Pleasure not in Strength of Horse, nor in Man's Legs doth lie.
8 But in all those that do him fear, the Lord hath his Delight:
   And such as do depend upon his Mercies shining Light.

PART II.

9 O praise the Lord, Jerusalem, thy God, O Sion, praise:
   For he the Bars hath forged strong, wherewith thy Gates he stays.
10 Thy Children in thee he hath blest, and in thy Borders he
   Doth settle Peace, and with the Flour of Wheat he filleth thee.
11 And his Command likewise upon the Earth he sendeth out:
   Also his Word with speedy Course doth swiftly run about.
12 He giveth Snow like Wool, and Frost like Ashes scatters wide:
   Like Morsels cast his Ice, the Cold thereof who can abide.
13 He sendeth forth his mighty Word, and melteth them again:
   His Wind he makes to blow, and then the Waters flow amain.
14 The Doctrine of his holy Word to Jacob he doth shew:
   His Statutes and his Judgments he gives Israel to know.
15 With any Nation he hath not so dealt, nor have they known
   His secret Judgments, ye therefore praise ye the Lord alone.

PSALM CXLVIII. J. H.

1 GIVE Laud unto the Lord, From Heav'n that is so high
   Praise him in Deed and Word, Above the starry Sky;
   And also ye.
   His Angels all, Armies royal,
   Praise joyfully.

2 Praise him both Moon and Sun, Which are so clear and bright:
   The same of you be done, Ye glitt'ring Stars of Light.
   And you no less,
   Ye Heav'ns most fair, Clouds of the Air,
   His Laud express.

3 For at his Word they were All formed as we see:
   At his Voice did appear, All Things in their Degree.
   Which he set fast:
   To them he made A Law and Trade
   Always to last.

4 Extol and praise God's Name On Earth, ye Dragons fell,
   All Deeps do ye the same, For it becomes ye well;
   The same do ye,
   Fire, Hail, Ice, Snow, And Storms that blow
   At his Decree.

5 The Hills and Mountains all, And Trees that fruitful are:
   The Cedars great and tall, His worthy Praise declare;
   Beasts and Cattle,
   Yea, Birds of Wing, And Worms creeping,
   That on Earth dwell.

PSALM CXLIX, CL.

All Kings both great and small, / With all their pompous Train;
Princes and Judges all, / That in the World remain,
Exalt his Name:
Young Men and Maids, / Old Men and Babes,
Do ye the same.

For his Name shall we prove / To be most excellent,
Whose Praise is far above / The Earth and Firmament;
For sure he shall
Exalt with Bliss / The Horn of his,
And help them all.

His Saints all shall forth tell / His Praise and Worthiness:
The Sons of Israel, / Each one both more and less;
And also they
That with Good-will / His Words fulfil,
And him obey.

PSALM CXLIX. N.

SING ye unto the Lord our God, / a new rejoicing Song:
And let the Praise of him be heard / his holy Saints among,
Let Israel rejoice in God, / and Praises to him sing:
And let the Seed of Sion be / most joyful in their King.

Let them sound Praise with Voice and Lute / unto his holy Name:
And with the Timbrel and the Harp / sing Praises to the same,
For why? the Lord his Pleasure all / hath in his People set:
And by Deliv'rance he will raise / the Meek to Glory great.

With Glory and with Honour now / let all his Saints rejoice:
Aloud upon their Beds also / advance their singing Voice,
And in their Mouths let be the high / Praises of God the Lord:
And in their Hands likewise a sharp / and a two-edged Sword.

To plague the Heathen, and correct / the People with their Hands:
To bind their stately Kings in Chains, / their Lords in Iron Bands,
To execute on them the Doom / that written was before:
This Honour all his Saints shall have, / praise ye the Lord therefore.

PSALM CL. N.

YIELD unto God the mighty Lord, / Praise in his Holiness:
And in the Firmament of his / great Pow'r praise him no less,
Advance his Name, and praise him in / his mighty Acts always:
According to his Excellence / and Greatness give him Praise.

His Praises with the princely Noise / of sounding Trumpets blow:
Praise him upon the Viol, and / upon the Harp also,
Praise him with Timbrel and with Flute, / Organs and Virginals:
With sounding Cymbals praise ye him, / praise him with loud Cymbals.

Whatever hath the Benefit / of Breathing, praise the Lord:
To praise his great and holy Name, / agree with one Accord.

The End of the PSALMS.

VENI CREATOR.

COME Holy Ghost, eternal God,
Both from the Father and the Son,
Visit our Minds, and into us
That for all Truth and Godliness
proceeding from above:
the God of Peace and Love.
thy heav'nly Grace inspire:
we may have true Desire.

Thou art the very Comforter
The heav'nly Gift of God most high,
The Fountain and the living Spring
The Fire so bright, the Love so sweet,
in all Grief and Distress :
which no Tongue can express.
of Joy celestial:
and Unction spiritual.

Thou in thy Gifts art manifold,
In faithful Hearts writing thy Law,
According to thy Promise made,
That thro' thy Help the Praise of God
wherebyChrist'sChurch doth stand:
the Finger of God's Hand.
thou givest Speech with Grace:
may found in ev'ry Place.

O Holy Ghost, into our Souls
Enflame our Hearts with fervent Love
Our Weakness strengthen and confirm
That neither Devil, World, nor Flesh,
send down thy heav'nly Light :
to serve God Day and Night.
which feeble is and frail:
against us may prevail.

Our Enemies put far from us,
Peace in our Hearts with God and Man,
And grant, O Lord, that thou being,
We may eschew the Snares of Sin,
and grant us to obtain
the best and truest Gain.
our Leader and our Guide,
and never from thee slide.

To us such Plenty of thy Grace,
That thou may'st be our Comforter
Of Strife and all Dissention, Lord,
Tye fast the Knots of Peace and Love
good Lord grant, we thee pray,
at the last dreadful Day.
do thou dissolve the Bands :
thro'out all Christian Lands.

Grant us, O Lord, thro' thee to know,
That of his dear beloved Son
And that with perfect Faith also
The Spirit of them both alway,
the Father most of Might :
we may attain the Sight.
we may acknowledge thee,
one God in Persons three.

The humble Suit of a Sinner.

O Lord, on whom I do depend,
And when thy Will and Pleasure is,
Thou seest my Sorrows what they are,
And there is none that can remove,
behold my careful Heart :
release me of my Smart.
my Grief is known to thee:
or take the same from me;

But only thou whose Aid I crave,
To ease all those that come to thee
And since thou seest my restless Eyes,
Attend unto my Suit, O Lord,
whose Mercy still is prest,
for Succour and for Rest.
my Tears and grievous Groan,
mark my Complaint and Moan.

For Sin hath so enclosed me,
That I am now remediless,
For mortal Man cannot release,
But only Christ, my Lord and God,
and compass'd me about,
if Mercy help not out.
or mitigate my Pain :
who for my Sins was slain.

Whose bloody Wounds are yet to see,
Yet do thy Saints behold them, Lord,
Tho' Sin doth hinder me a While,
I shall enjoy the Sight of him
tho' not with mortal Eye :
and so I trust shall I.
when thou shalt see it Good,
who shed for me his Blood.

9 And as thy Angels and thy Saints do now behold the same:
So trust I to possess that Place, with them to praise thy Name.
10 But whilst I live here in this Vale where Sinners do frequent,
Assist me ever with thy Grace my Sins still to lament.
11 Lest that I tread the Sinners Path, and give them my Consent
To dwell with them in Wickedness, whereto Nature is bent.
12 Only thy Grace must be my Stay, let that with me remain:
For if I fail, then of myself I cannot rise again.
13 Wherefore this is yet once again, my Suit and my Request:
To grant me Pardon for my Sin, that I in thee may rest.
14 Then shall my Heart and Tongue also be Instruments of Praise:
And in thy Church and House of Saints sing Psalms to thee always.

The Song of Zacharias, called Benedictus.

1 THE only Lord of Israel be praised evermore:
For thro' his Visitation and his Mercy kept in Store,
2 His People now he hath redeem'd, that long have been in Thrall:
And spread abroad his saving Health upon his Servants all.

3 In David's House, his Servant true, according to his Mind:
And also his anointed King, as we in Scripture find.
4 As by his holy Prophets all he often did declare,
The which were since the World began, his Way for to prepare.

5 That we might be delivered from those that make Debate,
Ev'n from the Hands of Enemies, and all that do us hate.
6 The Mercy which he promised our Fathers to fulfil:
And think upon his Cov'nant made according to his Will.

7 And also to perform the Oath which he before had sworn
To Abraham our Father dear, for us that were forlorn:
8 That he would give himself for us, and us from Bondage bring
Out of the Hands of all our Foes to serve our heav'nly King.

9 And that without all Kind of Fear also in Righteousness:
And Likewise for to lead our Lives in stedfast Holiness.
10 And thou, O Child, who now art born, and of the Lord elect,
Shalt Prophet of the Highest be, his Way for to direct.

11 For thou shalt go before his Face, for to prepare his Ways;
And also for to teach his Will and Pleasure all thy Days.
12 To give them Knowledge how that their Salvation now is near:
And that Remission of their Sins is thro' his Mercy dear.

13 Whereby the Day-spring from on high descended from his Seat:
To give Light unto them that sat in Darkness very great.
14 To lighten those that shadow'd be with Death, and are oppress'd
And also for to guide our Feet the Way to Peace and Rest.

The Song of the Blessed Virgin Mary, called Magnificat.

1 MY Soul doth magnify the Lord, my Spirit evermore
Rejoiceth in the Lord my God, who is my Saviour.
2 And that because he did regard, and had Respect unto
The low Estate of his Hand-maid, and let the Mighty go.

3 For now behold all Nations, and the Generations all,
From this Time forth for evermore shall me right blessed call.
4 Because he hath me magnify'd, who is the Lord of Might:
Whose Name be ever sanctify'd, and praised Day and Night.

5 For with his Mercy and his Grace all Men he did inflame:
Thro'out the Generations all that fear his holy Name.
6 He shew'd Strength with his mighty Arm, and made the Proud to start:
With all Imaginations that were in their wicked Heart.
7 He hath put down the mighty Ones from their supernal Seat:
And did exalt the meek in Heart, ev'n from their low Estate.
8 The Hungry he replenished with all Things that were good:
And thro' his Pow'r he made the Rich Oft-times to want their Food.
9 And calling to Remembrance his great Mercy very well,
Hath holpen up most graciously his Servant Israel.
10 According to his Promise made to Abraham before:
And to his Seed successively to stand for evermore.

The Lamentation of a Sinner.

1 O Lord, turn not thy Face away from him that lies prostrate,
Lamenting sore his sinful Life before thy Mercy Gate.
2 Which thou dost open wide to those that do lament their Sin:
O shut it not against me, Lord, but let me enter in.
3 Call me not to a strict Account how I have lived here:
For then I know right well, O Lord, most vile I shall appear.
4 I need not to confess my Life, for surely thou canst tell
What I have been, and what I am, thou knowest very well.
5 O Lord, thou know'st what Things be past, also the Things that be:
Thou know'st also what is to come, Nothing is hid from thee.
6 Before the Heav'ns and Earth were made, thou knew'st what Things were then:
As all Things else that have been done among the Sons of Men.
7 And can the Things that I have done be hidden from thee then?
No, no, thou know'st them all, O Lord, where they were done and when.
8 Wherefore with Tears I come to thee, to beg and to entreat:
Ev'n as a Child that hath done Ill, and feareth to be beat.
9 So come I to the Throne of Grace, where Mercy doth abound:
Desiring Mercy for my Sin, to heal my deadly Wound.
10 O Lord, I need not to repeat what I do beg or crave:
For thou dost know before I ask, the Thing that I would have.
11 Mercy, good Lord, Mercy I ask, this is the total Sum:
For Mercy, Lord, is all my Suit, O let thy Mercy come.

The Lamentation.

1 O Lord, in thee is all my Trust, give ear unto my woful Cry:
Refuse me not that am unjust, but cast on me thy heav'nly Eye.
2 Behold how I do still lament my Sins wherein I do offend:
Shall I for them have Punishment, since thee to please I do intend.
3 No, no, thy Will is not so bent to deal with Sinners in thine Ire:
But when in Heart they do repent, with Speed thou grantest their Desire:
4 To thee therefore still will I cry, to wash away my sinful Crimes
Thy Blood, O Lord, is not yet dry, but that it may help me in Time.
5 Haste then, O Lord, therefore I pray, to pour on me the Gifts of Grace
That when this Life shall pass away, in Heav'n with thee I may have Place.
6 Where thou dost reign eternally with God, who once thee down did send:
Where Angels do incessantly sing Praise to thee World without End.

A

A Thankfgiving after the Receiving of the Lord's Supper.

1. THE Lord be thanked for his Gifts, and Mercies evermore,
That he doth fhew unto his Saints, to him be Laud therefore.
2. Our Tongues cannot fo praife the Lord as he doth right deferve:
Our Hearts cannot of him fo think as he doth us preferve.
3. His Benefits they be fo great to us who are but Sin,
That at our Hands a Recompence he cannot hope to win.
4. O finful Man, that thou fhouldft have fuch Mercies of the Lord!
Who doft deferve moft worthily of him to be abhorr'd.
5. Nought elfe but Sin and Wretchednefs doth reft within our Hearts:
And ftubbornly againft the Lord we daily aft our Parts.
6. The Sun that in the Firmament is fet for us a Light,
Doth fhew itfelf more clear and pure than we be in his Sight.
7. The Heav'ns above, and all therein, more holy are than we:
They ferve the Lord in their Eftate, each one in his Degree.
8. They do not ftrive for Mafterfhip, nor light their Office fet:
But ferve the Lord, and do his Will, there's Nothing can them let.
9. Alfo the Earth, and all therein, of God doth ftand in Awe,
Obferving the Creator's Will, by fkilful Nature's Law.
10. The Sea and all that is therein, doth bend when God doth beck,
Spirits beneath do tremble all, and fear his wrathful Check.
11. But we (alas!) for whom all thefe were made them for to rule,
Do not fo know or love the Lord as doth the Ox and Mule.
12. A Law he gave us for to know what was his holy Will:
He would us Good, but we would not avoid the Thing that's ill.
13. Not one of us that feeketh out the Lord of Life to pleafe:
Nor doth the Thing that might us lead to Chrift and quiet Eafe.
14. Thus we are all his Enemies, we can it not deny:
And he again of his Good-will would not that we fhould die.
15. Therefore when Remedy was none to bring us unto Life,
The Son of God our Flefh did take to end our mortal Strife.
16. And all the Law of God the Lord he fully did obey:
And for our Sins upon the Crofs his Blood our Debts did pay.
17. And that we never fhould forget what Good for us he wrought,
A Sign he left our Eyes to tell, that he our Bodies bought.
18. In Bread and Wine here vifible unto thy Eyes and Tafte:
His Mercies great thou may'ft record, if that his Grace thou haft.
19. As once the Corn did live and grow, and was cut down with Sithe,
And threfhed out with many Stripes, out of his Hufk to drive;
20. And as the Mill with Violence did tear it out fo fmall,
And make it like to earthly Duft, not fparing it at all.
21. And as the Oven with Fire hot doth clofe it up with Heat,
And all this done, as I have faid, that it fhould be our Meat:
22. So was the Lord in his ripe Age cut down by cruel Death
His Soul he gave in Torments great, and yielded up his Breath.
23. Becaufe that he to us might be an everlafting Bread:
With much Reproach and Troubles great, on Earth his Life he led.
24. And as the Grapes in pleafant Time are preffed very fore,
And plucked down when they be ripe, and let to grow no more:

25 Becaufe

25 Because the Juice that in them is as comfortable Drink
   We might receive, and joyful be when Sorrows make us shrin
26 So was the Blood of Christ press'd out also with Nails and Spear:
   The Juice thereof doth save all those that rightly do him fear.
27 And as the Corns by Unity into one Loaf are knit:
   So is the Lord and his whole Church, tho' he in Heav'n do sit.
28 As many Grapes make but one Wine, so should we be but one
   In Faith and Love in Christ above, and into Christ alone.
29 Leading a Life without all Strife, in Quiet, Rest and Peace:
   From Envy and from Malice both, our Hearts & Tongues should cease.
30 Which if we do, then shall we show that we his Chosen be:
   By Faith in him to lead a Life as always willed he.
31 And that we may so do indeed, God send us all his Grace:
   Then after Death we shall be sure with him to have a Place.

The Twelve Articles of the Christian Faith.

1 ALL my Relief and Confidence is in the Lord of Might:
   The Father who all Things hath made the Day and also Night.
2 The Heav'ns and Firmament likewise, and also every Star:
   The Earth and all that is therein, which pass Man's Reason far.
3 And in like Manner I believe in Christ our Lord his Son,
   Co-equal with the Deity, and Man in Flesh and Bone.
4 Conceived by the Holy Ghost, his Word doth me assure,
   And of his Mother Mary born, yet she a Virgin pure.
5 Because Mankind to Satan was for Sin in Bond and Thrall,
   He came and offer'd up himself to Death to save us all.
6 And suffering most grievous Pain, then Pilate being Judge,
   Was crucify'd upon the Cross, and thereat did not grudge.
7 And so he died in the Flesh, but quick'ned by the Spirit:
   His Body then was buried, that we might Life inherit.
8 His Soul did after this descend into the lower Parts:
   A Dread to wicked Spirits, but Joy unto faithful Hearts.
9 And on the third Day of his Death, he rose to Life again,
   That so he might be glorify'd, and freed from Grief and Pain,
10 Ascending up above the Heav'ns, to sit in Glory still,
   On God's Right-hand his Father dear, according to his Will.
11 Until the Day of Judgment, when he shall return again:
   With Angel's Pow'r, tho' of that Day we ignorant remain.
12 To judge all People righteously, whom he hath dearly bought:
   The Living and the Dead also, whom he hath made of Nought.
13 And in the Holy Ghost also, Author of Purity:
   In Trinity the Third Person, believe I stedfastly:
14 The Catholick and holy Church, that God's Word doth maintain:
   And holy Scripture doth allow, which Satan doth disdain.
15 And also I do trust to have by Jesus Christ his Death,
   Release and Pardon of my Sins, and that only by Faith:
16 What Time all Flesh shall rise again before the Lord of Might:
   And see him with their outward Eyes which now do give them Light:
17 Then shall our Saviour Jesus Christ, the Sheep and Goats divide,
   That he may give eternal Life to those whom he hath try'd.

18 Within

18 Within his Realm celeſtial, in Glory for to reſt:
With all his holy Company of Saints and Angels bleſt.
19 Who ſerve the Lord Omnipotent, and him always adore:
To whom be all Dominion, and all Praiſe for evermore.

PRESERVE us Lord, by thy dear Word From Turk and Pope defend us, Lord:
Both which would thruſt out of his Our Lord Chriſt Jeſus, thy dear Son.
Throne
Lord Jeſus Chriſt, ſhew us thy Might, That thou art Lord of Lords by Right:
Thy poor afflicted Flock defend, That we may praiſe thee without End.

God, Holy Ghoſt, the Comforter, Be our Patron, Help and Succour:
Give us one Mind, and perfect Peace, All Gifts of Grace in us increaſe.
Thou living God in Perſons Three, Thy Name be prais'd in Unity:
In all our Need ſo us defend, That we may praiſe thee without End.

The Lord's Prayer, or Pater Noſter.

1 OUR Father which in Heaven art, Lord, Hallowed be thy Name.
Thy Kingdom come. Thy Will be done, in Earth, ev'n as the ſame
2 In Heaven is. Give us, O Lord, our daily Bread this Day.
As we forgive our Debtors, ſo forgive our Debts we pray:
3 Into Temptation lead us not, from Evil keep us from:
For Kingdom, Power, and Glory is thine to Eternity.

GLORIA PATRI.

To Father, Son, and Holy Ghoſt, all Glory be therefore:
As in Beginning was, is now, and ſhall be evermore.

ANOTHER.

To Father, Son, and Holy Ghoſt, immortal Glory be:
As was, and is, and ſhall be ſtill, to all Eternity.

ANOTHER.

All Glory to the Trinity, that is of Mighties moſt:
To God the living Father, and the Son and Holy Ghoſt.
As it hath been in all the Time that hath been heretofore:
As it is now, and ſo ſhall be, henceforth for evermore.

To the HUNDREDTH PSALM Tune.

To Father, Son, and Holy Ghoſt, all Praiſe and Glory be therefore,
As in Beginning was, is now, and ſo ſhall be for evermore.

F I N I S.

A New Version

OF THE

PSALMS

OF

DAVID,

fitted to the TUNES used in CHURCHES.

BY

N. BRADY, D. D. Chaplain in Ordinary, and N. TATE, Esq; Poet-Laureat to His Majesty.

(With Permission of the Stationer's Company.)

BIRMINGHAM,

Printed by JOHN BASKERVILLE, 1762.

(Price One Shilling and Sixpence in Sheets.)

May *the* 23d, 1698.

*H*IS *Majefty having Allowed and Permitted the Ufe of a* New Verfion of the Pfalms of *David*, by Dr. *Brady* and Mr. *Tate, in all* Churches, Chapels and Congregations; *I cannot do lefs than wifh a good Succefs to this* Royal Indulgence; *For I find it a* WORK *done with fo much* Judgment *and* Ingenuity, *that I am perfuaded, it may take off that unhappy Objection, which has hitherto lain againft the* Singing Pfalms; *and difpofe that Part of Divine Service to much more Devotion. And I do heartily recommend the Ufe of* this Verfion *to all my Brethren within my Diocefe.*

H. LONDON.

An Alphabetical TABLE, shewing how to find each PSALM by its Beginning.

A	Psalm
AGAINST all those	35
As pants the Hart	42
At length by certain	73
B.	
Behold, O God	79
Bless God, my Soul	104
Bless God, ye Servants	134
D.	
Defend me, Lord	31
Deliver me, O Lord	59
Do thou, O God	56
F.	
For ever bless'd	144
For thee, O God	63
From lowest Depths	130
From my Youth	129
G.	
Give ear, thou Judge	55
God in the great	82
God is our Refuge	46
God's Temple crowns	87
H.	
Had not the Lord	124
Happy the Man	41
Have Mercy, Lord	51
Hear, O my People	78
He's blest, whose Sins	32
He that has God	91
Hold not thy Peace	83
How blest are they	119
How blest is he	1
How good and pleasant	92
How long wilt	13
How num'rous, Lord	3
How vast must	133
I.	
Jehovah reigns, let all	97
Jehovah reigns, let therefore	99
I'll celebrate thy	30
In deep Distress	120
In Judah the	76
In thee I put	71
In vain, O Man	52
Judge me, O Lord	26
Just Judge of Heav'n	43
I waited meekly	40
L.	
Let all the Just	33
Let all the Lands	66
Let all the list'ning	49

	Psalm
Let David, Lord	132
Let God, the God	68
Lord, hear my Cry	61
Lord, hear my Pray'r	143
Lord, hear the Voice	5
Lord, hear the Voice	64
Lord, let thy just	72
Lord, not to us	115
Lord, save me, for	54
Lord, thou hast	85
Lord, who's the	15
M.	
My crafty Foe with	36
My God, my God	22
My Soul for Help	62
My Soul, inspir'd	103
My Soul with	116
N.	
No Change of Times	18
O.	
O all ye People	47
O come, loud Anthems	95
Of Mercy's never	101
O God, my gracious	69
O God, my Heart	108
O God of Hosts	84
O God, to whom	94
O God, who hast	60
O God, whose	109
O Israel's Shepherd	80
O Lord, I am not	131
O Lord, my God	7
O Lord, my Rock	28
O Lord, our Fathers	44
O Lord, the Saviour	90
O Lord, that art my	4
O Lord, to my	70
On thee who dwell'st	123
O praise the Lord with	135
O praise the Lord, for	111
O praise the Lord in	150
O praise the Lord and	146
O praise the Lord with Hymns	147
O praise the Lord with one Consent	139
O praise ye the Lord	140
O render Thanks	105
O render Thanks to	106
O thou, to whom all	8
O 'twas a joyful	122
Praise

An Alphabetical TABLE, &c.

P.	Psalm
Praise ye the Lord	111
Preserve me, Lord	140
Protect me from my	16

R.	
Resolv'd to watch	39

S.	
Save me, O God	69
Since godly Men	12
Since I have plac'd	11
Sing to the Lord	96
Sing to the Lord	98
Speak, O ye Judges	58
Sure, wicked Fools	14

T.	
Thee I'll extol	145
The Heavens declare	19
The King, O Lord,	21
The Lord hath spoke	50
The Lord himself	23
The Lord, the only	48
The Lord to thy	20
The Lord unto my	110
That Man is blest who stands	112
The Man is blest who fears	128
The wicked Fools	53
This spacious Earth	24
Tho' wicked Men	37
Thou, Lord, by	139
Thy chast'ning Wrath	38
Thy dreadful Anger	6
Thy Mercies, Lord	89
Thy Mercy, Lord	57
Through all the	34
To bless thy chosen	67

	Psalm
Thy Presence why	10
To celebrate thy	9
To God I cry'd	77
To God, in whom	25
To God our never	81
To God the mighty	136
To God with mournful	142
To God your grateful	107
To my Complaint	86
To my just Plea	17
To thee, my God	88
To thee, O God	75
To thee, O Lord	141
To Sion's Hill	121

W.	
We build with	127
When I pour out	102
When Isr'el by	114
When Sion's God	126
When we our	137
While I the King's	45
Whom should I fear	27
Who place on Sion's	125
Why hast thou cast	74
With chearful	117
With Glory clad	93
With my whole	138
With one Consent	100
With restless and	2

Y.	
Ye boundless Realms	148
Ye Princes that	29
Ye Saints and Servants	113

DIREC-

DIRECTIONS
ABOUT THE
TUNES and MEASURES

ALL Pſalms of this Verſion in the *Common Meaſure* of Eights and Sixes (that is, where the firſt and third Lines of the ſingle Stanza conſiſt of eight Syllables each, the ſecond and fourth Lines of ſix Syllables each) may be ſung to any of the moſt uſual Tunes: namely, *York*-tune, *Windſor*-tune, St. *David*'s, *Lichfield*, *Canterbury*, *Martyrs* St. *Mary*'s, alias *Hackney*, St. *Ann*'s-tune, &c.

As the Old 25 Pſalm, may be ſung the New 25, 31, 51, 67, 130, 142.

As the Old 113, the 37, 46, 50, 63, 76, 91 110, 113, 120.

As the Old 148, the 136, 148.

As the Old 104, the 149.

The Pſalms in this Verſion of four Lines in a ſingle Stanza, and eight Syllables in each Line (in Pſalms of Praiſe or Chearfulneſs) may properly be ſung as the Old 100 Pſalm, or to the Tune of the Old 125 Pſalm, ſecond Metre.

The Penitential or Mournful Pſalms in the ſame Meaſure, may be ſung as the Old 51 Pſalm; which Tunes, with all the fore-mentioned, are printed in the *Supplement* to this New Verſion.

A New

A New Version of the PSALMS, &c.

PSALM I.

HOW blest is he who ne'er consents by ill Advice to walk;
Nor stands in Sinners Ways, nor sits where Men profanely talk.
2 But makes the perfect Law of God his Business and Delight;
Devoutly reads therein by Day, and meditates by Night.
Like some fair Tree, which fed by Streams with timely Fruit does bend,
He still shall flourish, and Success all his Designs attend.
Ungodly Men and their Attempts no lasting Root shall find;
Untimely blasted and dispers'd like Chaff before the Wind.
Their Guilt shall strike the Wicked dumb before the Judge's Face;
No formal Hypocrite shall then amongst the Saints have place.
For God approves the just Man's Ways, to Happiness they tend;
But Sinners and the Paths they tread, shall both in Ruin end.

PSALM II.

WITH restless and ungovern'd Rage. why do the Heathen storm?
Why in such rash Attempts engage as they can ne'er perform.
The great in Counsel and in Might, their various Forces bring;
Against the Lord they all unite, and his anointed King.
Must we submit to their Commands? presumptuously they say:
No, let us break their slavish Bands, and cast their Chains away.
But God who sits inthron'd on high, and sees how they combine,
Does their conspiring Strength defy, and mocks their vain Design.
Thick Clouds of Wrath divine shall break on his rebellious Foes:
And thus will he in Thunder speak to all that dare oppose.
" Though madly you dispute my Will, " the King that I ordain,
" Whose Throne is fix'd on Sion's Hill, " shall there securely reign."
Attend, O Earth, whilst I declare God's uncontrol'd Decree;
" Thou art my Son, this Day my Heir " have I begotten thee.
" Ask and receive thy full Demands, " thine shall the Heathen be;
" The utmost Limits of the Lands " shall be possess'd by thee.
" Thy threat'ning Sceptre thou shalt shake, " and crush them ev'ry where;
" As massy Bars of Iron break " the Potter's brittle Ware."
Learn then, ye Princes, and give ear, ye Judges of the Earth;
Worship the Lord with holy Fear, rejoice with awful Mirth.
Appease the Son with due Respect, your timely Homage pay;
Lest he revenge the bold Neglect, incens'd by your Delay.
If but in part his Anger rise, who can endure the Flame?
Then blest are they whose Hope relies on his most holy Name.

PSALM III.

HOW num'rous, Lord, of late are grown the Troublers of thy Peace!
And as their Numbers hourly rise, so does their Rage increase.
Insulting they my Soul upbraid, and him whom I adore;
The God in whom he trusts, say they, shall rescue him no more.
But thou, O Lord, art my Defence; on thee my Hopes rely;
Thou art my Glory, and shalt yet lift up my Head on high.
Since, whensoe'er in my Distress to God I made my Pray'r,
He heard me from his holy Hill, why should I now despair?

B   5 Guarded

5 Guarded by him, I laid me down my sweet Repose to take:
  For I through him securely sleep, through him in Safety wake.
6 No Force nor Fury of my Foes my Courage shall confound,
  Were they as many Hosts as Men, that have beset me round.
7 Arise and save me, O my God, who oft hast own'd my Cause,
  And scatter'd oft these Foes to me and to thy righteous Laws.
8 Salvation to the Lord belongs, he only can defend;
  His Blessing he extends to all that on his Pow'r depends.

PSALM IV.

1 O Lord, that art my righteous Judge, to my Complaint give Ear;
  Thou still redeem'st me from Distress, have Mercy, Lord, and hear.
2 How long will ye, O Sons of Men, to blot my Fame devise?
  How long your vain Designs pursue, and spread malicious Lies?
3 Consider, that the righteous Man is God's peculiar Choice;
  And when to him I make my Pray'r, he always hears my Voice.
4 Then stand in awe of his Commands, flee ev'ry Thing that's ill;
  Commune in private with your Hearts, and bend them to his Will.
5 The Place of other Sacrifice let Righteousness supply;
  And let your Hope, securely fixt, on God alone rely.
6 While worldly Minds impatient grow more prosp'rous Times to see,
  Still let the Glories of thy Face shine brightly, Lord, on me.
7 So shall my Heart o'erflow with Joy more lasting and more true,
  Than theirs, who Stores of Corn and Wine successively renew.
8 Then down in Peace I'll lay my Head, and take my needful Rest;
  No other Guard, O Lord, I crave, of my Defence possest.

PSALM V.

1 LORD, hear the Voice of my Complaint, accept my secret Pray'r;
2 To thee alone, my King, my God, will I for Help repair.
3 Thou in the Morn my Voice shalt hear; and with the dawning Day
  To thee devoutly I'll look up, to thee devoutly pray.
4 For thou the Wrongs that I sustain canst never, Lord, approve;
  Who from thy sacred Dwelling-place all Evil dost remove.
5 Not long shall stubborn Fools remain unpunish'd in thy View:
  All such as act unrighteous Things thy Vengeance shall pursue.
6 The sland'ring Tongue, O God of Truth, by thee shall be destroy'd,
  Who hat'st alike the Man in Blood and in Deceit employ'd.
7 But when thy boundless Grace shall me to thy lov'd Courts restore,
  On thee I'll fix my longing Eyes, and humbly there adore.
8 Conduct me by thy righteous Laws, for watchful is my Foe:
  Therefore, O Lord, make plain the Way wherein I ought to go.
9 Their Mouth vents nothing but Deceit, their Heart is set on Wrong;
  Their Throat is a devouring Grave, they flatter with their Tongue.
10 By their own Counsels let them fall, oppress'd with Loads of Sin;
  For they against thy righteous Laws have harden'd Rebels been.
11 But let all those who trust in thee, with Shouts their Joy proclaim
  Let them rejoice whom thou preserv'st, and all that love thy Name.
12 To righteous Men, the righteous Lord his Blessing will extend,
  And with his Favour all his Saints, as with a Shield defend.

PSALM VI, VII.

PSALM VI.

1 THY dreadful Anger, Lord, restrain, and spare a Wretch forlorn;
   Correct me not in thy fierce Wrath, too heavy to be borne.
2 Have Mercy, Lord, for I grow faint, unable to endure
   The Anguish of my aking Bones, which thou alone canst cure.
3 My tortur'd Flesh distracts my Mind, and fills my Soul with Grief;
   But, Lord, how long wilt thou delay to grant me thy Relief!
4 Thy wonted Goodness, Lord, repeat, and ease my troubled Soul;
   Lord, for thy wond'rous Mercy's sake, vouchsafe to make me whole.
5 For after Death no more can I thy glorious Acts proclaim;
   No Pris'ners of the silent Grave can magnify thy Name.
6 Quite tir'd with Pain, with groaning faint, no Hope of Ease I see;
   The Night, that quiets common Griefs, is spent in Tears by me.
7 My Beauty fades, my Sight grows dim, my Eyes with Weakness close;
   Old Age o'ertakes me, whilst I think on my insulting Foes.
8 Depart, ye Wicked; in my Wrongs ye shall no more rejoice;
   For God, I find, accepts my Tears, and listens to my Voice.
9, 10 He hears, and grants my humble Pray'r; and they that with my Fall,
   Shall blush and rage to see that God protects me from them all.

PSALM VII.

1 O Lord, my God, since I have plac'd my Trust alone in thee,
   From all my Persecutors Rage do thou deliver me.
2 To save me from my threat'ning Foe, Lord, interpose thy Pow'r;
   Lest, like a savage Lion, he my helpless Soul devour.
3, 4 If I am guilty, or did e'er against his Peace combine;
   Nay, if I have not spar'd his Life, who fought unjustly mine,
5 Let them to persecuting Foes my Soul become a Prey;
   Let them to Earth tread down my Life, in Dust my Honour lay.
6 Arise, and let thine Anger, Lord, in my Defence engage;
   Exalt thyself above thy Foes, and their insulting Rage:
   Awake, awake, in my Behalf, the Judgment to dispense,
   Which thou hast righteously ordain'd for injur'd Innocence.
7 So to thy Throne adoring Crowds shall still for Justice fly;
   O! therefore for their Sakes resume thy Judgment-Seat on high.
8 Impartial Judge of all the World, I trust my Cause to thee;
   According to my just Deserts, so let thy Sentence be.
9 Let wicked Arts and wicked Men, together be o'erthrown;
   But guard the Just, thou God, to whom the Hearts of both are known.
10, 11 God he protects, not only me, but all of upright Heart;
   And daily lays up Wrath for those who from his Laws depart.
12 If they persist, he whets his Sword, his Bow stands ready bent;
13 Ev'n now with swift Destruction wing'd, his pointed Shafts are sent.
14 The Plots are fruitless which my Foe unjustly did conceive:
15 The Pit he digg'd for me has prov'd his own untimely Grave.
16 On his own Head his Spite returns, whilst I from Harm am free!
   On him the Violence is fall'n, which he design'd for me.
17 Therefore will I the righteous Ways of Providence proclaim;
   I'll sing the Praise of God most High, and celebrate his Name.

PSALM VIII, IX.

PSALM VIII.

1 O Thou, to whom all Creatures bow   within this earthly Frame,
   Thro' all the World how great art thou! how glorious is thy Name!
   In Heav'n thy wond'rous Acts are sung,   nor fully reckon'd there;
2 And yet thou mak'st the Infant-Tongue   thy boundless Praise declare:
   Thro' thee the Weak confound the Strong, and crush their haughty Foes;
   And so thou quell'st the wicked Throng, that thee and thine oppose.
3 When Heav'n, thy beauteous Work on high, employs my wond'ring Sight;
   The Moon, that rightly rules the Sky,   with Stars of feebler Light;
4 What's Man (say I) that, Lord, thou lov'st to keep him in my Mind?
   Or what his Offspring, that thou prov'st to them so wond'rous kind?
5 Him next in Pow'r thou did'st create   to thy celestial Train;
6 Ordain'd with Dignity and State,   o'er all thy Works to reign.
7 They jointly own his pow'rful Sway;   the Beasts that prey or graze;
8 The Bird that wings its airy Way;   the Fish that cuts the Seas.
9 O thou, to whom all Creatures bow   within this earthly Frame,
   Thro' all the World how great art thou! how glorious is thy Name!

PSALM IX.

1 TO celebrate thy Praise, O Lord,   I will my Heart prepare;
   To all the list'ning World thy Works,   thy wond'rous Works declare.
2 The Thought of them shall to my Soul   exalted Pleasures bring;
   Whilst to thy Name, O thou most High, triumphant Praise I sing.
3 Thou mad'st my haughty Foes to turn   their Backs in shameful Flight;
   Struck with thy Presence down they fell, they perish'd at thy Sight.
4 Against insulting Foes advanc'd   thou did'st my Cause maintain;
   My Right asserting from thy Throne,   where Truth and Justice reign.
5 The Insolence of Heathen Pride   thou hast reduc'd to Shame;
   Their wicked Offspring quite destroy'd, and blotted out their Name.
6 Mistaken Foes! your haughty Threats   are to a Period come:
   Our City stands, which you design'd   to make our common Tomb.
7, 8 The Lord for ever lives, who has   his righteous Throne prepar'd,
   Impartial Justice to dispense,   to punish or reward.
9 God is a constant sure Defence   against oppressing Rage;
   As Troubles rise, his needful Aids   in our Behalf engage.
10 All those who have his Goodness prov'd will in his Truth confide;
   Whose Mercy ne'er forsook the Man   that on his Help rely'd.
11 Sing Praises therefore to the Lord;   from Sion his Abode,
   Proclaim his Deeds, till all the World confess no other God.

PART II.

12 When he enquiry makes for Blood,   he'll call the Poor to mind:
   The injur'd humble Man's Complaint   Relief from him shall find.
13 Take pity on my Troubles, Lord,   which spiteful Foes create,
   Thou that hast rescu'd me so oft   from Death's devouring Gate.
14 In Sion then I'll sing thy Praise,   to all that love thy Name;
   And with loud Shouts of grateful Joy   thy saving Pow'r proclaim.
15 Deep in the Pit they digg'd for me,   the Heathen Pride is laid;
   Their guilty Feet to their own Snare   insensibly betray'd.
16 Thus by the just Returns he makes   the mighty Lord is known;
   While wicked Men by their own Plots   are shamefully o'erthrown.

PSALM X, XI.

17 No single sinner shall escape by Privacy obscur'd;
   Nor Nation from his just Revenge by Numbers be secur'd.
18 His suff'ring Saints, when most distrest, he ne'er forgets to aid;
   Their Expectation shall be crown'd, though for a Time delay'd.
19 Arise, O Lord, assert thy Pow'r, and let not Man o'ercome;
   Descend to Judgment, and pronounce the guilty Heathen's Doom.
20 Strike Terror thro' the Nations round, till, by consenting Fear,
   They to each other, and themselves, but mortal Men appear.

PSALM X.

1 THY Presence why withdraw'st thou, Lord? why hid'st thou now thy Face,
     When dismal Times of deep Distress call for thy wonted Grace?
2 The wicked, swell'd with lawless Pride, have made the Poor their Prey,
   O let them fall by those Designs which they for others lay.
3 For straight they triumph, if Success their thriving Crimes attend:
   And sordid Wretches, whom God hates, perversly they commend.
4 To own a Pow'r above themselves their haughty Pride disdains;
   And therefore in their stubborn Mind no Thought of God remains.
5 Oppressive Methods they pursue, and all their Foes they slight;
   Because thy Judgments unobserv'd are far above their Sight.
6 They fondly think their prosp'rous State shall unmolested be;
   They think their vain Designs shall thrive, from all Misfortune free.
7 Vain and deceitful is their Speech, with Curses fill'd and Lies;
   By which the Mischief of their Heart they study to disguise.
8 Near public Roads they lie conceal'd, and all their Art employ,
   The Innocent and Poor at once to rifle and destroy.
9 Not Lions, couching in their Dens, surprise their heedless Prey
   With greater Cunning, or express more savage Rage than they.
10 Sometimes they act the harmless Man, and modest Looks they wear;
   That so deceiv'd, the Poor may less their sudden Onset fear.

PART II.

11 For God they think, no Notice takes of their unrighteous Deeds;
   He never minds the suff'ring Poor, nor their Oppression heeds.
12 But thou, O Lord, at length arise; stretch forth thy mighty Arm;
   And, by the Greatness of thy Pow'r. defend the Poor from Harm.
13 No longer let the Wicked vaunt, and proudly boasting say,
   " Tush, God regards not what we do, " he never will repay."
14 But sure thou seest, and all their Deeds impartially dost try;
   The Orphan therefore and the Poor on thee for Aid rely.
15 Defenceless let the Wicked fall, of all their Strength bereft;
   Confound, O God, their dark Designs, till no Remains are left.
16 Assert thy just Dominion, Lord, which shall for ever stand;
   Thou who the Heathen didst expel from this thy chosen Land.
17 Thou dost the humble Suppliants hear that to thy Throne repair;
   Thou first prepar'st their Hearts to pray, and then accept'st their Pray'r.
18 Thou in thy righteous Judgment weigh'st the Fatherless and Poor;
   That so the Tyrants of the Earth may prosecute no more.

PSALM XI.

1 SINCE I have plac'd my Trust in God, a Refuge always nigh,
   Why should I, like a tim'rous Bird, to distant Mountains fly?
                                                      2 Behold,

PSALM XII, XIII, XIV.

2 Behold, the Wicked bend their Bow, and ready fix their Dart;
Lurking in Ambush to destroy the Man of upright Heart.
3 When once the firm Assurance fails which public Faith imparts,
'Tis Time for Innocence to fly from such deceitful Arts.
4 The Lord hath both a Temple here, and righteous Throne above;
Where he surveys the Sons of Men, and how their Counsels move.
5 If God, the Righteous, whom he loves, for Trial does correct;
What must the Sons of Violence, whom he abhors, expect?
6 Snares, Fire, and Brimstone on their Heads shall in one Tempest show'r;
This dreadful Mixture his Revenge into their Cup shall pour.
7 The righteous Lord with righteous Deeds with signal Favour grace;
And to the upright Man disclose the Brightness of his Face.

PSALM XII.

1 SINCE godly Men decay, O Lord, do thou my Cause defend:
For scarce these wretched Times afford one just and faithful Friend.
2 One Neighbour now can scarce believe what t'other doth impart:
With flatt'ring Lips they all deceive, and with a double Heart.
3 But Lips that with Deceit abound can never prosper long;
God's righteous Vengeance will confound the proud blaspheming Tongue.
4 In vain those foolish Boasters say, " our Tongues are sure our own
" With doubtful Words we'll still betray, " and be control'd by none."
5 For God, who hears the suff'ring Poor, and their Oppression knows,
Will soon arise and give them Rest, in spite of all their Foes.
6 The Word of God shall still abide, and void of Falshood be;
As is the Silver sev'n Times try'd, from drossy Mixture free.
7 The Promise of his aiding Grace shall reach its purpos'd End;
His Servants from this faithless Race he ever shall defend.
8 Then shall the Wicked be perplex'd, nor know which Way to fly;
When those whom they despis'd and vex'd, shall be advanc'd on high.

PSALM XIII.

1 HOW long wilt thou forget me, Lord? Must I for ever mourn?
How long wilt thou withdraw from me? oh! never to return?
2 How long shall anxious Thoughts my Soul, and Grief my Heart oppress;
How long my Enemies insult, and I have no Redress?
3 O hear! and to my longing Eyes restore thy wonted Light;
And suddenly, or I shall sleep in everlasting Night.
4 Restore me, lest they proudly boast 'twas their own Strengh o'ercam
Permit not them that vex my Soul to triumph in thy Shame.
5 Since I have always plac'd my Trust beneath thy Mercy's Wing,
Thy saving Health will come, and then my Heart with Joy shall spring
6 Then shall my Song, with Praise inspir'd, to thee my God ascend;
Who to thy Servant in Distress such Bounty didst extend.

PSALM XIV.

1 SURE, wicked Fools must needs suppose that God is nothing but a Nam
Corrupt and lewd their Practice grows, no Breast is warm'd with holy Flam
2 The Lord look'd down from Heav'n's high Tow'r, and all the Sons of Men did vie
To see if any own'd his Pow'r, if any Truth or Justice knew.

PSALM XV, XVI.

3 But all, he saw, were gone afide, all were degen'rate grown and bafe;
None took Religion for their Guide, not one of all the finful Race.
4 But can thefe Workers of Deceit be all fo dull and fenfelefs grown;
That they, like Bread, my People eat, and God's Almighty Pow'r difown?
5 How will they tremble then for Fear, when his juft Wrath fhall them o'ertake?
For, to the Righteous, God is near, and never will their Caufe forfake.
6 Ill Men in vain with Scorn expofe thofe Methods which the Good purfue;
Since God a Refuge is for thofe whom his juft Eyes with Favour view.
7 Would he his faving Pow'r employ, to break his People's fervile Band!
Then Shouts of univerfal Joy, fhould loudly echo through the Land.

PSALM XV.

1 LORD, who's the happy Man that may to thy bleft Courts repair?
Not, Stranger-like, to vifit them, but to inhabit there?
2 'Tis he, whofe ev'ry Thought and Deed by Rules of Virtue moves;
Whofe gen'rous Tongue difdains to fpeak the Thing his Heart difproves.

3 Who never did a Slander forge his Neighbour's Fame to wound;
Nor hearken to a falfe Report, by Malice whifper'd round.
4 Who Vice, in all its Pomp and Pow'r, can treat with fuch Neglect;
And Piety, tho' cloth'd in Rags, religioufly refpect.

Who to his plighted Vows and Truft has ever firmly ftood;
And tho' he promife to his Lofs he makes his Promife good.
5 Whofe Soul in Ufury difdains his Treafure to employ;
Whom no Rewards can ever bribe, the Guiltlefs to deftroy.

6 The Man who by his fteady Courfe has Happinefs infur'd,
When Earth's Foundation fhakes, fhall ftand, by Providence fecur'd.

PSALM XVI.

1 PROTECT me from my cruel Foes and fhield me, Lord, from Harm;
Becaufe my Truft I ftill repofe on thy Almighty Arm.
2 My Soul all Help but thine does flight, all Gods but thee difown;
Yet can no Deeds of mine requite the Goodnefs thou haft fhown.

3 But thofe that ftrictly virtuous are, and love the Thing that's right,
To favour always and prefer fhall be my chief Delight,
4 How fhall their Sorrows be increas'd, who other Gods adore?
Their bloody Off'rings I deteft, their very Names abhor.

5 My Lot is fall'n in that bleft Land where God is truly known;
He fills my Cup with lib'ral Hand; 'tis he fupports my Throne.
6 In Nature's moft delightful Scene my happy Portion lies;
The Place of my appointed Reign all other Lands out-vies.

7 Therefore my Soul fhall blefs the Lord, whofe Precepts give me Light,
And private Counfel ftill afford in Sorrow's difmal Night.
8 I ftrive each Action to approve to his all-feeing Eye;
No Danger fhall my Hopes remove, becaufe he ftill is nigh.

9 Therefore my Heart all Grief defies, my Glory does rejoice;
My Flefh fhall reft, in hope to rife, wak'd by his powerful Voice.
10 Thou, Lord, when I refign my Breath, my Soul from Hell fhalt free;
Nor let thy holy One in Death the leaft Corruption fee.

11 Thou fhalt the Paths of Life difplay, which to thy Prefence lead;
Where Pleafures dwell without allay, and Joys that never fade.

PSALM

PSALM XVII, XVIII.

PSALM XVII.

1 TO my juſt Plea and ſad Complaint, attend, O righteous Lord,
   And to my Pray'r, as 'tis unfeign'd, a gracious Ear afford.
2 As in thy Sight I am approv'd, ſo let my Sentence be;
   And with impartial Eyes, O Lord, my upright Dealing ſee,

3 For thou haſt ſearch'd my Heart by Day, and viſited by Night;
   And on the ſtricteſt Trial found its ſecret Motions right.
   Nor ſhall thy Juſtice, Lord, alone my Heart's Deſigns acquit:
   For I have purpos'd that my Tongue ſhall no Offence commit.

4 I know what wicked Men would do their Safety to maintain;
   But me thy juſt and mild Commands from bloody Paths reſtrain.
5 That I may ſtill, in ſpite of Wrongs, my Innocence ſecure;
   O guide me in thy righteous Ways, and make my Footſteps ſure.

6 Since heretofore I ne'er in vain to thee my Pray'r addreſt;
   O now, my God, incline thine Ear to this my juſt Requeſt.
7 The Wonders of thy Truth and Love in my Defence engage,
   Thou whoſe Right-hand preſerves thy Saints from their Oppreſſors Rage.

PART II.

8, 9 O! keep me in thy tend'reſt Care; thy ſhelt'ring Wings ſtretch out,
    To guard me ſafe from ſavage Foes, that compaſs me about.
10 O'er grown with Luxury, incloſ'd in their own Fat they lie;
   And with a proud blaſpheming Mouth both God and Man defy.

11 Well may they boaſt; for they have now my Paths incompaſs'd round;
   Their Eyes at watch, their Bodies bow'd, and couching on the Ground.
12 In Poſture of a Lion ſet, when greedy of his Prey;
   Or a young Lion, when he lurks within a covert Way.

13 Ariſe, O Lord, defeat their Plots, their ſwelling Rage control;
   From wicked Men, who are thy Sword, deliver thou my Soul;
14 From worldly Men, thy ſharpeſt Scourge, whoſe Portion's here below;
   Who, fill'd with earthly Stores, aſpire no other Bliſs to know;

15 Their Race is num'rous, that partake their Subſtance while they live:
   Their Heirs ſurvive, to whom they may the vaſt Remainder give.
16 But I, in Uprightneſs, thy Face ſhall view without control;
   And, waking, ſhall its Image find reflected in my Soul.

PSALM XVIII.

1,2 NO Change of Times ſhall ever my firm Affection, Lord, to thee;
     ſhock
   For thou haſt always been a Rock, a Fortreſs and Defence to me.
   Thou my Deliv'rer art, my God; my Truſt is in thy mighty Pow'r;
   Thou art my Shield from Foes abroad, At Home my Safe-guard and my Tow'r.

3 To thee I'll ſtill addreſs my Pray'r, (to whom all Praiſe we juſtly owe;)
   So ſhall I, by thy watchful Care, be guarded from thy treach'rous Foe.
4, 5 By Floods of wicked Men diſtreſs'd, with deadly Sorrows compaſs'd round,
    With dire infernal Pangs oppreſs'd, in Death's unwieldy Fetters bound.

6 To Heav'n I made my mournfull'ray'r, to God addreſs'd my humble Moan;
   Who graciouſly inclin'd his Ear, and heard me from his lofty Throne.

PART

PSALM XVIII.

PART II.

7 When God arose to take my Part, the conscious Earth did quake for Fear;
From their firm Posts the Hills did start, nor could his dreadful Fury bear.
8 Thick Clouds of Smoke disperst abroad, Ensigns of Wrath before him came;
Devouring Fire around him glow'd, that Coals were kindled at its Flame.

9 He left the beauteous Realms of Light, whilst Heav'n bow'd down its awful Head;
Beneath his Feet substantial Night was like a sable Carpet spread.
10 The Chariot of the King of Kings, which active Troops of Angels drew,
On a strong Tempest's rapid Wings, with most amazing Swiftness flew.

11,12 Black watry Mists & Clouds conspir'd with thickest Shades his Face to veil;
But at his Brightness soon retir'd, and fell in Show'rs of Fire and Hail.
13 Thro' Heav'n's wide Arch a thund'ring God's angry Voice did loudly roar;
Peal,
While Earth's sad Face, with Heaps of Hail and Flakes of Fire, was cover'd o'er.

14 His sharpen'd Arrows round he threw, which made his scatter'd Foes retreat;
Like Darts, his nimble Light'nings flew, and quickly finish'd their Defeat.
15 The deep its secret Stores disclos'd; the World's Foundations naked lay,
By his avenging Wrath expos'd, which fiercely rag'd that dreadful Day.

PART III.

16 The Lord did on my Side engage, from Heav'n (his Throne) my Cause upheld;
And snatch'd me from the furious Rage of threat'ning Waves that proudly swell'd.
17 God his resistless Pow'r employ'd, my strongest Foes Attempts to break;
Who else with Ease had soon destroy'd the weak Defence that I could make.

18 Their subtle Rage had near prevail'd, when I distrest and friendless lay;
But still when other Succours fail'd, God was my firm Support and Stay.
19 From Dangers that inclos'd me round, he brought me forth, and set me free:
For some just Cause his Goodness found, that mov'd him to delight in me,

20 Because in me no Guilt remains, God does his gracious Help extend;
My Hands are free from bloody Stains, therefore the Lord is still my Friend.
21, 22 For I his Judgements kept in Sight; in his just Paths I always trod;
I never did his Statutes flight, nor loosly wander'd from my God.

23, 24 But still my Soul, sincere and pure, did ev'n from darling Sins refrain;
His Favours therefore yet endure, because my Heart and Hands are clean.

PART IV.

25, 26 Thou suit'st, O Lord, thy righteous to various Paths of Human-kind;
Ways
They who for Mercy merit Praise, with thee shall wond'rous Mercy find.
Thou to the Just shalt Justice shew, the Pure thy Purity shall see;
Such as perversly chuse to go, shall meet with due Returns from thee.

27, 28 That he the humble Soul will save, and crush the Haughty's boasted Might,
In me the Lord an Instance gave, whose Darkness he has turn'd to Light.
29 On his firm Succour I rely'd, and did o'er num'rous Foes prevail;
Nor fear'd, whilst he was on my Side, the best defended Walls to scale.

30 For God's Designs shall still succeed; his Word will bear the utmost Test;
He's a strong Shield to all that need, and on his sure Protection rest.
31 Who then deserves to be ador'd, but God, on whom my Hopes depend?
Or who, except the mighty Lord, can with resistless Pow'r defend?

PART

PSALM XIX.

PART V.

32, 33 'Tis God that girds my Armour on, and all my juſt Deſigns fulfils;
Thro' him my Feet can ſwiftly run, and nimbly climb the ſteepeſt Hills,
34 Leſſons of War from him I take, and manly Weapons learn to wield;
Strong Bows of Steel with Eaſe I break, forc'd by my ſtronger Arms to yield.

35 The Buckler of his ſaving Health protects me from aſſaulting Foes;
His Hand ſuſtains me ſtill, my Wealth and Greatneſs from his Bounty flows.
36 My Goings he enlarg'd abroad, till then to narrow Paths confin'd;
And, when in ſlipp'ry Ways I trod, the Method of my Steps deſign'd.

37 Thro' him I num'rous Hoſts defeat, and flying Squadrons captive take;
Nor from my fierce Purſuit retreat, till I a final Conqueſt make.
38 Cover'd with Wounds, in vain they try, their vanquiſh'd Heads again to rear;
Spite of their boaſted Strength they lie beneath my Feet, and grovel there.

39 God, when freſh Armies take the Field, recruits my Strength, my Courage warms;
He makes my ſtrong Oppoſers yield, ſubdu'd by my prevailing Arms.
40 Through him the Necks of proſtrate Foes my conqu'ring Feet in Triumph preſs;
Aided by him, I root out thoſe who hate and envy my Succeſs.

41 With loud Complaints a'l Friends they try'd, but none was able to defend;
At length to God for Help they cry'd, but God would no Aſſiſtance lend.
42 Like flying Duſt which Winds purſue, their broken Troops I ſcatter'd round:
Their ſlaughter'd Bodies forth I threw, like loathſome Dirt that clogs the Ground.

PART VI.

43 Our factious Tribes, at Strife till now, by God's Appointment me obey;
The Heathen to my Scepter bow, and foreign Nations own my Sway.
44 Remoteſt Realms their Homage ſend, when my ſucceſsful Name they hear;
Strangers for my Commands attend, charm'd with Reſpect, or aw'd by Fear.

45 All to my Summons tamely yield, or ſoon in Battle are diſmay'd;
For ſtronger Holds they quit the Field, and ſtill in ſtrongeſt Holds afraid.
46 Let the eternal Lord be prais'd, the Rock on whoſe Defence I reſt!
O'er higheſt Heav'ns his Name be rais'd, who me with his Salvation bleſs'd!

47 'Tis God that ſtill ſupports my Right, his juſt Revenge my Foes purſues;
'Tis he, that with reſiſtleſs Might, fierce Nations to my Yoke ſubdues.
48 My univerſal Safeguard, he! from whom my laſting Honours flow;
He made me great, and ſet me free, from my remorſeleſs bloody Foe.

49 Therefore to celebrate his Fame, my grateful Voice to Heav'n I'll raiſe;
And Nations, Strangers to his Name, ſhall thus be taught to ſing his Praiſe;
50 " God to his King Deliv'rance ſends, " ſhews his Anointed ſignal Grace;
" His Mercy evermore extends " to David and his promis'd Race.

PSALM XIX.

1 THE Heav'ns declare thy Glory, Lord, which that alone can fill?
The Firmament and Stars expreſs their great Creator's Skill.
2 The Dawn of each returning Day, freſh Beams of Knowledge brings;
From darkeſt Night's ſucceſſive Rounds divine Inſtructions ſprings.

3 Their pow'rful Language to no Realm or Region is confin'd:
'Tis Nature's Voice, and underſtood alike by all Mankind.
4 Their Doctrine does its ſacred Senſe thro' Earth's Extent diſplay:
Whoſe bright Contents the circling Sun does round the World convey.

5 No Bridegroom, for his Nuptials dreſt, has ſuch a chearful Face;
No Giant does like him rejoice, to run his glorious Race.
6 From Eaſt to Weſt, from Weſt to Eaſt, his reſtleſs Courſe he goes:
And thro' his Progreſs chearful Light and vital Warmth beſtows.

PART II.

7 God's perfect Law converts the Soul, reclaims from falſe Deſires;
With ſacred Wiſdom his ſure Word the Ignorant inſpires.
8 The Statutes of the Lord are juſt, and bring ſincere Delight;
His pure Commands, in Search of Truth, aſſiſt the feebleſt Sight.
9 His perfect Worſhip here is fix'd, on ſure Foundations laid:
His equal Laws are in the Scales of Truth, and Juſtice weigh'd,
10 Of more Eſteem than golden Mines, or Gold refin'd with Skill;
More ſweet than Honey, or the Drops than from the Comb diſtil.
11 My truſty Counſellors they are, and friendly Warnings give;
Divine Rewards attend on thoſe who by thy Precepts live.
12 But what frail Man obſerves, how oft he does from Virtue fall?
O cleanſe me from my ſecret Faults, thou God that knows them all.
13 Let no preſumptuous Sin, O Lord, Dominion have o'er me;
That, by thy Grace preſerv'd, I may the great Tranſgreſſion flee.
14 So ſhall my Pray'r and Praiſes be with thy Acceptance bleſt;
And I ſecure on my Defence, my Strength and Saviour, reſt.

PSALM XX.

1 THE Lord to my Requeſt attend, and hear thee in Diſtreſs:
The Name of Jacob's God defend, and grant thy Arms Succeſs.
2 To aid thee from on high repair, and Strength from Sion give;
3 Remember all thy Off'rings there, Thy Sacrifice receive.
4 To compaſs thy own Heart's Deſire thy Counſels ſtill direct;
May kindly all Events conſpire to bring them to effect.
5 To thy Salvation, Lord, for Aid we chearfully repair,
With Banners in thy Name diſplay'd, " the Lord accept thy Pray'r.
6 Our Hopes are fix'd, that now the Lord our Sov'reign will defend,
From Heav'n reſiſtleſs Aid afford, and to his Pray'r attend.
7 Some truſt in Steeds for War deſign'd, on Chariots ſome rely;
Againſt them all we'll call to mind the Pow'r of God moſt high.
8 But from their Steeds and Chariots thrown, Behold them thro' the Plain,
Diſorder'd, broke and trampled down, whilſt firm our Troops remain
9 Still ſave us, Lord, and ſtill proceed our rightful Cauſe to bleſs,
Hear, King of Heav'n, in Times of Need, the Pray'rs that we addreſs.

PSALM XXI.

1 THE King, O Lord, with Songs of Praiſe ſhall in thy Strength rejoice.
With thy Salvation crown'd ſhall raiſe to Heav'n his chearful Voice.
2 For thou, whate'er his Lips requeſt, not only didſt impart;
But haſt with thy Acceptance bleſt the Wiſhes of his Heart.
3 Thy Goodneſs and thy tender Care have all his Hopes out-gone;
A Crown of Gold thou mad'ſt him wear, and ſet'ſt it firmly on,
4 He pray'd for Life, and thou, O Lord, didſt his ſhort Span extend;
And graciouſly to him afford a Life that ne'er ſhall end.

5 Thy

PSALM XXII.

5 Thy sure Defence thro' Nations round has spread his glorious Name;
   And his successful Actions crown'd   with Majesty and Fame.
6 Eternal Blessings thou bestow'st,   and mak'st his Joys increase;
   Whilst thou to him unclouded show'st the Brightness of thy Face.

PART II.

7 Because the King on God alone   for timely Aid relies;
   His Mercy still supports his Throne, and all his Wants supplies.
8 But, righteous Lord, thy stubborn Foes shall feel thy heavy Hand;
   Thy vengeful Arm shall find out those that hate thy mild Command.
9 When thou against them dost engage,   thy just but dreadful Doom,
   Shall, like a glowing Oven's Rage,   their Hopes and them consume.
10 Nor shall thy furious Anger cease,   or with their Ruin end;
   But root out all their guilty Race,   and to their Seed extend.
11 For all their Thoughts were set on Ill, their Hearts on Malice bent;
   (But thou with watchful Care did'st still the ill Effects prevent.)
12 In vain by shameful Flight they'll try to 'scape thy dreadful Might;
   While thy swift Darts shall faster fly, and gall them in their Flight.
13 Thus, Lord, thy wond'rous Strength disclose, and thus exalt thy Fame;
   Whilst we glad Songs of Praise compose to thy Almighty Name.

PSALM XXII.

1 MY God, my God, why leav'st thou me when I with Anguish faint?
   O why so far from me remov'd,   and from my loud Complaint?
2 All Day, but all the Day unheard,   to thee do I complain:
   With Cries implore Relief all Night, but cry all Night in vain.
3 Yet thou art still the righteous Judge of Innocence opprefs'd;
   And therefore Isr'el's Praises are   of Right to thee addrefs'd.
4, 5 On thee our Ancestors rely'd,   and thy Deliv'rance found;
   With pious Confidence they pray'd,   and with Success were crown'd.
6 But I am treated like a Worm,   like none of human Birth:
   Not only by the Great revil'd,   but made the Rabble's Mirth.
7 With Laughter all the gazing Crowd   my Agonies survey,
   They shoot the Lip, they shake the Head, and thus deriding say;
8 " In God he trusted, boasting oft   " that he was Heav'n's Delight;
   " Let God come down to save him now, " and own his Favourite."

PART II.

9 Thou mad'st my teeming Mother's Womb a living Offspring bear;
   When but a Suckling at the Breast,   I was thy early Care.
10 Thou, Guardian-like, didst shield from Wrongs my helpless Infant Days;
   And since hast been my God and Guide, thro' Life's bewilder'd Ways.
11 Withdraw not then so far from me,   when Trouble is so nigh:
   O send me Help! thy Help, on which   I only can rely.
12 High pamper'd Bulls, a frowning Herd, from Bason's Forest met;
   With Strength proportion'd to their Rage, have me around befet.
13 They gape on me, and ev'ry Mouth   a yawning Grave appears;
   The Defart Lion's savage Roar   less dreadful is than theirs.

PART III.

14 My Blood like Water's spill'd, my Joints are rack'd and out of Frame;
   My Heart dissolves within my Breast, like Wax before the Flame.

15 My

PSALM XXIII.

My Strength like Potter's Earth is parch'd, my Tongue cleaves to my Jaws;
And to the silent Shades of Death My fainting Soul withdraws.

Like Blood-hounds to surround me, they in packt Assemblies meet;
They pierc'd my inoffensive Hands, they pierc'd my harmless Feet.
My Body's rack'd till all my Bones distinctly may be told:
Yet such a Spectacle of Woe, as Pastime they behold.

As Spoil my Garments they divide, Lots for my Vesture cast:
Therefore approach, O Lord, my Strength, and to my Succour haste.
From their sharp Swords protect thou me, (of all but Life bereft!)
Nor let thy Darling in the Pow'r of cruel Dogs be left.

To save me from the Lion's Jaws, thy present Succour send;
As once from goring Unicorns, thou did'st my Life defend.
Then to my Brethren I'll declare the Triumphs of thy Name,
In Presence of assembled Saints, thy Glory thus proclaim.

" Ye Worshippers of Jacob's God, " all you of Isr'el's Line.
" O praise the Lord, and to your Praise " sincere Obedience join.
" He ne'er disdain'd on low Distress " to cast a gracious Eye;
" Nor turn'd from Poverty his Face, " but hears its humble Cry."

PART IV.

5 Thus in thy sacred Courts will I my chearful Thanks express,
In Presence of thy Saints perform the Vows of my Distress.
6 The meek Companions of my Grief shall find my Table spread,
And all that seek the Lord shall be with Joys immortal fed.

7 Then shall the glad converted World to God their Homage pay;
And scatter'd Nations of the Earth one sov'reign Lord obey.
8 'Tis his supreme Prerogative o'er Subject-Kings to reign:
'Tis just that he should rule the World, who does the World sustain.

9 The Rich, who are with Plenty fed, his Bounty must confess;
The Sons of Want, by him reliev'd, their gen'rous Patron bless.
With humble Worship to his Throne they all for Aid resort;
That Pow'r which first their Beings gave, can only them support.

0, 31 Then shall a chosen spotless Race devoted to his Name,
To their admiring Heirs his Truth and glorious Acts proclaim.

PSALM XXIII.

THE Lord himself, the mighty Lord, vouchsafes to be my Guide;
The Shepherd by whose constant Care my Wants are all supply'd.
In tender Grass he makes me Feed, and gently there repose;
Then leads me to cool Shades, and where refreshing Waters flows.

He does my wand'ring Soul reclaim, and to his endless Praise,
Instruct with humble Zeal to walk in his most righteous Ways.
I pass the gloomy Vale of Death from Fear and Danger free;
For there his aiding Rod and Staff defend and comfort me.

In Presence of my spiteful Foes he does my Table spread,
He crowns my Cup with chearful Wine, with Oil anoints my Head.
Since God does thus his wond'rous Love through all my Life extend,
That Life to him I will devote, and in his Temple spend.

PSALM XXIV, XXV.

PSALM XXIV.

1 THIS spacious Earth is all the Lord's, the Lord's her Fulness is;
The World, and they that dwell therein, by sov'reign Right are his.
2 He fram'd and fix'd it on the Seas, and his Almighty Hand,
Upon inconstant Floods has made the stable Fabric stand.

3 But for himself this Lord of all, one chosen Seat design'd:
O! who shall to that sacred Hill deserv'd Admittance find?
4 The Man whose Hands and Heart are pure, whose Thoughts from Pride are
Who honest Poverty prefers to gainful Perjury.

5 This, this is he, on whom the Lord shall show'r his Blessings dov
Whom God his Saviour shall vouchsafe with Righteousness to crown,
6 Such is the Race of Saints, by whom the sacred Courts are trod;
And such the Proselytes that seek the Face of Jacob's God.

7 Erect your Heads, eternal Gates, unfold, to entertain
The King of Glory: see, he comes with his celestial Train.
8 Who is the King of Glory? who? the Lord for Strength renow:
In Battle mighty, o'er his Foes eternal Victor crown'd.

9 Erect your Heads, ye Gates, unfold in State to entertain
The King of Glory: see, he comes with all his shining Train.
10 Who is the King of Glory? who? the Lord of Hosts renown'd:
Of Glory he alone is King, who is with Glory crown'd.

PSALM XXV.

1, 2 TO God, in whom I trust, I lift my Heart and Voice;
O let me not be put to Shame, nor let my Foes rejoice.
3 Those who on thee rely let no Disgrace attend;
Be that the shameful Lot of such as wilfully offend.

4, 5 To me thy Truth impart, and lead me in thy Way;
For thou art he that brings me Help, on thee I wait all Day.
6 Thy Mercies and thy Love, O Lord, recal to mind;
And graciously continue still, as thou wert ever kind.

7 Let all my youthful Crimes be blotted out by thee;
And for thy wond'rous Goodness sake, in Mercy think on me.
8 His Mercy and his Truth the righteous Lord displays,
In bringing wand'ring Sinners Home, and teaching them his Ways.

9 He those in Justice guides who his Direction seek;
And in his sacred Paths shall lead the Humble and the Meek.
10 Thro' all the Ways of God both Truth and Mercy shine,
To such as with religious Hearts to his blest Will incline.

PART II.

11 Since Mercy is the Grace that most exalts thy Fame,
Forgive my heinous Sin, O Lord, and so advance thy Name.
12 Whoe'er with humble Fear to God his Duty pays,
Shall find the Lord a faithful Guide in all his righteous Ways.

13 His quiet Soul with Peace shall be for ever blest,
And by his num'rous Race the Land successively possest.
14 For God to all his Saints his secret Will imparts,
And does his gracious Cov'nant write in their obedient Hearts.

PSALM XXVI, XXVII.

5 To him I lift my Eyes,
Who breaks the strong and treach'rous Snare,
5 O turn, and all my Griefs
For I am compass'd round with Woes,
and wait his timely Aid,
which for my Feet was laid.
in Mercy, Lord, redress;
and plung'd in deep Distress.

7 The Sorrows of my Heart
O from this dark and dismal State
8 Do thou with tender Eyes
Acquit me, Lord, and from my Guilt
to mighty Sums increase:
my troubled Soul release!
my sad Affliction see;
intirely set me free.

9 Consider, Lord, my Foes.
What lawless Force and Rage they use,
10 Protect and set my Soul
Nor let me be asham'd, who place
how vast their Numbers grow!
what boundless Hate they show!
from their fierce Malice free;
my stedfast Trust in thee.

Let all my righteous Acts
Because my firm and constant Hope
11 To Isr'el's chosen Race
And in the midst of all their Wants
to full Perfection rise,
on thee alone relies.
continue ever kind:
let them thy Succour find.

PSALM XXVI.

JUDGE me, O Lord, for I the Paths
I cannot fail, who all my Trust
4 Search, prove my Heart, whose Innocence
For I have kept thy Grace in view
of Righteousness have trod;
repose on thee, my God.
will shine the more 'tis try'd;
and made thy Truth my Guide.

I never for Companions took
No Hypocrite with all his Arts,
I hate the busy plotting Crew,
And shun their wicked Company,
the Idle or Prophane:
could e'er my Friendship gain.
who make distracted Times;
as I avoid their Crimes.

I'll wash my Hands in Innocence,
That when thy Altar I approach,
8 My Thanks I'll publish there, and tell
That Seat affords me most Delight,
and bring a Heart so pure;
my Welcome shall secure.
how thy Renown excels;
in which thy Honour dwells.

Pass not on me the Sinners Doom,
Who others Rights by secret Bribes,
But I will walk in Paths of Truth,
Protect me therefore, and to me
who Murder make their Trade;
or open Force invade.
and Innocence pursue:
thy Mercies, Lord, renew.

In spite of all assaulting Foes
And shall survive amongst thy Saints,
I still maintain my Ground:
thy Praises to resound.

PSALM XXVII.

WHOM should I fear, since God to me
Since strongly he my Life supports,
With fierce Intent my Flesh to tear,
They stumbled, and their lofty Crests
is saving Health and Light?
what can my Soul affright?
when Foes beset me round,
were made to strike the Ground.

Through him my Heart, undaunted, dares
Through him in doubtful Straits of War,
Henceforth within his House to dwell
His wond'rous Beauty there to view,
with num'rous Hosts to cope;
for good Success I hope.
I earnestly desire,
and his blest Will inquire.

For there may I with Comfort rest,
And safe as on a Rock abide,
Whilst God o'er all my haughty Foes
And I my joyful Off'ring bring,
in Times of deep Distress,
in that secure Recess;
my lofty Head shall raise,
and sing glad Songs of Praise.

PSALM XXVIII, XXIX.
PART II.

7 Continue, Lord, to hear my Voice,
 In Mercy all my Pray'rs receive,
8 When thou to seek thy glorious Face
 " Thy glorious Face I'll always seek,"
9 Then hide not thou thy Face, O Lord,
 My God and Saviour, leave not him
10 Tho' all my Friends and nearest Kin
 Yet thou whose Love excels them all,

11 Instruct me in thy Paths, O Lord,
 Lest envious Men, who watch my Steps,
12 Lord, disappoint my cruel Foes,
 Whose lying Lips and bloody Hands

13 I trusted that my future Life
 Or else my fainting Soul had sunk
14 God's Time with patient Faith expect,
 With inward Strength; do thou thy Part,

whene'er to thee I cry;
nor my Request deny;
thou kindly dost advise;
my grateful Heart replies.
nor me in Wrath reject;
thou didst so oft protect.
their helpless Charge forsake,
wilt Care and Pity take.

my Ways directly guide,
should see me tread aside.
defeat their ill Desire,
against my Peace conspire.

should with thy Love be crown'd
with Sorrow compass'd round,
and he'll inspire thy Breast
and leave to him the rest.

PSALM XXVIII.

1 O Lord, my Rock, to thee I cry,
  O answer, or I shall become
2 Regard my Supplication, Lord,
 With weeping Eyes and lifted Hands

3 Let me escape the Sinners Doom,
 And ever speak the Person fair,
4 According to their Crimes Extent,
 Relentless be to them, as they

5 Since they the Works of God despise,
 His Wrath shall utterly destroy,
6 But I, with due Adknowledgment,
 From whom the Cries of my Distress

7 My Heart its Confidence repos'd,
 In him I trusted, and return'd
 As he has made my Joys complete,
 The chearful Tribute of my Thanks,

8 " His aiding Pow'r supports the Troops
 " 'Twas he advanc'd me to the Throne,
9 Preserve thy Chosen, and proceed
 With Plenty prosper them in Peace;

in Sighs consume thy Breath;
like those that sleep in Death.
the Cries that I repeat,
before thy Mercy Seat.

who make a Trade of Ill,
whose Blood they mean to spill.
let Justice have its Course;
have sinn'd without Remorse.

nor will his Grace adore,
and build them up no more.
his Praises will resound,
a gracious Answer found.

in God, my Strength and Shield,
triumphant from the Field.
'tis just that I should raise
and thus resound his Praise:

" that my just Cause maintain:
" 'tis he secures my Reign,"
thine Heritage to bless;
in Battle with Success.

PSALM XXIX.

1 YE Princes that in Might excel,
  God's glorious Actions loudly tell,
2 To his great Name fresh Altars raise,
 Him in his holy Temple praise,

3 'Tis he that with amazing Noise
 The Ocean trembles at his Voice,
4, 5 How full of Pow'r his Voice appears!
 Which from their Roots tall Cedars tears,

6 They, and the Hills on which they grow,
 And leap, like Hinds that bounding go,

your grateful Sacrifice prepare;
his wond'rous Pow'r to all declare.
devoutly due Respect afford;
where he's with solemn State ador'd.

the wat'ry Clouds in sunder breaks;
when he from Heav'n in Thunder speaks
with what majestic Terror crown'd!
and strews their scatter'd Branches round

are sometimes hurried far away;
or Unicorns in youthful Play.

PSALM XXX, XXXI.

8 When God in Thunder loudly speaks, and scatter'd Flames of Lightning sends,
the Forest nods, the Desart quakes, and stubborn Kadesh lowly bends.

He makes the Hinds to cast their Young, and leaves the Beasts dark Coverts bare;
While those that to his Courts belong, securely sing his Praises there.
11 God rules the angry Floods on high; his boundless Sway shall never cease,
His People he'll with Strength supply, and bless his own with constant Peace.

PSALM XXX.

I'LL celebrate thy Praises, Lord,   who didst thy Pow'r employ
To raise thy drooping Head, and check my Foes insulting Joy.
3 In my Distress I cry'd to thee,   who kindly didst relieve,
And from the Grave's expecting Jaws   my hopeless Life retrieve.

Thus to his Courts ye Saints of his   with Songs of Praise repair;
With me commemorate his Truth,   and providential Care.
His Wrath has but a Moment's Reign,   his Favour no Decay;
Your Night of Grief is recompens'd   with Joy's returning Day.

But I in prosp'rous Days presum'd;   no sudden Change I fear'd,
Whilst in thy Sun-shine of Success   no low'ring Cloud appear'd.
But soon I found thy Favour, Lord,   my Empire's only Trust;
For when thou hid'st thy Face, I saw   my Honour laid in Dust.

Then, as I vainly had presum'd,   my Error I confess'd,
And thus with supplicating Voice;   thy Mercy's Throne address'd:
" What Profit is there in my Blood,   " conjeal'd by Death's cold Night?
" Can silent Ashes speak my Praise,   " thy wond'rous Truth recite?

Hear me, O Lord, in Mercy hear,   " thy wonted Aid extend;
" Do thou send Help, on whom alone   " I can for Help depend."
'Tis done! thou hast my mournful Scene to Songs and Dances turn'd;
Invested me in Robes of State,   who late in Sackcloth mourn'd.

Exalted thus, I'll gladly sing   thy Praise in grateful Verse;
And, as thy Favours endless are,   thy endless Praise rehearse.

PSALM XXXI.

DEFEND me, Lord, from Shame,   for still I trust in thee;
As just and righteous is thy Name,   from Danger set me free.
Bow down thy gracious Ear,   and speedy Succour send;
Do thou my stedfast Rock appear,   to shelter and defend.

Since thou, when Foes oppress,   my Rock and Fortress art,
To guide me forth from this Distress, thy wonted Help impart.
Release me from the Snare   which they have closely laid,
Since I, O God, my Strength repair   to thee alone for Aid.

To thee, the God of Truth,   my Life, and all that's mine,
(For thou preserv'dst me from my Youth) I willingly resign.
All vain Designs I hate,   of those that trust in Lyes;
And still my Soul in ev'ry State,   to God for Succour flies.

PART II.

Those Mercies thou hast shown   I'll chearfully express;
For thou hast seen my Straits, and known my Soul in deep Distress.
When Keilah's treach'rous Race   did all my Strength enclose,
Thou gav'st my Feet a larger Space   to shun my watchful Foes.

PSALM XXXII.

9 Thy Mercy, Lord, display, and hear my just Complaint;
For both my Soul and Flesh decay, with Grief and Hunger faint.
10 Sad Thoughts my Life oppress, my Years are spent in Groans;
My Sins have made my Strength decrease, and ev'n consum'd my Bones.

11 My Foes my Suff'rings mock'd, my Neighbours did upbraid;
My Friends at Sight of me were shock'd, and fled as Men dismay'd.
12 Forsook by all am I, as dead, and out of mind:
And like a shatter'd Vessel lie, whose Parts can ne'er be join'd.

13 Yet sland'rous Words they speak, and seem my Pow'r to dread,
Whilst they together Counsel take, my guiltless Blood to shed.
14 But still my stedfast Trust, I on thy Help repose;
That thou, my God, art good and just, my Soul with Comfort knows.

PART III.

15 Whate'er Events betide, thy Wisdom times them all;
Then, Lord, thy Servant safely hide from those that seek his Fall.
16 The Brightness of thy Face to me, O Lord, disclose;
And, as thy Mercies still increase, preserve me from my Foes.

17 Me from Dishonour save who still have call'd on thee;
Let that, and Silence in the Grave, the Sinner's Portion be.
18 Do thou their Tongues restrain, whose Breath in Lyes are spent
Who false Reports, with proud Disdain, against the Righteous vent.

19 How great thy Mercies are to such as fear thy Name!
Which thou, for those that trust thy Care, dost to the World proclaim.
20 Thou keep'st them in thy Sight, from proud Oppressors free;
From Tongues that do in Strife delight they are preserv'd by thee.

21 With Glory and Renown God's Name be ever bless'd;
Whose Love in Keilah's well-fenc'd Town was wond'rously express'd!
22 I said in hasty Flight, "I'm banish'd from thine Eyes
Yet still thou keep'st me in thy Sight, and heard'st my earnest Cries.

23 O all ye Saints, the Lord with eager Love pursue,
Who to the Just will Help afford, and give the Proud their due.
24 Ye that on God rely, couragiously proceed:
For he will still your Hearts supply with Strength in Time of Need.

PSALM XXXII.

1 HE's blest, whose Sins have Pardon gain'd no more in Judgment to appear;
2 Whose Guilt Remission has obtain'd, and whose Repentance is sincere.
3 While I conceal'd the fretting Sore, my Bones consum'd without Relief
All Day did I with Anguish roar, but no Complaint asswag'd my Grief.

4 Heavy on me thy Hand remain'd, by Day and Night alike distress'd:
Till quite of vital Moisture drain'd, like Land with Summer's Drought oppr'st
5 No sooner I my Wound disclos'd, the Guilt that tortur'd me within,
But thy Forgiveness interpos'd, and Mercy's healing Balm pour'd in.

6 True Penitents shall thus succeed, who seek thee whilst thou may'st be found
And from the common Deluge freed, shall see remorseless Sinners drown'd.
7 Thy Favour, Lord, in all Distress, my Tow'r of Refuge I must own;
Thou shalt my haughty Foes suppress, and me with Songs of Triumph crown.

8 In my Instruction then confide, you that would Truth's safe Path desi'e
Your Progress I'll securely guide, and keep you in my watchful Eye.

PSALM XXXIII, XXXIV.

9 Submit yourselves to Wisdom's Rule,   like Men that Reason have attain'd;
   Not like th' ungovern'd Horse and Mule,   whose Fury must be curb'd and reign'd.
10 Sorrows on Sorrows multiply'd,   the harden'd Sinners shall confound;
   But them who in his Truth confide   Blessings of Mercy shall surround.
11 His Saints that have perform'd his Laws,   their Life in Triumphs shall employ;
   Let them (as they alone have Cause)   in grateful Raptures shout for Joy.

PSALM XXXIII.

1 LET all the Just to God with Joy   their chearful Voices raise,
   For well the Righteous it becomes   to sing glad Songs of Praise.
2, 3 Let Harps, and Psalteries, and Lutes   in joyful Consort meet;
   And new-made Songs of loud Applause   the Harmony complete.
4, 5 For faithful is the Word of God,   his Works with Truth abound;
   He Justice loves, and all the Earth   is with his Goodness crown'd.
6 By his Almighty Word at first   Heav'n's glorious Arch was rear'd
   And all the beauteous Hosts of Light   at his Command appear'd.
7 The swelling Floods, together roll,   he makes in Heaps to lie;
   And lays, as in a Storehouse safe,   the wat'ry Treasures by.
8, 9 Let Earth and all that dwell therein   before him trembling stand:
   For when he spake the Word, 'twas made,   'twas fix'd at his Command.
10 He, when the Heathens closely plot,   their Counsels undermines;
   His Wisdom ineffectual makes   the People's rash Designs.
11 Whate'er the mighty Lord decrees   shall stand for ever sure;
   The settled Purpose of his Heart   to Ages shall endure.

PART II.

12 How happy then are they to whom   the Lord for God is known!
   Whom he from all the World besides   has chosen for his own!
13, 14, 15 He all the Nations of the Earth   from Heav'n his Throne survey'd;
   He saw their Works, and view'd their Thoughts,   by him their Hearts were made.
16, 17 No King is safe by num'rous Hosts,   their Strength the Strong deceives;
   No manag'd Horse, by Force or Speed,   His warlike Rider saves:
18, 19 'Tis God, who those that trust in him   beholds with gracious Eyes;
   He frees their Soul from Death, their Want   in Time of Dearth supplies.
20, 21 Our Soul on God with Patience waits   our Help and Shield is he!
   Then, Lord, let still our Hearts rejoice,   because we trust in thee.
22 The Riches of thy Mercy, Lord,   do thou to us extend;
   Since we for all we want or wish,   on thee alone depend.

PSALM XXXIV.

1 THRO' all the changing Scenes of Life,   in Trouble and in Joy,
   The Praises of my God shall still   my Heart and Tongue employ.
2 Of his deliv'rance I will boast,   till all that are distrest,
   From my Example comfort take,   and charm their Griefs to rest.
3 O magnify the Lord with me,   with me exalt his Name:
4 When in Distress to him I call'd,   he to my Rescue came.
5 Their drooping Hearts were soon refresh'd,   who look'd to him for Aid;
   Desir'd Success in ev'ry Face   a chearful Air display'd.
6 " Behold (say they) behold the Man   " whom Providence reliev'd:
   " So dangerously with Woes beset,   " so wond'rously retriev'd."
7 The Hosts of God encamp around   the Dwellings of the Just;
   Deliv'rance he affords to all   who on his Succour trust.

80

PSALM XXXV.

8 O make but Trial of his Love, Experience will decide
How bless'd they are, and only they, who in his Truth confide.
9 Fear him, ye Saints, and you will then have nothing else to fear;
Make you his Service your Delight, he'll make your Wants his Care.
10 While hungry Lions lack their Prey, the Lord will Food provide
For such as put their Trust in him, and see their Needs supply'd.

PART II.

11 Approach, ye piously dispos'd, and my Instruction hear,
I'll teach you the true Discipline of his religious Fear.
12 Let him who length of Life desires, and prosp'rous Days would see,
13 From sland'ring Language keep his Tongue, his Lips from Falshood free.
14 The crooked Paths of Vice decline, and Virtue's Ways pursue;
Establish Peace where 'tis begun, and where 'tis lost renew.
15 The Lord from Heav'n beholds the Just with favourable Eyes;
And when distress'd, his gracious Ear is open to their Cries:
16 But turns his wrathful Look on those whom Mercy can't reclaim.
To cut them off, and from the Earth blot out their hated Name.
17 Deliv'rance to his Saints he gives, when his Relief they crave:
18 He's nigh to heal the broken Heart, and contrite Spirit save.
19 The Wicked oft, but still in vain, against the Just conspire;
20 For under their Affliction's Weight he keeps their Bones intire.
21 The wicked from their wicked Arts their Ruin shall derive;
Whilst righteous Men, whom they detest, shall them in theirs survive.
22 For God preserves the Souls of those who on his Truth depend,
To them and their Posterity, his Blessings shall descend.

PSALM XXXV.

1 AGAINST all those that strive with me, O Lord, assert my Right;
With such as War unjustly wage do thou my Battles fight.
2 Thy Buckler take, and bind thy Shield upon thy warlike Arm;
Stand up, my God, in my Defence, and keep me safe from Harm.
3 Bring forth thy Spear, and stop their Course that haste my Blood to spill:
Say to my Soul " I am thy Health, " and will preserve thee still."
4 Let them with shame be cover'd o'er, who my Destruction fought:
And such as did my Harm devise be to confusion brought.
5 Then shall they fly, dispers'd like Chaff before the driving Wind:
God's vengeful Minister of Wrath shall follow close behind.
6 And when thro' dark and slipp'ry Ways they strive his Rage to shun,
His vengeful Ministers of Wrath shall goad them as they run.
7 Since unprovok'd by any Wrong, they hid their treach'rous Snare;
And for my harmless Soul a Pit did without Cause prepare.
8 Surpris'd by Mischiefs unforeseen. by their own Arts betray'd;
Their Feet shall fall into the Net, which they for me had laid.
9 Whilst my glad Soul shall God's great Name for this Deliv'rance bless;
And by his saving Health secur'd, its grateful Joy express.
10 My very Bones shall say, O Lord, who can compare with thee,
Who sett'st the poor and helpless Man from strong Oppressors free?

PART II.

11 False Witnesses with forg'd Complaints, against my Truth combin'd;
And to my Charge such Things they laid as I had ne'er design'd.

PSALM XXXVI.

12 The Good which I to thee hath done, with Evil they repaid;
    And did, by Malice undeserv'd, my harmless Life invade.
13 But as for me, when they were sick, I still in Sackcloth mourn'd:
    I pray'd and fasted, and my Pray'r to my own Breast return'd.
14 Had they my Friends or Brethren been, I could have done no more;
    Nor with more decent Signs of Grief, a Mother's loss deplore.

15 How diff'rent did their Carriage prove, in Times of my Distress?
    When they, in Crowds together met, did Savage Joy express.
    The Rabble too in num'rous Throngs, by their Examples came;
    And ceas'd not with reviling Words, to wound my spotless Fame.

16 Scoffers that noble Tables haunt, and earn their Bread with lyes,
    Did gnash their Teeth, and sland'rous Jests maliciously devise.
17 But, Lord, how long wilt thou look on? on my Behalf appear;
    And save my guiltless Soul, which they, like rav'ning Beasts would tear.

PART III.

18 So I before the list'ning World, shall grateful Thanks express;
    And where the great Assembly meets, thy Name with Praises bless.
19 Lord, suffer not thy causeless Foes, who me unjustly hate,
    With open Joy, or secret Signs, to mock my sad Estate.

20 For they, with Hearts averse to Peace, industriously devise,
    Against the Men of quiet Minds : to forge malicious Lyes.
21 Nor with these private Arts content, aloud they vent their Spite,
    And say " At last we found him out, " he did it in our Sight."

22 But thou, who dost both them and me with righteous Eyes survey,
    Assert my Innocence, O Lord, and keep not far away,
23 Stir up thyself in my Behalf, to Judgment, Lord, awake;
    Thy righteous Servant's Cause, O God, to thy Decision take.

24 Lord, as my Heart has upright been, let me thy Justice find;
    Nor let my cruel Foes obtain the Triumph they design'd.
25 O let them not amongst themselves, in boasting Language say,
    " At length our Wishes are complete, " at last he's made our Prey."

26 Let such as in my Harm rejoic'd, for Shame their Faces hide;
    And foul Dishonour wait on those that proudly me defy'd:
27 Whilst they with chearful Voices shout, who my just Cause befriend:
    And bless the Lord, who loves to make Success his Saints attend.

28 So shall my Tongue thy Judgments sing, inspir'd with grateful Joy;
    And chearful Hymns in Praise of thee, shall all my Days employ.

PSALM XXXVI.

1 **M**Y crafty Foe with flatt'ring Art, his wicked Purpose would disguise;
    But Reason whispers to my Heart, no Fear of God before his Eyes.
2 He sooths himself, retir'd from Sight, secure he thinks his treach'rous Game;
    Till his dark Plots expos'd to Light, their false Contriver brand with Shame.

3 In Deeds he is my Foe confess'd, whilst with his Tongue he speaks me fair:
    True Wisdom's banish'd from his Breast, and Vice has sole Dominion there.
4 His wakeful Malice spends the Night in forging his accurst Designs;
    His obstinate ungen'rous Spite, no execrable Means declines.

5 But, Lord, thy Mercy, my sure Hope, the highest Orb of Heav'n transcends,
    Thy sacred Truth's unmeasur'd Scope beyond the spreading Skies extends.

6 Thy

PSALM XXXVII.

6 Thy Justice like the Hills remains; unfathom'd Depths thy Judgments are;
Thy Providence the World sustains, the whole Creation is thy Care.
7 Since of thy Goodness all partake, with what Assurance should the Just
Thy shelt'ring Wings their Refuge make, and Saints to thy Protection trust?
8 Such Guests shall to thy Courts be led, to Banquet on thy Love's Repast,
And drink, as from a Fountain's Head, of Joys that shall for ever last.
9 With thee the Springs of Life remain, thy Presence is eternal Day;
10 O let thy Saints thy Favour gain; to upright Hearts thy Truth display.
11 Whilst Pride's insulting Foot would spurn and wicked Hand my Life surprize;
12 Their Mischiefs on themselves return; down, down they're fall'n no more to rise.

PSALM XXXVII.

1 THO' wicked Men grow rich or great,
Yet let not their successful State,
Thy Anger or thy Envy raise:
2 For they, cut down like tender Grass,
Or like young Flow'rs, away shall pass,
Whose blooming Beauty soon decays.

3 Depend on God, and him obey,
So thou within the Land shall stay,
Secure from Danger and from Want:
4 Make his Commands thy chief Delight,
And he, thy Duty to requite,
Shall all thy earnest Wishes grant.

5 In all thy Ways trust thou the Lord,
And he will needful help afford,
To perfect ev'ry just Design:
6 He'll make like Light, serene and clear,
Thy clouded Innocence appear,
And as a mid-day Sun to shine.

7 With quiet Mind on God depend,
And patiently for him attend;
Nor let thy Anger fondly rise,
Tho' wicked Men with Wealth abound,
And with Success the Plots are crown'd,
Which they maliciously devise.

8 From Anger cease, and Wrath forsake,
Let no ungovern'd Passion make
Thy wav'ring Heart espouse their Crime;
9 For God shall sinful Men destroy,
Whilst only they the Land enjoy,
Who trust on him, and wait his Time.

10 How soon shall wicked Men decay!
Their Place shall vanish quite away,
Nor by the strictest Search be found:
11 Whilst humble Souls possess the Earth,
Rejoicing still with godly Mirth,
With Peace and Plenty always crown'd.

PART II.

12 With sinful Crowds with false Design,
Against the righteous Few combine,
And gnash their Teeth, and threat'ning stand,
13 God shall their empty Plots deride,
And laugh at their defeated Pride;
He sees their Ruin near at hand.
14 They draw the Sword, and bend the Bow,
The Poor and Needy to o'erthrow,
And Men of Upright Lives to slay:
15 But their strong Bows shall soon be broke,
Their sharpen'd Weapon's mortal Stroke
Thro' their own Hearts shall force its Way.
16 A little, with God's Favour blest,
That's by one righteous Man possest,
The Wealth of many bad excels:

17 For God supports the just Man's Cause,
But as for those who break his Laws,
Their unsuccessful Pow'r he quells.
18 His constant Care the Upright guides,
And over all their Life presides,
Their Portion shall for ever last;
19 They, when Distress o'erwhelms the Earth,
Shall be unmov'd, and even in Dearth
The happy Fruits of Plenty taste.
20 Not so the wicked Men, and those,
Who proudly dare, God's Will oppose:
Destruction is their hapless Share:
Like Fat of Lambs, their Hopes and they
Shall in an Instant melt away,
And vanish into Smoke and Air.

PART III.

21 While Sinners brought to sad Decay,
Still borrow on, and never pay,
The Just have Will and Pow'r to give;
22 For such as God vouchsafes to bless,
Shall peaceably the Earth possess.
And those he curses shall not live.

PSALM XXXVIII.

23 The good Man's Way is God's Delight,
He orders all the Steps aright
Of him that moves by his Command;
24 Tho' he sometimes may be diſtreſs'd,
Yet ſhall he ne'er be quite oppreſs'd,
For God upholds him with his Hand.

25 From my firſt Youth till Age prevail'd,
I never ſaw the Righteous fail'd,
Or Want o'ertake his num'rous Race;
26 Becauſe Compaſſion fill'd his Heart,
And he did chearfully impart, (creaſe.
God made his Offspring's Wealth in-

27 With Caution ſhun each wicked Deed,
In Virtue's Ways with Zeal proceed,
And ſo prolong your happy Days :
28 For God, who Judgment loves, does ſtill
Preſerve his Saints ſecure from Ill,
While ſoon the wicked Race decays.

29, 30, 31 The Upright ſhall poſſeſs the
His Portion ſhall for Ages ſtand; (Land
His Mouth with Wiſdom is ſupply'd,
His Tongue by Rules of Judgment moves,
His Heart the Law of God approves,
Therefore his Footſteps never ſlide.

PART IV.

32 In wait the watchful Sinner lies,
In vain the Righteous to ſurpriſe;
In vain his Ruin does decree;
33 God will not him defenceleſs leave,
To his Revenge expos'd; but ſave,
And when he's ſentenc'd, ſet him free.

34 Wait ſtill on God, keep his Command,
And thou exalted in the Land,
Thy bleſt Poſſeſſion ne'er ſhall quit:
The Wicked ſoon deſtroy'd ſhall be,
And at his diſmal Tragedy,
Thou ſhalt a ſafe Spectator ſit.

35 The Wicked I in Pow'r have ſeen
And like a Bay-tree freſh and green,
That ſpreads its pleaſant Branches round:

36 But he was gone as ſwift as Thought,
And tho' in ev'ry Place I ſought,
No Sign or Track of him I found.

37 Obſerve the perfect Man with Care,
And mark all ſuch as upright are:
Their rougheſt Days in Peace ſhall en'd:
38 While on the latter end of thoſe
Who dare God's ſacred Will oppoſe,
A common Ruin ſhall attend.

39 God to the Juſt will Aid afford,
Their only Safe-guard is the Lord.
Their Strength in Time of Need is he;
40 Becauſe on him they ſtill depend,
The Lord will timely Succour ſend,
And from the Wicked ſet them free.

PSALM XXXVIII.

1 THY chaſt'ning Wrath, O Lord, reſtrain,
Nor let at once on me the Storm
2 In ev'ry wretched Part of me
Thy heavy Hand's afflicting Weight

3 My Fleſh is one continu'd Wound,
Betwixt my Puniſhment and Guilt
4 My Sins which to a Deluge ſwell,
And for my feeble Strength to bear

5 Stench and Corruption fill my Wounds
6 With Trouble I am warp'd and bow'd,
7 A loath'd Diſeaſe afflicts my Loins,
8 With Sickneſs worn, I groan and roar,

Tho' I deſerve it all;
of thy Diſpleaſure fall.
thy Arrows deep remain;
I can no more ſuſtain.

Thy Wrath ſo fiercely glows;
my Bones have no repoſe.
my ſinking Head o'erflow,
too vaſt a Burden grow.

my Folly's juſt Return,
and all Day long I mourn.
infecting ev'ry Part :
thro' Anguiſh of my Heart.

PART II.

9 But, Lord, before thy ſearching Eyes
And ſure my Groans have been too loud,
10 My Heart's oppreſt, my Strength decay'd,
11 Friends, Lovers, Kinſmen gaze aloof

12 Mean while the Foes that ſeek my Life,
Vent Slanders, and contrive all Day

all my Deſires appear :
not to have reach'd thine Ear.
my Eyes depriv'd of Light :
on ſuch a diſmal Sight.

their Snares to take me ſet :
to forge ſome new Deceit.

13 But

PSALM XXXIX, XL.

13 But I, as if both deaf and dumb, nor heard, nor once reply'd;
14 Quite deaf and dumb, like one whose Tongue with conscious Guilt is ty'd.

15 For, Lord, to thee I do appeal, my Innocence to clear;
Assur'd that thou the righteous God, my injur'd Cause wilt hear.
16 " Hear me, said I, lest my proud Foes " a spiteful Joy display,
" Insulting if they see my Foot, " but once to go astray."

17 And with continual Grief opprest, to think I now begin:
18 To thee, O Lord, I will confess, to thee bewail my Sin.
19 But whilst I languish, my proud Foes their Strength and Vigour boast;
And they who hate me without Cause, are grown a dreadful Host.

20 Ev'n they, whom I oblig'd, return my Kindness with Despite;
And are my Enemies, because I choose the Path that's right.
21 Forsake me not, O Lord, my God, nor far from me depart;
22 Make haste to my Relief, O thou, who my Salvation art.

PSALM XXXIX.

1 RESOLV'D to watch o'er all my Ways, I kept my Tongue in awe;
I curb'd my hasty Words when I the prosp'rous Wicked saw.
2 Like one that's dumb I silent stood, and did my Tongue refrain
From good Discourse; but that Restraint increas'd by inward Pain.

3 My Heart did glow, which working Thoughts did hot and restless make,
And warm Reflections fann'd the Fire, till thus at length I spake:
4 Lord, let me know my Term of Days, how soon my Life will end;
The num'rous Train of Ills disclose which this frail State attend.

5 My Life, thou know'st is but a Span, a Cypher sums my Years;
And ev'ry Man in best Estate, but Vanity appears.
6 Man, like a Shadow, vainly Walks, with fruitless Cares opprefs'd;
He heaps up Wealth, but cannot tell by whom 'twill be poffefs'd.

7 Why then should I on worthless Toys with anxious Care attend?
On thee alone my stedfast Hope shall ever, Lord, depend.
8, 9 Forgive my Sins, nor let me scorn'd by foolish Sinners be;
For I was dumb, and murmur'd not, because 'twas done by thee.

10 The dreadful Burden of thy Wrath in Mercy soon remove;
Lest my frail Flesh too weak to bear the heavy Load should prove.
11 For when thou chast'nest Man for Sin, thou mak'st his Beauty fade,
(So vain a Thing is he) like Cloth by fretting Moths decay'd.

12 Lord, hear my Cry, accept my Tears, and listen to my Prayer;
Who sojourn like a Stranger here, as all my Fathers were.
13 O spare me yet a little Time, my wasted Strength restore;
Before I vanish quite from hence, and shall be seen no more.

PSALM XL.

1 I Waited meekly for the Lord, 'till he vouchsaf'd a kind Reply;
Who did his gracious Ear afford, and heard from Heav'n my humble Cry.
2 He took me from the dismal Pit, when founder'd deep in miry Clay;
On solid Ground he plac'd my Feet, and suffer'd not my Steps to stray.

3 The Wonders he for me has wrought shall fill my Mouth with Songs of Praise;
And others, to his Worship brought, to Hopes of like Deliv'rance raise.
4 For Blessings shall that Man reward who on th' Almighty Lord relies;
Who treats the Proud with Disregard, and hates the Hypocrite's Disguise.

5 Who

PSALM XLI.

Who can the wond'rous Works recount, which thou, O God, for us haft wrought?
The Treasures of thy Love furmount the Pow'r of Numbers, Speech and Thought.
I've learn'd that thou haft not defir'd Off'rings and Sacrifice alone;
Nor Blood of guiltlefs Beafts requir'd, for Man's Tranfgreffion to atone.

I therefore come—come to fulfil the Oracles thy Books impart:
'Tis my Delight to do thy Will; thy Law is written in my Heart.

PART II.

In full Affemblies I have told thy Truth and Righteoufnefs at large:
Nor did, thou know'ft, my Lips with-hold from utt'ring what thou gav'ft in charge.
Nor kept within my Breaft confin'd, thy Faithfulnefs and faving Grace;
But preach'd thy Love for all defign'd, that all might that and Truth embrace.

Then let thefe Mercies I declar'd to others, Lord, extend to me;
Thy Loving-Kindnefs my Reward, thy Truth my fafe Protection be.
For I with Troubles am diftreft, too vaft and numberlefs to bear;
Nor lefs with Loads of Guilt oppreft, that plunge and fink me to Defpair.

As foon, alas! may I recount the Hairs on this afflicted Head:
My vanquifht Courage they furmount, and fill my drooping Soul with Dread.

PART III.

But, Lord, to my Relief draw near, for never was more preffing Need!
In my Deliv'rance, Lord, appear, and add to that Deliv'rance Speed.
Confufion on their Heads return, who to deftroy my Soul combine;
Let them, defeated, blufh and mourn, enfnar'd in their own vile Defign.

Their Doom let Deffolation be, with Shame their Malice be repaid,
Who mock'd my Confidence in thee, and Sport of my Affliction made.
While thofe who humbly feek thy Face to joyful Triumphs fhall be rais'd;
And all who prize thy faving Grace, with me refound, The Lord be prais'd.

Thus, wretched tho' I am, and poor, of me th' Almighty Lord takes care,
Thou, God, who only can'ft reftore, to my Relief with Speed repair.

PSALM XLI.

HAPPY the Man, whofe tender Care relieves the Poor diftreft:
When he's by Troubles compafs'd round, the Lord fhall give him Reft.
The Lord his Life, with Bleffings crown'd, In Safety fhall prolong;
And difappoint the Will of thofe that feek to do him Wrong.

If he in languifhing Eftate oppreft with Sicknefs lie;
The Lord will eafy make his Bed, and inward Strength fupply.
Secure of this, to thee, my God, I thus my Pray'r addrefs'd;
" Lord, for thy Mercy, heal my Soul, " tho' I have much tranfgrefs'd;

My cruel Foes, with fland'rous Words, attempt to wound my Fame;
" When fhall he die (fay they) and Men " forget his very Name?"
Suppofe they formal Vifits make, it's all but empty Show;
They gather Mifchief in their Hearts, and vent it where they go.

8 With private Whifpers, fuch as thefe, to hurt me they devife;
" A fore Difeafe afflicts him now, " he's fall'n, no more to rife."
My own familiar Bofom Friend, on whom I moft rely'd,
Has me, whofe daily Gueft he was, with open Scorn defy'd.

But thou, my fad and wretched State, in Mercy, Lord, regard;
And raife me up, that all their Crimes may meet their juft Reward.
By this, I know, thy gracious Ear is open when I call;
Becaufe thou fuffer'ft not my Foes to triumph in my Fall.

PSALM XLII, XLIII, XLIV.

12 Thy tender Care secures my Life from Danger and Disgrace;
And thou vouchsaf'st to set me still before thy glorious Face.
13 Let therefore Isr'el's Lord and God from Age to Age be bles'd;
And all the People's glad Applause with loud Amens express'd.

PSALM XLII.

1 AS pants the Hart for cooling Streams when heated in the Chace,
So longs my Soul, O God, for thee, and thy refreshing Grace,
2 For thee, my God, the living God, my thirsty Soul doth pine;
O when shall I behold thy Face, thou Majesty divine!

3 Tears are my constant Food, while thus insulting Foes upbraid,
"Deluded Wretch, where's now thy God? "and where his promis'd Aid
4 I sigh when-e'er my musing Thoughts those happy Days present,
When I with Troops of pious Friends thy Temple did frequent.

When I advanc'd with Songs of Praise, my solemn Vows to pay,
And led the lawful sacred Throng that kept the Festal Day.
5 Why restless, why cast down, my Soul? trust God, and he'll employ
His Aid for thee; and change these Sighs to thankful Hymns of Joy.

6 My Soul's cast down, O God, but thinks on thee and Sion still;
From Jordan's Bank, from Herman's Heights and Missar's humbler Hill.
7 One Trouble calls another on, and bursting o'er my Head,
Fall spouting down, till round my Soul a roaring Sea is spread.

8 But when thy Presence, Lord of Life, has once dispell'd this Storm,
To thee I'll midnight Anthems sing, and all my Vows perform.
9 God of my Strength, how long shall I like one forgotten, mourn?
Forlorn, forsaken, and expos'd to my Oppressor's Scorn.

10 My Heart is pierc'd, as with a Sword, whilst thus my Foes upbraid,
"Vain Boaster where is now thy God? "and where his promis'd Aid?
11 Why restless, why cast down, my Soul? hope still, and thou shalt sing
The Praise of him who is thy God, thy Health's eternal Spring.

PSALM XLIII.

1 JUST Judge of Heav'n, against my Foes do thou assert my injur'd Right:
O set me free, my God from those that in Deceit and Wrong delight.
2 Since thou art still my only Stay, why leav'st thou me in deep Distress?
Why go I mourning all the Day, whilst me insulting Foes oppress?

3 Let me with Light and Truth be bless, be these my Guides, and lead the Way
Till on thy holy Hill I rest, and in thy sacred Temple pray,
4 Then will I there fresh Altars raise to God, who is my only Joy;
And well-tun'd Harps with Songs of Praise shall all my grateful Hours employ.

5 Why then cast down, my Soul, and why so much opprest with anxious Care?
On God, thy God, for Aid rely, who will thy ruin'd State repair.

PSALM XLIV.

1 O Lord, our Fathers oft have told in our attentive Ears,
Thy Wonders in their Days perform'd and elder Times than theirs:
2 How thou, to plant them here, didst drive the Heathen from this Land;
Dispeopled by repeated Strokes of thy avenging Hand.

3 For, not their Courage, nor their Sword, to them Possession gave,
Nor Strength, that from unequal Force their fainting Troops could sa-
But thy Right-hand and pow'rful Arm, whose Succour they implor'd,
Thy Presence with the chosen Race, who thy great Name ador'd.

PSALM XLV.

As thee their God our Fathers own'd, thou art our Sov'reign King;
O therefore, as thou didst to them, to us Deliv'rance bring.
Thro' thy victorious Name our Arms the proudest Foes shall quell,
And crush 'em with repeated Strokes as oft as they rebel.

I'll neither trust my Bow nor Sword, when I in Fight engage;
But thee, who hast our Foes subdu'd, and sham'd their spiteful Rage.
To thee the Triumph we ascribe, from whom the Conquest came;
In God we will rejoice all Day, and ever bless his Name.

PART II.

But thou hast cast us off, and now most shamefully we yield;
For thou no more vouchsaf'st to lead our Armies to the Field.
o Since when, to every upstart Foe we turn our Backs in Fight;
And with our Spoil their Malice feast who bear us ancient Spite.

1 To Slaughter doom'd, we fall like Sheep, into their butch'ring Hands:
Or (what's more wretched yet) survive dispers'd thro' Heathen Lands.
2 Thy People thou hast sold for Slaves, and set their Price so low,
That not thy Treasure by the Sale, but their Disgrace might grow.

3, 14 Reproach'd by all the Nations round, the Heathen's By-word grown,
Whose Scorn of us is both in Speech and mocking Gestures shown.
5 Confusion strikes me blind, my Face in conscious Shame I hide,
6 While we are scoff'd, and God blasphem'd by their licentious Pride.

PART III.

7 On us this Heap of Woes is fall'n, all this we have endur'd;
Yet have not, Lord, renounc'd thy Name, or Faith to thee abjur'd.
8 But in thy righteous Paths have kept our Heart and Steps with Care;
9 Tho' thou hast broken all our Strength, and we almost despair.

o Could we, forgetting thy great Name, on other Gods rely,
1 And not the Searcher of all Hearts the treach'rous Crime descry;
2 Thou seest what Suff'rings for thy Sake, we ev'ry Day sustain;
All slaughter'd, or reserv'd like Sheep appointed to be slain.

3 Awake, arise; let seeming Sleep no longer thee detain;
Nor let us, Lord, who sue to thee, for ever sue in vain.
4 O wherefore hidest thou thy Face from our afflicted State?
5 Whose Souls and Bodies sink to Earth, with Grief's oppressive Weight.

6 Arise, O Lord, and timely haste to our Deliv'rance make;
Redeem us, Lord,——if not for ours, yet for thy Mercy's Sake.

PSALM XLV.

WHILE I the King's loud Praise rehearse, indited by my Heart,
My Tongue is like the Pen of him that writes with ready Art.
How matchless is thy Form, O King! thy Mouth with Grace o'erflows:
Because fresh Blessings God on thee eternally bestows.

Gird on thy Sword, most mighty Prince, and clad thy rich Array,
With glorious Ornaments of Pow'r majestic Pomp display.
Ride on in State, and still protect the Meek, the Just and True;
Whilst thy Right-hand with swift Revenge does all thy Foes pursue.

How sharp thy Weapons are to them that dare thy Pow'r oppose!
Down, down they fall, while thro' their Heart the feather'd Arrow goes.
But thy firm Throne, O God, is fix'd for ever to endure;
Thy Scepter's Sway shall always last, by righteous Laws secure.

7 Be-

PSALM XLVI, XLVII.

7 Becaufe thy Heart, by Juftice led, did upright Ways approve,
And hated ftill the crooked Paths where wand'ring Sinners rove.
Therefore did God, thy God, on thee the Oil of Gladnefs fhed;
And has above thy Fellows round advanc'd thy lofty Head.

8 With Caffia, Aloes and Myrrh thy Royal Robes abound;
Which from the ftately Wardrobe brought fpread grateful Odours round.

9 Among the honourable Train did princely Virgins wait:
The Queen was plac'd at thy Right-hand, In Golden Robes of State.

PART II.

10 But thou, O Royal Bride, give ear, and to my Words attend;
Forget thy Native Country now, and ev'ry former Friend.

11 So fhall thy Beauty charm the King, nor fhall his Love decay;
For he is now become thy Lord, to him due Rev'rence pay.

12 The Tyrian Matrons rich and proud fhall humble Prefents make;
And all the wealthy Nations fue thy Favour to partake.

13 The King's fair Daughter's beauteous Soul all inward Graces fill;
Her Raiment is of pureft Gold, adorn'd with coftly Skill.

14 She in her Nuptial Garment drefs'd, with Needles richly wrought,
Attended by her Virgin Train, fhall to the King be brought,

15 With all the State of folemn Joy the Triumph moves along,
Till with wide Gates the Royal Court receives the pompous Throng.

16 Thou, in thy Royal Father's Room, muft princely Sons expect;
Whom thou to diff'rent Realms may'ft fend to govern and protect.

17 Whilft this my Song to future Times tranfmits thy glorious Name;
And makes the World, with one Confent, thy lafting Praife proclaim.

PSALM XLVI.

1 GOD is our Refuge in Diftrefs, 7 The Lord of Hofts conducts our Arms,
A prefent Help when Dangers prefs; Our Tow'r of Refuge in Alarms,
In him undaunted we'll confide: Our Fathers Guardian-God and ours

2, 3 Tho' Earth were from her Center toft, 8 Come, fee the Wonders he hath wrought
And Mountains in the Ocean loft. On Earth what Deffolation brought;
Torn piece-meal by the roaring Tide. 9 How he has calm'd the jarring World:

4 A gentler Stream with Gladnefs ftill He broke the Warlike Spear and Bow;
The City of our Lord fhall fill, With them the thund'ring Chariots too
The Royal Seat of God moft high: Into devou'ring Flames were hurl'd.

5 God dwells in Sion, whofe fair Tow'rs 10 Submit to God's Almighty Sway,
Shall mock th'Affaults of earthly Pow'rs, For him the Heathen fhall obey,
While his Almighty Aid is nigh. And Earth her Sov'reign Lord confefs.

6 In Tumults when the Heathen rag'd, 11 The God of Hofts conducts our Arms,
And Kingdoms War againft us wag'd, Our Tow'r of Refuge in Alarms,
He thunder'd and difpers'd their As to our Fathers in Diftrefs.
Pow'rs:

PSALM XLVII.

1, 2 O All ye People, clap your and with triumphant Voices fing;
Hands,
No Force the mighty Pow'r withftands of God the univerfal King.

3, 4 He fhall oppofing Nations quell, and with Succefs our Battles fight;
Shall fix the Place where we muft dwell, the Pride of Jacob, his Delight.

5, 6 Gor

PSALM XLVIII, XLIX.

5, 6 God is gone up, our Lord and King, with Shouts of Joy and Trumpets Sound;
To him repeated Praises sing, and let the chearful Song go round.
7, 8 Your utmost Skill in Praise be shown, for him who all the World commands;
Who sits upon his righteous Throne, and spreads his Sway o'er Heathens Lands.
9 Our Chiefs and Tribes, that far from hence t'adore the God of Ab'ram came,
Found him their constant sure Defence, How great and glorious is his Name!

PSALM XLVIII.

1 THE Lord, the only God, is great, and greatly to be prais'd;
In Sion on whose happy Mount His sacred Throne is rais'd.
2 Her Tow'rs, the Joy of all the Earth, with beauteous Prospect rise:
On her North-side th' Almighty King's Imperial City lies.
3 God in her Palaces is known, his Presence is her Guard.
4 Confed'rate Kings withdrew their Siege, and of Success despair'd.
5 They view'd her Walls, admir'd and fled, with Grief and Terror struck,
6 Like Women whom the sudden Pangs of Travail had o'ertook.
7 No wretched Crew of Mariners appear like them forlorn,
When Fleets from Tarshish wealthy Coasts, by Eastern Winds are torn.
8 In Sion we have seen perform'd a Work that was foretold,
In Pledge that God, for Times to come, his City will uphold.
9 Not in our Fortresses and Walls, did we, O God, confide,
But on the Temple fix'd for Hopes in which thou dost reside.
10 According to thy Sov'reign Name, thy Praise thro' Earth extends;
Thy pow'rful Arm, as Justice guides, chastises or defends.
11 Let Sion's Mount with Joy resound, her Daughters all be taught,
In Songs his Judgments to extol, who this Deliv'rance wrought.
12 Compass her Walls in solemn Pomp, your Eyes quite round her cast;
Count all her Tow'rs, and see if there you find one Stone displac'd.
13 Her Forts and Palaces survey, observe their Order well;
That with Assurance, to her Heirs, this Wonder you may tell.
14 This God is ours, and will be ours, whilst we in him confide;
Who as he has preserv'd us now, 'till Death will be our Guide.

PSALM XLIX.

1, 2 LET all the list'ning World attend, and my Instructions hear;
Let High and Low, and Rich and Poor, with joint Consent give Ear.
3 My Mouth with sacred Wisdom fill'd, shall good Advice impart,
The sound Result of prudent Thoughts, digested in my Heart.
4 To Parables of weighty Sense, I will my Ear incline;
Whilst to my tuneful Harp I sing dark Words of deep Design.
5 Why should my Courage fail in Times of Danger and of Doubt?
When Sinners that would me supplant have compass'd me about?
6 Those Men that all their Hope and Trust in Heaps of Treasure place,
And boast and triumph when they see their ill-got Wealth increase.
7 Are yet unable from the Grave their dearest Friend to free;
Nor can by Force of costly Bribes reverse God's firm Decree.
8, 9 Their vain Endeavours they must quit, the Price is held too high;
No Sums can purchase such a Grant, that Man should never die.
10 Not Wisdom can the Wise exempt, nor Fools their Folly save;
But both must perish, and in Death their Wealth to others leave.

PSALM L.

11 For tho' they think their stately Seats
shall ne'er to Ruin fall;
But their Remembrance last, in Lands
which by their Names they call;
12 Yet shall their Fame be soon forgot,
how great soe'er their State;
With Beasts their Memory and they
shall share one common Fate.

PART II.

13 How great their Folly is, who thus
absurd Conclusions make!
And yet their Children unreclaim'd,
repeat the gross Mistake.
14 They all, like Sheep to Slaughter led,
the Prey of Death are made;
Their Beauty, while the Just rejoice,
within the Grave shall fade.

15 But God will yet redeem my Soul,
and from the greedy Grave
His greater Pow'r shall set me free,
and to himself receive.
16 Then fear not thou, when worldly Men
in envy'd Wealth abound,
Nor tho' their prosp'rous House increase,
with State and Honour crown'd.

17 For when they're summon'd hence by Death,
they leave all this behind;
No Shadow of their former Pomp
within the Grave they find:
18 And yet they thought their State was blest,
caught in the Flatt'rer's Snare,
Who praises those that slight all else,
and of themselves take care.

19 In their Forefather's Steps they tread;
and when, like them, they die,
Their wretched Ancestors and they
in endless Darkness lie.
20 For Man, how great soe'er his State,
unless he's truly wise,
As, like a sensual Beast he lives,
so, like a Beast he dies.

PSALM L.

1,2 THE Lord hath spoke, the mighty God
Hath sent his Summons all abroad,
From dawning Light, till Day declines;
The list'ning Earth his Voice hath heard,
And he from Sion hath appear'd,
Where Beauty in Perfection shines.

3,4 Our God shall come, and keep no more
Misconstru'd Silence as before;
But wasting Flames before him send;
Around shall Tempests fiercely rage,
While he does Heav'n and Earth engage
His just Tribunal to attend.

5,6 Assemble all my Saints to me,
(Thus runs the great Divine Decree)
That in my lasting Cov'nant live;
And Off'rings bring with constant Care;
(The Heav'n his Justice shall declare,
For God himself shall Sentence give.)

7 Attend my People, Isra'l, hear;
Thy strong Accuser, I'll appear;
Thy God, the only God am I;
8 'Tis not of Off'rings I complain,
Which, daily in my Temple slain,
My sacred Altar did supply.

9 Will this alone Atonement make?
No Bullock from thy Stall I'll take,
Nor He-Goat from thy Fold accept;
10 The Forest Beasts that range alone,
The Cattle too are all my own,
That on a thousand Hills are kept.

11 I know the Fowls that build their Nests
In craggy Rocks; and savage Beasts,
That loosely haunt the open Fields:
12 If seiz'd with Hunger I could be,
I need not seek Relief from thee,
Since the World's mine, and all it yields.

13 Think'st thou that I have any need
On slaughter'd Bulls, and Goats to feed,
To 'eat their Flesh, and drink their Blood?
14 The Sacrifices I require
Are Hearts which Love and Zeal inspire,
And Vows which strictest Care make good.

15 In Time of Trouble call on me,
And I will set thee safe and free;
And thou Returns of Praise shalt make:
16 But to the Wicked thus saith God,
How dar'st thou teach my Laws abroad,
Or in thy Mouth my Cov'nant take?

17 For stubborn thou, confirm'd in Sin,
Hast Proof against Instruction been,
And of my Word didst lightly speak:
18 When

PSALM LI.

18 When thou a fubtle Thief did fee,
 Thou gladly didft with him agree,
 And with Adult'rers didft partake.

19 Vile Slander is thy chief Delight,
 Thy Tongue, by envy mov'd, and Spite,
 Deceitful Tales doth hourly fpread:

20 Thou doft with hatefulScandals wound
 Thy Brother, and with Lyes confound
 The Offspring of thy Mother's Bed:

21 Thefe Things didft thou, whom ftill I ftrove
 To gain with Silence and with Love;

Till thou didft wickedly furmife,
That I was fuch a one as thou;
But I'll reprove and fhame thee now,
And fet thy Sins before thine Eyes.

22 Mark this, ye wicked Fools, left I
 Let all my Bolts of Vengeance fly,
 Whilft none fhall dare your Caufe to own:

23 Who praifes me due Honour gives;
 And to the Man that juftly lives
 My ftrong Salvation fhall be fhown.

PSALM LI.

1 HAVE Mercy, Lord, on me,
 Let me oppreft with Loads of Guilt,
2, 3 Wafh off my foul Offence,
 For I confefs my Crime, and fee

4 Againft thee, Lord, alone,
 Have I tranfgrefs'd, and tho' condemn'd,
5 In Guilt each Part was form'd
 In Guilt I was conceiv'd, and born

6 Yet thou, whofe fearching Eye
 In fecret did with Wifdom's Laws,
7 With Hyffop, purge me, Lord,
 I fhall with Snow in Whitenefs vie,

8 Make me to hear with Joy,
 That fo the Bones which thou haft broke,
9, 10 Blot out my crying Sins,
 Create in me a Heart that's clean,

as thou wert ever kind;
thy wonted Mercy find.
and cleanfe me from my Sin;
how great my Guilt has been.

and only in thy Sight.
muft own thy Judgments right.
of all this finful Frame;
the Heir of Sin and Shame.

doth inward Truth require,
my tender Soul infpire.
and fo I clean fhall be:
when purify'd by thee.

thy kind forgiving Voice;
may with frefh Strength rejoice.
nor me in Anger view;
an upright Mind renew.

PART II.

11 Withdraw not thou my Help,
 Nor let thy holy Spirit take
12 The Joy thy Favour gives
 And thy free Spirit's firm Support

13 So I thy righteous Ways
 Whilft my Advice fhall wicked Men
14 My Guilt of Blood remove,
 And my glad Tongue fhall loudly tell

15 Do thou unlock my Lips,
 So fhall my Mouth thy wond'rous Praife
16 Could Sacrifice atone,
 But on fuch Off'rings thou difdain'ft

17 A broken Spirit is
 By him a broken contrite Heart
18 Let Sion Favour find,
 And thy own City flourifh long,

19 The Juft fhall then attend,
 And Sacrifice of choiceft Kind

nor caft me from thy Sight;
its everlafting Flight.
let me again obtain;
my fainting Soul fuftain.

to Sinners will impart,
to thy juft Laws convert.
my Saviour and my God;
thy righteous Acts abroad.

with Sorrow clos'd and Shame;
to all the World proclaim,
whofe Flocks and Herds fhould die;
to caft a gracious Eye.

by God moft highly priz'd;
fhall never be defpis'd.
of thy Good-will affur'd;
by lofty Walls fecur'd.

and pleafing Tribute pay:
upon thy Altar lay.

PSALM

PSALM LII, LIII, LIV, LV.

PSALM LII.

1 IN vain, O Man of lawlefs Might, thou boaſt'ſt thyſelf in Ill:
Since God, the God in whom I truſt, vouchſafe's his Favour ſtill.
2 Thy wicked Tongue doth ſland'rous Tales maliciouſly deviſe:
And ſharper than a Razor ſet, it wounds with treach'rous Lyes.

3, 4 Thy Thoughts are more on Ill than Good, on Lyes than Truth employ'd;
Thy Tongue delights in Words, by which the Guiltleſs are deſtroy'd.
5 God ſhall for ever blaſt thy Hopes, and ſnatch thee ſoon away;
Nor in thy Dwelling-Place permit, nor in the World to ſtay.

6 The Juſt, with pious Fear, ſhall ſee the Downfall of thy Pride;
And'at thy ſudden Ruin laugh, and thus thy Fall deride:
7 "See there the Man that haughty was, " who proudly God defy'd,
" Who truſted in his Wealth, and ſtill " on wicked Arts rely'd."

8 But I am like thoſe Olive-Plants, that ſhade God's Temple round;
And hope with his indulgent Grace to be for ever crown'd.
9 So ſhall my Soul with Praiſe, O God, extol thy wond'rous Love;
And on thy Name with Patience wait; for this thy Saints approve.

PSALM LIII.

1 THE wicked Fools muſt ſure ſuppoſe that God is but a Name:
This groſs Miſtake their Practice ſhows ſince Virtue all diſclaim.
2 The Lord look'd down from Heav'n's high Tow'r the Sons of Men to view;
To ſee if any own'd his Pow'r, or Truth or Juſtice knew.

3 But all he ſaw, were backwards gone, degen'rate grown, and baſe;
None for Religion car'd, not one of all the ſinful Race.
4 But are thoſe Workers of Deceit ſo dull and ſenſeleſs grown,
That they, like Bread, my People eat, and God's juſt Pow'r diſown?

5 Their cauſeleſs Fears ſhall ſtrangely grow; and they, deſpis'd of God,
Shall ſoon be foil'd; his Hand ſhall throw their ſhatter'd Bones abroad.
6 Would he his ſaving Pow'r employ, to break our ſervile Band,
Loud Shouts of univerſal Joy ſhould eccho through the Land.

PSALM LIV.

1, 2 LORD, ſave me, for thy glorious Name, and in thy Strength appear,
To judge my Cauſe, accept my Pray'r, and to my Words give Ear.
3 Mere Strangers, whom I never wrong'd, to ruin me deſign'd;
And cruel Men, that fear no God againſt my Soul combin'd.

4, 5 But God takes Part with all my Friends, and he's the ſureſt Guard;
The God of Truth ſhall give my Foes their Falſhood's juſt Reward;
6 While I my grateful Off'rings bring, and Sacrifice with Joy;
And in his Praiſe my Time to come. delightfully employ.

7 From dreadful Danger and Diſtreſs the Lord hath ſet me free;
Thro' him ſhall I of all my Foes the juſt Deſtruction ſee.

PSALM LV.

1 GIVE ear, thou Judge of all the Earth, and liſten when I pray;
Nor from thy humble Suppliant turn thy glorious Face away.
2 Attend to this my ſad Complaint, and hear my grievous Moans,
Whilſt I my mournful Caſe declare with artleſs Sighs and Groans.

3 Hark! how the Foe inſults aloud, how fierce Oppreſſors rage!
Whoſe ſland'rous Tongues with wrathful Hate againſt my Fame engage.

4, 5 My

PSALM LVI.

4, 5 My Heart is rack'd with Pain, my Soul
  With Fear and Trembling compafs'd round
  with deadly Frights diftreft;
  with Horror quite oppreft.
6 How often wifh'd I then, that I
  That I might take my fpeedy Flight,
  the Dove's fweet Wings could get;
  and feek a fafe Retreat!
7, 8 Then would I wander far from hence,
  Till all this furious Storm were fpent,
  and in wild Defarts ftray,
  this Tempeft paft away.

PART II.

9 Deftroy, O Lord, their ill Defigns,
  For through the City my griev'd Eyes
  their Counfels foon divide:
  have Strife and Rapine 'fpy'd.
10 By Day and Night on ev'ry Wall
  And in the Midft of all her Strength,
  they walk'd their conftant Round;
  are Grief and Mifchief found.

11 Whoe'er thro' ev'ry Part fhall roam,
  Deceit and Guile their conftant Pofts
  will frefh Diforders meet;
  maintain in ev'ry Street,
12 For 'twas not any open Foe
  For then I could with Eafe have borne
  that falfe Reflections made;
  the bitter Things he faid:

'Twas none who Hatred had profeft,
  For then I had withdrawn myfelf
  that did againft me rife;
  from his malicious Eyes.
13, 14 But 'twas ev'n thou, my Guide, my Friend,
  Whofe fweet Advice I valu'd moft,
  whom tend'reft Love did join;
  whofe Pray'rs were mix'd with mine

15 Sure, Vengeance equal to their Crimes
  And fudden Death requite thofe Ills,
  fuch Traitors muft furprife;
  they wickedly devife!
16, 17 But I will call on God, who ftill
  At Morn, and Noon, and Night I'll pray,
  fhall in my Aid appear;
  and he my Voice fhall hear.

PART III.

18 God has releas'd my Soul from thofe
  And made a num'rous Hoft of Friends
  that did with me contend;
  my righteous Caufe defend.
19 For he who was my Help of old,
  And punifh them whofe profp'rous State
  fhall now his Suppliant hear;
  makes them no God to fear.

20 Whom can I truft, if faithlefs Men
  To ruin me, their peaceful Friend,
  perfidioufly devife
  and break the ftrongeft Ties?
21 Tho' foft and melting are their Words,
  Their Speeches are more fmooth than Oil,
  their Hearts with War abound;
  and yet like Swords they wound.

22 Do thou, my Soul, on God depend,
  He aids the Juft, whom to fupplant
  and he fhall thee fuftain;
  the Wicked ftrive in vain.
23 My Foes, that trade in Lyes and Blood,
  Whilft I for Health and Length of Days
  fhall all untimely die;
  on thee, my God, rely.

PSALM LVI.

1 DO thou, O God, in Mercy help,
  To crufh me with repeated Wrongs,
  for Man my Life purfues;
  he daily Strife renews.
2 Continually my fpiteful Foes
  Thou fee'ft, who fit'ft enthron'd on high,
  to ruin me combine;
  what mighty Numbers join.

3 But tho' fometimes furpriz'd by Fear,
  Yet ftill for Succour I depend
  (on Danger's firft Alarm)
  on thy Almighty Arm.
4 God's faithful Promife I fhall praife,
  In God I truft, and trufting him,
  on which I now rely:
  the Arm of Flefh defy.

5 They wreft my Words, and make 'em fpeak
  Their Thoughts are all with reftlefs Spite,
  a Senfe they never meant:
  on my Deftruction bent.
6 In clofe Affemblies they combine,
  They watch my Steps, and lie in wait,
  and wicked Projects lay;
  to make my Soul their Prey,

Shall

PSALM LVII, LVIII.

7 Shall such Injustice still escape?
Let thy just Wrath (too long provok'd)
8 Thou numb'rest all my wand'ring Steps,
My very Tears are treasur'd up,
9 When therefore I invoke thy Aid,
For I am well assur'd that God
10, 11 I'll trust God's Word, and so despise
12 To thee, O God, my Vows are due,
13 Thou hast retriev'd my Soul from Death;
The Life thou hast so oft preserv'd,
That thus protected by thy Pow'r,
And in the Service of my God

O righteous God, arise:
this impious Race chastise.
since first compell'd to flee:
and register'd by thee.
my Foes shall be o'erthrown;
my righteous Cause will own.
the Force that Man can raise:
to thee I'll render Praise:
and thou wilt still secure
and make my Footsteps sure.
I may this Light enjoy,
my length'ned Days employ.

PSALM LVII.

1 THY Mercy, Lord, to me extend,
And to thy Wings for Shelter haste;
2 To thy Tribunal, Lord, I'll fly,
Who Wonders hast for me begun,
3 From Heav'n protect me by thine Arm,
To my Relief thy Mercy send,
4 For I with savage Men converse,
With Men whose Teeth are Spears, their Words

On thy Protection I depend;
'Till this outragious Storm is past.
Thou sov'reign Judge and God most high;
And wilt not leave thy Work undone.
And shame all those who seek my Harm;
And Truth, on which my Hopes depend.
Like angry Lions wild and fierce,
Invenom'd Darts, and two-edg'd Swords.

5 Be thou, O God, exalted high;
So let it be on Earth display'd,
6 To take me they their Net prepar'd,
But fell themselves, by just Decree,
7 O God, my Heart is fix'd, 'tis bent
And with my Heart, my Voice I'll raise
8 Awake my Glory; Harp and Lute,
And I, my tuneful Part to take,
9 Thy Praises, Lord, I will resound
10 Thy Mercy highest Heav'n transcends,
11 Be thou, O God, exalted high;
So let it be on Earth display'd,

And, as thy Glory fills the Sky,
'Till thou art here, as there, obey'd.
And had almost my Soul ensnar'd,
Into the Pit they made for me.
Its thankful Tribute to present;
To thee, my God, in Songs of Praise.
No longer let your Strings be mute;
Will with the early Dawn awake.
To all the list'ning Nations round:
Thy Truth beyond the Clouds extends.
And as thy Glory fills the Sky,
Till thou art here, as there, obey'd.

PSALM LVIII.

1 SPEAK, O ye Judges of the Earth,
Or, must not Innocence appeal
2 Your wicked Hearts and Judgments are
Your griping Hands, by weighty Bribes
3 To Virtue Strangers from the Womb,
They prattled Slander, and in Lyes
4 No Serpent of parch'd Afric's Breed
The drowsy Adder will as soon
5 Unmov'd by good Advice, and deaf
From whom the skilful Charmer's Voice
6 Defeat, O God, their threat'ning Rage,
Disarm these growing Lion's Jaws,
7 Let now their Insolence, at Height,
Their shiver'd Darts deceive their Aim,

if just your Sentence be,
to Heav'n from your Decree?
alike by Malice sway'd:
to Violence betray'd.
their Infant-steps went wrong?
employ'd their lisping Tongue.
does ranker Poison bear;
unlock his sullen Ear.
as Adders they remain;
can no Attention gain.
and timely break their Pow'r:
ere practis'd to devour.
like ebbing Tides be spent;
when they their Bow have bent.

8 Like

PSALM, LIX, LX.

8 Like Snails let them diffolve to Slime; like hafty Births become,
Unworthy to behold the Sun, and dead within the Womb.
9 Ere Thorns can make the Flefh-pots boil, tempeftuous Wrath fhall come
From God, and fnatch 'em hence alive, to their eternal Doom.
10 The Righteous fhall rejoice to fee their Crimes fuch Vengeance meet,
And Saints in Perfecutors Blood, fhall dip their harmlefs Feet.
11 Tranfgreffors then with Grief fhall fee juft Men Rewards obtain;
And own a God, whofe Juftice will the guilty Earth arraign.

PSALM LIX.

1 DELIVER me, O Lord my God, from all my fpiteful Foes;
In my Defence oppofe thy Pow'r to theirs who me oppofe.
2 Preferve me from a wicked Race, who make a Trade of Ill;
Protect me from remorfelefs Men. who feek my Blood to fpill.
3 They lie in wait, and mighty Pow'rs againft my Life combine:
Implacable; yet, Lord, thou know'ft for no Offence of mine.
4 In hafte they run about, and watch my guiltlefs Life to take:
Look down, O Lord, on my Diftrefs, and to my Help awake!
5 Thou, Lord of Hofts, and Ifr'el's God, their Heathen Rage fupprefs;
Relentlefs Vengeance take on thofe who ftubbornly tranfgrefs.
6 At Ev'ning to befet my Houfe like growling Dogs they meet;
While others thro' the City range, and ranfack ev'ry Street.
7 Their Throats envenom'd Slander breathe, theirTongues arefharpen'dSwords;
Who hears (fay they) or hearing dares reprove our lawlefs Words?
8 But from thy Throne thou fhalt, O Lord, their baffled Plots deride;
And foon to Scorn and Shame expofe their boafted heathen Pride.
9 On thee I wait, 'tis on thy Strength for Succour I depend:
'Tis thou, O God, art my Defence, who only canft defend.
10 Thy Mercy, Lord, which has fo oft from Danger fet me free,
Shall crown my Wifhes, and fubdue My haughty Foes to me.
11 Deftroy 'em not, O Lord, at once, reftrain thy vengeful Blow,
Left we, ingratefully, too foon forget their Overthrow.
Difperfe 'em thro' the Nations round by thy avenging Pow'r.
Do thou bring down their haughty Pride, O Lord, our Shield and Tow'r.
12 Now, in the Height of all their Hopes, their Arrogance chaftife;
Whofe Tongues have finn'd without Reftraint, and Curfes join'd with Lyes.
13 Nor fhalt thou, whilft their Race endures, thine Anger, Lord, fupprefs,
That diftant Lands, by their juft Doom may Ifr'el's God confefs.
14 At Ev'ning let them ftill perfift like growling Dogs to meet,
Still wander all the City round, and traverfe ev'ry Street.
15 Then, as for Malice now they do, for Hunger let them ftray,
And yell their vain Complaints aloud, defeated of their Prey.
16 Whilft early I thy Mercy fing, thy wond'rous Pow'r confefs;
For thou haft been my fure Defence, my Refuge in Diftrefs.
17 To thee with never-ceafing Praife, O God, my Strength, I'll fing;
Thou art my God, the Rock from whence my Health and Safety fpring.

PSALM LX.

1 O God, who haft ourTroops difperft, Forfaking thofe who left thee firft,
As we thy juft Difpleafure mourn, To us in Mercy, Lord, return.

2 Our

PSALM LXVI.

3 Our Sins (tho' numberless) in vain To stop thy flowing Mercy try;
Whilst thou o'erlook'st the guilty Stain, And washest out the crimson Dye.
4 Blest is the Man, who near thee plac'd, Within thy sacred Dwelling lives!
Whilst we at humbler Distance taste The vast Delights thy Temple gives.

5 By wond'rous Acts, O God, most just, Have we thy gracious Answer found;
In thee remotest Nations trust, And those whom stormy Waves surround.
6, 7 God, by his Strength, sets fast the Hills, And does his matchless Pow'r engage,
With which the Seas loud Waves he stills, And angry Crowds tumultuous rage.

PART II.

8 Thou, Lord, dost barb'rous Lands dismay, When they thy dreadful Tokens view:
With Joy they see the Night and Day, Each others Track by Turns pursue.
9 From out thy unexhausted Store Thy Rain relieves the thirsty Ground;
Makes Lands, that barren were before, With Corn and useful Fruits abound.

10 On rising Ridges, down it pours, And ev'ry furrow'd Valley fills;
Thou mak'st them soft with gentle In which a blest Increase distils.
Show'rs
11 Thy Goodness does the circling Year With fresh returns of Plenty crown;
And where thy glorious Paths appear, Thy fruitful Clouds drop Fatness down.

12 They drop on barren Forests, chang'd By them to Pastures fresh and green:
The Hills about in Order rang'd, In beauteous Robes of Joy are seen.
13 Large Flocks with fleecy Wool adorn The chearful Downs; the Vallies bring
A plentious Crop of full-ear'd Corn, And seem for Joy to shout and sing.

PSALM LXVI.

1, 2 LET all the Lands with Shouts of Joy· to God their Voices raise;
Sing Psalms in Honour of his Name, and spread his glorious Praise.
3 And let them say, how dreadful, Lord, in all thy Works art thou!
To thy great Pow'r thy stubborn Foes shall all be forc'd to bow.

4 Thro' all the Earth the Nations round shall thee their Good confess;
And with glad Hymns their awful Dread of thy great Name express.
5 O come, behold the Works of God, and then with me, you'll own,
That he to all the Sons of Men, has wond'rous Judgments shown.

6 He made the Sea become dry Land, thro' which our Fathers walk'd;
Whilst to each other of his Might with Joy his People talk'd.
7 He by his Pow'r for ever rules; his Eyes the World survey;
Let no presumptuous Man rebel against his sov'reign Sway.

PART II.

8, 9 O all ye Nations, bless our God, and loudly speak his Praise;
Who keeps our Soul alive, and still confirms our stedfast Ways.
10 For thou hast try'd us, Lord, as Fire does try the precious Ore;
11 Thou brought'st us into Straits, where we oppressing Burdens bore.

12 Insulting Foes did us, their Slaves, thro' Fire and Water chace;
But yet at last thou brought'st us forth into a wealthy Place.
13 Burnt-Off'rings to thy House I'll bring, and there my Vows I'll pay,
14 Which I with solemn Zeal did make in Trouble's dismal Day.

15 Then shall the richest Incense smoke, the fattest Rams shall fall;
The choicest Goats from out the Fold, and Bullocks from the Stall.
16 O come, all ye that fear the Lord, attend with heedful Care;
Whilst I what God for me has done, with grateful Joy declare.

17, 18 As

PSALM LXVII, LXVIII.

17, 18 As I before his Aid implor'd, so now I praise his Name;
Who, if my Heart had harbour'd Sin, would all my Pray'rs disclaim,
19 But God to me, whene'er I cry'd, his gracious Ear did bend;
And to the Voice of my Request with constant Love attend.

20 Then bless'd for ever be my God, who never, when I pray,
With-holds his Mercy from my Soul, nor turns his Face away.

PSALM LXVII.

1 TO bless thy chosen Race, in Mercy, Lord, incline;
And cause the Brightness of thy Face on all thy Saints to shine:
2 That so thy wond'rous Ways may thro' the World be known;
Whilst distant Lands their Tribute pays, and thy Salvation own.

3 Let diff'ring Nations join to celebrate thy Fame;
Let all the World, O Lord, combine to praise thy glorious Name.
4 O let them shout and sing, dissolv'd in pious Mirth,
For thou, the righteous Judge and King, shall govern all the Earth.

5 Let diff'ring Nations join to celebrate thy Fame ;
Let all the World, O Lord, combine to praise thy glorious Name.
6 Then shall the teeming Ground a large Increase disclose;
And we with Plenty shall be crown'd, which God, our God, bestows.

7 Then God upon our Land shall constant Blessings show'r,
And all the World in Awe shall stand of his resistless Pow'r.

PSALM LXVIII.

1 LET God, the God of Battle rise And scatter his presumptuous Foes;
Let shameful Rout their Host surprise, Who spitefully his Pow'r oppose.
2 As smoke in Tempest's Rage is lost, Or Wax into the Furnace cast,
So let their sacrilegious Host Before his wrathful Presence waste.

3 But let the Servants of his Will His Favour's gentle Beams enjoy;
Their upright Hearts let Gladness fill, And chearful Songs their Tongues employ.
4 To him your Voice in Anthems raise, Jehovah's awful Name he bears,
In him rejoice, extol his Praise, Who rides upon high rolling Spheres.

5 Him, from his Empire of the Skies, To this low World Compassion draws,
The Orphan's Claim to patronize, And judge the injur'd Widow's Cause.
6 'Tis God, who from a foreign Soil, Restores poor Exiles to their Home,
Makes Captives free, and fruitless Toil Their proud Oppressors righteous Doom.

7 'Twas so of old, when thou didst lead, In Person, Lord, our Armies forth,
Strange Terrors thro' the Desart spread, Convulsions shook th' astonish'd Earth.
8 The breaking Clouds did Rain distil, And Heav'n's high Arches shook with Fear:
How then shall Sinai's humble Hill, Of Isr'el's God the Presence bear?

9 Thy Hand at famisht Earth's Complaint, Reliev'd her from celestial Stores;
And when thy Heritage was faint, Asswag'd the Drought with plenteous Show-
10 Where Savages had rang'd before, At Ease thou mad'st our Tribes reside; ('rs.
And in the Desart, for the Poor, Thy gen'rous Bounty did provide.

PART II.

11 Thou gav'st the Word, we sally'd forth, And in that pow'rful Word o'ercame;
While Virgin-troops with Songs of Mirth In State our Conquest did proclaim.
12 Vast Armies, by such Gen'rals led, As yet had ne'er receiv'd a Foil,
Forsook their Camp with sudden Dread, And to our Women left the Spoil.

PSALM LXVIII.

13 Tho' Egypt's Drudges you have been, Your Army's Wings shall shine as bright
   As Doves in Golden Sun-shine seen,   Or silver'd o'er with paler Light.
14 'Twas so when God's Almighty Hand   O'er scatter'd Kings the Conquest won;
   Our Troops drawn up on Jordan's Strand, High Salmon's glitt'ring Snow out-shone.

15 From thence to Jordan's farther Coast, And Bashan's Hill we did advance:
   No more her Height shall Bashan boast, But that she's God's Inheritance.
16 But wherefore (tho' the Honour's great) Should this, O Mountains, swell your Pride;
   For Sion is his chosen Seat,   Where he for ever will reside.

17 His Chariots numberless, his Pow'rs   Are heav'nly Hosts that wait his Will;
   His Presence now fills Sion's Tow'rs, As once it honour'd Sinai's Hill.
18 Ascending high, in Triumph thou   Captivity hast Captive led
   And on thy People didst bestow   The Spoil of Armies, once their Dread.

Ev'n Rebels shall partake thy Grace,   And humble Proselytes repair
To worship at thy Dwelling-Place,   And all the World pay Homage there.
19 For Benefits each Day bestow'd,   Be daily his great Name ador'd;
20 Who is our Saviour and our God,   Of Life and Death the sov'reign Lord.

21 But Justice for his harden'd Foes   Proportion'd Vengeance hath decreed,
   To wound the hoary Head of those   Who in presumptuous Crimes proceed.
22 The Lord has thus, in Thunder spoke; "As I subdu'd proud Bashan's King,
   "Once more I'll break my People's Yoke, " And from the Deep my Servants bring.
23 "Their Feet shall with a Crimson Flood "Of slaughter'd Foes be cover'd o'er,
   " Nor Earth receive such impious Blood, " But leave for Dogs th' unhallow'd Gore.

PART III.

24 When marching to thy blest Abode,   The wond'ring Multitude survey'd
   The pompous State of thee O God,   In Robes of Majesty array'd."
25 Sweet-singing Levites led the Van,   Loud Instruments brought up the Rear;
   Between both Troops a Virgin Train   With Voice and Timbrel charm'd the Ear.

26 This was the Burden of their Song,   " In full Assemblies bless the Lord,
   " All, who to Isr'el's Tribes belong, " The God of Isr'el's Praise record."
27 Nor little Benjamin alone   From neighb'ring Bounds did there attend.
   Nor only Judah's nearer Throne,   Her Counsellors in State did send.

But Zebulon's remoter Seat,   And Naphthali's more distant Coast,
(The grand Procession to compleat)   Sent up their Tribes a princely Host.
28 Thus God to Strength & Union brought Our Tribes, at Strife till that blest Hour;
   This Work, which thou, O God, hast   Confirm with fresh Recruits of Pow'r.
   wrought,

29 To visit Salem, Lord, descend,   And Sion thy terrestrial Throne;
   Where Kings with Presents shall attend, And thee with offer'd Crowns atone.
30 Break down the Spearmen's Ranks, who Like pamper'd Herds of savage Might,
   threat
   Their Silver'd-armour'd Chiefs defeat, Who in destructive War delight.

31 Egypt shall then to God stretch forth Her Hands, and Afric Homage bring:
32 The scatter'd Kingdoms of the Earth   Their common Sov'reign's Praises sing.
33 Who mounted on the loftiest Sphere   Of ancient Heav'n, sublimely rides;
   From whence his dreadful Voice we hear, Like that of warning Winds and Tides.

34 Ascribe ye Pow'r to God most high,   Of humble Isr'el he takes Care;
   Whose Strength from out the dusky Sky Darts shining Terrors thro' the Air.
35 How dreadful are the sacred Courts,   Where God has fix'd his earthly Throne!
   His Strength his feeble Saints supports; To God give Praise, and him alone.

PSALM

PSALM LXIX.

PSALM LXIX.

SAVE me, O God, from Waves that roll,
And press to overwhelm my Soul.
With painful Steps in Mire I tread, And Deluges o'erflow my Head,
With restless Cries my Spirits faint, My Voice is hoarse with long Complaint,
My Sight decays with tedious Pain, Whilst for my Good I wait in vain.

My Hairs, tho' num'rous, are but few, Compar'd with Foes that me pursue
With groundless Hate, grown now of Might To execute their lawless Spite,
They force, me guiltless, to resign As Rapine, what by Right was mine.
Thou, Lord, my Innocence dost see, Nor are my Sins conceal'd from thee.

Lord God of Hosts, take timely Care, Let for my Sake thy Saints despair;
Since I have suffer'd for thy Name Reproach, and hid my Face in Shame.
A Stranger to my Country grown; Nor to my nearest Kindred known;
A Foreigner, expos'd to Scorn By Brethren of my Mother born.

For Zeal to thy lov'd House and Name Consumes me like devouring Flame,
Concern'd at their Affronts to thee, More than at Slanders cast on me.
My very Tears and Abstinence They construe in a spiteful Sense ;
When cloth'd with Sackcloth for their sake, They me their common Proverb make.

Their Judges make my Wrongs their Jest, Those Wrongs they ought to have redrest !
How should I then expect to be From Libels of lewd Drunkards free.
But, Lord, to thee I will repair For Help with humble timely Pray'r :
Relieve me from thy Mercy's Store, Display thy Truth's deserving Pow'r.

From threat'ning Dangers me relieve, And from the Mire my Feet retrieve ;
From spiteful Foes in Safety keep, And snatch me from the raging Deep.
Controul the Deluge e'er it spread, And roll its Waves above my Head;
Nor deep Destruction's yawning Pit To close her Jaws on me permit.

Lord, hear the humble Pray'r I make, For thy transcending Goodness Sake;
Relieve the Supplicant once more From thy abounding Mercy's Store.
Nor from thy Servant hide thy Face; Make haste, for desp'rate is my Case :
Thy timely Succour interpose, And shield me from remorseless Foes.

Thou know'st what Infamy and Scorn, I from my Enemies have born,
Nor can their close dissembled Spite, Or darkest Plots escape thy Sight.
Reproach & Grief have broke my Heart, I look'd for some to take my Part;
To pity or relieve my Pain, But look'd (alas !) for both in vain !

With Hunger pin'd for Food I call, Instead of Food, they gave me Gall ;
And when with Thirsts my Spirits sink, They gave me Vinegar to drink.
Their Table therefore to their Health Shall prove a Snare, a Trap their Wealth ;
Perpetual Darkness seize their Eyes, And sudden Blasts their Hopes surprise.

On them thou shalt thy Fury pour, Till thy fierce Wrath their Race devour.
And make their House a dismal Cell, Where none will e'er vouchsafe to dwell.
For new Afflictions they procur'd, For him who had thy Stripes endur'd;
And made the Wounds thy Scourge had torn To bleed afresh with sharper Scorn.

Sin shall to Sin their Steps betray, Till they to Truth have lost the Way.
From Life thou shalt exclude their Soul, Nor with the Just their Names enrol.
But me, howe'er distrest and poor, Thy strong Salvation shall restore :
Thy Pow'r with Songs I'll then proclaim, And celebrate with Thanks thy Name.

PSALM LXX, LXXI.

31 Our God shall this more highly prize Than Herds or Flocks in Sacrifice;
32 Which humble Saints with Joy shall see, And hope for like Redress with me.
33 For God regards the Poor's Complaint, Sets Pris'ners free from close Restraint;
34 Let Heav'n, Earth, Sea, their Voices raise, And all the World resound his Praise.

35 For God will Sion's Walls erect, Fair Judah's Cities he'll protect,
Till all her scatter'd Sons repair To undisturb'd Possession there.
36 This Blessing they shall, at their Death, To their religious Heirs bequeath;
And they to endless Ages more, Of such as his blest Name adore.

PSALM LXX.

1 O Lord, to my Relief draw near, for never was more pressing Need;
For my Deliv'rance, Lord, appear, and add to that Deliv'rance Speed.
2 Confusion on their Heads return, who to destroy my Soul combine;
Let them, defeated, blush and mourn, ensnar'd in their own vile Design.

3 Their Doom let Desolation be, with Shame their Malice be repaid.
Who mock'd my Confidence in thee, and Sport of my Afflictions made.
4 While those who humbly seek thy Face, to joyful Triumphs shall be rais'd,
And all who prize thy saving Grace with me shall sing, The Lord be prais'd.

5 Thus wretched tho' I am and poor, the mighty Lord of me takes care,
Thou God, who only can'st restore, to my Relief with Speed repair.

PSALM LXXI.

1, 2 IN thee I put my stedfast Trust, defend me, Lord, from Shame;
Incline thine Ear, and save my Soul, for righteous is thy Name.
3 Be thou my strong abiding Place, to which I may resort;
'Tis thy Decree that keeps me safe; thou art my Rock and Fort.

4, 5 From cruel and ungodly Men protect and set me free,
For from my earliest Youth 'till now my Hope has been in thee.
6 Thy constant Care did safely guard my tender infant Days;
Thou took'st me from my Mother's Womb, to sing thy constant Praise.

7, 8 While some on me with Wonder gaze, thy Hand supports me still;
Thy Honour therefore and thy Praise my Mouth shall always fill.
9 Reject not then thy Servant, Lord, when I with Age decay,
Forsake me not, when worn with Years, my Vigour fades away.

10 My Foes, against my Fame and me, with crafty Malice speak;
Against my Soul, they lay their Snares, and mutual Counsel take.
11 His God, say they, forsakes him now, on whom he did rely:
Pursue and take him, whilst no Hope of timely Aid is nigh.

12 But thou, my God, withdraw not far, for speedy Help I call;
13 To Shame and Ruin bring my Foes that seek to work my Fall.
14 But as for me, my stedfast Hope shall on thy Pow'r depend,
And I in grateful Songs of Praise, my Time to come will spend.

PART II.

15 Thy righteous Acts and saving Health my Mouth shall still declare;
Unable yet to count them all, tho' summ'd with utmost Care.
16 While God vouchsafes me his Support, I'll in his Strength go on;
All other Righteousness disclaim, and mention his alone.

17 Thou, Lord, hast taught me from my Youth to praise thy glorious Name?
And ever since thy wond'rous Works have been my constant Theme.

18 Then

PSALM LXXII.

18 Then now forsake me not when I am gray and feeble grown,
'Till I to these and future Times, thy Strength and Pow'r have shown.
19 How high thy Justice soars, O God! how great and wond'rous are
The mighty Works which thou hast done! who may with thee compare?
20 Me, whom thy Hand had sorely press'd, thy Grace shall yet relieve;
And from the lowest Depth of Woe with tender Care retrieve.
21 Thro' thee my Time to come shall be with Pow'r and Greatness crown'd,
And me, who dismal Years have past, thy Comforts shall surround.
22 Therefore with Psaltery and Harp thy Truth, O Lord, I'll praise;
To thee, the God of Jacob's Race, my Voice in Anthems raise.
23 Then Joy shall fill my Mouth, and Songs employ my chearful Voice;
My grateful Soul, by thee redeem'd shall in thy Strength rejoice.
24 My Tongue thy just and righteous Acts shall all the Day proclaim;
Because thou didst confound my Foes, and brought'st them all to Shame.

PSALM LXXII.

1 LORD, let thy just Decrees the King in all his Ways direct;
And let his Son throughout his Reign thy righteous Laws respect.
2 So shall he still thy People judge with pure and upright Mind,
Whilst all the helpless Poor shall him their just Protector find.
3 Then Hills and Mountains shall bring forth the happy Fruits of Peace;
Which all the Land shall own to be the Work of Righteousness;
4 Whilst he the poor and needy Race shall rule with gentle Sway;
And from their humble Necks shall take oppressive Yokes away.
5 In ev'ry Heart thy awful Fear shall then be rooted fast,
As long as Sun and Moon endure, or Time itself shall last.
6 He shall descend like Rain that chears the Meadows second Birth,
Or like warm Show'rs, whose gentle Drops refresh the thirsty Earth.
7 In his blest Days the Just and Good shall be with Favour crown'd,
The happy Land shall ev'ry where with endless Peace abound.
8 His uncontrol'd Dominion shall from Sea to Sea extend,
Begin at proud Euphrate's Streams, at Nature's Limits end.
9 To him the savage Nations round shall bow their servile Heads,
His vanquish'd Foes shall lick the Dust where he his Conquests spreads.
10 The Kings of Tarshish and the Isles shall costly Presents bring;
From spicy Sheba Gifts shall come, and wealthy Saba's King.
11 To him shall ev'ry King on Earth his humble Homage pay,
And diff'ring Nations gladly join to own his righteous Sway.
12 For he shall set the Needy free, when they for Succour cry,
Shall save the Helpless and the Poor, and all their Wants supply.

PART II.

13 His Providence, for needy Souls, shall due Supplies prepare:
And over their defenceless Lives shall watch with tender Care.
14 He shall preserve and keep their Souls, from Fraud and Rapine free,
And in his Sight their guiltless Blood of mighty Price shall be.
15 Therefore shall God his Life and Reign to many Years extend,
Whilst Eastern Princes Tribute pay, and golden Presents send.
For him shall constant Pray'rs be made, thro' all his prosp'rous Days,
His just Dominion shall afford a lasting Theme of Praise.

PSALM LXXIII.

16 Of useful Grain, thro' all the Land, great Plenty shall appear;
A Handful sown on Mountain Tops a mighty Crop shall bear.
Its Fruit, like Cedars shook by Winds, a rattling Noise shall yield;
The City too shall thrive, and vie for Plenty with the Field.

17 The Mem'ry of his glorious Name thro' endless Years shall run;
His spotless Fame shall shine as bright and lasting as the Sun.
In him the Nations of the World shall be completely blest,
And his unbounded Happiness by ev'ry Tongue confest.

18 Then bless'd be God, the mighty Lord, the God whom Isr'el fears;
Who only wond'rous in his Works, beyond compare appears,
19 Let Earth be with his Glory fill'd; for ever bless his Name;
Whilst to his Praise the list'ning World their good Assent proclaim.

PSALM LXXIII.

1 AT length, by certain Proofs, 'tis plain that God will to his Saints be kind;
That all, whose Hearts are pure & clean, shall his protecting Favour find.
2, 3 Till this sustaining Truth I knew, my stagg'ring Feet had almost fail'd;
I griev'd the Sinners Wealth to view, and envy'd when the Fools prevail'd.
4, 5 They to the Grave in Peace descend, and whilst they live are hale and strong;
No Plagues or Troubles them offend, which oft to other Men belong.
6, 7 With Pride, as with a Chain, they're held,
Their Eyes stand out with Fatness swell'd, and Rapine seem their Robe of State;
they grow beyond their Wishes great.
8, 9 With Hearts corrupt and lofty Talk, oppressive Methods they defend;
Their Tongue thro' all the Earth does walk, their Blasphemies to Heav'n ascend.
10 And yet admiring Crowds are found, who servile Visits duly make,
Because with Plenty they abound, of which their flatt'ring Slaves partake.
11 Their fond Opinions these pursue, till they with them prophanely cry,
" How should the Lord our Actions view, " Can he perceive who dwells so high?"
12 Behold the Wicked! these are they who openly their Sins profess;
And yet their Wealth's increas'd each Day, and all their Actions meet Success.
13, 14 Then have I cleans'd my Heart (said I) and wash'd my Hands from Guilt in vain,
If all the Day opprefs'd I lie, and ev'ry Morning suffer Pain.
15 Thus did I once to speak intend; but if such Things I rashly say,
Thy Children, Lord, I must offend, and basely should their Cause betray.

PART II.

16, 17 To fathom this my Thoughts I bent, but found the Case too hard for me,
'Till to the House of God I went, then I their End did plainly see.
18 How high foe'er advanc'd, they all on slipp'ry Places loosely stand;
Thence into Ruin headlong fall, cast down by thy avenging Hand.
19, 20 How dreadful and how quick their Fate! despis'd by thee, when they're destroy'd;
As waking Men with Scorns do treat the Fancies that their Dreams employ'd.
21, 22 Thus was my Heart with Grief opprefs'd, my Reins were rack'd with restless Pains;
So stupid was I, like a Beast, who no reflecting Thought retains.
23, 24 Yet still thy Presence me supply'd, and thy Right-hand Assistance gave,
Thou first shalt with my Counsel guide, and then to Glory me receive.
25 Whom then in Heav'n, but thee alone, have I, whose Favour I require?
Throughout the spacious Earth there's none that I besides thee can desire.

26 My

PSALM LXXIV.

26 My trembling Flesh and aking Heart may often fail to succour me;
But God shall inward Strength impart, and my eternal Portion be.
27 For they that far from thee remove, shall into sudden Ruin fall;
If after other Gods they rove, thy Vengeance shall destroy them all.

28 But as for me, 'tis good and just that I should still to God repair;
In him I always put my Trust, and will his wond'rous Works declare.

PSALM LXXIV.

1 WHY hast thou cast us off, O God! wilt thou no more return?
O why against thy chosen Flock, does thy fierce Anger burn?
2 Think on thy ancient Purchase, Lord, the Land that is thy own;
By thee redeem'd; and Sion's Mount, where once thy Glory shone.

3 O come, and view our ruin'd State! how long our Troubles last!
See! how the Foe with wicked Rage has laid thy Temple waste!
4 Thy Foes blaspheme thy Name; where late thy zealous Servants pray'd;
The Heathen there, with haughty Pomp, their Banners have display'd.

5, 6 Those curious Carvings which did once advance the Artist's Fame,
With Ax and Hammer they destroy, like Works of vulgar Frame.
7 Thy holy Temple they have burnt; and what escap'd the Flame,
Has been prophan'd, and quite defac'd. tho' sacred to thy Name.

8 Thy Worship wholly to destroy, maliciously they aim'd;
And all the sacred Places burn'd where we thy Praise proclaim'd.
9 Yet of thy Presence thou vouchsaf'st no tender Signs to send;
We have no Prophet now that knows when this sad State shall end.

PART II.

10 But, Lord, how long wilt thou permit th' insulting Foe to boast?
Shall all the Honour of thy Name for evermore be lost?
11 Why hold'st thou back thy strong Right-hand? and on thy patient Breast,
When Vengeance calls to stretch it forth, so calmly let's it rest?

12 Thou heretofore, with kingly Pow'r, in our Defence hast fought;
For us, throughout the wand'ring World, hast great Salvation wrought.
13 'Twas thou, O God, that didst the Sea by thy own Strength divide;
Thou break'st the wat'ry Monster's Head, thy Waves o'erwhelm'd their Pride.

14 The greatest, fiercest of them all, that seem'd the Deep to sway;
Was by thy Pow'r destroy'd, and made to savage Beasts a Prey.
15 Thou clav'st the solid Rock, and mad'st the Waters largely flow;
Again, thou mad'st thro' parting Streams thy wand'ring People go.

16 Thine is the chearful Day, and thine the black return of Night;
Thou hast prepar'd the glorious Sun, and ev'ry feebler Light:
17 By thee the Borders of the Earth in perfect Order stand;
The Summer's Warmth, the Winter's Cold, attend on thy Command.

PART III.

18 Remember, Lord, how scornful Foes have daily urg'd our Shame;
And how the foolish People have blasphem'd thy holy Name.
19 O free thy mourning Turtle-Dove, by sinful Crowds beset;
Nor the Assembly of thy Poor. for evermore forget.

20 Thy ancient Cov'nant, Lord, regard, and make thy Promise good;
For now each Corner of the Land is fill'd with Men of Blood.
21 O let not the Opprest return, with Sorrow cloath'd and Shame;
But let the Helpless and the Poor for ever Praise thy Name.

22 Arise,

PSALM LXXV, LXXVI.

22 Arise, O God, in our Behalf,
Remember how insulting Fools
23 Make thou the Boastings of thy Foes
Whose Insolence, if unchastis'd,

thy Cause and ours maintain;
each Day thy Name prophane!
for ever, Lord, to cease;
will more and more increase.

PSALM LXXV.

1 TO thee, O God, my tender Praise,
   For, that thy Name to us is nigh,
2 In Isr'el when my Throne is fix'd,
3 The Land with Discord shakes, but I

to thee with Thanks repair:
thy wond'rous Works declare.
with me shall Justice reign:
the sinking Frame sustain.

4 Deluded Wretches I advis'd
And warn'd bold Sinners that they should
5 Bear not yourselves so high, as if
Submit your stubborn Necks, and learn

their Errors to redress,
their swelling Pride suppress.
no Pow'r could yours restrain;
to speak with less Disdain.

6 For that Promotion, which to gain
From neither East nor West, nor yet
7 For God the great Disposer is,
Who casts the Proud to Earth, and lifts

your vain Ambition strives,
from Southern Climes arrives.
and sov'reign Judge alone,
the Humble to a Throne.

8 His Hand holds forth a dreadful Cup,
The deadly Mixture, which his Wrath
Of this his Saints sometimes may taste,
The bitter Dregs, and be condemn'd

with Purple Wine 'tis crown'd;
deals out to Nations round,
but wicked Men shall squeeze
to drink the very Lees.

9 His Prophet, I, to all the World
The Justice then of Jacob's God,
10 The Wicked's Pride I will reduce,
Exalt the Just, and seat him high,

this Message will relate;
my Song shall celebrate.
their Cruelty disarm!
above the Reach of Harm.

PSALM LXXVI.

1 IN Judah the Almighty's known,
   (Almighty thereby Wonders shown)
   His Name in Jacob does excel:
2 His Sanctuary in Salem stands,
Their Majesty that Heav'n commands,
In Sion condescends to dwell.

3 He brake the Bow and Arrows there,
The Shield, the temper'd Sword and Spear,
There slain the mighty Army lay;
4 Whence Sion's Fame thro' Earth is spread,
Of greater Glory, greater Dread,
Than Hills where Robbers lodge their Prey.

5 Their valiant Chiefs, who came for Spoil,
Themselves met there a shameful Foil.
Securely down to Sleep they lay,
But wak'd no more; their stoutest Band
Ne'er lifted one resisting Hand
'Gainst his that did their Legions slay.

6 When Jacob's God began to frown,
Both Horse, and Charioteers, o'erthrown,
Together slept in endless Night:
7 When thou, whom Heav'n and Earth revere,
Dost once with wrathful Look appear,
What mortal Pow'r can stand thy Sight.

8 Pronounc'd from Heav'n, Earth heard its Doom, (come,
Grew hush'd with Fear, when thou didst
9 The Meek with Justice to restore;
10 The Wrath of Man shall yield thee Praise,
Its last Attempts but serve to raise
the Triumphs of Almighty Pow'r.

11 Vow to the Lord, ye Nations, bring
Vow'd Presents to the Eternal King;
Thus to his Name due Rev'rence pay,
12 Who proudest Potentates can quell,
To earthly Kings more terrible
Than to their trembling Subjects they.

PSALM

PSALM LXXVII, LXXVIII.

PSALM LXXVII.

1 TO God I cry'd, who to my Help did graciously appear;
 In Trouble's difmal Day I fought my God with humble Pray'r.
2 All Night my feſt'ring Wound did run, no Med'cine gave Relief;
 My Soul no comfort would admit, my Soul indulg'd her Grief.

3 I thought on God, and Favours paſt, but that increas'd my Pain;
 I found my Spirit more oppreſt, the more I did complain.
4 Thro' ev'ry Watch of tedious Night thou keep'ſt my Eyes awake;
 My Grief is ſwell'd to that Exceſs I ſigh but cannot ſpeak.

5 I call to mind the Days of old with ſignal Mercy crown'd,
 Thoſe famous Years of ancient Times, for Miracles renown'd.
6 By Night I recollect my Songs on former Triumphs made,
 Then ſearch, conſult, and aſk my Heart where's now that wond'rous Aid?

7 Has God for ever caſt us off? Withdrawn his Favours quite?
8 Are both his Mercy and his Truth retir'd to endleſs Night?
9 Can his long-pracliſ'd Love forget its wonted Aids to bring!
 Has he in Wrath ſhut up and ſeal'd his Mercy's healing Spring?

10 I ſaid, my Weakneſs hints theſe Fears, but I'll my Fears diſband;
 I'll yet remember the moſt high, and Years of his Right-hand.
11 I'll call to mind his Works of old, the Wonders of his Might;
12 On them my Heart ſhall meditate, my Tongue ſhall then recite.

13 Safe lodg'd from human ſearch on high, O God, thy Counſels are!
 Who is ſo great a God as ours? who can with him compare?
14 Long ſince a God of Wonders thee thy reſcu'd People found:
15 Long ſince haſt thou thy choſen Seed with ſtrong Deliv'rance crown'd.

16 When thee, O God, the Waters ſaw, the frighted Billows ſhrunk;
 The troubled Depths themſelves for Fear, beneath their Channels ſunk.
17 The Clouds pour'd down, while rending Skies did with their Noiſe conſpire;
 Thy Arrows all abroad were ſent, wing'd with avenging Fire.

18 Heav'n with thy Thunders Voice was torn, whilſt all the lower World
 With Light'nings blaz'd; Earth ſhook and ſeem'd from her Foundations hurl'd.
19 Thro' rolling Streams thou find'ſt thy Way, thy Paths in Waters lie;
 Thy wond'rous Paſſage, where no Sight thy Footſteps can deſcry.

20 Thou led'ſt thy People, like a Flock, ſafe thro' the deſart Land.
 By Moſes, their meek ſkilful Guide, and Aaron's ſacred Hand.

PSALM LXXVIII.

HEAR, O my People; to my Law devout Attention lend;
 Let the Inſtruction of my Mouth deep in your Hearts deſcend.
My Tongue, by Inſpiration taught, ſhall Parables unfold,
Dark Oracles, but underſtood, and own'd for Truths of old.

Which we from ſacred Regiſters of ancient Times have known,
And our Fore-fathers pious Care to us has handed down.
We will not hide them from our Sons; our Offspring ſhall be taught
The Praiſes of the Lord, whoſe Strength has Works of Wonders wrought.

For Jacob he this Law ordain'd, this League with Iſr'el made,
With Charge, to be from Age to Age, from Race to Race convey'd.
That Generations yet to come ſhould to their unborn Heirs
Religiouſly tranſmit the ſame, and they again to theirs.

PSALM LXXVIII.

7 To teach 'em that in God alone their Hope fecurely ftands;
That they fhould ne'er his Works forget, but keep his juft Commands.
8 Left, like their Fathers they might prove a ftiff Rebellious Race,
Falfe-hearted, fickle to their God, unftedfaft in his Grace.
9 Such were revolting Ephraim's Sons, who tho' to Warfare bred,
And fkilful Archers arm'd with Bows, from Field ignobly fled.
10, 11 They falfify'd their League with God, his Orders difobey'd;
Forgot his Works and Miracles before their Eyes difplay'd.
12 Nor Wonders which their Fathers faw, did they in Mind retain;
Prodigious Things in Egypt done, and Zoan's fertile Plain.
13 He cut the Seas to let them pafs, reftrain'd the prefling Flood;
While pil'd in Heaps, on either Side, the folid Waters ftood.
14 A wond'rous Pillar led them on, compos'd of Shade and Light;
A fhelt'ring Cloud it prov'd by Day, a leading Fire by Night.
15 When Drought oppreft them, where no Stream the Wildernefs fupply'd,
He cleft the Rock, whofe flinty Breaft diffolv'd into a Tide.
16 Streams from the folid Rock he brought, which down in Rivers fell,
That, trav'ling with their Camp, each Day renew'd the Miracle.
17 Yet there they finn'd againft him more, provoking the moft High;
In that fame Defart where he did their fainting Souls fupply.
18 They firft incens'd him in their Hearts, that did his Pow'r diftruft,
And long'd for Meat, not urg'd by Want, but to indulge their Luft.
19 Then utter'd their blafpheming Doubts, " Can God, fay they, prepare
" A Table in the Wildernefs, " fet out with various Fare?
20 " He fmote the flinty Rock, ('tis true) " and gufhing Streams enfu'd;
" But can he Corn and Flefh provide " for fuch a Multitude?"
21 The Lord with Indignation heard: from Heav'n avenging Flame
On Jacob fell, confuming Wrath on thanklefs Ifr'el came.
22 Becaufe their unbelieving Hearts in God wou'd not confide:
Nor truft his Care, who had from Heav'n, their Wants fo oft fupply'd.
23 Tho' he had made his Clouds difcharge Provifions down in Show'rs;
And when Earth fail'd, reliev'd their Needs from his celeftial Stores.
24 Tho' tafteful Manna was rain'd down their Hunger to relieve;
Tho' from the Stores of Heav'n they did fuftaining Corn receive.
25 Thus Man with Angels facred Food, ingrateful Man was fed;
Not fparingly, for ftill they found a plenteous Table fpread.
26 From Heav'n he made an Eaft-Wind blow, then did the South command,
27 To rain down Flefh like Duft, and Fowls like Seas unnumber'd Sand.
28 Within their Trenches he let fall the lufcious eafy Prey,
And all around their fpreading Camp their feather'd Booty lay.
29 They fed, were fill'd, he gave 'em Leave their Appetites to feaft;
30, 31 Yet ftill their wanton Luft crav'd on, nor with their Hunger ceas'd.
But whilft in their luxurious Mouths, they did their Dainties chew,
The Wrath of God fmote down their Chiefs, and Ifr'el's Chofen flew.

PART II.

32 Yet ftill they finn'd, nor would afford his Miracles Belief;
33 Therefore thro' fruitlefs Travels he confum'd their Lives in Grief.
34 When fome were flain, the reft return'd to God with early Cry;
35 Own'd him the Rock of their Defence, their Saviour, God moft High.

36 But

PSALM LXXVIII.

But this was feign'd Submiffion all,
Their Heart was ftill perverfe, nor would
Yet, full of Mercy, he forgave,
But turn'd his kindled Wrath afide,
their Heart their Tongue bely'd;
firm in his League abide.
nor did with Death chaftife;
or would not let it rife.

For he remember'd they were Flefh
A murm'ring Wind that's quickly paft
How oft did they provoke him there,
In that fame Defart where he did
that could not long remain;
and ne'er returns again.
how oft his Patience grieve,
their fainting Soul relieve?

They tempted him by turning back,
When Ifr'el's God refus'd to be
Nor call'd to mind the Hand and Day
His Signs in Egypt, wond'rous Works
and wickedly repin'd,
by their Defires confin'd.
that their Redemption brought;
in Zoan's Valley wrought.

He turn'd their Rivers into Blood,
And rather chofe to die of Thirft
He fent devouring Swarms of Flies,
Locufts and Caterpillars reap'd
that Man and Beaft forbore,
than drink the putrid Gore.
Hoarfe Frogs annoy'd their Soil;
the Harveft of their Toil.

Their Vines with batt'ring Hail were broke,
Lightning and Hail made Flocks and Herds
He turn'd his Anger loofe, and fet
And, with their Plagues, bad Angels fent
with Froft the Fig-tree dies;
one gen'ral Sacrifice.
no Time for it to ceafe;
their Torments to increafe.

He clear'd a Paffage for his Wrath
The Murrain on their Firftlings feiz'd
The deadly Peft from Beaft to Man,
It flew their Heirs, their eldeft Hopes,
to ravage uncontrol'd;
in ev'ry Field and Fold,
from Field and City came;
thro' all the Tents of Ham.

But his own Tribe, like folded Sheep,
And them conducted like a Flock,
He led 'em on, and in their Way,
But march'd fecurely thro' thofe Deeps
he brought from their Diftrefs,
throughout the Wildernefs.
no Caufe of Fear they found;
in which their Foes were drown'd.

Nor ceas'd his Care, 'till them he brought
And to his holy Mount, the Prize
To them the out-caft Heathen's Land
And in their Foes abandon'd Tents
fafe to his promis'd Land,
of his victorious Hand.
he did by Lot divide;
made Ifr'el's Tribes refide.

PART III.

Yet ftill they tempted, ftill provok'd
Nor would to practice his Commands
But in their faithlefs Fathers fteps
They turn'd afide, like Arrows fhot
the Wrath of God moft High;
their ftubborn Hearts apply.
perverfly chofe to go;
from fome deceitful Bow.

For him to Fury they provok'd
And with their graven Images
When God heard this, on Ifr'el's Tribes,
He quitted Shilo, and the Tents
with Altars fet on high;
inflam'd his Jealoufy.
his Wrath and Hatred fell;
where once he chofe to dwell.

To vile Captivity his Ark,
His People to the Sword he gave,
Deftructive War their ableft Youth
No Virgin was to th' Altar led,
his Glory to difdain,
nor would his Wrath reftrain.
untimely did confound;
with Nuptial Garlands crown'd.

In Fight the Sacrificer fell,
And Widows who their Death fhould mourn
Then, as a Giant, rouz'd from Sleep,
Shouts out aloud, the Lord awak'd,
the Prieft a Victim bled;
themfelves of Grief were dead.
whom Wine had throughly warm'd,
and his proud Foe alarm'd.

PSALM LXXIX, LXXX.

66 He smote their Hosts, that from the Field a scatter'd Remnant came,
 With Wounds imprinted on their Backs of everlasting Shame:
67 With Conquests crown'd, he, Joseph's Tents and Ephraim's Tribe forsook;
68 But Judah chose, and Sion's Mount for his lov'd dwelling took.

69 His Temple he erected there, with Spires exalted high,
 While deep and fixt, as that of Earth, the strong Foundations lie.
70 His faithful Servant David too, he for his Choice did own,
 And from the Sheep-folds him advanc'd to sit on Judah's Throne.

71 From tending on the teeming Ewes, he brought him forth to feed
 His own Inheritance, the Tribes of Isr'el's chosen Seed.
72 Exalted thus, the Monarch prov'd a faithful Shepherd still;
 He fed them with an upright Heart, and guided them with Skill.

PSALM LXXIX.

1 BEHOLD, O God, how Heathen Hosts have thy Possession seiz'd:
 Thy sacred House they have defil'd, thy holy City raz'd.
2 The mangled Bodies of thy Saints abroad unbury'd lay;
 Their Flesh expos'd to savage Beasts, and rav'nous Birds of Prey.

3 Quite thro' Jerus'lem was their Blood like common Water shed;
 And none were left alive to pay last Duties to the Dead.
4 The neighb'ring Lands our small Remains with loud Reproaches wound;
 And we a Laughing-stock are made to all the Nations round.

5 How long wilt thou be angry, Lord, must we for ever mourn?
 Shall thy devouring jealous Rage, like Fire, for ever burn?
6 On foreign Lands that know not thee, thy heavy Vengeance show'r,
 Those sinful Kingdoms let it crush that have not own'd thy Pow'r.

7 For their devouring Jaws have prey'd on Jacob's chosen Race;
 And to a barren Desart turn'd their fruitful dwelling place.
8 O think not on our former Sins, but speedily prevent
 The utter Ruin of thy Saints, almost with Sorrow spent.

9 Thou God of our Salvation, help, and free our Souls from Blame;
 So shall our Pardon and Defence exalt thy glorious Name.
10 Let Infidels, that scoffing say, where is the God they boast?
 In Vengeance for thy Daughter'd Saints, perceive thee to their Cost.

11 Lord, hear the sighing Pris'ners Moan, thy saving Pow'r extend:
 Preserve the Wretches doom'd to die, from that untimely End.
12 On them, who us oppress, let all our Suff'rings be repaid;
 Make their Confusion sev'n Times more than what on us they laid.

13 So we, thy People and thy Flock, shall ever praise thy Name;
 And with glad Hearts our grateful Thanks. from Age to Age proclaim.

PSALM LXXX.

1 O Isr'el's Shepherd, Joseph's Guide, our Pray'rs to thee vouchsafe to hear;
 Thou that dost on the Cherubs ride, again in solemn State appear.
2 Behold how Benjamin expects, with Ephraim and Manasseh join'd,
 In our Deliv'rance, the Effects of thy resistless Strength to find.

3 Do thou convert us, Lord, do thou the Lustre of thy Face display;
 And all the Ills we suffer now like scatter'd Clouds shall pass away.
4 O thou whom Heav'nly Hosts obey, how long shall thy fierce Anger burn?
 How long thy suff'ring People pray and to their Pray'rs have no Return?

5 When

PSALM LXXXI.

5 When hungry, we are forc'd to drench our scanty Food in Floods of Woe;
   When dry, our raging Thirst we quench with Streams of Tears that largely flow.
6 For us the Heathen Nations round, as for a common Prey, contest;
   Our Foes with spiteful Joy abound, and at our lost Condition jest.
7 Do thou convert us, Lord, do thou the Lustre of thy Face display;
   And all the Ills we suffer now, like scatter'd Clouds shall pass away.

PART II.

8 Thou brought'st a Vine from Egypt's Land, and casting out the Heathen Race,
   Didst plant it with thy own Right-hand, and firmly fix it in their Place.
9 Before it thou prepar'd'st the Way, and mad'st it take a lasting Root;
   Which, blest with thy indulgent Ray, o'er all the Land did widely shoot.
10,11 The Hills were cover'd with its Shade its goodly Boughs did Cedars seem;
   Its Branches to the Seas were spread, and reach'd to proud Euphrate's Stream.
12 Why then hast thou its Hedge o'er- which thou hast made so firm and strong?
   thrown,
   While all its Grapes, defenceless grown, are pluck'd by those that pass along.
13 See how the bristling Forest-Boar with dreadful Fury lays it waste;
   Hark how the savage Monsters roar, and to their helpless Prey make haste.

PART III.

14 To thee, O God of Hosts, we pray; thy wonted Goodness, Lord, renew:
   From Heav'n thy Throne this Vine survey, and her sad State with Pity view.
15 Behold the Vineyard, made by thee, which thy Right-hand did guard so long;
   And keep that Branch from Danger free, which for thyself thou mad'st so strong.
16 To wasting Flames 'tis made a Prey, And all its spreading Boughs cut down;
   At thy Rebuke they soon decay, And perish at thy dreadful Frown.
17 Crown thou the King with good Success, 'By thy Right-hand secur'd from Wrong;
   The Son of Man in Mercy bless, Whom for thyself thou mad'st so strong.
18 So shall we still continue free From whatsoe'er deserves thy Blame;
   And if once more reviv'd by thee, Will always praise thy holy Name.
19 Do thou convert us, Lord, do thou the Lustre of thy Face display;
   And all the Ills we suffer now, Like scatter'd Clouds, shall pass away.

PSALM LXXXI.

1 **T**O God, our never-failing Strength, with loud Applauses sing;
   And jointly make a chearful Noise to Jacob's awful King.,
2 Compose a Hymn of Praise, and touch your Instruments of Joy:
   Let Psalteries and pleasant Harps your grateful Skill employ.
3 Let Trumpets at the great New Moon their joyful Voices raise,
   To celebrate th' appointed Time, the solemn Day of Praise.
4 For this a Statute was of old, which Jacob's God decreed,
   To be with pious Care observ'd by Isr'el's chosen Seed.
5 This he for a Memorial fix'd when freed from Egypt's Land,
   Strange Nations barb'rous Speech we heard, but could not understand.
6 " Your burthen'd Shoulders I reliev'd, (thus seems our God to say)
   " Your servile Hands by me were freed " from lab'ring in the Clay.
7 " Your Ancestors with Wrongs opprest, " to me for Aid did call;
   " With Pity I their Suff'rings saw, " and set them free from all.
   " They sought for me, and from the Cloud " in Thunder I reply'd;
   " At Meribah's contentious Stream " their Faith and Duty try'd.

PSALM LXXXII, LXXXIII.

PART II.

8 " While I my solemn Will declare, " my chosen People, hear;
" If thou, O Isr'el, to my Words " wilt bend thy list'ning Ear;
9 " Then shall no God besides myself " within thy Coasts be found;
" Nor shalt thou worship any God " of all the Nations round.
10 " The Lord thy God am I, who thee " brought forth from Egypt's Land;
" 'Tis I that all thy just Desires " supply with lib'ral Hand.
11 " But they, my chosen Race, refus'd " to hearken to my Voice;
" Nor would rebellious Isr'el's Sons " make me their happy Choice."

12 So I, provok'd, resign'd them up to ev'ry Lust a Prey,
And, in their own perverse Designs, permitted them to stray.
13 O that my People wisely would my just Commandments heed!
And Isr'el in thy righteous Ways with pious Care proceed!
14 Then should my heavy Judgments fall on all that them oppose,
And my avenging Hand be turn'd against their num'rous Foes.
15 Their Enemies and mine, should all before my Footstool bend;
But as for them, their happy State shall never know an End.
16 All Parts with Plenty shall abound; with finest Wheat their Field:
The barren Rocks, to please their Taste, should richest Honey yield.

PSALM LXXXII.

1   GOD in the great Assembly stands, where his impartial Eye,
    In State surveys the earthly Gods, and does their Judgments try.
2, 3 How dare you then unjustly judge, or be to Sinners kind?
Defend the Orphans and the Poor, let such your Justice find.

4 Protect the humble helpless Man, reduc'd to deep Distress,
And let not him become a Prey to such as would oppress.
5 They neither know, nor will they learn, but blindly rove and stray;
Justice and Truth, the World's Support, thro' all the Land decay.

6 Well then may God in Anger say, " I've call'd you by my Name;
" I've said y'are Gods, the Sons and Heirs. " of my immortal Fame.
7 " But ne'ertheless your unjust Deeds " to strict Account I'll call;
" You all shall die like common Men, " like other Tyrants fall."

8 Arise, and thy just Judgment, Lord, throughout the Earth display;
And all the Nations of the World shall own thy righteous Sway.

PSALM LXXXIII.

1   HOLD not thy Peace, O Lord our God, no longer silent be;
    Nor with consenting quiet Looks our Ruin calmly see!
2 For lo! the Tumults of thy Foes o'er all the Land are spread;
And they that hate thy Saints and thee lift up their threat'ning Head.

3 Against thy zealous People, Lord, they craftily combine;
And to destroy the chosen Saints have laid their close Design.
4 " Come, let us cut them off, say they, " their Nation quite deface;
" That no Remembrance may remain " of Isr'el's hated Race,"

5 Thus they against thy People's Peace consult with one Consent;
And diff'ring Nations, jointly leagu'd, their common Malice vent.
6 The Ishm'elites that dwell in Tents, with warlike Edom join'd,
And Moab's Sons our Ruin vow, with Hagar's Race combin'd.

7 Proud

PSALM LXXXIV.

7 Proud Ammon's Offspring, Gebal too, with Amalek confpire;
   The Lords of Paleſtine, and all the wealthy Sons of Tyre:
8 All theſe the ſtrong Aſſyrian King their firm Ally have got,
   Who with a pow'rful Army aids th' inceſtuous Race of Lot.

PART II.

9 But let ſuch Vengeance come to them, as once to Midian came;
   To Jabin and proud Siſera, at Kiſhon's fatal Stream.
10 When thy Right-hand their num'rous Hoſts near Endor did confound,
   And left their Carcaſſes for Dung to feed the hungry Ground.
11 Let all their mighty Men the Fate of Zeb and Oreb ſhare;
   As Zebah and Zalmunnah, ſo let all their Princes fare.
12 Who, with the ſame Deſign inſpir'd, thus vainly boaſting ſpake,
   " In firm Poſſeſſion for ourſelves " let us God's Houſes take."
13 To Ruin let them haſte, like Wheels which downwards ſwiftly move:
   Like Chaff before the Winds, let all their ſcatter'd Forces prove,
14, 15 As Flames conſume dry Wood, or Heath that on parch'd Mountains grows,
   So let thy fierce purſuing Wrath with Terror ſtrike thy Foes.
16, 17 Lord, ſhroud their Faces with Diſgrace, that they may own thy Name;
   Or them confound, whoſe harden'd Hearts thy gentler Means diſclaim.
18 So ſhall the wond'ring World confeſs that thou, who claim'ſt alone
   Jehovah's Name, o'er all the Earth hath rais'd thy lofty Throne.

PSALM LXXXIV.

1 O God of Hoſts, the mighty Lord, how lovely is the Place
   Where thou, inthron'd in Glory, ſhew'ſt the Brightneſs of thy Face!
2 My longing Soul faints with Deſire, to view thy bleſt Abode;
   My panting Heart and Fleſh cry out for thee the living God.
3 The Birds, more happy far than I, around thy Altars throng;
   Securely there they build, and there ſecurely hatch their Young.
4 O Lord of Hoſts, my King and God, how highly bleſt are they,
   Who in thy Temple always dwell, and there thy Praiſe diſplay!
5 Thrice happy they, whoſe Choice has thee their ſure Protection made;
   Who long to tread the ſacred Ways that to thy Dwelling lead!
6 Who paſs thro' Baca's thirſty Vale, yet no Refreſhment want;
   Their Pools are fill'd with Rain, which thou at their Requeſt doſt grant.
7 Thus they proceed from Strength to Strength and ſtill approach more near;
   Till all on Sion's holy Mount, before their God appear.
8 O Lord, the mighty God of Hoſts, my juſt Requeſt regard;
   Thou God of Jacob, let my Pray'r be ſtill with Favour heard.
9 Behold, O God, for thou alone canſt timely aid diſpenſe;
   On thy anointed Servant look, be thou his ſtrong Defence,
10 For in thy Courts one ſingle Day 'tis better to attend,
   Than, Lord, in any Place beſides a thouſand Days to ſpend.
   Much rather in God's Houſe will I the meaneſt Office take,
   Than in the wealthy Tents of Sin my pompous Dwelling make.
11 For God who is our Sun and Shield, will Grace and Glory give;
   And no good Thing will he with-hold from them that juſtly live.
12 Thou God, who heav'nly Hoſts obey, how highly bleſt is he,
   Whoſe Hope and Truſt, ſecurely plac'd, is ſtill repos'd on thee!

PSALM LXXXV, LXXXVI.

PSALM LXXXV.

1 LORD, thou haft granted to thy Land, the Favours we implor'd;
And faithful Jacob's captive Race haft gracioufly reftor'd.
2, 3 Thy People's Sins thou haft abfolv'd, and all their Guilt defac'd:
Thou haft not let thy Wrath flame on, nor thy fierce Anger laft.

4 O God our Saviour, all our Hearts to thy Obedience turn;
That quench'd with our repenting Tears, thy Wrath no more may burn.
5, 6 For why fhould'ft thou be angry ftill and Wrath fo long retain?
Revive us, Lord, and let thy Saints thy wonted Comfort gain.

7 Thy gracious Favour, Lord, difplay, which we have long implor'd;
And, for thy wond'rous Mercies fake, thy wonted Aid afford.
8 God's Anfwer patiently I'll wait, for he, with glad Succefs,
(If they no more to Folly turn) his mourning Saints will blefs.

9 To all that fear his holy Name his fure Salvation's near;
And in its former happy State our Nation fhall appear.
10 For Mercy now with Truth is join'd, and Righteoufnefs with Peace,
Like kind Companions abfent long, (Heav'n with friendly Arms embrace.

11, 12 Truth from the Earth fhall fpring, whilft fhall Streams of Juftice pour;
And God, from whom all Goodnefs flows, fhall endlefs Plenty fhow'r.
13 Before him Righteoufnefs fhall march, and his juft Paths prepare;
Whilft we his holy Steps purfue, with conftant Zeal and Care.

PSALM LXXXVI.

1 TO my Complaint, O Lord my God, thy gracious Ear incline;
Hear me, diftreft and deftitute of all Relief but thine!
2 Do thou, O God, preferve my Soul, that does thy Name adore;
Thy Servant keep, and him, whofe Truft relies on thee, reftore.

3 To me, who daily thee invoke, thy Mercy, Lord, extend:
4 Refresh thy Servant's Soul, whofe Hopes on thee alone depend.
5 Thou, Lord, art good, not only good, but prompt to Pardon too;
Of plenteous Mercy to all thofe who for thy Mercy fue.

6 To my repeated humble Pray'r, O Lord, attentive be!
7 When troubled I on thee will call, for thou wilt anfwer me.
8 Among the Gods there's none like thee, O Lord, alone divine!
To thee as much inferior they, as are their Works to thine.

9 Therefore their great Creator thee the Nations fhall adore,
Their long-mifguided Pray'rs and Praife to thy bleft Name reftore.
10 All fhall confefs thee great, and great the Wonders thou haft done:
Confefs thee God, the God fupreme, confefs thee God alone.

PART II.

11 Teach me thy Way, O Lord, and I from Truth fhall ne'er depart;
In rev'rence to thy facred Name devoutly fix my Heart.
12 Thee will I praife, O Lord my God, praife thee with Heart fincere,
And to thy everlafting Name eternal Trophies rear.

13 Thy boundlefs Mercy fhewn to me tranfcends my Pow'r to tell,
For thou haft oft redeem'd my Soul from loweft Depths of Hell.
14 O God, the Sons of Pride and Strife have my Deftruction fought,
Regardlefs of thy Pow'r, that oft has my Deliv'rance wrought.

PSALM LXXXVII, LXXXVIII, LXXXIX.

15 But thou thy conſtant Goodneſs didſt to my Aſſiſtance bring;
Of Patience, Mercy, and of Truth, thou everlaſting Spring!
16 O bounteous Lord, thy Grace and Strength to me thy Servant ſhow;
Thy kind Protection, Lord, on me thine Handmaid's Son beſtow.

17 Some Signal give, which my proud Foes may ſee with Shame and Rage,
When thou, O Lord, for my Relief and Comfort doſt engage.

PSALM LXXXVII.

1 GOD's Temple crowns the holy Mount;
the Lord there condeſcends to dwell:
2 His Sion's Gates in his Account,
our Iſr'el's faireſt Tents excel.
3 Fame glorious Things of thee ſhall ſing,
O City of th' Almighty King!

4 I'll mention Rabab with due Praiſe,
in Babylon's Applauſes join,
The Fame of Ethiopia raiſe,
with that of Tyre and Paleſtine.
And grant that ſome amongſt them born,
Their Age and Country did adorn.

5 But ſtill of Sion I'll aver,
that many ſuch from her proceed;
Th' Almighty ſhall eſtabliſh her.
6 His gen'ral Liſt ſhall ſhew, when read,
That ſuch a Perſon there was born,
And ſuch did ſuch an Age adorn.

7 He'll Sion find with Numbers fill'd
of ſuch as merit high Renown;
For Hand and Voice Muſician's ſkill'd,
and (her tranſcending Fame to crown)
Of ſuch ſhe ſhall Succeſſions bring,
Like Waters from a living Spring.

PSALM LXXXVIII.

1 TO thee, my God and Saviour, I By Day and Night addreſs my Cry;
2 Vouchſafe my mournful Voice to hear, To my Diſtreſs incline thine Ear:
3 For Seas of Trouble me invade, My Soul draws nigh to Death's cold Shade.
4 Like one whoſe Strength & Hopes are fled, They number me among the Dead.

5 Like thoſe, who, ſhrouded in the Grave, From thee no more Remembrance have;
6 Caſt off from thy ſuſtaining Care, Down to the Confines of Deſpair.
7 Thy Wrath has hard upon me lain, Afflicting me with reſtleſs Pain;
Me all thy Mountain Waves have preſt, Too weak, alas! to bear the leaſt.

8 Remov'd from Friends, I ſigh alone, In a loath'd Dungeon laid, where none
A Viſit will vouchſafe to me, Confin'd, paſt Hopes of Liberty.
9 My Eyes from weeping never ceaſe, They waſte, but ſtill my Griefs increaſe;
Yet daily, Lord, to thee I've pray'd, With-out-ſtretch'd Hands invok'd thy Aid.

10 Wilt thou by Miracle revive The Dead whom thou forſook'ſt alive?
From Death reſtore thy Praiſe to ſing, Whom thou from Priſon would'ſt not bring
11 Shall the mute Grave thy Love confeſs? A mould'ring Tomb thy Faithfulneſs?
12 Thy Truth and Pow'r Renown obtain, When Darkneſs and Oblivion reign?

13 To thee, O Lord, I cry, forlorn, My Pray'r prevents the early Morn.
14 Why haſt thou, Lord, my Soul forſook, Nor once vouchſaf'd a gracious Look?
15 Prevailing Sorrows bear me down, Which from my Youth with me have grown;
Thy Terrors paſt diſtract my Mind, And Fears of blacker Days behind.

16 Thy Wrath has burſt upon my Head, Thy Terrors fill my Soul with Dread;
17 Environ'd as with Waves combin'd, And for a gen'ral Deluge join'd.
18 My Lovers, Friends, Familiars, all Remov'd from Sight and out of Call,
To dark Oblivion all retir'd, Dead, or at leaſt ſo me expir'd.

PSALM LXXXIX.

1 THY Mercies, Lord, ſhall be my Song, my Song on them ſhall ever dwell;
To Ages yet unborn my Tongue thy never-failing Truth ſhall tell.

PSALM LXXXIX.

2 I have affirm'd, and still maintain, thy Mercy shall for ever last;
 Thy Truth that does the Heav'ns sustain, like them shall stand for ever fast.
3 Thus spak'st thou by thy Prophet's Voice, " with David I a League have made,
 " To him my Servant and my Choice, " my solemn Oath this Grant convey'd.
4 " While Earth, and Seas, & Skies endure, " thy Seed shall in thy Sight remain;
 " To them thy Throne I will ensure, " they shall to endless Ages reign."
5 For such stupend'ous Truth and Love both Heav'n and Earth just Praises owe,
 By Choirs of Angels sung above, and by assembled Saints below.
6 What Seraph of celestial Birth to vie with Isr'el's God shall dare?
 Or who among the Gods of Earth, with our Almighty Lord compare?
7 With Rev'rence and religious Dread, his Saints should to his Temple press;
 His Fear thro' all their Hearts should who his Almighty Name confess;
  spread,
8 Lord God of Armies, who can boast of Strength or Pow'r like thine renown'd?
 Of such a num'rous faithful Host, as that which does thy Throne surround?
9 Thou dost the lawless Sea control, and change the Prospect of the Deep:
 Thou mak'st the sleeping Billows roll, thou mak'st the rolling Billows sleep.
10 Thou brak'st in Pieces Rahab's Pride, and didst oppressing Pow'r disarm:
 Thy scatter'd Foes have dearly try'd the Force of thy resistless Arm.
11 In thee the sov'reign Right remains of Earth and Heav'n; thee, Lord, alone
 The World, and all that it contains, their Maker and Preserver own.
12 The Poles on which the Globe does rest, were form'd by thy creating Voice;
 Tabor and Hermon, East and West, in thy sustaining Pow'r rejoice.
13 Thy Arm is mighty, strong thy Hand, yet, Lord, thou dost with Justice reign;
14 Possest of absolute Command, thou Truth and Mercy dost maintain.
15 Happy, thrice happy they, who hear thy sacred Trumpet's joyful Sound;
 Who may at Festivals appear, with thy most glorious Presence crown'd.
16 Thy Saints shall always be o'erjoy'd, who on thy sacred Name rely;
 And, in thy Righteousness employ'd, above their Foes be rais'd on high.
17 For in thy Strength they shall advance, whose Conquests from thy Favour spring
18 The Lord of Hosts is our Defence, and Isr'el's God our Isr'el's King.
19 Thus spak'st thou by thy Prophet's " A mighty Champion I will send;
  Voice,
 " From Judah's Tribe have I made choice " of one who shall the rest defend,
20 " My Servant David I have found, " with holy Oil anointed him;
21 " Him shall the Hand support that " and guard that gave the Diadem.
  crown'd,
22 " No Prince from him shall Tribute force " no Son of Strife shall him annoy;
23 " His spiteful Foes I will disperse " and them before his Face destroy.
24 " My Truth and Grace shall him sustain; " his Armies in well order'd Ranks,
25 " Shall conquer from the Tyrian Main " to Tygris and Euphrates Banks.
26 " Me for his Father he shall take, " his God and Rock of Safety call;
27 " Him I my first-born Son will make, " and earthly Kings his Subjects all.
28 " To him my Mercy I'll secure, " my Cov'nant make for ever fast; (last.
29 " His Seed for ever shall endure, " his Throne, 'till Heav'n dissolves, shall
       PART II.
30 " But if his Heirs my Law forsake, " and from my sacred Precepts stray,
31 " If they my righteous Statutes break, " nor strictly my Commands obey.
32 " Their Sins I'll visit with a Rod, " and for their Folly make them smart;
33 " Yet will not cease to be their God, " nor from my Truth, like them, depart.
              34 " My

PSALM XC.

34 "My Cov'nant I will ne'er revoke, "but in Remembrance faſt retain;
"The Thing that once my Lips have "ſhall in eternal Force remain.
ſpoke
35 "Once have I ſworn, but once for all, "and made my Holineſs the Tie,
"That I my Grant will ne'er recall, "nor to my Servant David lie.
36 "WhoſeThrone and Race, the conſtant "ſhall, like his Courſe, eſtabliſht ſee;
Sun
37 "Of this my Oath, thou conſcious "in Heav'n my faithful Witneſs be."
Moon,
38 Such was thy gracious Promiſe, Lord, but thou haſt now our Tribes forſook,
Thy own Anointed haſt abhor'd, and turn'd on him thy wrathful Look.
39 Thou ſeemeſt to have render'd void the Cov'nant with thy Servant made,
Thou haſt his Dignity deſtroy'd, and in the Duſt his Honour laid.
40 Of Strong-holds thou haſt him bereft, and brought his Bulwarks to Decay,
41 His Frontier Coaſt defenceleſs left, a public Scorn and common Prey.
42 His Ruin does glad Triumphs yield to Foes advanc'd by thee to Might;
43 Thou haſt his conqu'ring Sword un- his Valour turn'd to ſhameful Flight.
ſteel'd,
44 His Glory is to Darkneſs fled, his Throne is levell'd with the Ground:
45 His Youth to wretched Bondage led, with Shame o'erwhelm'd and Sorrow
drown'd.

46 How long ſhall we thy Abſence mourn? wilt thou for ever, Lord, retire?
Shall thy conſuming Anger burn till that and we at once expire?
47 Conſider, Lord, how ſhort a Space thou doſt for mortal Life ordain;
No Method to prolong the Race, but loading it with Grief and Pain.

48 What Man is he that can control Death's ſtrict, unalterable Doom?
Or reſcue from the Grave his Soul, the Grave that muſt Mankind intomb?
49 Lord, where's thy Love, thy boundleſs The Oath to which thy Truth did ſeal,
Grace,
Conſign'd to David and his Race, the Grant which Time ſhould ne'er repeal?
50 See how thy Servants treated are with Infamy, Reproach and Spite;
Which in my ſilent Breaſt I bear from Nations of licentious Might.
51 How they, reproaching thy great Name, have made thy Servant's Hope their Jeſt;
52 Yet thy juſt Praiſes we'll proclaim, and ever ſing, the Lord be bleſt.
Amen, Amen.

PSALM XC.

1 O Lord, the Saviour and Defence of us thy choſen Race,
From Age to Age thou ſtill haſt been our ſure abiding Place.
2 Before thou brought'ſt the Mountains forth, or th' Earth and World didſt frame,
Thou always wert the mighty God, and ever art the ſame.

3 Thou turneſt Man, O Lord, to Duſt, of which he firſt was made;
And when thou ſpeak'ſt the Word, Return, 'tis inſtantly obey'd.
4 For in thy Sight a thouſand Years are like a Day that's paſt,
Or like a Watch in Dead of Night, whoſe Hours unminded waſte.

5 Thou ſweep'ſt us off as with a Flood, we vaniſh hence like Dreams;
At firſt we grow like Graſs that feels the Sun's reviving Beams.
6 But howſoever freſh and fair its Morning Beauty ſhows;
'Tis all cut down, and wither'd quite, before the Ev'ning cloſe.

7, 8 We by thine Anger are conſum'd, and by thy Wrath diſmay'd:
Our publick Crimes and ſecret Sins before thy Sight are laid.

9 Be-

PSALM XCI.

9 Beneath thy Anger's sad Effects
Our unregarded Years break off,
our drooping Days we spend;
like Tales that quickly end.

10 Our Term of Time is seventy Years,
But if, with more than common Strength,
Yet then our boasted Strength decays,
So soon the slender Thread is cut.
an Age that few survive;
to Eighty we arrive;
to Sorrow turn'd and Pain;
and we no more remain.

PART II.

11 But who thy Anger's dread Effects
And yet thy Wrath does fall or rise,
12 So teach us, Lord, the uncertain Sum
That to true Wisdom all our Hearts
does, as he ought, revere?
as more or less we fear.
of our short Days to mind,
may ever be inclin'd.

13 O to thy Servant, Lord, return,
As we of our Misdeeds, do thou
14 To satisfy and chear our Souls,
That we may all our Days to come,
and speedily relent!
of our just Doom repent.
thy early Mercy send;
in Joy and Comfort spend.

15 Let happy Times, with large Amends,
Or equal at the least the Term
16 To all thy Servants, Lord, let this
And to our Offspring, yet unborn,
dry up our former Tears;
of our afflicted Years.
thy wond'rous Works be known,
thy glorious Pow'r be shown.

17 Let thy bright Rays upon us shine,
The glorious Work we have in Hand
give thou our Work Success;
do thou vouchsafe to bless.

PSALM XCI.

1 HE that has God his Guardian made,
shall under the Almighty Shade,
Secure and undisturb'd abide,
2 Thus to my Soul, of him I'll say,
He is my Fortress and my Stay,
My God, in whom I will confide.

3 His tender Love and watchful Care
Shall free thee from the Fowler's Snare,
And from the noisome Pestilence:
4 He over thee his Wings shall spread,
And cover thy unguarded Head:
His Truth shall be thy strong Defence.

5 No Terrors, that surprise by Night,
Shall thy undaunted Courage fright,
Nor deadly Shafts that fly by Day;
6 Nor Plague of unknown Rise, that kills
In Darkness, nor infectious Ills,
That in the hottest Season slay.

7 A thousand at thy Side shall die,
At thy Right-hand ten thousand lie,
While thy firm Health untouch'd remains:
8 Thou only shalt look on and see
The Wicked's sad Catastrophe,
And count the Sinner's mournful Gains.

9 Because (with well-plac'd Confidence)
Thou mak'st the Lord thy sure Defence,
And on the Highest dost rely;
10 Therefore no Ill shall thee befall,
Nor to thy healthful Dwelling shall
Any infectious Plague draw nigh.

11 For he, throughout thy happy Days,
To keep thee safe in all thy Ways,
shall give his Angels strict Commands:
12 And they, lest thou should'st chance to meet
With some rough Stone to wound thy Feet,
Shall bear thee safely in their Hands.

13 Dragons and Asps that thirst for Blood,
And Lions roaring for their Food,
Beneath his conqu'ring Feet shall lie,
14 Because he lov'd and honour'd me,
Therefore (says God) I'll set him free,
And fix his glorious Throne on high.

15 He'll call; I'll answer when he calls,
And rescue him when Ill befalls:
Increase his Honour and his Wealth:
16 And when with undisturb'd Content,
His long and happy Life is spent,
His End I'll crown with saving Health,

PSALM XCII, XCIII, XCIV.

PSALM XCII.

1 HOW good and pleasant must it be to thank the Lord most high!
    And with repeated Hymns of Praise, his Name to magnify!
2 With ev'ry Morning's early Dawn, his Goodness to relate;
    And of his constant Truth each Night, the glad Effects repeat.

3 To ten-string'd Instruments we'll sing, with tuneful Psalt'ries join'd;
    And to the Harp, with solemn Sounds, for sacred Use design'd.
4 For thro' thy wond'rous Works, O Lord, thou mak'st my Heart rejoice;
    The Thoughts of them shall make me glad, and shout with chearful Voice.

5, 6 How wond'rous are thy Works, O Lord, how deep are thy Decrees!
    Whose winding Tracks in secret laid, no stupid Sinner sees.
7 He little thinks, when wicked Men, like Grass, look fresh and gay,
    How soon their short-liv'd Splendor must for ever pass away.

8, 9 But thou, my God, art still most high; and all thy lofty Foes,
    Who thought they might securely sin, shall be o'erwhelm'd with Woes.
10 Whilst thou exalt'st my sov'reign Pow'r, and mak'st it largely spread;
    And with refreshing Oil anoint'st my consecrated Head.

11 I soon shall see my stubborn Foes to utter Ruin brought;
    And hear the dismal End of those who have against me fought.
12 But righteous Men, like fruitful Palms, shall make a glorious Show;
    As Cedars that on Lebanon in stately Order grow.

13, 14 These planted in the House of God, within his Courts shall thrive;
    Their Vigour and their Lustre both shall in old Age revive.
15 Thus will the Lord his Justice shew; and God, my strong Defence,
    Shall due Rewards to all the World impartially dispense.

PSALM XCIII.

1 WITH Glory clad, with Strength array'd, the Lord, that o'er all Nature reigns,
    The World's Foundation strongly laid, and the vast Fabric still sustains.
2 How surely stablisht is thy Throne! which shall no Change of Period see;
    For thou, O Lord, and thou alone, art God from all Eternity.

3, 4 The Floods, O Lord, lift up their Voice, and toss the troubled Waves on high;
    But God above can still their Noise, and make the angry Sea comply.
5 Thy Promise, Lord, is ever sure; and they that in thy House would dwell,
    That happy Station to secure, must still in Holiness excel.

PSALM XCIV.

1, 2 O God, to whom Revenge belongs, thy Vengeance now disclose;
    Arise, thou Judge of all the Earth, and crush thy haughty Foes.
3, 4 How long, O Lord, shall sinful Men their solemn Triumphs make?
    How long their wicked Actions boast? and insolently speak?

5, 6 Not only they thy Saints oppress, but unprovok'd they spill
    The Widows and the Strangers Blood, and helpless Orphans kill.
7 " And yet the Lord shall ne'er perceive, " (prophanely thus they speak)
    " Nor any Notice of our Deeds " the God of Jacob take."

8 At length, ye stupid Fools, your Wants endeavour to discern,
    In Folly will you still proceed, and Wisdom never learn?
9, 10 Can he be deaf who form'd the Ear, or blind who fram'd the Eye?
    Shall Earth's great Judge not punish those who his known Will defy?

PSALM XCV.

11 He fathoms all the Thoughts of Men, to him their Hearts lie bare;
His Eye surveys them all, and sees how vain their Counsels are.

PART II.

12 Blest is the Man whom thou, O Lord, in Kindness dost chastise;
And by thy sacred Rules to walk dost lovingly advise.
13 This Man shall Rest and Safety find in Seasons of Distress;
Whilst God prepares a Pit for those that stubbornly transgress.
14 For God will never from his Saints his Favour wholly take;
His own Possession and his Lot, he will not quite forsake.
15 The World shall then confess thee just, in all that thou hast done;
And those that choose thy upright Ways, shall in those Paths go on.
16 Who will appear in my Behalf, when wicked Men invade?
Or who, when Sinners would oppress, my righteous Cause shall plead?
17, 18, 19 Long since had I in Silence slept, but that the Lord was near,
To stay me when I slipt; when sad, my troubled Heart to chear.
20 Wilt thou, who art a God most just, their sinful Throne sustain,
Who make the Law a fair Pretence their wicked Ends to gain?
21 Against the Lives of righteous Men they form their close Design;
And Blood of Innocents to spill, in solemn League combine.
22 But my Defence is firmly plac'd in God the Lord most High;
He is my Rock, to which I may for Refuge always fly.
23 The Lord shall cause their ill Designs on their own Heads to fall;
He in their Sins shall cut them off, our God shall slay them all.

PSALM XCV.

1 O Come, loud Anthems let us sing, Loud thanks to our Almighty King,
For we our Voices high should raise When our Salvation's Rock we praise,
2 Into his Presence let us haste, To thank him for his Favours past;
To him address in joyful Songs, The Praise that to his Name belongs.
3 For God the Lord, enthron'd in State, Is, with unrival'd Glory, great;
A King superior far to all, Whom, by his Title, God we call.
4 The Depths of Earth are in his Hand, Her secret Wealth at his Command;
The strength of Hills that threat the skies Subjected to his Empire lies.
5 The rolling Ocean's vast Abyss By the same sov'reign Right is his;
'Tis mov'd by his Almighty Hand, That form'd and fix'd the solid Land.
6 O let us to his Courts repair, And bow with Adoration there,
Down on our Knees devoutly all Before the Lord our Maker fall.
7 For he's our God, our Shepherd he, His Flock and Pasture-sheep are we;
If then you'll (like his Flock) draw near, To-Day, if you his Voice will hear.
8 Let not your harden'd Hearts renew Your Fathers Crimes and Judgments too;
Nor here provoke my Wrath, as they In Desart Plains of Meribah!
9 When thro' the Wilderness they mov'd, And me with fresh Temptations prov'd;
They still, thro' Unbelief, rebell'd, While they my wond'rous Works beheld.
10, 11 They, forty Years, my Patience Tho' daily I their Wants reliev'd;
griev'd,
Then—'Tis a faithless Race, I said, Whose Heart from me has always stray'd;
They ne'er will tread my righteous Path, Therefore to them in settled Wrath,
Since they despis'd my Rest, I swear, That they shall never enter there.

PSALM

PSALM XCVI, XCVII, XCVIII.

PSALM XCVI.

1 SING to the Lord a new-made Song,
Let Earth, in one assembled Throng,
Her common Patron's Praise resound.
2 Sing to the Lord, and bless his Name,
From Day to Day his Praise proclaim,
Who us has with Salvation crown'd.
3 To heathen Lands his Fame rehearse,
His Wonders to the Universe.

4 He's great, and greatly to be prais'd;
In Majesty and Glory rais'd
Above all other Deities:
5 For Pageantry and Idols all,
Are they whom Gods the Heathen call;
He only rules who made the Skies.
6 With Majesty and Honour crown'd,
Beauty & Strength his Throne surround;

7 Be therefore both to him restor'd
By you who have false Gods ador'd,
Ascribe due Honour to his Name;
8 Peace-Off'rings on his Altar lay,
Before his Throne your Homage pay,
Which he, and he alone, can claim.
9 To worship at his sacred Court
Let all the trembling World resort.

10 Proclaim aloud, Jehovah reigns,
Whose Pow'r the Universe sustains,
And banisht Justice will restore;
11 Let therefore Heav'n new Joys confess,
And heav'nly Mirth let Earth express,
Its loud Applause the Ocean roar;
Its mute Inhabitants rejoice,
And for this Triumph find a Voice.

12 For Joy let fertile Valleys sing,
The chearful Groves their Tribute bring;
The tuneful Choir of Birds awake,
13 The Lord's Approach to celebrate,
Who now sets out, with awful State,
His Circuit thro' the Earth to take:
From Heav'n to judge the World he's come,
With Justice to reward and Doom.

PSALM XCVII.

1 JEHOVAH reigns, let all the Earth in his just Government rejoice;
Let all the Isles, with sacred Mirth, in his Applause unite their Voice.
2 Darkness and Clouds of awful Shade his dazling Glory shroud in State;
Justice and Truth his Guards are made, and fix'd by his Pavilion wait.

3 Devouring Fire before his Face, his Foes around with Vengeance strook;
4 His Lightnings set the World on Blaze. Earth saw it, and with Terror shook.
5 The proudest Hills his Presence felt, their Height nor Strength could Help afford,
The proudest Hills like Wax did melt in Presence of th' Almighty Lord.

6 The Heav'ns, his Righteousness to show, with Storms of Fire our Foes pursu'd;
And all the trembling World below, have his descending Glory view'd.
7 Confounded be their impious Host, who make the Gods to whom they pray;
All who of Pageant Idols boast, to him, ye Gods, your Worship pay.

8 Glad Sion of thy Triumph heard, and Judah's Daughters were o'erjoy'd;
Because thy righteous Judgments, Lord, have Pagan-Pride and Pow'r destroy'd.
9 For thou, O God, art seated high, above Earth's Potentates enthron'd;
Thou, Lord, unrivall'd in the Sky, Supreme by all the Gods art own'd.

10 You, who to serve this Lord aspire, abhor what's ill, and Truth esteem:
He'll keep his Servants Souls ent're, and them from wicked Hands redeem.
11 For Seeds are sown of glorious Light, a future Harvest for the Just;
And Gladness for the Heart that's right, to recompense his pious Trust.

12 Rejoice, ye Righteous in the Lord, Memorials of his Holiness,
Deep in your faithful Breasts record, and with your thankful Tongues confess.

PSALM XCVIII.

1 SING to the Lord a new-made Song, who wond'rous Things has done;
With his Right-hand and holy Arm the Conquest he has won.

PSALM XCIX, C, CI.

2 The Lord has thro' th' astonisht World
And made his righteous Acts appear
    display'd his saving Might,
    in all the Heathens Sight.

3 Of Isr'el's House his Love and Truth
Wide Earth's remotest Parts the Pow'r
    have ever mindful been:
    of Isr'el's God have seen.

4 Let therefore Earth's Inhabitants
And all with universal Joy,
    their chearful Voices raise,
    resound their Maker's Praise.

5 With Harp and Hymns soft Melody,
6 The Trumpet and shrill Cornets Sound,
7 Let the loud Ocean roar her Joy,
  The Earth and her Inhabitants
    into the Consort bring,
    before the Almighty King,
    with all that Seas contain;
    join Consort with the Main.

8 With Joy let Riv'lets swell to Streams,
And echoing Vales, from Hill to Hill,
    to spreading Torrents they;
    redoubled Shouts convey;

9 To welcome down the World's great Judge,
And, with impartial Equity,
    who does with Justice come,
    both to Reward and Doom.

PSALM XCIX.

1 JEHOVAH reigns, let therefore all
   On Cherubs Wings he sits enthron'd:
2 On Sion's Hill he keeps his Court,
  Yet thence his Sovereignty extends
    the guilty Nations quake;
    let Earth's Foundation shake.
    his Palace makes her Tow'rs;
    supreme o'er earthly Pow'rs.

3 Let therefore all with Praise address
  And with his unresisted Might,
    his great and dreadful Name;
    his Holiness proclaim.

4 For Truth and Justice, in his Reign,
His Judgments are with Righteousness
    of Strength and Pow'r take Place;
    dispens'd to Jacob's Race.

5 Therefore exalt the Lord our God,
And with his unresisted Might,
    before his Footstool fall;
    his Holiness extol.

6 Moses and Aaron thus of old,
Amongst his Prophets Samuel thus
    among his Priests ador'd;
    his sacred Name implor'd.

Distrest, upon the Lord, they call'd,
But, as with Rev'rence they implor'd,
    who ne'er their Suit deny'd;
    he graciously reply'd.

7 For with their Camp, to guide their March,
They kept his Laws, and to his Will
    the cloudy Pillar mov'd:
    obedient Servants prov'd.

8 He answer'd them, forgiving oft
And those who rashly them oppos'd,
    his People for their Sake,
    did sad Examples make.

9 With Worship at his sacred Courts
For he, who only holy is,
    exalt our God and Lord;
    alone should be ador'd.

PSALM C.

1,2 WITH one Consent let all the Earth
  Glad Homage pay with awful Mirth,
3 Convinc'd that he is God alone,
  We, whom he chooses for his own.
    to God their chearful Voices raise;
    and sing before him Songs of Praise;
    from whom both we and all proceed;
    the Flock that he vouchsafes to feed.

4 O enter then his Temple-Gate,
And still your grateful Hymns repeat,
    thence to his Courts devoutly press,
    and still his Name with Praises bless.

5 For he's the Lord, supremely good,
His Truth which always firmly stood,
    his Mercy is for ever sure,
    to endless Ages shall endure.

PSALM CI.

1 OF Mercy's never-failing Spring,
   And since they both to thee belong,
2 When, Lord, thou shalt with me reside,
  With blameless life myself I'll make
    And stedfast Judgment I will sing;
    To thee, O Lord, address my Song.
    Wise Discipline my Reign shall guide,
    A Pattern for my Court to take.

PSALM CII.

3 No ill Design will I pursue, Nor those my Fav'rites make that do,
4 Who to Reproof bears no Regard, Him I will totally discard.
5 The private Slanderer shall be In public Justice doom'd by me:
  From haughty Looks I'll turn aside, And mortify the Heart of Pride;

6 But Honesty, call'd from her Cell, In Splendor at my Court shall dwell:
  Who Virtue's Practice make their Care, Shall have the first Preferments there.
7 No Politics shall recommend His Country's Foe to be my Friend:
  None e'er shall to my Favour rise By flatt'ring or malicious Lyes.

8 All those who wicked Courses take, An early Sacrifice I'll make;
  Cut off, destroy, till none remain God's holy City to profane.

PSALM CII.

1 WHEN I pour out my Soul in Pray'r, do thou, O Lord, attend,
  To thy eternal Throne of Grace let my sad Cry ascend.
2 O hide not thou thy glorious Face in Times of deep Distress,
  Incline thine Ear, and when I call my Sorrows soon redress.

3 Each cloudy Portion of my Life, like scatter'd Smoke expires;
  My shrivel'd Bones are like a Hearth, that's parch'd with constant Fires.
4 My Heart like Grass, that feels the Blast of some infectious Wind,
  Does languish so with Grief, that scarce my needful Food 1 mind.

5 By reason of my sad Estate, I spend my Breath in Groans;
  My Flesh is worn away, my Skin scarce hides my starting Bones.
6 I'm like a Pelican become, that does in Desarts mourn;
  Or like an Owl, that sits all Day on barren Trees forlorn.

7 In Watching or in restless Dreams the Night by me is spent;
  As by those solitary Birds that lonesome Roofs frequent.
8 All Day by railing Foes I'm made the Subject of their Scorn;
  Who all, possest with furious Rage, have my Destruction sworn.

9 When grov'ling on the Ground I lie, opprest with Grief and Fears,
  My Bread is strew'd with Ashes o'er, my Drink is mix'd with Tears.
10 Because on me with double Weight thy heavy Wrath does lie;
   For thou, to make my Fall more great, didst lift me up on high.

11 My Days, just hast'ning to their End, are like an Ev'ning Shade;
   My Beauty does, like with'red Grass, with waning Lustre fade,
12 But thy eternal State, O Lord, no Length of Time shall waste;
   The Mem'ry of thy wond'rous Works, from Age to Age shall last.

13 Thou shalt arise, and Sion view with an unclouded Face;
   For now her Time is come, thy own appointed Day of Grace.
14 Her scatter'd Ruins by thy Saints with Pity are survey'd;
   They grieve to see her lofty Spires in Dust and Rubbish laid,

15, 16 The Name and Glory of the Lord all Heathen Kings shall fear;
   When he shall Sion build again, and in full State appear.
17, 18 When he regards the Poor's Request, nor slights their earnest Pray'r;
   Our Sons for this recorded Grace, shall his just Praise declare.

19 For God, from his Abode on high, his gracious Beams display'd;
   The Lord from Heav'n his lofty Throne, has all the Earth survey'd.
20 He list'ned to the Captives Moans, he heard their mournful Cry,
   And freed by his resistless Pow'r the Wretches doom'd to die.

21 That they in Sion, where he dwells, might celebrate his Fame,
   And through the holy City sing loud Praises to his Name.

PSALM CIII, CIV.

22 When all the Tribes assembling there, their solemn Vows address,
And neighb'ring Lands, with glad Consent, the Lord their God confess.
23 But ere my Race is run, my Strength thro' his fierce Wrath decays;
He has, when all my Wishes bloom'd, cut short my hopeful Days.
24 Lord, end not thou my Life, said I, when half is scarcely past;
Thy Years from worldly Changes free, to endless Ages last.
25 The strong Foundations of the Earth of old by thee were laid;
Thy Hands the beauteous Arch of Heav'n with wond'rous Skill have made.
26, 27 Whilst thou for ever shalt endure, they soon shall pass away;
And, like a Garment often worn, shall tarnish and decay.

Like that, when thou ordain'st their Change, to thy Command they bend;
But thou continu'st still the same, nor have thy Years an End.
28 Thou to the Children of thy Saints shalt lasting Quiet give;
Whose happy Race, securely fixt, shall in thy Presence live.

PSALM CIII.

1, 2 **M**Y Soul, inspir'd with sacred God's Holy Name for ever bless:
Love,
Of all his Favours mindful prove, and still thy grateful Thanks express.
3, 4 'Tis he that all thy Sins forgives, and after Sickness makes thee sound;
From Danger he thy Life retrieves, by him with Grace and Mercy crown'd.
5, 6 He with good Things my Mouth sup- thy Vigour, Eagle-like, renews;
plies,
He, when the guiltless Suff'rer cries, his Foe with just Revenge pursues.
7 God made of old his righteous Ways to Moses and our Fathers known;
His Works to his eternal Praise, were to the Sons of Jacob shown.
8 The Lord abounds with tender Love, and unexampled Acts of Grace:
His waken'd Wrath does slowly move; his willing Mercy flows apace.
9, 10 God will not always harshly chide, but with his Anger quickly part;
And loves his Punishments to guide, more by his Love than our Desert.
11 As high as Heav'n its Arch extends, above this little Spot of Clay;
So much his boundless Love transcends, the small Respects that we can pay.
12, 13 As far as 'tis from East to West, so far has he our Sins remov'd;
Who with a Father's tender Breast, has such as fear him always lov'd.
14, 15 For God, who all our Frame surveys, considers that we are but Clay;
How fresh soe'er we seem, our Days like Grass or Flow'rs must fade away.
16, 17 Whilst they are nipt with sudden nor can we find their former Place;
Blasts,
God's faithful Mercy ever lasts, to those that fear him, and their Race.
18 This shall attend on such as still proceed in his appointed Way;
And who not only know his Will; but to his just Obedience pay.
19, 20 The Lord, the universal King, in Heav'n has fixt his lofty Throne:
To him, ye Angels, Praises sing, in whose great Strength his Pow'r is shown.

Ye that his just Commands obey, and hear and do his sacred Will!
21 Ye Hosts of his, this Tribute pay, who still what he ordains fulfil.
22 Let every Creature jointly bless the mighty Lord; and thou my Heart
With gateful Joy thy Thanks express, and in this Consort bear thy Part.

PSALM CIV.

1 **B**LESS God, my Soul; thou, Lord, possesset Empire without Bounds;
alone,
With Honour thou art crown'd thy Throne eternal Majesty surrounds.

2 With

PSALM CIV.

2 With Light thou doſt thyſelf enrobe, and Glory for a Garment take:
Heav'n's Curtains ſtretch beyond the Globe thy Canopy of State to make.

3 God builds on liquid Air, and forms his Palace-Chambers in the Skies;
The Clouds his Chariots are, the Storms the ſwift-wing'd Steeds with which he flies.
4 As bright as Flame, and ſwift as Wind, his Miniſters Heav'n's Palace fill,
To have their ſundry Taſks aſſign'd; all proud to ſerve their Sov'reign's Will.

5, 6 Earth on her Center fixt he ſet, her Face with Waters overſpread:
Nor proudeſt Mountains dar'd, as yet, to lift above the Waves their Head.
7 But when thy awful Face appear'd th' inſulting Waves diſpers'd; they fled,
When once thy Thunder's Voice they heard, and by their Haſte confeſs'd their Dread.

8 Thence up, by ſecret Tracts they creep, and, guſhing from the Mountain's Side,
Thro' Valleys travel to the Deep, appointed to receive their Tide.
9 There haſt thou fixt the Ocean's Bounds, the threat'ning Surges to repel;
That they no more o'erpaſs their Mounds, nor to a ſecond Deluge ſwell.

PART II.

10 Yet thence in ſmaller Parties drawn, the Sea recovers her loſt Hills;
And ſtarting Springs from ev'ry Lawn, ſurprize the Vales with plenteous Rills.
11 The Field's tame Beaſts are thither led, weary with Labour, faint with Drought;
And Aſſes on wild Mountains bred, have Senſe to find theſe Currents out.
12 There ſhady Trees, from ſcorching Beams yield Shelter to the feather'd Throng;
They drink, & to the bounteous Streams return the Tribute of their Song.
13 His Rains from Heav'n parcht Hills recruit, that ſoon tranſmit the liquid Store;
Till Earth is burden'd with her Fruit, and Nature's Lap can hold no more.

14 Graſs for our Cattle to devour, he makes the Growth of ev'ry Field;
Herbs for Man's Uſe, of various Pow'r, that either Food or Phyſick yield.
15 With cluſter Grapes he crowns the Vine, to chear Man's Heart oppreſt with Cares;
Gives Oil that makes his Face to ſhine, and Corn, that waſted Strength repairs.

PART III.

16 The Trees of God, without the Care or Art of Man, with Sap are fed:
The Mountain-Cedar looks as fair as thoſe in Royal Gardens bred.
17 Safe in the lofty Cedar's Arms the Wand'rers of the Air may reſt:
The hoſpitable Pine from Harms protects the Stork, her pious Gueſt.
18 Wild Goats the craggy Rock aſcend, its tow'ring Heights their Fortreſs make,
Whoſe Cells in Labyrinths extend, where feebler Creatures Refuge take.
19 The Moon's inconſtant Aſpect ſhows th' appointed Seaſons of the Year;
Th' inſtructed Sun his Duty knows, his Hours to riſe and diſappear.

20, 21 Darkneſs he makes the Earth to ſhroud, when Foreſt-Beaſts ſecurely ſtray;
Young Lions roar their Wants aloud to Providence that ſends them Prey.
22 They range all Night, on Slaughter bent, 'till ſummon'd by the riſing Morn,
To ſculk in Dens, with one Conſent, the conſcious Ravagers return.
23 Forth to the Tillage of his Soil, the Huſbandman ſecurely goes,
Commencing with the Sun his Toil, with him returns to his Repoſe.
24 How various, Lord, thy Works are found for which thy Wiſdom we adore!
The Earth is with thy Treaſure crown'd, 'till Nature's Hand can graſp no more.

PSALM CV.

PART IV.

25 But still the vast unfathom'd Main, of Wonders a new Scene supplies,
Whose Depths Inhabitants contain of ev'ry Form and ev'ry Size.
26 Full-freighted Ships from ev'ry Port, there cut their unmolested Way;
Leviathan, whom there to sport thou mad'st, has Compass there to play.

27 These various Troops of Sea and Land, in Sense of common Want agree;
All wait on thy dispensing Hand, and have their daily Alms from thee.
28 They gather what thy Stores disperse, without their Trouble to provide;
Thou op'st thy Hand, the Universe, the craving World is all supply'd.

29 Thou for a Moment hid'st thy Face, the num'rous Ranks of Creatures mourn:
Thou tak'st their Breath, all Nature's Race forthwith to Mother-Earth return.
30 Again thou send'st thy Spirit forth, t'inspire the Mass with vital Seed;
Nature's restor'd, and Parent-Earth smiles on her new-created Breed.

31 Thus thro' successive Ages stands firm fixt, thy providential Care;
Pleas'd with the Work of thy own Hands, thou dost the Wastes of Time repair.
32 One Look of thine, one wrathful Look, Earth's panting Breast with Terror fills;
One Touch from thee with Clouds of Smoke, in Darkness shrouds the proudest Hills.

33 In praising God, while he prolongs my Breath, I will that Breath employ;
34 And join Devotions to my Songs, sincere, as in him is my Joy.
35 While Sinners from Earth's Face are hurl'd, my Soul, praise thou his holy Name,
Till, with thy Song, the list'ning World join Consort, and his Praise proclaim.

PSALM CV.

1 O Render Thanks, and bless the Lord, invoke his sacred Name:
Acquaint the Nations with his Deeds, his matchless Deeds proclaim.
2 Sing to his Praise in lofty Hymns, his wond'rous Works rehearse;
Make them the Theme of your Discourse, and Subject of your Verse.

3 Rejoice in his Almighty Name, alone to be ador'd;
And let their Hearts o'erflow with Joy, that humbly seek the Lord.
4 Seek ye the Lord, his saving Strength devoutly still implore;
And, where he's ever present, seek his Face for evermore.

5 The Wonders that his Hands have wrought keep thankfully in Mind;
The righteous Statutes of his Mouth, and Laws to us assign'd.
6 Know ye his Servant Abr'am's Seed, and Jacob's chosen Race,
7 He's still our God, his Judgments still throughout the Earth take Place.

8 His Cov'nant he has kept in Mind for num'rous Ages past;
Which yet, for thousand Ages more, in equal Force shall last.
9 First sign'd to Abr'am, next by Oath to Isaac made secure;
10 To Jacob and his Heirs a Law for ever to endure.

11 That Canaan's Land should be their Lot, when yet but few they were:
12 But few in Number, and those few all friendless Strangers there.
13 In Pilgrimage, from Realm to Realm, securely they remov'd;
14 Whilst proudest Monarchs for their sakes severely he reprov'd.

15 " These mine Anointed are, said he, " let none my Servants wrong;
" Nor treat the poorest Prophet ill, " that does to me belong."
16 A Dearth at last, by his Command, did thro' the Land prevail,
Till Corn, the chief Support of Life, sustaining Corn did fail.

17 But

PSALM CV.

17 But his indulgent Providence had pious Joseph sent,
   Sold into Egypt, but their Death who sold him to prevent.
18 His Feet with heavy Chains were crush'd, with Calumny his Fame;
19 Till God's appointed Time and Word to his Deliv'rance came.
20 The King his sov'reign Orders sent, and rescu'd him with Speed;
   Whom private Malice had confin'd, the People's Ruler freed.
21 His Court, Revenues, Realm, were all subjected to his Will:
22 His greatest Princes to control, and teach his Statesmen Skill.

PART II.

23 To Egypt then, invited Guests, half-famish'd Isr'el came;
   And Jacob held, by Royal Grant, the fertile Soil of Ham.
24 Th' Almighty there with such Increase his People multiply'd;
   Till with their proud Oppressors they in Strength and Number vy'd.
25 Their vast Increase th' Egyptians Hearts with jealous Anger fir'd,
   Till they his Servants to destroy by treach'rous Arts conspir'd.
26 His Servant Moses then he sent, his chosen Aaron too;
27 Impower'd with Signs and Miracles, to prove their Mission true.
28 He call'd for Darkness, Darkness came, Nature his Summons knew;
29 Each Stream and Lake transform'd to Blood, the wond'ring Fishes flew.
30 In putrid Floods, throughout the Land, the Pest of Frogs were bred;
   From noisome Fens sent up to croak at Pharaoh's Board and Bed.
31 He gave the Sign, and Swarms of Flies came down in cloudy Hosts;
   Whilst Earth's enliv'ned Dust below bred Lice through all their Coasts.
32 He sent them batt'ring Hail for Rain, and Fire for cooling Dew;
33 He smote their Vines and Forest Plants, and Garden's Pride o'erthrew.
34 He spake the Word and Locusts came, with Caterpillar's join'd,
   They prey'd upon the poor Remains the Storm had left behind.
35 From Trees to Herbage they descend; no verdent Thing they spare;
   But like the naked Fallow-Field, leave all the Pastures bare.
36 From Fields to Villages and Towns, commission'd Vengeance flew;
   One fatal Stroke their eldest Hopes and Strength of Egypt flew.
37 He brought his Servants forth, enrich'd with Egypt's borrow'd Wealth;
   And, what transcends all Treasure else, enrich'd with vig'rous Health.
38 Egypt rejoyc'd, in Hopes to find her Plagues with them remov'd;
   Taught dearly now to fear worse Ills, by those already prov'd.
39 Their shrouding Canopy by Day, a journeying Cloud was spread;
   A fiery Pillar all the Night their Desart Marches led.
40 They long'd for Flesh, with Ev'ning Quails he furnish'd ev'ry Tent;
   From Heav'n's own Granary, each Morn, the Bread of Angels sent.
41 He smote the Rock, whose flinty Breast pour'd forth a gushing Tide,
   Whose flowing Streams where-e'er they march'd the Desart's Drought supply'd.
42 For still he did on Abr'am's Faith an ancient League reflect;
43 He brought his People forth with Joy, with Triumph his Elect.
44 Quite rooting out their Heathen Foes, from Canaan's fertile Soil,
   To them in cheap Possession gave the Fruit of others Toil.
45 That they his Statutes might observe, his sacred Laws obey;
   For Benefits so vast let us our Songs of Praise repay.

PSALM CVI.

PSALM CVI.

1 O Render Thanks to God above, The Fountain of eternal Love;
Whose Mercy firm thro' Ages past Has flood, and shall for ever last.
2 Who can his mighty Deeds express, Not only vast but numberless?
What mortal Eloquence can raise His Tribute of immortal Praise?

3 Happy are they, and only they, Who from thy Judgments never stray,
Who know what's right, not only so, But always practice what they know.
4 Extend to me that Favour, Lord, Thou to thy Chosen dost afford;
When thou return'st to set them free, Let thy Salvation visit me.

5 O may I worthy prove, to see Thy Saints in full Prosperity!
That I the joyful Choir may join, And count thy People's Triumph mine.
6 But ah! can we expect such Grace, Of Parents vile, the viler Race;
Who their Misdeeds have acted o'er, And with new Crimes increas'd the Score?

7 Ingrateful they, no longer thought On all his Works in Egypt wrought;
The Red-Sea they no sooner view'd, But they their base Distrust renew'd.
8 Yet he, to vindicate his Name, Once more to their Deliv'rance came,
To make his sov'reign Pow'r be known, That he is God, and he alone.

9 To Right and Left at his Command, The parting Deep disclos'd her Sand;
Where firm and dry the Passage lay, As through some parch'd and desart Way.
10 Thus rescu'd from their Foes they were, Who closely press'd upon the Rear;
11 Whose Rage pursu'd them to those That prov'd the rash pursuers Graves.
Waves

12 The wat'ry Mountains sudden Fall O'erwhelm'd proud Pharaoh, Host and all;
This Proof did stupid Isr'el move To own God's Truth, and praise his Love.

PART II.

13 But soon these Wonders they forgot, And for his Counsel waited not;
14 But lusting in the Wilderness, Did him with fresh Temptations press.
15 Strong Food at their Request he sent, But made their Sin their Punishment;
16 Yet still his Saints they did oppose, The Priest and Prophet whom he chose.

17 But Earth, the Quarrel to decide, Her vengeful Jaws extending wide,
Rash Dathan to her Centre drew, With proud Abiram's factious Crew
18 The rest of those who did conspire To kindle wild Sedition's Fire,
With all their impious Train became A Prey to Heav'n's devouring Flame.

19 Near Horeb's Mount a Calf they made, And to the molten Image pray'd;
20 Adoring what their Hands did Frame, They chang'd their Glory to their Shame.
21 Their God and Saviour they forgot, And all his Works in Egypt wrought;
22 His Signs in Ham's astonisht Coast, And where proud Pharaoh's troops were lost.

23 Thus urg'd, his vengeful Hand he rear'd, But Moses in the Breach appear'd;
The Saint did for the Rebels pray, And turn'd Heav'ns kindled Wrath away.
24 Yet they his pleasant Land despis'd, Nor his repeated Promise priz'd;
25 Nor did th' Almighty's Voice obey, But when God said, Go up, would stay.

26, 27 This seal'd their Doom without To perish in the Wilderness;
Redress,
Or else to be by Heathens Hands O'erthrown and scatter'd thro' the Lands.

PART III.

28 Yet unreclaim'd this stubborn Race, Baal-Peor's Worship did embrace;
Became his impious Guests and fed On Sacrifices to the Dead.
29 Thus they persisted to provoke God's Vengeance to the final Stroke
'Tis come;—the deadly pest is come To execute their gen'ral Doom.

30 Bu-

PSALM CVII.

30 But Phineas, fir'd with holy Rage, (Th' Almighty's Vengeance to aſſwage,
    Did by two bold Offenders fall, Th' Atonement make that ranſom'd all.
31 As him a heav'nly Zeal had mov'd, So Heav'n the zealous Act approv'd;
    To him confirming, and his Race, The Prieſthood he ſo well did Grace.

32 At Meribah God's Wrath they mov'd, Who Moſes for their Sakes reprov'd:
33 Whoſe patient Soul they did provoke, Till raſhly the meek Prophet ſpoke.
34 Nor when poſſeſt of Canaan's Land, Did they perform their Lord's Command,
    Nor his commiſſion'd Sword employ The guilty Nations to deſtroy.

35 Nor only ſpar'd the Pagan Crew, But, mingling, learnt their Voices too;
36 And worſhip to thoſe Idols paid Which them to fatal Snares betray'd.
37, 38 To Devils they did Sacrifice Their Children with relentleſs Eyes,
    Approach'd their Altars thro' a Flood, Of their own Sons and Daughters Blood.

    No cheaper Victims would appeaſe Canaan's remorſeleſs Deities;
    No Blood her Idols reconcile, But that which did the Land defile.

PART IV.

39 Nor did theſe ſavage Cruelties The harden'd Reprobates ſuffice;
    For after their Hearts Luſt they went, And daily did new Crimes invent.
40 But Sins of ſuch infernal Hue God's Wrath againſt his People drew,
    Till he, their once indulgent Lord, His own Inheritance abhor'd.

41 He then defenceleſs did expoſe To their inſulting Heathen Foes;
    And made them on the Triumphs wait, Of thoſe who bore them greateſt Hate.
42 Nor thus his Indignation ceas'd, Their Liſt of Tyrants he increas'd,
    Till they, who God's mild Sway declin'd, Were made the Vaſſals of Mankind.

43 Yet when diſtreſt, they did repent, His Anger did as oft relent;
    But freed, they did his Wrath provoke, Renew'd their Sins, and he their Yoke.
44 Nor yet implacable he prov'd, Nor heard their wretched Cries unmov'd.
45 But did to mind his Promiſe bring, And Mercy's inexhauſted Spring.

46 Compaſſion too he did impart E'en to their Foes obdurate Heart,
    And Pity for their Suff'rings bred In thoſe who them to Bondage led.
47 Still ſave us, Lord, and Iſr'el's Bands Together bring from Heathen Lands;
    So to thy Name our Thanks we'll raiſe, And ever Triumph in thy Praiſe.

48 Let Iſr'el's God be ever bleſt, his Name eternally confeſt;
    Let all his Saints with full Accord, Sing loud Amens—Praiſe ye the Lord.

PSALM CVII.

1 TO God your grateful Voices raiſe, who does your daily Patron prove;
    And let your never-ceaſing Praiſe attend on his eternal Love.
2, 3 Let thoſe give Thanks whom he from of proud oppreſſing Foes releas'd;
    Bands
    And brought them back from diſtant from North and South, and Weſt and Eaſt,
    Lands,

4, 5 Thro' lonely deſart Ways they went, nor could a peopled City find;
    Till quite with Thirſt and Hunger ſpent; their fainting Soul within them pin'd.
6 Then ſoon to God's indulgent Ear did they their mournful Cry addreſs,
    Who graciouſly vouchſaf'd to hear, and freed them from their deep Diſtreſs.

7 From crooked Paths he led them forth, and in the certain Way did guide,
    To wealthy Towns of great Reſort, where all their Wants were well ſupply'd.
8 O then that all the Earth with me, would God for this his Goodneſs praiſe!
    And for the mighty Works which he thro'out the wond'ring World diſplays!

9 For he from Heav'n the ſad Eſtate of longing Souls with Pity views;
    To hungry Souls that pant for Meat, his Goodneſs daily Food renews.

PART

PSALM CVII.

PART II.

10 Some lie, with Darknefs compafs'd round   in Death's uncomfortable Shade;
And with unweildy Fetters bound,   by preffing Cares more heavy made;
11, 12 Becaufe God's Counfel they defy'd,   and lightly priz'd his holy Word,
With thefe Afflictions they were try'd;   they fell, and none could Help afford.

13 Then foon to God's indulgent Ear,   did they their mournful Cry addrefs;
Who gracioufly vouchfaf'd to hear,   and freed them from their deep Diftrefs.
14 From difmal Dungeons, dark as Night,   and Shades as black as Death's Abode,
He brought them forth to chearful Light,   and welcome Liberty beftow'd.

15 O then that all the Earth, with me   would God for this his Goodnefs praife!
And for the mighty Works which he   thro'out the wond'ring World difplays!
16 For he with his Almighty Hand   the Gates of Brafs in Pieces broke;
Nor could the maffy Bars withftand,   or temper'd Steel refift his Stroke.

PART III.

17 Remorfelefs Wretches, void of Senfe,   with bold Tranfgreffions God defy;
And for their multiply'd Offence,   oppreft with fore Difeafes lie:
18 Their Soul, a Prey to Pain and Fear,   abhors to tafte the choiceft Meats,
And they by faint Degrees draw near   to Death's inhofpitable Gates.

19 Then ftrait to God's indulgent Ear,   do they their mournful Cry addrefs;
Who gracioufly vouchfafes to hear,   and frees them from their deep Diftrefs.
20 He all their fad Diftempers heals,   his Word both Health and Safety gives;
And when all human Succour fails,   from near Deftruction them retrieves.

21 O then that all the Earth, with me,   would God for this his Goodnefs praife!
And for the mighty Works which he   thro'out the wond'ring World difplays!
22 With Off'rings let his Altars flame,   whilft they their grateful Thanks exprefs!
And with loud Joy his holy Name   for all his Acts of Wonder blefs.

PART IV.

23, 24 They that in Ships, with Courage   o'er fwelling Waves their Trade purfue;
bold,
Do God's amazing Works behold,   and in the Deep his Wonders view.
25 No fooner his Command is paft,   but forth a dreadful Tempeft flies,
Which fweeps the Sea with rapid Hafte,   and makes the ftormy Billows rife.

26 Sometimes the Ships, tofs'd up to Heav'n,   on Tops of mounting Waves appear;
Then down the fteep Abyfs are driv'n,   whilft ev'ry Soul diffolves with Fear.
27 They reel and ftagger too and fro,   like Men with Fumes of Wine oppreft;
Nor do the fkilful Seamen know,   which Way to fteer, what Courfe is beft.

28 Then ftrait to God's indulgent Ear   they do their mournful Cry addrefs;
Who gracioufly vouchfafes to hear,   and frees them from their deep Diftrefs.
29, 30 He does the raging Storm appeafe,   and makes the Billows calm and ftill:
With Joy they fee their Fury ceafe,   and their intended Courfe fulfil.

31 O then that all the Earth, with me,   would God for this his Goodnefs praife;
And for the mighty Works, which he   thro'out the wond'ring World difplays!
32 Let them, where all the Tribes refort,   advance to Heav'n his glorious Name,
And in the Elders fov'reign Court,   with one Confent his Praife proclaim.

PART V.

33, 34 A fruitful Land, where Streams   God's juft Revenge, where People fin,
abound,
will turn to dry and barren Ground,   to punifh thofe that dwell therein.

PSALM CVIII, CIX.

35, 36 The parcht and desart Heath he makes
  to flow with Streams and springing Wells:
Which for his Lot the Hungry takes,
  and in strong Cities safely dwells.
37, 38 He sows the Field, the Vineyard plants,
  which gratefully his Toil repay;
Nor can, whilst God his Blessing grants,
  his fruitful Seed or Stock decay.
39 But when his Sins Heav'n's Wrath provoke,
  his Health and Substance fade away;
He feels th' Oppressor's gauling Yoke,
  and is of Grief the wretched Prey.
40 The Prince that slights what God commands,
  expos'd to Scorn, must quit his Throne;
And over wild and desart Lands,
  where no Path offers, stray alone.
41 Whilst God, from all afflicting Cares,
  sets up the humble Man on high:
And makes in Time his num'rous Heirs
  with his increasing Flocks to vye.
42, 43 Then Sinners shall have nought to say
  the Just a decent Joy shall show;
The Wise these strange Events shall weigh,
  and thence God's Goodness fully know.

PSALM CVIII.

1 O God, my Heart is fully bent,
  to magnify thy Name;
My Tongue with chearful Songs of Praise,
  shall celebrate thy Fame,
2 Awake, my Lute; nor thou, my Harp,
  thy warbling Notes delay;
Whilst I with early Hymns of Joy,
  prevent the dawning Day.
3 To all the list'ning Tribes, O Lord,
  thy Wonders I will tell;
And to those Nations sing thy Praise
  that round about us dwell:
4 Because thy Mercy's boundless Height
  the highest Heav'n transcends;
And far beyond th' aspiring Clouds
  thy faithful Truth extends.
5 Be thou, O God, exalted high
  above the starry Frame;
And let the World, with one Consent,
  confess thy glorious Name.
6 That all thy chosen People Thee
  their Saviour may declare.
Let thy Right-hand protect me still,
  and answer thou my Pray'r.
7 Since God himself has said the Word,
  whose Promise cannot fail,
With Joy I Sechem will divide,
  and measure Succoth's Vale:
8 Gilead is mine, Manasseh too;
  and Ephraim owns my Cause:
Their Strength my Regal Pow'r supports,
  and Judah gives my Laws.
9 Moab I'll make my servile Drudge,
  on vanquisht Edom tread;
And thro' the proud Philistine Lands
  my conqu'ring Banners spread.
10 By whose Support and Aid shall I
  their well-fenc'd City gain?
Who will my Troops securely lead
  thro' Edom's guarded Plain?
11 Lord, wilt not thou assist our Arms,
  which late thou didst forsake?
And wilt not thou, of these our Hosts,
  once more the Guidance take?
12 O to thy Servants in Distress
  thy speedy Succour send:
For vain it is on human Aid
  for Safety to depend.
13 The valiant Acts shall we perform,
  if thou thy Pow'r disclose,
For God it is, and God alone,
  that treads down all our Foes.

PSALM CIX.

1 O God, whose former Mercies make
  my constant Praise thy due,
Hold not thy Peace, but my sad State
  with wonted Favour view.
2 For sinful Men, with lying Lips,
  deceitful Speeches frame,
And with their study'd Slanders seek
  to wound my spotless Fame.

3 Their

PSALM CIX.

3 Their reſtleſs Hatred prompts them ſtill, malicious Lies to ſpread;
   And all againſt my Life combine, by cauſeleſs Fury led.
4 Thoſe whom with tend'reſt Love I us'd, my chief Oppoſers are;
   Whilſt I of other Friends bereft, reſort to thee by Pray'rr
5 Since Miſchief, for the Good I did, their ſtrange Reward does prove:
   And Hatred's the Return they make for undiſſembled Love;
6 Their guilty Leader ſhall be made to ſome ill Man a Slave;
   And when he's try'd, his mortal Foe for his Accuſer have.
7 His Guilt when Sentence is pronounc'd, ſhall meet a dreadful Fate;
   Whilſt his rejected Pray'r but ſerves his Crimes to aggravate.
8 He, ſnatch'd by ſome untimely Fate, ſhan't live out half his Days;
   Another, by divine Decree, ſhall on his Office ſeize.
9, 10 His Seed ſhall Orphans be, his Wife a Widow plung'd in Grief;
   His vagrant Children beg their Bread, where none can give Relief.
11 His ill-got Riches ſhall be made to Uſurers a Prey;
   The Fruit of all his Toil ſhall be by Strangers borne away.
12 None ſhall be found, that to his Wants their Mercy will extend,
   Or to his helpleſs Orphan-Seed the leaſt Aſſiſtance lend.
13 A ſwift Deſtruction ſoon ſhall ſeize on his unhappy Race;
   And the next Age his hated Name ſhall utterly deface.
14 The Vengeance of his Father's Sins upon his Head ſhall fall:
   God on his Mother's Crimes ſhall think, and puniſh him for all.
15 All theſe, in horrid Order rank'd, before the Lord ſhall ſtand,
   Till his fierce Anger quite cuts off their Mem'ry from the Land.

PART II.

16 Becauſe he never Mercy ſhew'd, but ſtill the Poor oppreſs'd;
   And ſought to ſlay the helpleſs Man, with heavy Woes diſtreſs'd.
17 Therefore the Curſe he lov'd to vent, ſhall his own Portion prove;
   And Bleſſing, which he ſtill abhor'd, ſhall far from him remove.
18 Since he in Curſing took ſuch Pride, like Water it ſhall ſpread
   Thro' all his Veins, and ſtick like Oil, with which his Bones are fed.
19 This, like a poiſon'd Robe, ſhall ſtill his conſtant Cov'ring be,
   Or an envenom'd Belt, from which he never ſhall be free.
20 Thus ſhall the Lord reward all thoſe that Ill to me deſign;
   That with malicious falſe Reports againſt my Life combine.
21 But for thy glorious Name, O God, do thou deliver me;
   And for thy gracious Mercy's Sake, preſerve and ſet me free.
22 For I, to utmoſt Straits reduc'd, am void of all Relief;
   My Heart is wounded with Diſtreſs, and quite pierc'd thro' with Grief.
23 I, like an Ev'ning Shade, decline, which vaniſhes apace;
   Like Locuſts up and down I'm toſt, and have no certain Place.
24, 25 My Knees with faſting are grown weak, my Body lank and lean;
   All that behold me ſhake their Heads, and treat me with Diſdain.
26, 27 But for thy Mercy's ſake, O Lord do thou my Foes withſtand;
   That all may ſee 'tis thy own Act, the Work of thy Right-hand.
28 Then let them curſe, ſo thou but bleſs; let Shame the Portion be
   Of all that my Deſtruction ſeek, while I rejoice in thee.
29 My Foe ſhall with Diſgrace be cloath'd, and ſpite of all his Pride:
   His own Confuſion, like a Cloak, the guilty Wretch ſhall hide.

30 But

PSALM CX, CXI, CXII.

50 But I to God, in grateful Thanks,
And where the great Assembly meets,
31 For him the Poor shall always find
And he shall from unrighteous Dooms
my chearful Voice will raise;
set forth his noble Praise.
their sure and constant Friend;
their guiltless Souls defend.

PSALM CX.

1 THE Lord unto my Lord thus spake,
" Till I thy Foes thy Foot-stool
make,
" sit thou, in State, at my Right-hand;
2 " Supreme in Sion thou shalt be,
" and all thy proud Oppressors see
" subjected to thy just Command.

3 " Thee, in thy Pow'r's triumphant Day,
" the willing Nations shall obey,
" and when thy rising Beams they view,
" Shall all (redeem'd from Error's Night)
" appear as numberless and bright
" as Chrystal Drops of Morning Dew."

4 The Lord has sworn, nor sworn in vain,
that like Melchizedeck's, thy Reign
and Priesthood shall no Period know:
5 No proud Competitor to sit
at thy Right-hand will he permit:
but in his Wrath crown'd Heads o'erthrow.

6 The sentenc'd Heathen he shall slay,
and fill with Carcasses his Way,
till he has struck Earth's Tyrant dead;
7 But in the High-way Brook shall first,
like a poor Pilgrim slake his Thirst,
and then in Triumph raise his Head.

PSALM CXI.

1 PRAISE ye the Lord; our God to
praise
With private Friends, and in the Throng
2 His Works, for greatness, tho' renown'd,
By those who seek for them aright,

3 His Works are all of matchless Fame,
His Truth, confirm'd thro' Ages past,
4 By Precept he has us enjoin'd,
And to Posterity record,

5 His Bounty, like a flowing Tide,
And he will ever keep in Mind
6 At once astonish and o'erjoy'd,
Whereby the Heathen were suppress'd,

7 Just are the Dealings of his Hands,
8 By Truth and Equity sustain'd,
9 He set his Saints from Bondage free,
For ever to remain the same:

10 Who Wisdom's sacred Prize would win,
Immortal Praise, and heav'nly Skill

My Soul her utmost Pow'r shall raise,

Of Saints my Praise shall be my Song.
His wond'rous Works with Ease are found
And in the pious Search delight.

And universal Glory claim;
Shall to eternal Ages last.
To keep his wond'rous Works in Mind,
That good and gracious is our Lord.

Has all his Servants Wants supply'd;
His Cov'nant with our Fathers sign'd.
They saw his matchless Pow'r employ'd;
And we their Heritage possess'd.

Immutable are his Commands:
And for eternal Rules ordain'd.
And then establish'd his Decree,
Holy and Rev'rend is his Name.

Must with the Fear of God begin:
Have they who know and do his Will.

PSALM CXII.
HALLELUJAH.

1 THAT Man is blest who stands in
Awe
2 His Seed on Earth shall be renown'd,
3 His House, the Seat of Wealth, shall be
His Justice free from all Decay,

4 The Soul that's fill'd with Virtue's Light,
To pity the Distress'd inclin'd,
5 His lib'ral Favours he extends,
Yet what his Charity impairs,

of God, and loves his sacred Law:
And with successive Honours crown'd,
An inexhausted Treasury;
Shall Blessings to his Heirs convey.

Shines brightest in Affliction's Night:
As well as Just to all Mankind.
To some he gives, to others lends:
He saves by Prudence in Affairs.

PSALM CXIII, CXIV, CXV.

6 Beset with threat'ning Dangers round, Unmov'd shall he maintain his Ground;
 The sweet Rememb'rance of the Just, Shall flourish when he sleeps in Dust.
7 Ill Tidings never can surprise His Heart that, fix'd, on God relies:
8 On Safety's Rock, he sits, and sees The Shipwreck of his Enemies.
9 His Hands, while they his Alms bestow'd, His Glory's future Harvest sow'd;
 Whence, he shall reap Wealth, Fame, A temp'ral and eternal Crown.
 Renown,
10 The Wicked shall his Triumph see, And gnash their Teeth in Agony,
 While their unrighteous Hopes decay, And vanish, with themselves, away.

PSALM CXIII.

1 YE Saints and Servants of the Lord, 6 Tho' 'tis beneath his State to view
 the Triumphs of his Name record, in highest Heav'n what Angels do,
2 His sacred Name for ever bless. yet he to Earth vouchsafes his Care:
3 Where'er the circling Sun displays, He takes the Needy from his Cell,
 His rising Beams or setting Rays, advancing him in Courts to dwell,
 Due Praise to his great Name address. Companion to the greatest there.

4 God thro' the World extends his Sway, 7 When childless Families despair,
 the Regions of eternal Day; he sends the Blessing of an Heir,
 but Shadows of his Glory are. to rescue their expiring Name;
5 To him, whose Majesty excels, Makes her that barren was to bear,
 Who made the Heav'n wherein he dwells, and joyfully her Fruit to rear;
 let no created Pow'r compare. O then extoll his matchless Fame!

PSALM CXIV.

1 WHEN Isr'el by th' Almighty (enrich'd with their Oppressor's Spoil)
 led,
 From Egypt march'd, and Jacob's Seed from Bondage in a foreign Soil;
2 Jehovah, for his Residence, chose out imperial Judah's Tent,
 His Mansion-Royal, and from thence thro' Isr'el's Camp his Orders sent.

3 The distant Sea with Terror saw, and from th' Almighty's Presence fled;
 Old Jordan's Streams, surpriz'd with Awe, retreated to their Fountain's Head,
4 The taller Mountains skipp'd like Rams, when Danger near the Fold they hear;
 The Hills skipp'd after them, like Lambs, affrighted by their Leader's Fear.

5 O Sea, what made your Tide withdraw, and naked leave your ouzy Bed?
 Why, Jordan, against Nature's Law, recoild'st thou to thy Fountain's Head?
6 Why, Mountains, did ye skip like Rams, when Danger does approach the Fold?
 Why after you the Hills like Lambs, when they their Leader's Flight behold?

7 Earth, tremble on; well may'st thou fear, thy Lord and Maker's Face to see;
 When Jacob's awful God draws near, 'tis Time for Earth and Seas to flee;
8 To flee from God, whose Nature's Law, confirms and cancels at his Will;
 Who Springs from flinty Rocks can draw and thirsty Vales with Water fill.

PSALM CXV.

1 LORD, not to us, we claim no Share, but to thy sacred Name
 Give Glory for thy Mercy's Sake, and Truth's eternal Fame.
2 Why should the Heathen cry, Where's now the God whom we adore?
3 Convince them that in Heav'n thou art, and uncontroul'd thy Pow'r.

4 Their Gods but Gold and Silver are, the Works of mortal Hands:
5 With speechless Mouth, and sightless Eyes, the molten Idol stands.
6 The Pageant has both Ears and Nose, but neither hears nor smells;
7 Its Hands and Feet nor feel, nor move, no Life within it dwells.

PSALM CXVI, CXVII.

8 Such senseless Stocks they are, that we can nothing like them find
But those who on their Help rely, and them for God's design'd.
9 O Isr'el, make the Lord your Trust, who is your Help and Shield;
10 Priests, Levites, trust in him alone, who only Help can yield.

11 Let all, who truly fear the Lord, on him they fear, rely;
Who them in Danger can defend, and all their Wants supply.
12, 13 Of us he oft has mindful been, and Isr'el's House will bless,
Priests, Levites, Proselytes, ev'n all who his great Name confess.

14 On you, and on your Heirs, he will increase of Blessings bring;
15 Thrice happy you, who Fav'rites are - of this Almighty King.
16 Heav'n's highest Orb of Glory, he his Empire's Seat design'd;
And gave this lower Globe of Earth a Portion to Mankind.

17 They who in Death and Silence sleep to him no Praise afford:
18 But we will bless for evermore our ever-living Lord.

PSALM CXVI.

1 MY Soul with grateful Thoughts of Love intirely is possest;
Because the Lord, vouchsaf'd to hear the Voice of my Request.
2 Since he has now his Ear inclin'd, I never will despair;
But still in all the Straits of Life to him address my Pray'r.

3 With deadly Sorrows compast round, with Pains of Hell opprest,
When Troubles seiz'd my aking Heart, and Anguish rack'd my Breast;
4 On God's Almighty Name I call'd, and thus to him I pray'd;
" Lord, I beseech thee save my Soul, " with Sorrows quite dismay'd."

5, 6 How just and merciful is God, how gracious is the Lord!
Who saves the Harmless, and to me does timely Help afford.
7 Then, free from pensive Cares, my Soul, resume thy wonted Rest;
For God has wond'rously to thee his bounteous Love exprest.

8 When Death alarm'd me, he remov'd my Dangers and my Fears;
My Feet from falling he secur'd, and dry'd my Eyes from Tears.
9 Therefore my Life's remaining Years, which God to me shall lend,
Will I in Praises to his Name, and in his Service spend.

10, 11 In God I trusted, and of him in greatest Straits did boast;
(For in my Flight all Hopes of Aid from faithless Men were lost.)
12, 13 Then what Return to him shall I for all his Goodness make?
I'll praise his Name, and with glad Zeal, the Cup of Blessing take.

14, 15 I'll pay my Vows amongst his Saints, whose Blood, (howe'er despis'd
By wicked Men) in God's Account is always highly priz'd.
16 By various Ties, O Lord, must I to thy Dominion bow;
Thy humble Handmaid's Son before, thy ransom'd Captive now!

17, 18 To thee I'll Off'rings bring of Praise; and whilst I bless thy Name,
The just Performance of my Vows To all thy Saints proclaim.
19 They in Jerusalem shall meet, and in thy House shall join,
To bless thy Name with one Consent, and mix their Songs with mine.

PSALM CXVII.

1 WITH chearful Notes let all the Earth to Heav'n their Voices raise;
Let all inspir'd with godly Mirth, sing solemn Hymns of Praise:
2 God's tender Mercy knows no Bound, his Truth shall ne'er decay,
Then let the willing Nations round their grateful Tribute pay.

PSALM CXVIII, CXIX.

PSALM CXVIII.

1, 2 O Praise the Lord, for he is good, his Mercies ne'er decay:
That his kind Favours ever last, let thankful Isr'el say.
3, 4 Their Sense of his eternal Love let Aaron's House express;
And that it never fails, let all that fear the Lord confess.

5 To God I made my humble Moan, with Troubles quite opprest;
And he releas'd me from my Straits, and granted my Request.
6 Since therefore God does on my Side so graciously appear,
Why should the vain Attempts of Men possess my Soul with Fear;

7 Since God with those that aid my Cause vouchsafes my Part to take,
To all my Foes I need not doubt a just Return to make.
8, 9 For better 'tis to trust in God, and have the Lord our Friend,
Than on the greatest human Pow'r for Safety to depend.

10, 11 Tho' many Nations closely leagu'd, did oft beset me round!
Yet by his boundless Pow'r sustain'd, I did their Strength confound.
12 They swarm'd like Bees, and yet their Rage was but a short-liv'd Blaze:
For whilst on God I still rely'd, I vanquish'd them with Ease.

13 When all united press'd me hard, in Hopes to make me fall:
The Lord vouchsaf'd to take my Part, and sav'd me from them all.
14 The Honour of my strange Escape to him alone belongs;
He is my Saviour and my Strength, he only claims my Songs.

15 Joy fills the Dwellings of the Just, whom God has sav'd from Harm;
For wond'rous Things are brought to pass by his Almighty Arm.
16 He, by his own resistless Pow'r, has endless Honour won:
The saving Strength of his Right-hand amazing Works has done.

17 God will not suffer me to fall, but still prolongs my Days;
That by declaring all his Works, I may advance his Praise.
18 When God had sorely me chastis'd, till quite of Hopes bereav'd;
His Mercy from the Gates of Death my fainting Life repriev'd.

19 Then open wide the Temple-Gates to which the Just repair;
That I may enter in and praise my great Deliv'rer there.
20, 21 Within those Gates of God's Abode to which the Righteous press;
Since thou hast heard and set me safe, thy holy Name I'll bless.

22, 23 That, which the Builders once refus'd, is now the Corner-Stone;
This is the wond'rous Work of God, the Work of God alone.
24, 25 This Day is God's; let all the Land exalt their chearful Voice:
Lord, we beseech thee, save us now, and make us still rejoice.

26 Him that approaches in God's Name, let all th' Assembly bless;
" We, that belong to God's own House, " have wish'd you good Success."
27 God is the Lord, through whom we all both Light and Comforts find;
Fast to the Altar's Horn, with Cords, the chosen Victim bind.

28 Thou art my Lord, O God, and still I'll praise thy holy Name;
Because thou only art my God, I'll celebrate thy Fame.
29 O then, with me, give Thanks to God, who still does gracious prove;
And let the Tribute of our Praise be endless as his Love.

PSALM CXIX.
ALEPH.

1 HOW blest are they who always keep the pure and perfect Way!
Who never from the sacred Paths of God's Commandments stray!
2 Thrice

PSALM CXIX.

2 Thrice bleſt who to his righteous Laws have ſtill obedient been!
And have with fervent humble Zeal his Favour ſought to win!
3 Such Men their utmoſt Caution uſe to ſhun each wicked Deed;
But in the Path which he directs with conſtant Care proceed.
4 Thou ſtrictly haſt enjoin'd us, Lord, to learn thy ſacred Will;
And all our Diligence employ thy Statutes to fulfil.
5 O then that thy moſt holy Will might o'er my Ways preſide!
And I the Courſe of all my Life by thy Direction guide!
6 Then with Aſſurance ſhould I walk, from all Confuſion free;
Convinc'd, with Joy, that all my Ways with thy Commands agree.
7 My upright Heart, ſhall my glad Mouth with chearful Praiſes fill;
When by thy righteous Judgments taught, I ſhall have learnt thy Will.
8 So to thy ſacred Laws ſhall I, all due Obſervance pay;
O then forſake me not, my God, nor caſt me quite away.

BETH.

9 How ſhall the Young preſerve their Ways from all Pollution free?
By making ſtill their Courſe of Life with thy Commands agree.
10 With hearty Zeal, for thee I ſeek, to thee for Succour pray;
O ſuffer not my careleſs Steps from thy right Paths to ſtray.
11 Safe in my Heart, and cloſely hid, thy Word, my Treaſure, lies;
To ſuccour me with timely Aid, when ſinful Thoughts ariſe.
12 Secur'd by that, my grateful Soul ſhall ever bleſs thy Name;
O teach me then by thy juſt Laws my future Life to frame.
13 My Lips, unlockt by pious Zeal, to others have declar'd,
How well the Judgments of thy Mouth deſerve our beſt Regard.
14 Whilſt in the Way of thy Commands, more ſolid Joy I found,
Than had I been with vaſt Increaſe of envy'd Riches crown'd.
15 Therefore thy juſt and upright Laws ſhall always fill my Mind;
And thoſe ſound Rules which thou preſcrib'ſt all due Reſpect ſhall find.
16 To keep thy Statutes undefac'd, ſhall be my conſtant Joy;
The ſtrict Remembrance of thy Word, ſhall all my Thoughts employ.

GIMEL.

17 Be gracious to thy Servant, Lord, do thou my Life defend,
That I, according to thy Word, my Time to come may ſpend.
18 Enlighten both my Eyes and Mind, that ſo I may diſcern
The wond'rous Things which they behold who thy juſt Precepts learn.
19 Tho' like a Stranger in the Land, from Place to Place I ſtray,
Thy righteous Judgments from my Sight remove not thou away.
20 My fainting Soul is almoſt pin'd, with earneſt Longing ſpent;
Whilſt always on the eager Search of thy juſt Will, intent.
21 Thy ſharp Rebuke ſhall cruſh the Proud, whom ſtill thy Curſe purſues;
Since they to walk in thy right Ways preſumptuouſly refuſe.
22 But far from me do thou, O Lord, Contempt and Shame remove;
For I thy ſacred Laws affect with undiſſembled Love.
23 Tho' Princes oft in Council met, againſt thy Servant ſpake;
Yet I, thy Statutes to obſerve, my conſtant Buſineſs make.
24 For thy Commands have always been my Comfort and Delight;
By them I learn, with prudent Care, to guide my Steps aright.

DALETH.

PSALM CXIX.

DALETH.

25 My Soul oppress'd with deadly Care, close to the Dust does cleave:
Revive me, Lord, and let me now thy promis'd Aid receive.
26 To thee I still declare my Ways, and thou inclin'dst thine Ear;
O teach me then my future Life by thy just Laws to steer.

27 If thou wilt make me know thy Laws, and by their Guidance walk,
The wond'rous Works which thou hast done shall be my constant Talk.
28 But see, my Soul within me sinks, prest down with weighty Care;
Do, thou, according to thy Word, my wasted Strength repair.

29 Far, far from me be all false Ways, and lying Arts remov'd!
But kindly grant I still may keep the Path by thee approv'd.
30 Thy faithful Ways, thou God of Truth, my happy Choice I've made;
Thy Judgments, as my Rule of Life, before me always laid.

31 My Care has been to make my Life, with thy Commands agree;
O then preserve thy Servant, Lord, from Shame and Ruin free.
32 So in the Way of thy Commands, shall I with Pleasure run,
And with a Heart enlarg'd with Joy, successfully go on.

HE.

33 Instruct me in thy Statutes, Lord, thy righteous Paths display!
And I from them, thro' all my Life, will never go astray.
34 If thou true Wisdom from above wilt graciously impart,
To keep thy perfect Laws I will devote my zealous Heart.

35 Direct me in the sacred Ways to which thy Precepts lead;
Because my chief Delight has been thy righteous Paths to tread.
36 Do thou to thy most just Commands incline my willing Heart:
Let no Desire of worldly Wealth from thee my Thoughts divert.

37 From those vain Objects turn my Eyes which this false World displays;
But give me lively Pow'r and Strength to keep thy righteous Ways.
38 Confirm the Promise which thou mad'st, and give thy Servant Aid,
Who to transgress thy sacred Laws is awfully afraid.

39 The foul Disgrace I justly fear, in Mercy, Lord remove;
For all the Judgments thou ordain'st are full of Grace and Love.
40 Thou know'st how, after thy Commands, my longing Heart does pant;
O then make haste to raise me up, and promis'd Succour grant.

VAU.

41 Thy constant Blessing, Lord, bestow, to cheer my drooping Heart;
To me, according to thy Word, thy saving Health impart.
42 So shall I, when my Foes upbraid, this ready Answer make;
" In God I trust, who never will " his faithful Promise break."

43 Then let not quite the Word of Truth be from my Mouth remov'd;
Since still my Ground of stedfast Hope thy just Decrees have prov'd.
44 So I to keep thy righteous Laws, with all my Study bend;
From Age to Age my Time to come in their Observance spend.

45 Ere long I trust to walk at large, from all Incumbrance free;
Since I resolv'd to make my Life with thy Commands agree.
46 Thy Laws shall be my comfort Talk; and Princes shall attend,
Whilst I the Justice of thy Ways with Confidence defend.

47 My

PSALM CXIX.

47 My longing Heart and ravish'd Soul
When in thy lov'd Commandments I
48 Then will I to thy just Decrees,
My Care and Business then shall be

shall both o'erflow with Joy;
my happy Hours employ.
lift up my willing Hands;
to study thy Commands.

ZAIN.

49 According to thy promis'd Grace,
Make good to me the Word, on which
50 That only Comfort in Distress
Thy Word, when Troubles hem'd me round,

thy Favour, Lord, extend;
thy Servant's Hopes depend.
did all my Griefs controul;
reviv'd my fainting Soul.

51 Insulting Foes did proudly mock,
Yet from thy Law, not all their Scoffs
52 Thy Judgments then, of ancient Date,
'Till ravish'd with such Thoughts, my Soul

and all my Hopes deride;
could make me turn aside.
I quickly call'd to mind!
did speedy Comfort find.

53 Sometimes I stand amaz'd, 'like one
To think how all my sinful Foes
54 But I thy Statutes and Decrees,
Whilst thro' strange Lands and Desarts wild

with deadly Horror struck,
have thy just Laws forsook.
my chearful Anthems made;
I like a Pilgrim stray'd.

55 Thy Name that chear'd my Heart by Day,
I then resolv'd by thy just Laws,
56 That Peace of Mind, which has my Soul
By strict Obedience to thy Will

has fill'd my Thoughts by Night;
to guide my Steps aright.
in deep Distress sustain'd,
I happily obtain'd.

CHETH.

57 O Lord, my God, my Portion thou,
Thy Words I stedfastly resolve
58 With all the Strength of warm Desires
Disclose, according to thy Word.

and sure Possession art;
to treasure in my Heart,
I did thy Grace implore;
thy Mercy's boundless Store.

59 With due Reflection and strict Care
And so, reclaim'd to thy just Paths,
60 I lost no Time, but made great haste,
To watch, that I might never more

on all my Ways I thought;
my wand'ring Steps I brought.
resolv'd, without Delay,
from thy Commandments stray.

61 Tho' num'rous Troops of sinful Men
Yet I thy pure and righteous Laws
62 In Dead of Night I will arise,
Convinc'd how much I always ought

to rob me have combin'd;
have ever kept in Mind.
to sing thy solemn Praise;
to love thy righteous Ways.

63 To such as fear thy holy Name
To all who their obedient Wills
64 O'er all the Earth thy Mercy, Lord,
O make me then, exactly learn,

myself I closely join,
to thy Commands resign.
abundantly is shed;
thy sacred Paths to tread.

TETH.

65 With me, thy Servant, thou hast dealt
Repeated Benefits bestow'd,
66 Teach me the sacred Skill, by which
Who in Belief of thy Commands

most graciously, O Lord,
according to thy Word.
right Judgment is attain'd,
have stedfastly remain'd.

67 Before Affliction stopt my Course,
But I have since been disciplin'd
68 Thou art, O Lord, supremely good,
On me, thy Statutes to discern,

my Footsteps went astray;
thy Precepts to obey.
and all thou dost is so;
the saving Skill bestow.

69 The Proud have forg'd malicious Lies
but my fixt Heart, without Reserve,

my spotless Fame to stain;
thy Precepts shall retain.

70 While

PSALM CXIX.

70 While pamper'd they, with profp'rous Ills, in fenfual Pleafures live,
My Soul can relifh no Delight but what thy Precepts give.
71 'Tis good for me that I have felt Affliction's chaft'ning Rod,
That I may duly learn and keep the Statutes of my God.
72 The Law that from thy Mouth proceeds of more Efteem they hold,
Than untouch'd Mines, than thoufand Mines of Silver and of Gold.

J O D.

73 To me, who am the Workmanfhip of thy Almighty Hands,
The heav'nly Underftanding give to learn thy juft Commands.
74 My Prefervation to thy Saints ftrong Comfort will afford,
To fee Succefs attend my Hopes, who trufted in thy Word.
75 That right thy Judgments are, I now by fure Experience fee,
And that in Faithfulnefs, O Lord, thou haft afflicted me.
76 O let thy tender Mercy now afford me needful Aid;
According to thy Promife, Lord, to me, thy Servant, made.
77 To me thy faving Grace reftore, that I again may live;
Whofe Soul can relifh no Delight but what thy Precepts give.
78 Defeat the Proud, who, unprovok'd, to ruin me have fought;
Who only on thy facred Laws employ my harmlefs Thought.
79 Let thofe that fear thy Name efpoufe my Caufe, and thofe alone,
Who have by ftrict and pious Search thy facred Precepts known.
80 In thy blefs'd Statutes let my Heart continue always found,
That Guilt and Shame, the Sinners Lot, may never me confound.

C A P H.

81 My Soul with long Expectance faints to fee thy faving Grace;
Yet ftill on thy unerring Word my Confidence I place.
82 My very Eyes confume and fail with waiting for thy Word:
O! when wilt thou thy kind Relief and promis'd Aid afford?
83 My Skin like fhrivel'd Parchment fhows, that long in Smoke is fet;
Yet no Afflictions me can force thy Statutes to forget.
84 How many Days muft I endure of Sorrow and Diftrefs?
When wilt thou Judgment execute on them who me opprefs?
85 The Proud have digg'd a Pit for me, that have no other Foes,
But fuch as are averfe to thee, and thy juft Laws oppofe.
86 With Right and Truth's eternal Laws all thy Commands agree;
Men perfecute me without Caufe, thou Lord, my helper be.
87 With clofe Defigns againft my Life they had almoft prevail'd;
But in Obedience to thy Will my Duty never fail'd.
88 Thy wonted Kindnefs, Lord, reftore, my drooping Heart to cheer;
That by thy righteous Staures, I my Life's whole Courfe may fteer.

L A M E D.

89 For ever and for ever, Lord, unchang'd thou doft remain;
Thy Word, eftablifh'd in the Heav'ns, does all their Orbs fuftain.
90 Thro' circling Ages, Lord, thy Truth immoveable fhall ftand,
As doth the Earth, which thou uphold'ft by thy Almighty Hand.
91 All Things the Courfe by thee ordain'd, ev'n to this Day fulfil:
They are thy faithful Subjects all, and Servants of thy Will.
92 Unlefs thy facred Law had been my Comfort and Delight,
I muft have fainted and expir'd in dark Afflictions Night.

PSALM CXIX.

93 Thy Precepts therefore from my Thoughts shall never, Lord, depart;
For thou, by them, hast to new Life restor'd my dying Heart.
94 As I am thine, entirely thine, protect me, Lord, from Harm;
Who have thy Precepts sought to know, and carefully perform.
95 The Wicked have their Ambush laid my guiltless Life to take:
But in the Midst of Danger I thy Word my Study make.
96 I've seen an End of what we call Perfection here below;
But thy Commandments, like thyself, no Change or Period know.

M E M.

97 The Love that to thy Laws I bear, no Language can display;
They with fresh Wonders entertain my ravish'd Thoughts all Day.
98 Through thy Commands I wiser grow than all my subtile Foes;
For thy sure Word does me direct, and all my Ways difpose.

99 From me my former Teachers now my abler Counsel take;
Because thy sacred Precepts I my'constant Study make.
100 In Understanding I excel the Sages of our Days;
Because by thy unerring Rules I order all my Ways.

101 My Feet, with Care, I have refrain'd, from ev'ry sinful Way,
That to thy sacred Word I might intire Obedience pay.
102 I have not from thy Judgments stray'd, by vain Desires misled;
For, Lord, thou hast instructed me thy righteous Paths to tread.

103 How sweet are all thy Words to me; O what divine Repast!
How much more grateful to my Soul than Honey to my Taste.
104 Taught by thy sacred Precepts, I with heav'nly Skill am blest;
Thro' which the treach'rous Ways of Sin I utterly detest.

N U N.

105 Thy Word is to my Feet a Lamp, the Way of Truth to shew;
A Watch-light to point out the Path, in which I ought to go.
106 I swear (and from my solemn Oath will never start aside;)
That in thy righteous Judgments I will stedfastly abide.

107 Since I with Griefs am sore opprest that I can bear no more,
According to thy Word, do thou my fainting Soul restore.
108 Let still my Sacrifice of Praise with thee Acceptance find;
And in thy righteous Judgments, Lord, instruct my willing Mind.

109 Tho' ghastly Dangers me surround, my Soul they cannot awe:
Nor, with continual Terrors, keep from thinking on thy Law.
110 My wicked and invet'rate Foes for me their Snares have laid;
Yet I have kept the upright Path, nor from thy Precepts stray'd.

111 Thy Testimonies I have made my Heritage and Choice;
For they, when other Comforts fail, my drooping Heart rejoice.
112 My Heart with early Zeal began thy Statutes to obey;
And till my Course of Life is done, shall keep thy upright Way.

S A M E C H.

113 Deceitful Thoughts and Practices I utterly detest?
But to thy Law Affection bear too great to be exprest.
114 My Hiding-Place, my Refuge-Tow'r, and Shield art thou, O Lord;
I firmly Anchor all my Hopes on thy unerring Word.

115 Hence ye that trade in Wickedness, approach not my Abode,
For firmly I resolve to keep the Precepts of my God.

116 Ac-

PSALM CXIX.

116 According to thy gracious Word, from Danger set me free;
Nor make me of those Hopes asham'd that I repose on thee.
117 Uphold me, so I shall be safe, and rescu'd from Distress;
To thy Decrees continually my just Respects address.
118 The Wicked thou hast trod to Earth, who from thy Statutes stray'd;
Their vile Deceit the just Reward of their own Falshood made.
119 The Wicked from thy holy Land thou dost, like Dross, remove;
I therefore, with such Justice charm'd, thy Testimonies love.
120 Yet with that Love they make me dread lest I should so offend,
When on Transgressors I behold thy Judgments thus descend.

A I N.

121 Judgment and Justice I have lov'd; O therefore, Lord, engage
In my Defence, nor give me up to my Oppressors Rage.
122 Do thou be Surety, Lord, for me; and so shall this Distress
Prove good for me; nor shall the Proud my guiltless Soul oppress.
123 My Eyes, alas! begin to fail, in long Expectance held,
Till thy Salvation they behold, and righteous Word fulfil'd.
124 To me, thy Servant, in Distress thy wonted Grace display,
And discipline my willing Heart thy Statutes to obey.
125 On me, devoted to thy Fear, thy sacred Skill bestow,
That of thy Testimonies I the full Extent may know.
126 'Tis Time, high Time for thee, O Lord, thy Vengeance to employ,
When Men with open Violence thy sacred Law destroy.
127 Yet their Contempt of thy Commands but makes their Value rise
In my Esteem, who purest Gold, compar'd with them despise.
128 Thy Precepts therefore I account in all Respects divine;
They teach me to discern the right, and all false Ways decline.

P E.

129 The Wonders which thy Laws contain, no Words can represent;
Therefore to learn and practise them, my zealous Heart is bent.
130 The very Entrance to thy Word celestial Light displays;
And Knowledge of true Happiness to simplest Minds conveys.
131 With eager Hopes I waiting stood, and fainted with Desire,
That of thy wise Commands I might the sacred Skill acquire.
132 With Favour, Lord, look down on me, who thy Relief implore;
As thou art wont to visit those that thy blest Name adore.
133 Directed by thy heav'nly Word, let all my Footsteps be;
Nor Wickedness of any Kind Dominion have o'er me.
134 Release, intirely set me free from persecuting Hands,
That unmolested I may learn and practise thy Commands.
135 On me, devoted to thy Fear, Lord, make thy Face to shine;
Thy Statutes both to know and keep, my Heart with Zeal incline.
136 My Eyes to weeping Fountains turn, whence briny Rivers flow,
To see Mankind against thy Laws in bold Defiance go.

T S A D D I.

137 Thou art the righteous Judge, in whom wrong'd Innocence may trust:
And, like thyself, thy Judgments, Lord, in all Respects are just.
138 Most just and true those Statutes were, which thou didst first decree;
And all with Faithfulness perform'd, succeeding Times shall be.

139 With

PSALM CXIX.

139 With Zeal my Flesh consumes away, my Soul with Anguish frets,
    To see my Foes contemn, at once, thy Promises and Threats.
140 Yet each neglected Word of thine, (howe'er by them despis'd)
    Is pure, and for eternal Truth by me, thy Servant, priz'd.
141 Brought, for thy Sake, to low Estate, Contempt from all I find;
    Yet no Affronts or Wrongs can drive thy Precepts from my Mind.
142 Thy Righteousness shall then endure, when Time itself is past;
    Thy Law is truth itself, that Truth which shall for ever last.
143 Tho' Trouble, Anguish, Doubts and Dreads to compass me unite,
    Beset with Dangers, still I make thy Precepts my Delight.
144 Eternal and unerring Rules thy Testimonies give:
    Teach me the Wisdom that will make my Soul for ever live.

K O P H.

145 With my whole Heart to God I call'd, Lord, hear my earnest Cry;
    And I, thy Statutes to perform, will all my Care apply.
146 Again more fervently I pray'd, O save me, that I may,
    Thy Testimonies truly know and stedfastly obey.
147 My earlier Pray'r the dawning Day prevented, while I cry'd
    To him on whose engaging Word my Hope alone rely'd.
148 With Zeal have I awak'd before the Midnight Watch was set,
    That I, of thy mysterious Word, might perfect Knowledge get.
149 Lord, hear my supplicating Voice, and wonted Favour show;
    O quicken me, and so approve thy Judgments ever true.
150 My persecuting Foes advance and hourly nearer draw;
    What Treatment can I hope from them who violate thy Law?
151 Tho' they draw nigh, my Comfort is, thou, Lord, art yet more near,
    Thou, whose Commands are righteous all thy Promises sincere.
152 Concerning thy divine Decrees my Soul has known of old,
    That they were true, and shall their Truth to endless Ages hold.

R E S C H.

153 Consider my Affliction, Lord, and me from Bondage draw:
    Think on thy Servant in Distress, who ne'er forgets thy Law.
154 Plead thou my Cause; to that and me thy timely Aid afford;
    With Beams of Mercy quicken me according to thy Word.
155 From harden'd Sinners thou remov'st Salvation far away;
    'Tis just thou shouldst withdraw from them who from thy Statutes stray.
156 Since great thy tender Mercies are to all who thee adore;
    According to thy Judgments, Lord, my fainting Hopes restore.
157 A num'rous Host of spiteful Foes against my Life combine;
    But all too few to force my Soul thy Statutes to decline.
158 Those bold Transgressors I beheld, and was with Grief oppress'd,
    To see with what audacious Pride thy Cov'nant they transgress'd.
159 Yet while they flight, consider, Lord, how I thy Precepts love:
    O therefore quicken me with Beams of Mercy from Above.
160 As from the Birth of Time thy Truth has held through Ages past,
    So shall thy righteous Judgments, firm, to endless Ages last.

S C H I N.

161 Tho' mighty Tyrants, without Cause, conspire my Blood to shed,
    Thy sacred Word has Pow'r alone to fill my Heart with Dread.

PSALM CXX, CXXI.

162 And yet that Word my joyful Breaſt
Nor Conqueſt, nor the Spoils of War,
with heav'nly Rapture warms,
have ſuch tranſporting Charms.

163 Perfidious Practices and Lies
But to thy Laws Affection bear,
164 Sev'n Times a Day, with grateful Voice,
Becauſe I find thy Judgments all
I utterly deteſt;
too vaſt to be expreſt,
thy Praiſes I reſound,
with Truth and Juſtice crown'd.

165 Secure, ſubſtantial Peace have they
No ſmiling Miſchief them can tempt,
166 For thy Salvation I have hop'd,
With chearful Zeal and ſtricteſt Care
who truly love thy Law:
nor frowning Danger awe,
and tho' ſo long delay'd,
all thy Commands obey'd.

167 Thy Teſtimonies I have kept,
Becauſe the Love I bore to them
168 From ſtrict Obſervance of thy Laws
Convinc'd that my moſt ſecret Ways
and conſtantly obey'd;
thy Service eaſy made.
I never yet withdrew,
are open to thy View.

T A U.

169 To my Requeſt and earneſt Cry
Inſpire my Heart with heav'nly Skill,
170 Let my repeated Pray'r at laſt
According to thy plighted Word
attend, O gracious, Lord;
according to thy Word.
before thy Throne appear;
for my Relief draw near.

171 Then ſhall my grateful Lips return
When thou thy Counſels haſt reveal'd,
172 My Tongue the Praiſes of thy Word
Becauſe thy Promiſes are all
the Tribute of their Praiſe,
and taught me thy juſt Ways.
ſhall thankfully reſound,
with Truth and Juſtice crown'd.

173 Let thy Almighty Arm appear
For I the Laws thou haſt ordain'd
174 My Soul has waited long to ſee
Nor Comfort knew, but what thy Laws,
and bring me timely Aid;
my Heart's free Choice have made.
thy ſaving Grace reſtor'd;
thy heav'nly Laws afford.

175 Prolong my Life, that I may ſing
Whoſe Juſtice from the Depth of Woes
176 Like ſome loſt Sheep I've ſtray'd, till I
Thou, therefore, Lord, thy Servant ſeek,
my great Reſtorer's Praiſe;
my fainting Soul ſhall raiſe.
deſpair my Way to find;
who keeps thy Laws in mind.

PSALM CXX.

1 IN deep Diſtreſs I oft have cry'd
To God, who never yet deny'd
To reſcue me oppreſs'd with Wrongs;
2 Once more, O Lord, Deliv'rance ſend,
From lying Lips my Soul defend,
And from the Rage of ſland'ring Tongues.

5 But O! how wretched is my Doom,
Who am a Sojourner become
In barren Meſech's deſart Soil!
With Kedar's wicked Tents encloſ'd,
To lawleſs Savages expos'd,
Who live on nought but Theft and Spoil.

3 What little Profit can accrue?
And yet what heavy Wrath is due,
O thou perfidious Tongue, to thee?
4 Thy Sting upon thyſelf ſhall turn;
Of laſting Flames that fiercely burn,
The conſtant Fuel thou ſhalt be.

6 My hapleſs Dwelling is with thoſe
Who Peace and Amity oppoſe,
And Pleaſure take in others Harms:
7 Sweet Peace is all I court and ſeek;
But when to them of Peace I ſpeak,
they ſtraight cry out, to Arms, to Arms.

PSALM CXXI.

1 TO Sion's Hill I lift my Eyes,
2 From Sion's Hill, and Sion's God,
3 Then, thou my Soul, in Safety reſt,
4 His watchful Care, that Iſr'el guards,
from thence expecting Aid;
who Heav'n and Earth has made.
thy Guardian will not ſleep;
will Iſr'el's Monarch keep.

5 Shel-

PSALM CXXII, CXXIII, CXXIV, CXXV.

5 Shelter'd beneath th' Almighty's Wings,
6 Where neither Sun nor Moon shall thee
7 From common Accidents of Life
   From the blind Strokes of Chance and Foes,

thou shalt securely rest,
by Day or Night molest.
his Care shall guard thee still;
that lie in wait to kill.

8 At Home, Abroad, in Peace, in War,
   Conduct thee thro' Life's Pilgrimage

thy God shall thee defend;
safe to thy Journey's End.

PSALM CXXII.

1 O 'Twas a joyful Sound to hear
     Up Isr'el, to the Temple haste,
2 At Salem's Courts we must appear
3 In strong and beauteous Order rang'd

our Tribes devoutly say,
and keep your festal Day.
with our assembled Pow'rs;
like her united Tow'rs.

4 'Tis thither by divine Command,
   Before his Ark to celebrate
5 Tribunals stand erected there,
   There stands the Courts and Palaces

the Tribes of God repair,
his Name with Praise and Pray'r.
where Equity takes Place,
of Royal David's Race.

6 O, pray we then for Salem's Peace,
   (Thou holy City of our God!)
7 May Peace within thy sacred Walls
   With Plenty and Prosperity

for they shall prosp'rous be,
who bear true Love to thee.
a constant Guest be found,
thy Palaces be crown'd.

8 For my dear Brethren's Sake, and Friends,
   I'll pray,—May Peace in Salem's Tow'rs
9 But most of all I'll seek thy Good,
   For Sion and the Temple's sake,

no less than Brethren dear,
a constant Guest appear.
and ever wish thee well,
where God vouchsafes to dwell.

PSALM CXXIII.

1, 2 ON thee, who dwell'st above the Skies,
   As Servants watch their Masters Hands,
3, 4 O then have Mercy on us, Lord,
   To us whom cruel Foes oppress,

For Mercy wait my longing Eyes;
And Maids their Mistresses Commands.
Thy gracious Aid to us afford,
Grown rich and proud by our Distress.

PSALM CXXIV.

1 HAD not the Lord, (may Isr'el say)
     2 Had he not then espous'd our Cause,
3, 4, 5 Their Wrath had swallow'd us alive,
   Their Spite and Pride's united Floods

been pleas'd to interpose;
when Men against us rose.
and rag'd without Control;
had quite o'erwhelm'd our Soul.

6 But prais'd be our eternal Lord,
   Nor to their savage Jaws gave up
7 Our Soul is like a Bird escap'd
   The Snare is broke, their Hopes are crost,

who rescu'd us that Day,
our threat'ned Lives a Prey.
from out the Fowler's Net;
and we at Freedom set.

8 Secure in his Almighty Name,
   Who, as he made both Heav'n and Earth,

our Confidence remains,
of both sole Monarch reigns.

PSALM CXXV.

1 WHO place on Sion's God their Trust,
     Like her immoveable be fixt
2 Look how the Hills on ev'ry Side
   So stands the Lord around his Saints

like Sion's Rock shall stand,
by his Almighty Hand.
Jerusalem enclose:
to guard them from their Foes.

3 The Wicked may afflict the Just,
   Nor force him by Despair to seek
4 Be good, O righteous God, to those
   The Heart that Innocence retains

but ne'er too long oppress,
base Means for his Redress.
who righteous Deeds affect,
let Innocence protect.

PSALM CXXVI, CXXVII, CXXVIII, CXXIX.

5 All those who walk in crooked Paths,   the Lord shall soon destroy;
Cut off th' Unjust, but crown the Saints   with lasting Peace and Joy.

PSALM CXXVI.

1 WHEN Sion's God her Sons recall'd   from long Captivity,
It seem'd at first a pleasing Dream   of what we wish'd to see.
2 But soon in unaccustom'd Mirth   we did our Voice employ,
And sung our great Creator's Praise   in thankful Hymns of Joy.

Our Heathen Foes repining stood,   yet were compell'd to own,
That great and wond'rous was the Work   our God for us had done.
3 'Twas great, say they, 'twas wond'rous great,   much more should we confess;
The Lord has done great Things, whereof   we reap the glad Success.

4 To us bring back the Remnant, Lord,   of Isr'el's captive Bands,
More welcome than refreshing Show'rs   to parcht and thirsty Lands.
5 That we, whose Work commenc'd in Tears,   may see our Labours thrive,
Till finish'd with Success, to make   our drooping Hearts revive.

6 Tho' he despond that sows his Grain,   yet doubtless he shall come
To bind his full-ear'd Sheaves, and bring   his joyful Harvest home.

PSALM CXXVII.

1 WE build with fruitless Cost, unless   the Lord the Pile sustain,
Unless the Lord, the City keep,   the Watchman wakes in vain.
2 In vain we rise before the Day,   and late to Rest repair,
Allow no Respite to our Toil,   and eat the Bread of Care.

Supplies of Life, with Ease to them,   he on his Saints bestows;
He crowns their Labours with Success,   their Nights with sound Repose.
3 Children, those Comforts of our Life,   are Presents from the Lord:
He gives a num'rous Race of Heirs   as Piety's Reward.

4 As Arrows in a Giant's Hand,   when marching forth to War;
Ev'n so the Sons of sprightly Youth,   their Parents Safeguard are.
5 Happy the Man, whose Quiver's fill'd   with these prevailing Arms;
He needs not fear to meet his Foe,   at Law, or War's Alarms.

PSALM CXXVIII.

1 THE Man is blest who fears the Lord,   nor only Worship pays;
But keeps his Steps confin'd with Care,   to his appointed Ways.
2 He shall upon the sweet Returns   of his own Labour feed:
Without Dependance live, and see   his Wishes all succeed.

3 His Wife, like a fair fertile Vine,   her lovely Fruit shall bring;
His Children, like young Olive Plants,   about his Table spring.
4, 5 Who fears the Lord shall prosper thus;   him Sion's God shall bless;
And grant him all his Days to see   Jerusalem's Success.

6 He shall live on, 'till Heirs from him   descend with vast Increase;
Much bless'd in his own prosp'rous State,   and more in Isr'el's Peace.

PSALM CXXIX.

1 FROM my Youth up, may Isr'el say,   they oft have me assail'd;
2 Reduc'd me oft to heavy Straits,   but never quite prevail'd.
3 They oft have plough'd my patient Back   with Furrows deep and long;
4 But our just God has broke their Chains,   and rescu'd us from Wrong.

5 Defeat, Confusion, shameful Rout   be still the Doom of those,
Their righteous Doom, who Sion hate,   and Sion's God oppose.
6 Like Corn upon our Houses Tops,   untimely let them fade:
Which too much Heat, and want of Root,   has blasted in the Blade:

PSALM CXXX, CXXXI, CXXXII.

Which in his Arms no Reaper takes, but unregarded leaves:
Nor Binder thinks it worth his Pains to fold it into Sheaves:
8 No Traveller that paſſes by, vouchſafes a Minute's Stop,
To give it one kind Look, or crave Heav'n's Bleſſing on the Crop.

PSALM CXXX.

1 FROM loweſt Depths of Woe, to God I ſent my Cry:
2 Lord! hear my ſupplicating Voice, and graciouſly reply.
3 Should'ſt thou ſeverely judge, who can the Trial bear;
4 But thou forgiv'ſt, leſt we deſpond, and quite renounce thy Fear.
5 My Soul with Patience waits for thee the living Lord:
My Hopes are on thy Promiſe built, thy never-failing Word.
6 My longing Eyes look out for thy enliv'ning Ray;
More duly than the Morning Watch, to 'ſpy the dawning Day.
7 Let Iſr'el truſt in God, no Bounds his Mercy knows;
The plenteous Source and Spring from whence eternal Succour flows.
8 Whoſe friendly Streams to us ſupplies in Want convey;
A healing Spring, a Spring to cleanſe and waſh our Guilt away.

PSALM CXXXI.

1 O Lord, I am not proud of Heart, nor caſt a ſcornful Eye;
Nor my aſpiring Thoughts employ in Things for me too high.
2 With Infant-Innocence thou know'ſt I have myſelf demean'd:
Compos'd to Quiet, like a Babe, that from the Breaſt is wean'd.

3 Like me let Iſr'el hope in God, his Aid alone implore:
Both now and ever truſt in him who lives for evermore.

PSALM CXXXII.

1 LET David, Lord, a conſtant Place in thy Remembrance find;
Let all the Sorrows he endur'd, be ever in thy Mind.
2 Remember what a ſolemn Oath to thee, his Lord, he ſwore;
How to the mighty God he vow'd, whom Jacob's Sons adore.

3, 4 I will not go into my Houſe, nor to my Bed aſcend;
No ſoft Repoſe ſhall cloſe my Eyes, nor Sleep my Eye-lids bend:
5 'Till for the Lord's deſign'd Abode I mark the deſtin'd Ground;
Till I a decent Place of Reſt for Jacob's God have found.

6 Th' appointed Place, with Shouts of Joy, at Ephrata we found:
And made the Wood and neighb'ring Fields, our glad Applauſe reſound.
7 O with due Rev'rence let us then, to his Abode repair:
And proſtrate at his Footſtool fall'n, pour out our humble Pray'r.

8 Ariſe, O Lord, and now poſſeſs thy conſtant Place of Reſt;
Be that not only with thy Ark, but with thy Preſence bleſt.
9, 10 Clothe thou thy Prieſts with Righteouſneſs, make thou thy Saints rejoice:
And for thy Servant David's ſake, hear thy Anointed's Voice.

11 God ſwear to David in his Truth, (nor ſhall his Oath be vain)
One of thy Offspring after thee upon thy Throne ſhall reign.
12 And if thy Seed my Cov'nant keep, and to my Laws ſubmit;
Their Children too upon thy Throne for evermore ſhall ſit.

13, 14 For Sion does in God's Eſteem, and other Seats excel;
His Place of everlaſting Reſt, where he deſires to dwell.
15, 16 Her Stores, ſays he, I will encreaſe, her Poor with Plenty bleſs;
Her Saints ſhall ſhout for Joy, her Prieſts my ſaving Health confeſs.

PSALM CXXXIII, CXXXIV, CXXXV.

17 There David's Pow'r shall long remain, in his successive Line:
And my anointed Servant there shall with fresh Lustre shine.
18 The Faces of his vanquish'd Foes Confusion shall o'erspread;
Whilst, with confirm'd Success, his Crown shall flourish on his Head.

PSALM CXXXIII.

1 HOW vast must their Advantage be! how great their Pleasure prove!
Who live like Brethren, and consent in Ounces of Love!
2 True Love is like that precious Oil which pour'd on Aaron's Head,
Ran down his Beard, and o'er his Robes its costly Moisture shed.

3 'Tis like refreshing Dew, which does on Hermon's Top distil;
Or like the early Drops that fall on Sion's fruitful Hill.
For God to all, whose friendly Hearts with mutual Love abound,
Has firmly promis'd length of Days with constant Blessings crown'd.

PSALM CXXXIV.

1 BLESS God, ye Servants that attend upon his solemn State;
That in his Temple, Night by Night, with humble Rev'rence wait.
2, 3 Within his House lift up your Hands, and bless his holy Name;
From Sion bless thy Isr'el, Lord, who Heav'n and Earth didst frame.

PSALM CXXXV.

1 O Praise the Lord with one Consent, and magnify his Name;
Let all the Servants of the Lord his worthy Praise proclaim.
2 Praise him all ye that in his House, attend with constant Care;
With those that to his utmost Courts, with humble Zeal repair.

3 For this our truest Int'rest is, glad Hymns of Praise to sing;
And with loud Songs to bless his Name, a most delightful Thing.
4 For God his own peculiar Choice the Sons of Jacob makes;
And Isr'el's Offspring for his own most valu'd Treasure takes.

5 That God is great, we often have by glad Experience found;
And seen how he with wond'rous Pow'r above all Gods is crown'd.
6 For he with unresisted Strength, performs his sov'reign Will;
In Heav'n and Earth, and wat'ry Stores that Earth's deep Caverns fill.

7 He raises Vapours from the Ground, which pois'd in liquid Air,
Fall down at last in Show'rs, thro' which his dreadful Lightnings glare,
8 He from his Store-house brings the Winds: and he with vengeful Hand,
The First-born slew of Man and Beast, thro' Egypt's mourning Land.

9 He dreadful Signs and Wonders shew'd thro' stubborn Egypt's Coasts;
Nor Pharaoh could his Plagues escape, nor all his num'rous Hosts.
10, 11 'Twas he that various Nations smote, and mighty Kings suppress'd:
Sihon and Og, and all beside, who Canaan's Lands possess'd.

12, 13 Their Land upon his chosen Race he firmly did entail;
For which his Fame shall always last, his Praise shall never fail.
14 For God shall soon his People's Cause with pitying Eyes survey;
Repent him of his Wrath, and turn his kindled Rage away.

15 Those Idols, whose false Worship spreads o'er all the Heathen Lands,
Are made of Silver and of Gold, the Work of human Hands.
16, 17 They move not their fictitious Tongues, nor see with polish'd Eyes:
Their counterfeited Ears are deaf, no Breath their Mouth supplies.

18 As senseless, as themselves, are they that all their Skill apply
To make them, or in dangerous Times, on them for Aid rely.

19 Thus

PSALM CXXXVI.

19 Their juſt Returns of Thanks to God
    Nor let the Prieſts of Aaron's Race
20 Their Senſe of his unbounded Love
    And let all thoſe that fear the Lord,
21 Let all with Thanks his wond'rous Works
    Let them in Salem, where he dwells,

let grateful Iſr'el pay;
to bleſs the Lord delay.
let Levi's Houſe expreſs:
his Name for ever bleſs.
in Sion's Courts proclaim:
exalt his holy Name.

PSALM CXXXVI.

1 TO God, the mighty Lord,
    To him due Praiſe afford
    For God does prove
    His boundleſs Love

Your joyful Thanks repeat;
As good as he is great:
Our conſtant Friend,
Shall never end.

2, 3 To him whoſe wond'rous Pow'r
    Whom earthly Kings adore,
    For God, &c.

All other Gods obey,
This grateful Homage pay.

4, 5 By his Almighty Hand
    The Heav'ns by his Command,
    For God, &c.

Amazing Works are wrought;
Were to Perfection brought.

6 He ſpread the Ocean round
    And made the riſing Ground
    For God, &c.

About the ſpacious Land:
Above the Waters ſtand.

7, 8, 9 Thro' Heav'n he did diſplay
    The Sun to rule by Day,
    For God, &c.

His num'rous Hoſts of Light;
The Moon and Stars by Night.

10, 11, 12 He ſtruck the firſt-born dead,
    And thence his People led
    For God, &c.

Of Egypt's ſtubborn Land:
With his reſiſtleſs Hand.

13, 14 By him the raging Sea,
    Diſcloſ'd a middle Way,
    For God, &c.

As if in Pieces rent,
Thro' which his People went.

15 Where ſoon he overthrew.
    Who daring to purſue,
    For God, &c.

Proud Pharaoh and his Hoſt,
Were in the Billows loſt.

16, 17, 18 Thro' Deſarts vaſt and wild
    And famous Princes foil'd,
    For God, &c.

He led the choſen Seed:
And made great Monarchs bleed.

19, 20 Sihon, whoſe potent Hand
    And Og, whoſe ſtern Command
    For God, &c.

Great Ammon's Scepter ſway'd,
Rich Baſhan's Land obey'd.

21, 22 And of his wond'rous Grace,
    He gave to Iſr'el's Race,
    For God, &c.

Their Lands, whom he deſtroy'd,
To be by them enjoy'd.

23, 24 He, in our Depth of Woes,
    And from our cruel Foes
    For God, &c.

On us with Favour thought;
In Peace and Safety brought.

25, 26 He does the Food ſupply
    To God who reigns on high,
    For God will prove
    His boundleſs Love

On which all Creatures live,
Eternal Praiſes give.
Our conſtant Friend;
Shall never end.

PSALM CXXXVII, CXXXVIII, CXXXIX.

PSALM CXXXVII.

1 WHEN we our wearied Limbs to rest,
  Sat down by proud Euphrates' Streams;
  We wept with doleful Thoughts opprest,
  and Sion was our mournful Theme.
2 Our Harps, that when with Joy we sung,
  were wont their tuneful Parts to bear,
  With silent Strings neglected hung
  on Willow-Trees that wither'd there.
3 Mean while our Foes, who all conspir'd
  to triumph in our slavish Wrongs,
  Music and Mirth of us requir'd,
  " Come, sing us one of Sion's Songs."
4 How shall we tune our Voice to sing,
  or touch our Harps with skilful Hands?
  Shall Hymns of Joy to God our King,
  be sung by Slaves in foreign Lands?
5 O Salem, our once happy Seat!
  when I of thee forgetful prove,
  Let then my trembling Hand forget
  the speaking Strings with Art to move!
6 If I to mention thee forbear,
  eternal Silence seize my Tongue:
  Or if I sing one chearful Air,
  till thy Deliv'rance is my Song.
7 Remember, Lord, how Edom's Race,
  in thy own City's fatal Day,
  Cry'd out, " Her stately Walls deface,
  " and with the Ground quite level lay."
8 Proud Babel's Daughter doom'd to be
  of Grief and Woe the wretched Prey;
  Blest is the Man who shall to thee
  the Wrongs thou lay'st on us, repay.
9 Thrice blest, who with just Rage possest,
  and deaf to all the Parents Moans,
  Shall snatch thy Infants from the Breast,
  and dash their Heads against the Stones.

PSALM CXXXVIII.

1 WITH my whole Heart, my God & King,
  thy Praise I will proclaim;
  Before the Gods with Joy I'll sing,
  and bless thy holy Name,
2 I'll worship at thy sacred Seat,
  and with thy Love inspir'd,
  The Praises of thy Truth repeat,
  o'er all thy Works admir'd.
3 Thou graciously inclin'st thine Ear,
  when I to thee did cry;
  And when my Soul was prest with Fear,
  didst inward Strength supply.
4 Therefore shall ev'ry earthly Prince
  thy Name with Praise pursue;
  Whom these admir'd Events convince,
  that all thy Works are true.
5 They all thy wond'rous Ways, O Lord,
  with chearful Songs shall bless;
  And all thy glorious Acts record,
  thy awful Pow'r confess.
6 For God, altho' enthron'd on high,
  does thence the Poor respect;
  The Proud far off, his scornful Eye
  beholds with just Neglect.
7 Tho' I with Troubles am opprest,
  he shall my Foes disarm,
  Relieve my Soul when most distress'd,
  and keep me safe from Harm.
8 The Lord, whose Mercies ever last,
  shall fix my happy State:
  And mindful of his Favours past,
  shall his own Work complete.

PSALM CXXXIX.

1,2 THOU, Lord, by strictest Search hast known
  My rising up, and lying down;
  My secret Thoughts are known to thee,
  Known long before conceiv'd by me.
3 Thine Eye my Bed and Path surveys,
  My public Haunts and private Ways;
4 Thou know'st what 'tis my Lips would vent,
  My yet unutter'd Words Intent.
5 Surrounded by thy Pow'r I stand,
  On ev'ry Side I find thy Hand.
6 O Skill, for human Reach too high!
  Too dazling bright for mortal Eye!
7 O could I so perfidious be,
  To think of once deserting thee!
  Where, Lord, could I thy Influence shun,
  Or whither from thy Presence run?

PSALM CXL.

8 If up to Heav'n I take my Flight, 'Tis there thou dwell'st enthron'd in Light;
Or drive to Hell's infernal Plains, 'Tis there Almighty Vengeance reigns.
9 If I the Morning's Wings could gain, And fly beyond the Western Main,
10 Thy swifter Hand would first arrive, And there arrest thy Fugitive.

11 Or should I try to shun thy Sight Beneath the sable Wings of Night;
One Glance from thee, one piercing Ray Would kindle Darkness into Day.
12 The Veil of Night is no Disguise, No Screen from thy all-searching Eyes;
Thro' mid-night Shades thou find'st thy As in the blazing Noon of Day.
  Way

13 Thou know'st the Texture of my Heart, My Reins and ev'ry vital Part,
Each single Thread, in Nature's Loom, By thee was cover'd in the Womb.
14 I'll praise thee, from whose Hands I A Work of such a curious Frame:
  came,
The Wonders thou in me hast shown My Soul with grateful Joy must own.

15 Thine Eyes my Substance did survey, While yet a lifeless Mass it lay;
In secret how exactly wrought, Ere from its dark Inclosure brought.
16 Thou didst the shapeless Embryo see, Its Parts were register'd by thee:
Thou saw'st the daily Growth they took, Form'd by the Model of thy Book.

17 Let me acknowledge too, O God, That since this Maze of Life I trod,
Thy Thoughts of Love to me surmount The Pow'r of Numbers to recount.
18 Far sooner could I reckon o'er The Sands upon the Ocean's Shore;
Each Morn, revising what I've done, I find th' Account but new begun.

19 The Wicked thou shalt slay, O God; Depart from me, ye Men of Blood,
20 Whose Tongues Heav'n's Majesty pro- And take th' Almighty's Name in vain.
  fane
21 Lord, hate not I their impious Crew, Who thee with Enmity pursue?
And does not Grief my Heart oppress, When Reprobates thy Laws transgress?
22 Who practice Enmity to thee Shall utmost Hatred have from me:
Such Men I utterly detest, As if they were my Foes profest.
23, 24 Search, try, O God, my Thoughts, If Mischief lurks in any Part;
  and Heart,
Correct me when I go astray, And guide me in thy perfect Way.

PSALM CXL.

1 PRESERVE me, Lord, from crafty Foes of treacherous Intent;
2 And from the Sons of Violence, on open Mischief bent.
3 Their sland'ring Tongue the Serpent's Sting in Sharpness does exceed;
Between their Lips the Gall of Asps and Adder's Venom breed.

4 Preserve me, Lord, from wicked Hands, nor leave my Soul forlorn,
A Prey to Sons of Violence, who have my Ruin sworn.
5 The Proud for me have laid their Snare, and spread their wily Net;
With Traps and Gins, where'er I move, I find my Steps beset.

6 But thus environ'd with Distress, thou art my God, I said;
Lord, hear my supplicating Voice, that calls to thee for Aid.
7 O Lord, the God, whose saving Strength kind Succour did convey:
And cover'd my advent'rous Head in Battle's doubtful Day.

8 Permit not their unjust Designs to answer their Desire;
Lest they, encourag'd by Success, to bolder Crimes aspire.
9 Let first their Chiefs the sad Effects of their Injustice mourn,
The Blast of their envenom'd Breath, upon themselves return.

PSALM CXLI, CXLII, CXLIII.

10 Let them, who kindled first the Flame, its Sacrifice become;
 The Pit they digg'd for me, be made their own untimely Tomb.
11 Tho' Slander's Breath may raise a Storm, it quickly will decay;
 Their Rage does but the Torrent swell that bears themselves away.
12 God will assert the poor Man's Cause, and speedy Succour give;
 The Just shall celebrate his Praise, and in his Presence live.

PSALM CXLI.

1 TO thee, O Lord, my Cries ascend, O haste to my Relief;
 And with accustom'd Pity hear the Accents of my Grief.
2 Instead of Off'rings, let my Pray'r like Morning Incense rise;
 My lifted Hands supply the Place of Ev'ning Sacrifice.

3 From hasty Language curb my Tongue, and let a constant Guard
 Still keep the Portal of my Lips with wary Silence barr'd.
4 From wicked Mens Designs and Deeds my Heart and Hands restrain;
 Nor let me in the Booty share of their unrighteous Gain.

5 Let upright Men reprove my Faults, and I shall think them kind:
 Like Balm that heals a wounded Head, I their Reproof shall find.
 And in Return, my fervent Pray'r I shall for them address,
 When they are tempted and reduc'd, like me, to sore Distress.

6 When sculking in Engeddi's Rock, I to their Chiefs appeal,
 If one reproachful Word I spoke, when I had Pow'r to kill:
7 Yet us they persecute to Death, our scatter'd Ruins lie
 As thick as from the Hewer's Ax, the sever'd Splinters fly.

8 But, Lord, to thee I still direct my supplicating Eyes;
 O leave not destitute my Soul, whose Trust on thee relies.
9 Do thou preserve me from the Snares, that wicked Hands have laid;
 Let them in their own Nets be caught, while my Escape is made.

PSALM CXLII.

1 TO God with mournful Voice, in deep Distress I pray'd;
 2 Made him the Umpire of my Cause, my Wrongs before him laid.
3 Thou didst my Steps direct, when my griev'd Soul despair'd;
 For where I thought to walk secure, they had their Traps prepar'd.

4 I look'd, but found no Friend to own me in Distress;
 All Refuge fail'd, no Man vouchsaf'd his Pity or Redress.
5 To God, at last, I pray'd, thou, Lord, my Refuge art;
 My Portion in the Land of Life, till Life itself depart.

6 Reduc'd to greatest Straits, to thee I make my Moan;
 O! save me from oppressing Foes, for me too pow'rful grown.
7 That I may praise thy Name, my Soul from Prison bring:
 Whilst of thy kind Regard to me assembled Saints shall sing.

PSALM CXLIII.

1 LORD, hear my Pray'r, and to my Cry thy wonted Audience lend;
 In thy accustom'd Faith and Truth a gracious Answer send.
2 Nor at thy strict Tribunal bring thy Servant to be try'd;
 For in thy Sight no living Man can e'er be justify'd.

3 The spiteful Foe pursues my Life, whose Comforts all are fled;
 He drives me into Caves as dark as Mansions of the Dead.
4 My Spirit therefore is o'erwhelm'd, and sinks within my Breast;
 My mournful Heart grows desolate, with heavy Woes opprest.

PSALM CLXIV.

5 I call to mind the Days of old,
My former Dangers and Escapes
6 To thee my Hands in humble Pray'r.
My Soul for thy Refreshment thirsts,

7 Hear me with Speed; my Spirit fails,
Lest I become forlorn like them
8 Thy Kindness early let me hear,
Teach me the Way where I should go,

9 Do thou, O Lord, from all my Foes,
A safe Retreat against their Rage,
10 Thou art my God, thy righteous Will
Let thy good Spirit conduct and keep

11 O! for the sake of thy great Name,
For thy Truth's sake, to me distress'd,
12 In Pity to my Suff'rings, Lord,
Slay them that persecute a Soul

and Wonders thou hast wrought:
employ my musing Thought.
I fervently stretch out;
like Land oppress'd with Drought.

thy Face no longer hide;
that in the Grave reside.
whose Trust on thee depends;
my Soul to thee ascends.

preserve and set me free;
my Soul implores from thee.
instruct me to obey:
my Soul in thy right Way.

revive my drooping Heart;
thy promis'd Aid impart.
reduce my Foes to Shame:
devoted to thy Name.

PSALM CXLIV.

1 FOR ever bless be God the Lord,
At once both Strength & Skill afford
2 His Goodness is my Fort and Tow'r,
In him I trust, whose matchless Pow'r

3 Lord, what's in Man, that thou should'st love
What in his Offspring could thee move
4 The Life of Man does quickly fade;
His Days are like a flying Shade,

5 In solemn State, O God, descend,
The smoaking Hills asunder rend,
6 Discharge thy dreadful Lightnings round,
Them with thy pointed Arrows wound,

7, 8 Do thou, O Lord, from Heav'n engage
And snatch me from the stormy Rage
Fight thou against my foreign Foes,
Who, tho' in solemn Leagues they close

9 So I to thee, O King of Kings,
And Instruments of various Strings,
10 " God doth to Kings his Aid afford,
" 'Tis he that from the murd'ring Sword,

11 Fight thou against my foreign Foes,
Who, tho' in solemn Leagues they close,
12 Then our young Sons like Trees shall grow
Our Daughters shall like Pillars show,

13 Our Garners fill'd with various Store,
Our Sheep increasing more and more,
14 Strong shall our labouring Oxen grow,
Whilst we no War nor Slav'ry know,

15 Thrice happy is that People's Case,
Who God's true Worship still embrace,

who does his needful Aid impart,
to wield my Arms with warlike Art.
my strong Deliv'rance and my Shield;
makes to my Sway fierce Nations yield.

such tender Care of him to take?

such great Account of him to make?
his Thoughts but empty are and vain,
of whose short Stay no Signs remain.

whilst Heav'n its lofty Head inclines,
of thy Approach the awful Signs.
and make my scatter'd Foes retreat;
and their Destruction soon complete.

thy boundless Pow'r my Foes to quell,
of threat'ning Waves that proudly swell.
who utter Speeches false and vain;
their sworn Engagements ne'er maintain.

in joyful Hymns my Voice shall raise:
shall help me thus to sing thy Praise:
" to them his sure Salvation sends;
" his Servant David still defends."

who utter Speeches false and vain;
their sworn Engagements ne'er maintain.
well planted in some fruitful Place;
design'd some royal Court to grace.

shall us and ours with Plenty feed,
shall thousands and ten thousands breed.
nor in their constant Labour faint:
and in our Streets hear no Complaint.

whose various Blessings thus abound;
and are with his Protection crown'd.

PSALM

PSALM CLXV, CLXVI.

PSALM CXLV.

1, 2 THEE I'll extol, my God and King, thy endless Praise proclaim:
This Tribute daily I will bring, and ever bless thy Name.
3 Thou, Lord, beyond compare art great, and highly to be prais'd;
Thy Majesty, with boundless Height, above our Knowledge rais'd.
4 Renown'd for mighty Acts, thy Fame to future Times extends;
From Age to Age thy glorious Name successively descends.
5, 6 Whilst I thy Glory and Renown and wond'rous Works express;
The World with me thy Might shall own, and thy great Pow'r confess.
7 The Praise that to thy Love belongs, they shall with Joy proclaim;
Thy Truth of all their grateful Songs shall be the constant Theme.
8 The Lord is good, fresh Acts of Grace his Pity still supplies:
His Anger moves with flowest Pace, his willing Mercy flies.
9, 10 Thy Love thro' Earth extends its Fame to all thy Works express:
These shew thy Praise, whilst thy great Name is by thy Servants blest.
11 They, with the glorious Prospect fir'd, shall of thy Kingdom speak;
And thy great Pow'r by all admir'd, their lofty Subject make.
12 God's glorious Works of ancient Date, shall thus to all be known;
And thus his Kingdom's royal State, with public Splendor shown.
13 His stedfast Throne from Changes free, shall stand for ever fast;
His boundless Sway no End shall see, but Time itself out-last.

PART II.

14, 15 The Lord does them support that fall, and makes the Prostrate rise;
For his kind Aid all Creatures call, who timely Food supplies.
16 Whate'er their various Wants require with open Hand he gives:
And so fulfils the just Desire of ev'ry Thing that lives.
17, 18 How holy is the Lord, how just! how righteous all his Ways!
How nigh to him, who with firm Trust for his Assistance prays!
19 He grants the full Desires of those who him with Fear adore,
And will their Troubles soon compose, when they his Aid implore.
20 The Lord preserves all those with Care whom grateful Love employs:
But Sinners, who his Vengeance dare, with furious Rage destroys.
21 My Time to come, in Praises spent, shall still advance his Fame;
And all Mankind with one Consent, for ever bless his Name.

PSALM CXLVI.

1, 2 O Praise the Lord, and thou, my Soul, for ever bless his Name;
His wond'rous Love while Life shall last, my constant Praise shall claim.
3 On Kings, the greatest Sons of Men, let none for Aid rely;
They cannot save in dang'rous Times, nor timely Help apply.
4 Depriv'd of Breath to Dust they turn, and there neglected lie;
And all their Thoughts and vain Designs together with them die.
5 Then happy he, who Jacob's God for his Protector takes:
Who still with well-plac'd Hope, the Lord his constant Refuge makes.
6 The Lord who made both Heav'n and Earth, and all that they contain,
Will never quit his stedfast Truth, nor make his Promise vain.
7 The Poor oppress'd from all their Wrongs are eas'd by his Decree:
He gives the Hungry needful Food, and sets the Pris'ners free.

PSALM CXLVII, CXLVIII.

8 By him the Blind receive their Sight, the Weak and Fall'n he rears;
With kind Regard and tender Love he for the Righteous cares.
9 The Strangers he preserves from Harm, the Orphan kindly treats,
Defends the Widow, and the Wiles of wicked Men defeats.
10 The God, that does in Sion dwell, is our eternal King:
From Age to Age his Reign endures, let all his Praises sing.

PSALM CXLVII.

1 O Praise the Lord with Hymns of Joy, and celebrate his Fame;
For pleasant, good, and comely 'tis to praise his holy Name.
2 His holy City God will build, tho' level'd with the Ground;
Bring back his People, tho' dispers'd thro' all the Nations round.

3, 4 He kindly heals the broken Hearts, and all their Wounds doth close;
He tells the Number of the Stars, their several Names he knows.
5, 6 Great is the Lord, and great his Pow'r, his Wisdom has no Bound;
The Meek he raises, and throws down the Wicked to the Ground.

7 To God, the Lord, a Hymn of Praise with grateful Voices sing;
To Songs of Triumph tune the Harp, and strike each warbling String.
8 He covers Heav'n with Clouds, and thence refreshing Rain bestows;
Thro' him, on Mountain Tops, the Grass with wond'rous Plenty grows.

9 He, savage Beasts, that loosely range, with timely Food supplies:
He feeds the Ravens tender Brood, and stops their hungry Cries.
10 He values not the warlike Steed, but does his Strength disdain:
The nimble Foot that swiftly runs, no Prize from him can gain.

11 But he, to him that fears his Name, his tender Love extends;
To him that on his boundless Grace with stedfast Hope depends.
12, 13 Let Sion and Jerusalem to God their Praise address;
Who fenc'd their Gates with massy Bars, and does their Children bless.

14, 15 Thro' all their Borders he gives Peace, with finest Wheat they're fed;
He speaks the Word, and what he wills, is done as soon as said.
16 Large Flakes of Snow, like fleecy Wool, descend at his Command:
And hoary Frost, like Ashes spread, is scatter'd o'er the Land.

17 When join'd to these, he does his Hail in little Morsels break;
Who can against his piercing Cold secure Defences make.
18 He sends his Word which melts the Ice; he makes his Wind to blow;
And soon the Streams, congeal'd before, in plenteous Currents flow.

19 By him his Statutes and Decrees to Jacob's Sons were shown;
And still to Isr'el's chosen Seed, his righteous Laws are known.
20 No other Nation this can boast, nor did he e'er afford
To Heathen Lands his Oracles, and Knowledge of his Word.
HALLELUJAH.

PSALM CXLVIII.

1, 2 YE boundless Realms of Joy, 3, 4 Thou Moon, that rul'st the Night,
Exalt your Maker's Fame, And Sun, that guid'st the Day;
His Praise your Song employ Ye glitt'ring Stars of Light,
Above the starry Frame; To him your Homage pay;
Your Voices raise, His Praise declare,
Ye Cherubim Ye Heav'ns above,
And Seraphim, And Clouds that move
To sing his Praise. In liquid Air.

5, 6 Let

PSALM CXLIX, CL.

5, 6 Let them adore the Lord,
And praise his holy Name,
By whose Almighty Word
They all from nothing came;
And all shall last
From Changes free;
His firm Decree
Stands ever fast.

7, 8 Let Earth her Tribute pay;
Praise him ye dreadful Whales,
And Fish, that thro' the Sea
Glide swift, with glitt'ring Scales;
Fire, Hail, and Snow,
And misty Air,
And Winds, that where
He bids them blow.

9, 10 By Hills and Mountains, (all
In graceful Concert join'd)
By Cedars stately tall,
And Trees for Fruit design'd;
By ev'ry Beast,
And creeping Thing,
And Fowl of Wing,
His Name be blest.

11, 12 Let all of Royal Birth,
With those of humbler Frame,
And Judges of the Earth,
His matchless Praise proclaim;
In this Design
Let Youths with Maids,
And hoary Heads
With Children join.

13 United Zeal be shown,
His wond'rous Fame to raise,
Whose glorious Name alone
Deserves our endless Praise.
Earth's utmost Ends
His Pow'r obey;
His glorious Sway
The Sky transcends.

14 His chosen Saints to grace,
He sets them up on high,
And favours Isr'el's Race,
Who still to him are nigh.
O therefore raise
Your grateful Voice
And still rejoice
The Lord to praise.

PSALM CXLIX.

1, 2 O Praise ye the Lord,
His Praise in the great
In our great Creator
And Children of Sion
prepare your glad Voice,
Assembly to sing.
let Isr'el rejoice;
be glad in their King.

3, 4 Let them his great Name
With Timbrel and Harp
Who always takes Pleasure
And with his Salvation
extol in the Dance;
his Praises express;
his Saints to advance,
the Humble to bless.

5, 6 With Glory adorn'd
To God, who their Beds
Their Mouths fill'd with Praises;
Whilst a two-edged Sword
his People shall sing
with Safety does shield;
of him their great King;
their Right-hand shall wield.

7, 8 Just Vengeance to take
To punish those Lands
With Chains as their Captives,
With Fetters of Iron
for Injuries past;
for Ruin design'd;
to tie their Kings fast,
their Nobles to bind.

9 Thus shall they make good,
The dreadful Decree
Such Honour and Triumph
O therefore for ever
when them they destroy,
which God does proclaim:
his Saints shall enjoy,
exalt his great Name.

PSALM CL.

1 O Praise the Lord in that blest Place,
Praise him in Heav'n, where he
his Face
2 Praise him for all the mighty Acts
His Kindness this Return exacts,
from whence his Goodness largely flows;
unveil'd in perfect Glory shows.

which he in our Behalf has done;
with which our Praise should equal run.

PSALM CL.

3 Let the shrill Trumpet's warlike Voice make Rocks and Hills his Praise rebound:
Praise him with Harp's melodious Noise, and gentle Psalt'ry's silver Sound.
4 Let Virgin-Troops soft Timbrels bring, and some with graceful Motion dance;
Let Instruments of various Strings, with Organs join'd, his Praise advance.
5 Let them who joyful Hymns compose, to Cymbals set their Songs of Praise;
Cymbals of common Use, and those that loudly sound on solemn Days.
6 Let all, that vital Breath enjoy, the Breath he does to them afford,
In just returns of Praise employ; let every Creature praise the Lord!

The End of the PSALMS.

GLORIA PATRI, &c.

COMMON MEASURE.

1. TO Father, Son, and Holy Ghost,
the God whom we adore,
Be Glory, as it was, is now,
and shall be evermore.

As PSALM 25.

2. To God the Father, Son,
and Spirit, Glory be;
As 'twas, and is, and shall be so
to all Eternity.

As the 100 PSALM.

3. To Father, Son, and Holy Ghost,
the God whom Earth and Heav'n adore,
Be Glory, as it was of old,
is now, and shall be evermore.

As the old 112th, and the last Part of the 113th PSALM Tune.

4. To Father, Son, and Holy Ghost,
The God whom Heav'ns triumphant Host,
and suff'ring Saints on Earth adore,
Be Glory, as in Ages past,
As now it is, and so shall last
when Time itself must be no more.

As PSALM 148.

5. To God the Father, Son,
And Spirit, ever blest,
Eternal Three in One,
All Worship be addrest,
As heretofore,
It was, is now,
And shall be so
For evermore.

As PSALM 149.

6. By Angels in Heav'n
of ev'ry Degree,
And Saints upon Earth,
All Praise be addrest
To God in three Persons,
One God ever blest;
As it has been, now is,
And always shall be.

FINIS.

www.ingramcontent.com/pod-product-compliance
Lightning Source LLC
Chambersburg PA
CBHW031818230426
43669CB00009B/1187